SOCRATES AND PHILOSOPHY
IN THE DIALOGUES OF PLATO

D1446276

In Plato's *Apology*, Socrates says he spent his life examining and questioning people on how best to live, while avowing that he himself
knows nothing important. Elsewhere, however, for example in Plato's
Republic, Plato's Socrates presents radical and grandiose theses. In
this book Sandra Peterson offers a new hypothesis which explains
the puzzle of Socrates' two contrasting manners. She argues that the
apparently confident doctrinal Socrates is in fact conducting the first
step of an examination: by eliciting his interlocutors' reactions, his
apparently doctrinal lectures reveal what his interlocutors believe is the
best way to live. She tests her hypothesis by close reading of passages
in the *Theaetetus*, *Republic*, and *Phaedo*. Her provocative conclusion,
that there is a single Socrates whose conception and practice of philosophy remain the same throughout the dialogues, will be of interest
to a wide range of readers in ancient philosophy and classics.

SANDRA PETERSON is Professor of Philosophy at the University of
Minnesota, Twin Cities.

SOCRATES AND PHILOSOPHY IN THE DIALOGUES OF PLATO

SANDRA PETERSON

CAMBRIDGE
UNIVERSITY PRESS

CAMBRIDGE UNIVERSITY PRESS
Cambridge, New York, Melbourne, Madrid, Cape Town,
Singapore, São Paulo, Delhi, Mexico City

Cambridge University Press
The Edinburgh Building, Cambridge CB2 8RU, UK

Published in the United States of America by Cambridge University Press, New York

www.cambridge.org
Information on this title: www.cambridge.org/9781107667990

First published 2011
3rd printing 2012
First paperback edition 2013

A catalogue record for this publication is available from the British Library

Library of Congress Cataloguing in Publication Data
Peterson, Sandra, 1940–
Socrates and philosophy in the dialogues of Plato / Sandra Peterson.
p. cm.
Includes bibliographical references and index.
ISBN 978-0-521-19061-9 (hardback)
1. Plato. Dialogues. 2. Socrates. 3. Philosophy. I. Title.
B395.P3865 2011
184 – dc22 2010052773

ISBN 978-0-521-19061-9 Hardback
ISBN 978-1-107-66799-0 Paperback

Why is my verse so barren of new pride?[1]
So far from variation or quick change?
Why, with the time, do I not glance aside
To new-found methods and to compounds strange?
Why write I still all one, ever the same,
And keep invention in a noted weed,[2]
That every word doth almost tell my name,
Showing their birth and where they did proceed?
O, know, sweet love, I always write of you,
And you and love are still my argument;
So all my best is dressing old words new,
Spending again what is already spent:
For as the sun is daily new and old,
So is my love still telling what is told.

(William Shakespeare, Sonnet 76)

[1] *pride* adornment.   [2] *noted weed* familiar garment.

Contents

Acknowledgments	*page*	xi
List of abbreviations		xiv
Preface		xv

1	Opposed hypotheses about Plato's dialogues	1
	1.1 A datum: the two different modes of speaking of Plato's Socrates	1
	1.2 Two hypotheses to explain the datum	3
	1.3 More on the grand hypothesis and my alternative	5
	1.4 One approach that leads naturally to my alternative hypothesis	7
	1.5 A second approach to my hypothesis from four observations	8
	1.6 This book's plan to discuss the Socrates of Plato's dialogues	12
	1.7 The author Plato and the character Socrates	14
	1.8 Plato and the reader	15

2	Socrates in the *Apology*	17
	2.1 Looking for the Socrates of the *Apology*	17
	2.2 The label "wise" is a terrible slander	19
	2.3 Socrates is neither an investigator of nature nor a sophist	24
	2.4 Socrates is not a sage	27
	2.5 The thoughtfulness (*phronêsis*) that Socrates considers so important	30
	2.6 The "greatest things"	32
	2.7 Why the label "wise" is a terrible slander	33
	2.8 Socrates in the *Apology* sometimes echoes his accusers	36
	2.9 While knowing nothing big, Socrates does know some things	42
	2.10 Socrates' knowledge that the god orders him to test people is not big	47
	2.11 The Socrates of the *Apology*	56

3	Socrates in the digression of the *Theaetetus*: extraction by declaration	59
	3.1 The digression and its setting	59
	3.2 The first part of the digression	61

3.3	An acute interpretative problem	62
3.4	Theodorus	66
3.5	Extraction by declaration	67
3.6	Reflections on the extraction from Theodorus	71
3.7	The second half of the digression: *homoiôsis theô(i)*	74
3.8	The solution to our problems about the digression	85
3.9	Conclusion: Theodorus again, and Theaetetus	86

4	Socrates in the *Republic*, part I: speech and counter-speech	90
4.1	Strangeness and discontinuity	90
4.2	Question and answer discussion in book 1	93
4.3	A different kind of conversation in books 2–10: speech against speech	98
4.4	A question about Glaucon and a temporary puzzle about Socrates	101
4.5	Jostling conventions: question-and-answer conversation within persuasive speech	103
4.6	Glaucon and Adeimantus require of Socrates a made-to-order speech	105
4.7	The city of books 2–10 is Glaucon's, built under a condition he imposes	107
4.8	The "best" city Socrates describes in the *Timaeus*	115
4.9	Three reasons against finding Socrates committed to his proposals in books 2–10	118

5	Socrates in the *Republic*, part II: philosophers, forms, Glaucon, and Adeimantus	120
5.1	When can we say that Socrates does not believe proposals he makes in books 2–10?	120
5.2	Socrates' depiction of the philosopher	121
5.3	Glaucon's agreements about forms in books 5–7 do not survive examination	125
5.4	What Adeimantus accepts concerning philosophers does not survive examination	136
5.5	What can we conclude from the description of the philosopher for Adeimantus?	146
5.6	The effect of distancing Socrates from the content of his speech in books 2–10	147
5.7	The characters of Glaucon and Adeimantus	149
5.8	The Socrates of the *Republic*	160
5.9	The piety of Socrates' speech to Plato's brothers and its worth for Plato's readers	163

6   Socrates in the *Phaedo*: another persuasion
    assignment   166
    6.1   The famous proposals of the Socrates of the *Phaedo*   166
    6.2   Setting and participants   166
    6.3   The emphasis on persuasion   172
    6.4   Remarks on the logical structure of Socrates' persuasive argument   176
    6.5   "True philosophers"   182
    6.6   Socrates is not among the "true philosophers" he describes   190
    6.7   Why is Socrates not more straightforward?   193

7   Others' conceptions of philosophy in the
    Euthydemus, *Lovers*, and *Sophist*   196
    7.1   Comparison of some accounts of philosophy   196
    7.2   The conception of philosophy of an unnamed observer in
          the *Euthydemus*   198
    7.3   The *Lovers* as a compendium of current conceptions of philosophy   201
    7.4   The setting of the *Sophist*   205
    7.5   The Eleatic visitor's conception of philosophy   207
    7.6   Why does the Eleatic visitor not count Socratic cleansing
          refutation as philosophy?   210

8   Socrates and Plato in Plato's dialogues   216
    8.1   Socrates in Plato's dialogues   216
    8.2   What does Socrates believe?   218
    8.3   Socrates and Plato according to Kahn   219
    8.4   The Delphic oracle and a problem for two views about
          Plato's development   220
    8.5   Development and Plato's creativity   221
    8.6   The testimony of Aristotle about doctrines of Plato   224
    8.7   More about Plato   229
    8.8   Something else to explain and a pure speculation   230
    8.9   A possible objection: the traditional interpretation of Plato 231
    8.10 Plato's doctrines   233
    8.11 The argument of love; Plato and the historical Socrates   234

9   Socrates and philosophy   236
    9.1   Which of Plato's dialogues call Socrates a philosopher?   236
    9.2   Classification of previously considered passages   237
    9.3   Some more statements from observers   238
    9.4   More passages in which Socrates suggests a conception of
          the philosopher   240
    9.5   Passages of Socrates' self-description   242
    9.6   Why did Socrates, as depicted, call his activity "philosophizing"?   244

9.7   One possible reason why Socrates calls his own activities
        "philosophizing"   246
9.8   Another possible reason why Socrates calls his activities
        "philosophizing"   248
9.9   Plato and philosophy: one view   250
9.10 Plato and philosophy: a second view   254
9.11 Socrates, philosophy, and Plato   259

Bibliography   262
Index of passages cited   277
General index   286

Acknowledgments

I am grateful to the University of Minnesota for the sabbatical leave of 2005–2006 that gave me time to work on this book. For research support during 2005–2007 while I held the John M. Dolan Professorship I am grateful to Asher Waldfogel, who endowed the Professorship in honor of his undergraduate teacher at the University of Minnesota. I am also grateful for Asher's sustained interest in my project.

I am grateful to the anonymous readers for Cambridge University Press for their careful reading of the manuscript. For her meticulous and insightful copy-editing I give many thanks to Barbara Docherty. I am most grateful to editor Hilary Gaskin for her attention.

The book's thesis that Plato's Socrates sometimes makes statements that reveal the thoughts of his interlocutors and do not express his own convictions first occurred to me while I was thinking about the *Phaedo* for an essay on Socrates' last words. The essay was for a conference in honor of Terry Penner on his 65th birthday. (He had been my adviser for a dissertation on Aristotle.) The inspiration of the splendid Penner Fest at the University of Wisconsin in 2001 was a starting point for my book.

Soon thereafter I became interested in the digression of the *Theaetetus*. Presenting work-in-progress for the Arizona Colloquium in Ancient Philosophy for 2004 was a most valuable experience. Presenting a revision for the John M. Dolan Memorial Conference at the University of Minnesota was also useful. Giving a paper for the Arizona Colloquium in 2005 helped me articulate my thoughts on book 2 of the *Republic*. Presenting a revision for a Sister Mona Riley lecture at St. Catherine University in St. Paul helped me to progress.

I am very grateful to the many hosts for those events, and grateful to the participants for many thought-provoking comments and energizing reactions.

When I realized that an overarching idea tied together my thoughts about the *Theaetetus* and the *Republic*, what I had written seemed to be a start on a book. I then studied the *Apology* to learn how Socrates thought of his whole life near its end. The ensuing *Apology* chapter was the most difficult part of the book to write. After I had written a chapter on conceptions of philosophy in several dialogues of Plato, I added a full chapter on the *Phaedo*.

More people than I can possibly acknowledge here have occasioned or influenced specific points in the book. The decades of students both graduate and undergraduate that worked through my questions about Plato's dialogues have my gratitude. Among them I thank especially Tom Doyle and Josh Kortbein for their responses to the first draft of the manuscript, and Christopher Moore for written comments on the entire manuscript. Many colleagues at the University of Minnesota and more widely in the profession have shown an interest that helped me. Here I will mention only Betty Belfiore, Norman Dahl, Gene Garver, and John Wallace to thank them for their questions and encouragement over the years.

I would like to record here my gratitude to schoolteachers who made possible my studies of ancient philosophy and whom I cannot now thank personally.

Donald Davidson's epistemology course that I attended as an undergraduate used the *Theaetetus* as a central text. The dialogue and Davidson's engagement with it made a lasting impression on me.

My first examples of scholars of ancient philosophy were G.E.L. Owen and John Ackrill, my teachers of Aristotle at Oxford. I continue to find surprising the consideration and time that they gave to me as a B.Phil. student. Although their massive learning could serve only as a distant beacon, they themselves were personal influences.

Ackrill was also the teacher of my first graduate class on Plato at Princeton, a seminar on the *Theaetetus* and *Sophist*. My second graduate class on Plato was a seminar on Plato's metaphysics taught by Gregory Vlastos. My last Plato class was on Plato's theory of forms, taught by Harold Cherniss. Vlastos had persuaded Cherniss, who had no obligation to teach, to offer the seminar. Vlastos participated in that memorable experience. I must also mention that Vlastos had given me helpful advice about my application in 1963 for graduate work in philosophy at Princeton. He gave extraordinary support and encouragement during my graduate studies and afterwards.

An even older debt is to Dr. Johanna Goetzl, my Latin teacher at San Mateo High School in California. Her generous offer to teach me ancient

Greek after school (and then her insistence on further after-school lessons in her native German) set me on the path that led to this book. I still remember the fun of our reading a lesson on participles based on a passage in Plato's *Lysis*.

I offer the book to the reader.

Abbreviations

DK   Diels, Hermann, 1882. *Die Fragmente der Vorsokratiker*, 3 vols., 9th edn., ed. Walther Krantz. Berlin; repr. 1966, Dublin

D.L.   Hicks, R.D., 1925. *Diogenes Laertius, Lives of Eminent Philosophers*, 2 vols. trans. R.D. Hicks, Cambridge, MA, repr. 1991

LSJ   Liddell, H.G., Scott, R., and Jones, H.S. eds., [1843] 1961. *A Greek–English Lexicon*. Oxford

OCD   Hornblower, Simon and Spawforth, Antony (eds.), 1999. *Oxford Classical Dictionary*, 3rd edn. Oxford

SSR   Giannantoni, Gabriele (ed.), 1990. *Socratis et Socraticorum Reliquiae*. Naples

VP   *Vita Pythagorica* = Hershbell, Jackson, and Dillon, John (eds. and trans.), 1991. *Iamblichus: On the Pythagorean Way of Life. Text, Translation, and Notes*. Atlanta

Preface

The Socrates of some of Plato's dialogues is the avowedly ignorant figure of the *Apology* who knows nothing important and who gave his life to examining himself and others. In contrast, the Socrates of other dialogues such as the *Republic* and *Phaedo* gives confident lectures on topics of which the examining Socrates of the *Apology* professed ignorance. It is a long-standing puzzle why Socrates acts so differently in different dialogues.

To explain the two different manners of Socrates a current widely accepted interpretation of Plato's dialogues offers this two-part, Plato-centered, hypothesis: (i) the character Socrates of the dialogues is always Plato's device for presenting Plato's own views; and (ii) Plato had different views at different times. The Socrates who confidently lectures presents these famous four doctrines: Plato's blueprint for the best state, Plato's "Theory of Forms," Plato's view that philosophy is the knowledge of those Forms that fits the knower for the highest government stations, and Plato's arguments for the immortality of the soul.

To explain Socrates' two different manners this book offers instead an interlocutor-centered hypothesis that the character Socrates, who is permanently convinced that he knows nothing great, has reason to conduct different kinds of examination with different interlocutors. With some, he is the avowedly ignorant questioner. With others, he has reason to appear to be a confident lecturer: the reaction of interlocutors to an apparently confident lecture reveals them. Revealing them is the first step of an examination of them. Throughout Plato's dialogues Socrates' philosophizing centrally involves examining.

This book discusses some putatively doctrinal passages that seem the greatest obstacles to its thesis of the constantly ignorant and examining Socrates. Details of each containing dialogue show that, appearing to instruct, Socrates is instead conducting the revelatory first step of an examination. The second step would be critical logical scrutiny of the beliefs revealed. We do not see that second step after these apparently doctrinal passages. Nevertheless, Socrates' practice in these passages is exactly the examination that he says in the *Apology* that he continually engaged in.

The book's argument has the result – important though negative – that the dialogues it considers give the reader no reason to believe that Socrates, as depicted, held the famous four doctrines or that Plato was endorsing them through his presentation of Socrates.

Since Socrates does not critically examine the famous four putatively Platonic teachings in the dialogues it considers, the book does some examining on his behalf. The book finds that the putative teachings it considers fail critical scrutiny. Their failure gives us reason for the stronger positive result that Socrates, as depicted, and hence Plato, would in fact reject the putative teachings.

CHAPTER I

Opposed hypotheses about Plato's dialogues

1.1 A DATUM: THE TWO DIFFERENT MODES OF SPEAKING OF PLATO'S SOCRATES

The Socrates of Plato's *Apology*, on trial for his life, announces an intention to his jurors:

While I breathe and am able, I will not stop philosophizing (*philosophôn*) . . . saying the sorts of things I usually do. (29d)[1]

His example of what he usually says is this:

Best of men – being an Athenian, from the city the greatest and most reputed for wisdom and strength – are you not ashamed that you are concerned about having as much money as possible, and reputation and honor, while you are not concerned for (*epimelê(i)*) nor do you think about thoughtfulness and truth and how your soul will be the best it can be? (29d–e)

He also says:

My total concern is to be practicing nothing unjust or impious. (32d)

We can then infer that concern for "how your soul will be . . . best" is for Socrates concern about how to live justly and piously.[2] So Socrates' usual address involves issuing a challenge about the rightness of your way of living.

Socrates further reports that his challenge can lead to examination and that the examination can lead to reproach under certain conditions:

And if one of you disputes this and says he is concerned, I won't directly let him off or go away, but I will question him and examine (*exetasô*) and test (*elegxô*) and if he does not seem to me to possess virtue, but says he does, I will reproach him that things that are worth the most he makes least of, but the more trivial things he makes more of. (29e–30a)

---

[1] Translations from the *Apology* are my own. The text is Duke *et al.* (1995).
[2] Vlastos (1971, 5–6) discusses this point.

So Socrates' philosophizing, his usual or habitual activity throughout his life, as he describes it in the *Apology*, has several components. First he makes a challenge. Then he examines: that is, he subjects his interlocutor to a test – an elenchus – concerning how he conducts his life. Then, under certain conditions, Socrates reproaches. The examination that can follow upon an initial challenge is evidently an especially important component, for Socrates elsewhere closely links philosophizing with examining (28e: "philosophizing . . . and examining (*exetazonta*)").

His examining others involves examining himself, since he says to his jurors that they have heard him "examining both myself and others" (38a).

At the end of the *Apology* Socrates further describes his lifelong activity:

[W]hen my sons grow up, punish them, paining them with these very same things with which I pained you, if they seem to you to care for money or something else before virtue, and if they are reputed to be something when they are nothing, reproach them just as I did you, that they do not care for what one ought, and they think they are something when they are worth nothing. (41e)

Here Socrates considers his constant activity to have involved paining people by reproaching them that they don't care about living in the best way and – a new detail – that they think they are something when they are worth nothing.

This Socrates of the *Apology* who describes himself as constantly examining seems to many readers to contrast with the Socrates of some of Plato's other dialogues.[3] The Socrates of certain other dialogues, for example, the *Phaedo* and the *Republic*, apparently enunciates and recommends to his audience extraordinary views that he does not examine with them. He is

---

[3] Sedley (1995, 3–26):

Later we tend to find Socrates – or whoever replaces him as main speaker – using his interlocutors as partners in the development of his own constructive proposals.

Kenny (2004, 37–39):

Plato's dialogues do not assign a consistent role or personality to the character called Socrates. In some dialogues he is predominantly a critical inquirer. In other dialogues . . . notably *Phaedo*, *Republic*, and *Symposium* . . . Socrates appears not as an inquiring questioner but as a teacher in full possession of a system of philosophy.

Kenny (2004, 41) contrasts "the didactic philosopher" of some dialogues with "the agnostic inquirer" of certain other dialogues. See also Shields (2003, 61):

[W]e must be struck by an important shift in Socrates' self-presentation across the Platonic corpus. [In some dialogues] Socrates professes his analytical ignorance . . . He is also agnostic about such important matters as *post-mortem* existence. This contrasts sharply with the Socrates of the *Phaedo*, who . . . retails proof after proof of the soul's immortality . . . Assuming that the Socrates of the *Phaedo* now represents Plato's views rather than those of the historical Socrates, we can identify a first major Platonic departure from Socrates. Plato, unlike Socrates, has not only positive convictions, but is prepared to argue for them at length.

an apparently doctrinal Socrates. I emphasize that the positive theses that this new Socrates offers to his interlocutors are controversial, and yet he leaves the theses quite unexamined. The fact is that Socrates appears to have contrasting manners of conversation in Plato's dialogues.

1.2 TWO HYPOTHESES TO EXPLAIN THE DATUM

Some readers think that the contrasting conversational manners of the depicted Socrates are irreconcilable.[4] Gregory Vlastos, for example, says this to account for the division between the Socrates who questions and examines, for example in the *Euthyphro*, and the Socrates who offers unexamined instruction, for example in *Republic* books 2–10:

> I submit that to make sense of so drastic a departure from what Plato had put into his portrayals of Socrates from the *Apology* to the *Gorgias*, we must hypothesize a profound change in Plato himself. If we believe that in any given dialogue Plato allows the persona of Socrates only what he (Plato) at that time considers true, we must suppose that when that persona discards the elenchus as the right method to search for the truth, this occurs only because Plato himself has now lost faith in that method.[5]

Vlastos explains further:

> This is the grand . . . hypothesis on which my whole interpretation of Socrates-in-Plato is predicated.[6]

---

[4] Robinson (1969a, 74) finds that there won't be an explanation only with reference to the historical figure of Socrates because the Socrates Plato depicts would have an unlikely fluctuation in views. He goes on to look for an explanation in terms of Plato's intentions in writing.

But Robinson (1953, 83) also finds that Plato did not fully have his material under his control and was unaware of his distortion of Socrates' views.

[5] Vlastos (1991a, 117).

[6] Vlastos (1991a, 117, n. 50). Vlastos' full phrase is "grand methodological hypothesis." Others had earlier taken what amounted to Vlastos' hypothesis as an unstated or understated assumption. They had not seemed to recognize it as a hypothesis needing testing against the content of the dialogues. For example, Guthrie (1978, vol. v, 5–6) says:

> Plato, for all his reverence for Socrates as the inspiration and starting point for his own reflections, is a more sophisticated philosopher and marks a new and fateful development in the history of thought . . . One gets a strong impression that he was an essentially different philosophical character from the master through whose mouth he so often expresses the results of his own maturer and more widely ranging mind . . . [T]o him Protagoras and Gorgias, Prodicus and Hippias, were still opponents whose challenge had not been adequately met; but to meet it called for something more radical and comprehensive than the simple ethical intellectualism of Socrates. It called for nothing less than a new vision of the whole of reality, involving metaphysics, human psychology, and not least cosmology, . . . Since he claimed to have found what Socrates all his life was seeking, and since the personal impact of Socrates had been for him an unforgettable experience of his most impressionable years, he could see nothing improper in putting into Socrates' mouth some (not all) of the discoveries which in his eyes provided . . . the answers to the questions that [Socrates] had asked.

And again,

[M]y hypothesis ... proposes that Plato in those early works of his, sharing Socrates' philosophical convictions, sets out to think through for himself their central affirmations, denials, and reasoned suspensions of belief ... Employing a literary medium which allows Socrates to speak for himself, Plato makes him say whatever *he* – Plato – thinks *at the time of writing* would be the most reasonable thing for Socrates to be saying just then in expounding and defending ... [Plato's] own philosophy ... The writer's overriding concern is always the philosophy ...

As Plato changes, the philosophical persona of his Socrates is made to change, absorbing the writer's new convictions ... [7]

Much interesting scholarship has accepted Vlastos' grand hypothesis as confirmed and has treated it as no longer a hypothesis but as a sort of axiom or datum.[8] Vlastos, however, emphasized that he was treating it as a hypothesis under testing throughout his writings:

That it is offered as hypothesis, not dogma or reported fact, should be plain. Such it will remain as I pursue it step by step. Of its truth the reader must be the judge.[9]

In the judgment of this reader, Vlastos' hypothesis is false. I propose a different hypothesis. Pursuing it, I have found that it more adequately accounts for the same features of Plato's dialogues for which Vlastos was attempting to account. Other readers may find it worth the effort to judge the adequacy of this different hypothesis.

My hypothesis is that the Socrates in any of Plato's dialogues is examining his interlocutor and so engaging in the central component of the complex activity, philosophizing, which Socrates calls in the *Apology* his habitual activity throughout life. But examination is itself a multi-stage activity. Its first step is revealing the interlocutor. Socrates' awareness of

---

[7] Vlastos (1991a, 50–53).

[8] Morgan (1992, 232–233) treating it as a datum, offers a nuanced statement:

That shift [in the portrayal of Socrates] may be either from a historically attentive portrait to one that employs Socrates as a Platonic mouthpiece or from an earlier to a later Platonic perception of Socrates.

Kraut (1992, 3–4) says:

How can Socrates be so opposed to himself: a seeker who professes ignorance about the one subject that absorbs him – the human good – and yet (in the *Republic* and elsewhere) a confident theoretician who speculates at length not only about morality, but also about knowledge, reality, politics, and the human soul?

Kahn (1996, 100) says: "In ... [the] great didactic dialogues [*Phaedo* and *Republic*] the ignorant inquirer of the *Apology* has almost disappeared."

[9] Vlastos (1991a, 53).

what is appropriate to reveal his interlocutors occasions Socrates' different speaking styles, tailored to different interlocutors in different dialogues. With certain interlocutors Socrates appears to be recommending teachings of which he is certain. With them he appears to be teaching in those very areas of which he disclaims knowledge in the *Apology*. That is because Socrates as depicted realizes that appearing to enunciate doctrine, and observing his interlocutor's receptivity to it, is the best way of revealing for certain interlocutors their beliefs and inclinations that need to be examined. Revealing a receptive interlocutor, Socrates thereby enacts the first stage of an examination. So in the apparently doctrinal dialogues we still see Socrates living the single-minded life of examination that he attributes to himself in the *Apology*.[10]

While I pursue my alternative hypothesis in this book, I will nevertheless be retaining some assumptions that underlie Vlastos' hypothesis. I retain the assumption that Plato's character Socrates has a special status: what Socrates says must be taken very seriously as our best clue to Plato's own convictions. I also retain the assumption that Plato's "overriding concern is always the philosophy." I will later discuss the force these assumptions have for me.[11]

1.3 MORE ON THE GRAND HYPOTHESIS AND MY ALTERNATIVE

Vlastos' grand hypothesis says that Plato enunciates, through the character Socrates, some striking teachings in dialogues written in the middle of Plato's writing career. For example, the *Republic* recommends a novel political system. The *Phaedo*, *Symposium*, *Phaedrus*, and *Republic* offer what the secondary literature calls "the theory of forms."[12] The *Republic* and *Phaedo* offer some specialized conceptions of what a philosopher is and does. The

---

[10] The recurrent Socrates that I find in all the dialogues is close to the Socrates that Vlastos (1991a) finds in the dialogues he considers early and to the Socrates that Brickhouse and Smith (1994, viii) find in the dialogues they consider early.

[11] Wolfsdorf (2008, 253) finds that the character even of the group of dialogues in which Vlastos finds the ignorant and examining Socrates is not consistent. Wolfsdorf believes it serves Plato's larger purpose – to do philosophy – to present an inconsistent Socrates. My chapter 7, n. 5 (p. 198) indicates why I do not find convincing Wolfsdorf's interesting argument that Socrates in the *Euthydemus* is "psychologically inconsistent or implausible" (2008, 255).

[12] Dancy (2004, 4) says:

   Socrates in certain dialogues produces arguments to defeat proposed definitions without committing himself to the idea that the things to be defined are to be found in an eternal, unchanging, and ontologically pure realm. In other dialogues definition takes more of a back seat, and Socrates does commit himself to that metaphysical view. The metaphysical view is the Theory of Forms.

Phaedo gives memorable arguments for the immortality of the soul. John Cooper comments about these offerings:

[It is] the overwhelming impression not just of [ancient readers] but of every modern reader of at least many of his dialogues, that Platonism... constitutes a systematic body of "philosophical doctrine" – about the soul and its immortality;... the eternal and unfaltering Forms whose natures structure our physical world and the world of decent human relations within it; the nature of love and the subservience of love in its genuine form to a vision of that eternal realm. These and many other substantive philosophical ideas to be explored in Plato's dialogues are his permanent contribution to our Western philosophical culture.[13]

Given this comment, it is remarkable that so many readers, including Plato scholars, find Plato's "permanent contribution to our Western philosophical culture" quite unbelievable.[14] I will later discuss the constituents of the Platonic "systematic body of 'philosophical doctrine'" in more detail. For now I simply record the reception by very many prominent readers. Readers find the political arrangements of the *Republic* loathsome.[15] Many readers agree that the theory of forms of the *Republic* and *Phaedo*, on the standard account of that theory, is a "baroque monstrosity."[16] The conception of the philosopher in the *Republic* excludes almost everyone. The conception of the philosopher in the *Phaedo* is unworkable for anyone living an ordinary life. And even first-year undergraduates who are convinced of their souls' immortality for reasons of their own find the *Phaedo's* arguments for the immortality of the soul to be foolish.

Here is one reader's statement of his incredulity about the views of Plato as expressed by a putatively doctrinal Socrates:

Plato's philosophical views are mostly false, and for the most part they are evidently false; his arguments are mostly bad, and for the most part they are evidently bad. Studying Plato... can... be a dispiriting business: for the most part, the student of Plato is preoccupied by a peculiar question – How and why did Plato come to entertain such exotic opinions, to advance such outré arguments?[17]

---

[13] Cooper (1997a, xxv). I have quoted selectively from one side of Cooper's very balanced account in order to outline more sharply the view I oppose.

[14] For example Sedley (2002, 41) says: "[M]ost of Plato's interpreters long ago abandoned any commitment to the truth of his doctrines..."

[15] Rowe (2007, 16) speaks of "in the *Republic*... all those appalling political proposals." Ackrill (2001, 230–251), while recognizing the hostility with which some readers have reacted to the *Republic*, defends it.

[16] I borrow the phrase "baroque monstrosity," for the theory of forms as traditionally understood from Meinwald (2008, 3). Speaking of interpreters who find the Theory of Forms hopelessly flawed, Meinwald (1992, 390) says, "[T]he attribution to Plato of a middle theory that can only be nonsense is a problem."

[17] Barnes (1995, xv–xvi).

For my alternative hypothesis this question does not arise, since my hypothesis does not suppose that the depicted Socrates who appears to assert exotic views and to assert weird arguments actually does so and in so doing speaks what Plato believes.

My alternative hypothesis that Socrates often speaks to reveal interlocutors who would profit from examination provokes its own different questions. For example: how do we tell when Socrates' apparent assertions in Plato's dialogues are not straightforward assertions or endorsements but are instead revelation of an interlocutor? I will answer that question with different details for each dialogue I consider. Subsequent chapters will find evidence hitherto overlooked that Socrates' apparent offering of doctrine is mere appearance. The evidence is often within what Socrates' interlocutors ask him to do. They sometimes request of him a particular type of contribution to the discussion, and he responds entirely literally. He has listened to his interlocutors much better than they seem to have listened to themselves.

There is also the question: why would Plato think that any readers would be interested in Socrates' revelation that various interlocutors are inclined toward "exotic opinions" and "outré arguments"? I will answer that question later.

As preliminary to outlining the plan of this book I consider briefly the naturalness of my alternative hypothesis from two slightly different approaches.

1.4 ONE APPROACH THAT LEADS NATURALLY TO MY ALTERNATIVE HYPOTHESIS

If one feels a need to explain certain dialogues' drastic departure from the portrayal of Socrates in other dialogues, then one has done some background reasoning as follows. There appears to be a departure. Therefore there is a departure. Therefore we should ask: how can we explain the departure?

But another approach is to reason differently from the same starting point. There appears to be a departure. But there are strong reasons to expect that there would not be a departure. After all, Plato does not change Socrates' physical description, the details of his biography, or his mannerisms of speech.[18] Socrates reports no conversion experiences – for example,

---

[18] Halliwell (1995, 87–121) reports on a recurring feature of Socrates' address to interlocutors. Through Socrates' distinctive use of vocatives, some common in and outside Plato's works, and some rare, "Plato has succeeded in turning such phrases into one strand of the peculiarly Socratic manner of focusing his attention upon his respondents" (1995, 100–101).

no conversion from his avowed ignorance about death in the *Apology* to the conclusions of the (unconvincing) arguments for immortality thirty days later in the *Phaedo* as he awaits execution. Therefore we should ask: how can we explain why there would seem to be a departure if there is no departure? Having asked that question, one is naturally led to suspect that apparent presentation of doctrine might be a way of examining, and to ask how that could be so.

1.5 A SECOND APPROACH TO MY HYPOTHESIS FROM FOUR OBSERVATIONS

A second approach begins from four observations after dwelling on which the hypothesis that the Socrates of Plato's dialogues is constantly the examining Socrates might, again, naturally occur to one as something worth testing in the way this book's chapters test it.

A first observation concerns the kind of question-and-answer discussion via which Socrates, as depicted in certain of Plato's dialogues – the aporetic or puzzle-raising dialogues – elicits views of his conversational partner. Such question-and-answer discussion does not at all commit Socrates the questioner to any of the premises of the arguments he constructs. Socrates is committed at most to the connection between the premises and the conclusion: it is his answerer who is responsible for any assertions in the course of the argument.[19]

A second observation is that serious study of certain arguments that Plato presents leaves a vivid impression that Plato's logical acumen is substantial. (My own favorite arguments are in the *Euthyphro*, *Hippias Major*, *Parmenides*, *Theaetetus*, and *Sophist*.[20]) Even as one makes this observation, one will be aware that Plato's writings have many other arguments, some of which one has not yet understood. And of course one's views would be better grounded if one understood everything. But there will not be sufficient reason to think that anyone else understands everything, either. So one may reasonably consider oneself warranted in starting from where one is, with one's very strong impression that Plato is capable of solid reasoning.

---

[19] The memorable formulation of Frede (1992) first made me think about this point. See also Stokes (2005). See chapter 4 (pp. 93–97) for some conventions of stylized question-and-answer discussion. Socrates and Alcibiades in *Alcibiades* I (113a–b) discuss the matter of who owns the answers in a question-and-answer conversation: they conclude that the answerer has full ownership.

[20] Ackrill (2001, 72–79) discusses some arguments of the *Sophist*. Dancy (2004, 137–147) discusses a complex argument in the *Euthyphro*, as does Cohen (1971).

Granted, capacities are not always actualized. And we have seen one opinion that Plato's arguments are "mostly bad." So the impression that we should expect Plato to reason expertly is not universal. But still one may reasonably start from one's own vivid impression.

Let us recall here a familiar distinction, among flawed arguments: some are flawed by invalidity because they rest on an objectionable pattern; others are flawed because they have a false premise, although they may have a valid pattern. In many instances one can most usefully view the arguments that Socrates elicits from his interlocutors as captured by this irreproachable, simple pattern. Socrates asks: "Do you accept that p?" (What "p" represents may be a complex conjunction of several premises.) Socrates asks. "Do you accept the conditional premise that if p, then q?" If his interlocutor assents to these questions, Socrates may conclude: "Then you must accept that q." The second question about the conditional is sometimes not stated by Socrates. Nevertheless, an interlocutor who accepts an inference to the conclusion that q from a certain premise that p has implicitly accepted the conditional – if p, then q – that yields the result that q. On occasion the conditional premise that underlies an argument that Socrates has extracted from an interlocutor is questionable. But the argument extracted from an interlocutor, and its flaw, belongs to the interlocutor, not to Socrates or Plato. Plato almost never has Socrates, as depicted, presenting invalid arguments. Socrates usually employs the simple inference pattern of *modus ponens* outlined above decisively.[21]

Although this overall form of many of Socrates' arguments is irreproachable and available to any ordinary thinker, the inner details of the arguments and the choice of premises display Plato's ingenuity.

To arrive at this observation that Plato can argue with outstanding ingenuity and care, one uses only one's simple reflective common sense. Plato's depicted Socrates, often deploying outstanding arguments in examination, is evidently convinced that such reasoning is nevertheless available to any patient interlocutor for self-scrutiny.

---

[21] The idea that Socrates sometimes elicits fallacious arguments for a purpose (Sprague 1962) can be preserved if we understand "fallacy" widely enough to include arguments whose inferential transitions are valid but which have false premises.

    The useful discussion in Klosko (1983, 363–374) would not agree that every argument Socrates elicits can legitimately be understood as inferentially irreproachable. But I think it is mind-clearing to recognize the power of our common human capacity to use *modus ponens* and to focus instead on what false conditional premises may be at work. Klosko (1983, 368–369) observes that Socrates and his interlocutor may understand the premises of an argument that Socrates extracts differently. Klosko seems to think Socrates unfair for not clarifying premises for his interlocutor. I think it revealing of, and a potential lesson for, the interlocutor if he accepts something unclear.

Having arrived at the observation that Plato could reason very well, one will naturally arrive at a two-part third observation. First, it is unlikely that a Plato who shows a mastery of critical examination would rely on conspicuously bad arguments to support his own unexamined convictions. And, second, it is quite difficult to believe any account of Plato that implies that he at some time in his life had views that would not withstand persistent commonsense examination of the sort that the Socrates of the aporetic dialogues uses. It then will become pretty much impossible for one to believe that Plato created – or at the least fully understood – the solid arguments of dialogues that according to the grand hypothesis were written early in his career and then declined into a middle phase in which he no longer had a grip on critical reasoning, and still later got his grip back. To arrive at the third observation is to be unable to accept that in mid-life writings Plato fell into ill-supported views that he used his old character Socrates to present.

I would like to make clear that the last observation is not a symptom of a disabling interpretative attitude. One interpreter of Plato gives this diagnosis of the attitude:

Some scholars may be suspected of dismissing this or that remark in a Platonic text as "ironic," without specific evidence, for no better reason than misplaced charity – the apparent desire to rescue Plato from believing something which they themselves find either naïve or distasteful.[22]

For one thing, I do not dismiss any remark on the ground of irony. And, so far as I can tell, my standard for what Plato could believe is not my personal impression of naïveté or distastefulness. My standard has been the thought – based on the evidence of certain dialogues – that Plato can employ the shared human capacity for commonsense examination – the reflective consideration that is available to an ordinary person – as well as anyone can. I assume that if an ordinary reader can see on the basis of commonsense reflection that an argument is bad, or that a proposal does not withstand examination because of inconsistent parts, Plato could see it too, and probably faster. I have not been supposing, anachronistically, that Plato had at his disposal logical developments after the nineteenth century.[23]

---

[22] Sedley (2002, 41).

[23] Beversluis (2006, 102, n. 27) worries about "misinterpretation by abstraction," which is "concluding that since you think a particular inference is fallacious, Plato thought so too." Beversluis says, citing a point made by Ryle (1966, 206–207):

We should indeed be alert to the possibility of a misplaced charity that desires to absolve Plato of naïveté. But there are other varieties of misplacement. There is the possibility of misplaced low expectations for reasoners in antiquity; there is a misplaced readiness to find quaint and charming errors among the ancients. I hope to be as alert to other misplaced attitudes as to misplaced charity.

A fourth observation is that Plato's choice to write dialogues in which he never has a speaking part suggests that he is reluctant to make pronouncements as an authority who is certain about what he recommends.[24] This in turn suggests, though of course it does not decisively imply, that it would be odd if a Plato reluctant to write as an authority yet in mid-career chose to present Socrates as an authoritative spokesperson, apparently to lend weight to Plato's new presentation of doctrine.[25]

I now put the four observations together. First, in the question-and-answer discussions of the aporetic dialogues Socrates is not responsible for any assertions, and he is not there presenting teachings that represent his convictions. Second, Plato can reason capably, early and late. Third, given Plato's demonstrated capabilities, he is unlikely to have had bad reasons for what he believed and endorsed; he is unlikely to have had views whose inconsistency would emerge quickly from commonsense examination. Fourth, Plato is reluctant to act as an authority presenting views of which he is certain.

These observations together naturally lead to the suspicion that the depicted Socrates of the putatively doctrinal dialogues with some memorably flimsy arguments and some unsustainable theses was not presenting Plato's convictions that Plato was recommending to the reader. That suspicion leads to the further suspicion that the Socrates of the apparently doctrinal dialogues might be doing something other than presenting doctrine. He might be no more responsible for his apparent doctrine than

[L]ogic was in its infancy in Plato's day – a fact which makes it unlikely that a clear distinction between a valid and an invalid inference pre-dated the writing of the early dialogues and therefore, ill-advised to assume that Plato "just knew from the start" the differences between good and bad arguments.

I think, on the contrary, that Socrates as depicted and therefore Plato had a sufficiently good grip on *modus ponens* and *modus tollens* to find his way in argument.

[24] Plato's avoiding the appearance of being an authority is another theme of Frede (1992).

[25] It is an oddity of Frede 1992 that though he observes Socrates' detachment from what he says in the aporetic dialogues, and Plato's greater detachment from what Socrates says, Frede nevertheless thinks that one can tell – presumably chiefly from the dialogues – that Socrates had certain views and that Plato came to hold different views from Socrates. Frede perhaps assumes Vlastos' methodological hypothesis, and perhaps relies on our scant testimony from Aristotle particularly as it relates to Platonic forms. I give my stance on Aristotle's testimony in chapter 8 (pp. 224–229).

the examining Socrates of the aporetic dialogues is responsible for what he elicits by questioning. Interlocutors receptive to lectures they have occasioned from Socrates might instead be responsible for what they applaud, just as interlocutors from whom Socrates elicits views by questioning are responsible for their answers. Having now suspected that Socrates is not presenting doctrine, one asks what he might be doing instead.

This book will argue, first, that study of some apparently doctrinal dialogues or passages shows that they lend themselves very well to my thought that many of the views Socrates enunciates should not attach to Socrates, but to his receptive interlocutors and, second, that these apparently doctrinal passages are likely beginnings of examinations.

To test my hypothesis that the Socrates of all of Plato's dialogues is the avowedly ignorant and examining Socrates I consider a selected few passages that initially seem to be the most difficult cases for the hypothesis.[26] The hypothesis that Socrates as depicted is starting an examination makes much better sense of these allegedly doctrinal passages than the hypothesis that he speaks as an authority and represents the newly confident Plato in a later stage of his writing career instructing his readers. I think that once I have presented my main idea for those few passages, readers can easily continue on by themselves to confirm that the hypothesis stands up to testing in connection with other passages or dialogues that initially appear to show a doctrinal Socrates and not an examining one.

1.6 THIS BOOK'S PLAN TO DISCUSS THE SOCRATES OF PLATO'S DIALOGUES

This is the plan of the book. In this introductory sketch I present conclusions for which the chapters, with close attention to the text, give the full arguments.

As preliminary to actual testing of my hypothesis chapter 2 spells out the hypothesis by studying the *Apology* to draw from it an account of the

---

[26] My overall hypothesis in its barest formulation has some similarity to the thesis of Christopher Rowe in various recent publications. For example, Rowe (2007, viii) says:

[I oppose the view] that Plato started as a Socratic but broke away in mid-career to become a Platonist. My own rival thesis is that Plato stayed a Socratic until the end.

And in Rowe (2006, 7–24) Rowe says: "The Socrates of books ii–x is still recognizably the same as the Socrates of book i."

That would summarize my view of the *Republic*. But my reasons for it will be very different from Rowe's, as is my own understanding of what it means to say that Plato remained a Socratic. My testing of my hypothesis will not be redundant.

Socrates who there sums up his life as the habitual activity of examining. Socrates' summary gives us something to look for in dialogues that depict other times in his life.

Chapter 3 tests my hypothesis against a famous passage of the *Theaetetus* (172b–177c), its so-called "digression," which seems to some readers to have a decidedly doctrinal Socrates. The Socrates of the *Theaetetus* digression, speaking to a secondary interlocutor, Theodorus, articulates a conception of the philosopher that is quite different from the conception of the *Apology*. Many interpreters have thought that Socrates in the *Theaetetus* embraces the digression's recommendation of how best to spend one's life. I will argue that Plato takes pains to identify the Socrates of the *Theaetetus* with the Socrates of the *Apology* who said he constantly philosophized, that is, examined. Moreover, Plato takes pains to show that the Socrates of the *Theaetetus* could not possibly embrace for his own life the digression's picture of the philosopher. Several details within the *Theaetetus* tell us that the digression reveals what the interlocutor Theodorus thinks a philosopher does. Theodorus' receptivity to the digression is a first step of examination that reveals what needs examination. (We do not see any further steps of examination of Theodorus.)

Chapters 4 and 5 test my hypothesis against the *Republic* and find that it explains the *Republic* well. My argument here is in two parts. Chapter 4 argues that the *Republic* gives us signs distinctive to it that Socrates is articulating views that appeal to his interlocutors rather than expressing his own convictions. For example, in book 2 the interlocutors request from Socrates a speech, a counter-speech as in a law-court, a response to their own speeches, to persuade them of an assigned conclusion. (Law-court speeches are not good evidence of the speaker's thoughts. They reveal what he thinks likely to persuade his jury.[27]) In books 2–10 Socrates gives his speech. Given the interlocutors' insistent request, and given several conditions on Socrates' speech that the interlocutors impose, we have good grounds to think that the city described in the *Republic* expresses Glaucon's and Adeimantus' aspirations and no reason to think it expresses Socrates'. Chapter 5 shows the incoherence of the account of philosophers and of the discussion of forms in book 5. Their incoherence gives us reason for the stronger conclusion that the *Republic*'s Socrates is in fact not endorsing them.

Chapter 6 tests my hypothesis against the *Phaedo*. The *Phaedo*'s interlocutors also bluntly ask Socrates to persuade them of a conclusion that

---

[27] See Dover (1994, 13–14).

they assign to him in advance. He undertakes to do as they ask, quite literally. The request to persuade someone of an assigned conclusion is not likely to inspire from the literal-minded Socrates a speech about his own convictions. The *Phaedo* also gives other indications that Socrates is articulating views that would persuade his interlocutors rather than expressing his own convictions. Moreover, the weakness both of the *Phaedo's* conception of philosophy as well as of its arguments for immortality give us reason for the stronger result that the depicted Socrates would reject them.

Chapter 7, the final piece of my main argument, is of a different type from the preceding ones. I discuss some conceptions of philosophy that characters other than Socrates articulate. These conceptions turn up in the *Lovers*, *Euthydemus* and *Sophist*. Socrates recognizes them as current conceptions of philosophy. For the *Lovers* and *Euthydemus* it will be obvious that although Socrates recognizes that others have those conceptions, Socrates does not live by those conceptions any more than he lives by the conceptions of philosophy he articulates in the *Theaetetus*, *Republic*, and *Phaedo*. Chapter 7 will also compare Socrates' conception of philosophy from the *Apology* with the conception that the Eleatic visitor of the *Sophist* presents while he rather pointedly refrains from including Socrates under it.

I.7 THE AUTHOR PLATO AND THE CHARACTER SOCRATES

Chapter 8 will review my progress on Socrates, consider some objections, and make some proposals about the author Plato. Chapter 9 will re-consider the question of what Socrates, as depicted, understood philosophy to be. Since the previous chapters will have considered Plato's presentation of conceptions of philosophy that belong to other interlocutors and that are at odds with the philosophizing that Socrates does, chapter 9 will ask why the Socrates of the *Apology* would choose to call his lifetime activity "philosophizing." His awareness that the word is widely used for activities alien to him makes his choice of it for his own activity not an obvious one.

I have already said that in treating my hypothesis about Plato, I retain a central presupposition of Vlastos' "grand hypothesis": I retain the assumption that Plato presents his own views through his depiction of the character Socrates.[28] While I do not take the extreme position that Socrates represents Plato by the direct device that any extended speech of Socrates' states beliefs of Plato, I can nevertheless almost fully concur with this assessment:

---

[28] Vlastos (1991a, 50).

The twin considerations that the dialogue's apparent argument (1) is legitimately attributable to the dialogue's author, and (2) is itself located in the questions and assertions of the primary speaker, surely suffice to make the primary speaker recognizably Plato's spokesperson. And that is why Plato's readers have always been able to set themselves the realistic goal of discovering his doctrines in his dialogues.[29]

I disagree with many interpreters on the matter of which exactly, among the many proposals that Socrates articulates, are his assertions. So I will disagree also on the matter of which exactly are the convictions of Plato's that we can locate in the dialogues.[30]

Terence Irwin suggests one way of helping to decide which are the convictions of Plato's that we can locate in his dialogues:

If . . . we find that a reasonably coherent philosophical outlook and a reasonably intelligible line of philosophical development can be ascribed to the Platonic Socrates, we have some grounds for claiming to have found Plato's views.[31]

As I understand Plato's character Socrates, the views to which he shows his commitment, and which seem to me a "reasonably coherent philosophical outlook," reduce to a very few, among which these are prominent: he does not know the greatest things; people who think they do know the greatest things are worth nothing; and his philosophizing consists in examining others and himself while acknowledging his profound ignorance. The reasonable coherence of this outlook, together with the failure of some other outlooks sketched in the dialogues to withstand commonsense examination, are some grounds for electing this outlook as Plato's.

Vlastos' assumption that Plato's "overriding concern is always the philosophy" I also retain.[32] Unlike Vlastos, I do not believe that concern with the philosophy was ever in opposition to concern to present a character Socrates who remains profoundly the same throughout the dialogues.[33]

1.8 PLATO AND THE READER

My hypothesis still faces the question why Plato thought that readers would be interested to watch a Socrates in occasional apparently doctrinal mode revealing interlocutors' sometimes exotic and often ill-supported beliefs

---

[29] Sedley (2002, 39).
[30] I take Socrates as always the most important of Plato's characters, even when entirely absent, as in the *Laws*. It would be a project for another occasion to explain how Plato's views emerge there.
[31] Irwin (2008, 85).
[32] Vlastos (1991a, 51): "The writer's overriding concern is always the philosophy."
[33] Wolfsdorf (2008, 253) makes that opposition.

that stand in need of examination that is not forthcoming in the dialogue that reveals those beliefs. The quality of being exotic has its own kind of interest, of course, but I think there is an answer closer to home that will emerge from my book. An anecdote from the ancient Plato interpreter, Plutarch, helps to make a start at that answer. Plutarch tells us, four times in his *Moralia*, that Plato asked himself – or, as Plutarch twice puts it, was accustomed to ask himself – "Am I not possibly like that?" Plutarch writes:

> Speakers, not only when they succeed, but also when they fail, render a service to hearers who are alert and attentive. For poverty of thought, emptiness of phrase, an offensive bearing, fluttering excitement combined with a vulgar delight at commendation, and the like, are more apparent to others when we are listening than in ourselves when we are speakers. Wherefore we ought to transfer our scrutiny from the speaker to ourselves, and examine whether we unconsciously commit such mistakes . . . And everyone ought to be ready ever to repeat to himself, as he observes the faults of others, the utterance of Plato, "Am I not possibly like them?" For as we see our own eyes brightly reflected in the eyes of those near us, so we must get a picture of our own discourse in the discourses of others, that we may not too rashly disdain others, and may give more careful attention to ourselves in the manner of speaking. (*Moralia*, "On Listening to Lectures," 40c–d)[34]

I do not know how Plutarch obtained this detail of Plato's biography. But if it is accurate, it would explain why Plato, and we too, should be interested in the life-guiding views of Socrates' interlocutors as revealed in the speeches of the Socrates who reflects his interlocutors back to themselves by speaking their inclinations for them. While interlocutors have an opportunity to see themselves better as they react to Socrates, Plato's readers have an opportunity to see themselves better as they react to the dialogues. Reacting to what appeals to Socrates' interlocutors, Plato's reader can ask, "Am I not possibly like that?" Plato prepares a reader who sees himself in the reflecting pool of the dialogues for critical self-examination. In this Plato stands toward his reader as Socrates stands toward his interlocutor.

---

[34] Translation of Babbitt (trans.) (2000, vol. 1). Plutarch's three other reports are in *Moralia* at (i) (Babbit (trans.), 2000) "Advice about Keeping Well" (129D); (ii) (Babbit (trans.), 2000) "How to Profit from One's Enemies" (88E); (iii) (Helmbold 1939) "On the Control of Anger" (463e).

CHAPTER 2

Socrates in the Apology

2.1 LOOKING FOR THE SOCRATES OF THE *APOLOGY*

Plato's *Apology* depicts Socrates' defense speech when he is on trial for his life. Its Socrates recounts the life that led to the charge against him. So the *Apology* is a natural starting point for formulating my hypothesis that the Socrates of Plato's dialogues that depict other times in Socrates' life is the same.

I do not first take my hypothesis as a datum and then try to understand the other dialogues to fit with it. My study of the *Apology* will sharpen my hypothesis by giving me a Socrates to look for in the other dialogues. I do not assume that I will find him. If my hypothesis is correct, my study of some other dialogues in which Socrates appears should confirm the hypothesis.

I do not take up the interesting question whether Plato intended the speech he wrote to correspond closely to what the historical Socrates said at his actual trial. Of course no one expects the depicted speech to be word-for-word the same as the actual speech. Even a team of note-takers, for which we have no evidence, would not have ensured total accuracy. At best, we'd expect only the outline and main content in Plato's *Apology* to be the same as the actual speech.

I mention, however, as relevant to that question a possibly revealing pun. Socrates says early on:

It would not be becoming, men, for someone of my age to come before you fabricating (*plattonti*) speeches (*logous*) like a youth. (17c)[1]

The phrase *plattonti logous* has the sound and effect of "Plato-ing speeches."[2] If the actual Socrates used that phrase, Plato's sensitive ear

---

[1] Translations from the *Apology* are my own, with debt to the many translators I cite. The Greek text is Duke *et al.* (1995).

[2] The Greek for Plato's name, *Platôn*, has one less tau than the verb and has the long vowel omega, preserved in the cases other than the nominative, instead of the short omicron of the verb form here. West (1979, 51) notices a possible pun, but doesn't explore its point.

could not have failed to notice the possibility for a pun.[3] As Plato wrote the phrase, it would become a punning indication to the reader that it would not be fitting for Socrates to be Plato-ing, that is, sounding like Plato and not like Socrates. If, on the other hand, the actual Socrates did not use that exact phrase, but Plato has supplied it, there is some likelihood of a deliberate pun to suggest to the reader that the Socrates depicted by Plato is not going to be giving a speech that represents Plato more than it does Socrates.[4]

---

[3] Wordplay between *Platôn* and *plattonti* does not require exact correspondence between the words. Compare some other wordplay in the *Apology*, on "Meletus" (24d7–9; 25c; 26b1–2); on "Hades" ("the unseen" (29b)); on *epistatên* and *epistêmôn* (20b4 and 20b5). On the latter, see Burnet's note on 20a8 (Burnet 1924). Wordplay elsewhere in Plato is at *Symposium* 185 ("when Pausanias paused") and 198c ("Gorgias' head," a play on the phrase "Gorgon's head"); *Protagoras* 336b, 362a (on "Callias"), *Gorgias* 463a (on "Polus"). For other examples of wordplay in Plato, see Tarrant (1946, 1958). Sprague (1994, 55–58) discusses some Platonic puns.

Plato's *Cratylus* etymologies show a sensitivity to the way language sounds. Compare wordplay on Plato's name by Timon the Hellenistic sillographer (poet of parodies). Diogenes Laertius (D.L. III 26) reports that Timon said, *hôs aneplasse Platôn ho peplasmena thaumata eidôs*. R.D. Hicks, the Loeb translator of D.L., attempts to preserve the wordplay, and translates "As Plato placed strange platitudes." Athenaeus in *Deipnosophists* (Gulick 1928/1987) quotes the same witticism, XI, 505e. *Thaumata*, the primary meaning of which is "wonders," also means "puppet-shows." The verb *plattein* or *plassein*, the source of our word "plastic," primarily means "mold," as in "to mold clay." It can also mean to fabricate, or imagine, or invent. Timon's *mot* is supposed to illustrate the point that Plato did not record conversations, but invented them.

De Boo (2001) locates much play on Plato's name in the *Republic*. (His overall view of Plato's writing differs greatly from mine.)

[4] On the question how accurate a picture of the historical Socrates the *Apology* gives, the essay of Morrison (2000) is useful though finally quite pessimistic. I note briefly and without of course having conclusive reasons for it my disagreement with one point in Morrison's essay. He says:

The *Apology* is not merely a masterful piece of writing. It is a quietly ironical parody of the standard defense-speech of its day. Socrates' speech contains an exordium, prosthesis, statement of the case, refutation, digression, and a peroration, the same formal parts which a student of rhetoric would have been taught to produce. This is a highly literary device. It fits Plato's massive literary talent and carefully developed skill at imitating many different styles. It does not very well fit Socrates the oral philosopher. (244)

I agree up to the last sentence. I expect that the depicted Socrates has heard many speeches (*Hippias Minor* and *Hippias Major* mention some). I expect that Socrates was an extremely good listener. de Stryker and Slings (1994, 19) estimate a composition time of five to ten years for the *Apology* and comment (1994, 7) that it would be an error to think the speech not deliberately artful.

I would add that it would be equally an error to assume that Plato's artful composition could not much reflect the actual speech. Its subject matter is the thoughtful life of Socrates. There seems to me a strong possibility that someone who had lived so deliberately and thoughtfully with so much attention to what he and others said would be at the age of seventy able to give a defense of his life that was not clumsy. Xenophon (*Apology* 3) has a relevant anecdote:

Hermogenes, . . . on seeing Socrates discussing any and every subject rather than the trial, . . . said, "Socrates, ought you not to be giving some thought to what defence you are going to make?" . . . Socrates had at first replied, "Why, do I not seem to you to have spent my whole life in preparing to defend myself?" Then when he asked "How so?" he had said, "Because all my life I have been guiltless of wrong-doing; and that I consider the finest preparation (*meletên*) for a defence." (Translation of Marchant and Todd 1923/1979)

Here I want only to understand as accurately as possible the speech-giver Plato portrays. I assume neither that Plato did nor that he did not intend the depicted speech closely to resemble the historically actual speech.

Socrates as depicted makes plain that he considers the label "wise" a great slander. He distinguishes certain old accusers (18a ("the first accusers"), 18e) from the new accusers who have made the formal charges on which he now stands trial ("the later accusers" (18b; 24b)). The first accusers, who say what is not true (18b), accuse him of being a wise man (18b: *sophos anêr*). These are the "more terrible" (*deinoteroi* 18b4) and "terrible" (18c2) accusers. Socrates says of this label, "wise:"

> I will try to demonstrate to you whatever this is that has brought me the name (*to . . . onoma*) and the slander. (20d)

It will emerge that the "and" in the phrase "the name and the slander" is appositional or explanatory.[5] It amounts to "that is to say." The name "wise" is precisely the slander.[6]

Socrates begins his explanation of how he got the bad name by revealing to the jury that his friend Chaerephon had asked the Delphic oracle if anyone was wiser than Socrates. The Delphic priestess replied, "No";[7] or possibly she actually uttered the sentence, "No one is wiser than Socrates." Socrates says:

> When I heard these things, I pondered them like this: "Whatever is the god saying, and what riddle is he posing? For I am conscious that I am wise neither in anything big nor in anything small (*oute mega oute smikron*). So whatever is he saying when he claims that I am wisest? Surely he is not saying something false, at least, for that is not sanctioned for him." And for a long time I was at an impasse about whatever he was saying. (21b)

Socrates' phrase "wise, neither in anything big nor in anything small," shows that there are various things to be wise about or to know about, some of them bigger than others. The bare word translated

---

[5] Denniston (1996, 291) discusses the appositional *kai*.

[6] Burnet (1924) on the passage says perhaps too unqualifiedly that *sophos anêr* "was not a compliment in the mouth of an Athenian of the fifth century B.C." Socrates doesn't take it as a compliment, when used by Athenians, as he will explain. Burnet sees that the name is the slander at 23a1: "[T]he name of *sophos* is the chief *diabolê*."

[7] Reeve (1989, 28–32) describes the likely procedure of the oracle – drawing a lot to answer a yes/no question.

"wise" – *sophos* – lacking any qualifying phrase, "in respect of such and such," might naturally apply to someone knowledgeable in any skill, or craft.[8] But also the bare word was used for the traditional sages or wise men (*Protagoras* 343b 6–7).

Socrates undertook to investigate the oracular pronouncement:

Very reluctantly I turned to some such investigation of it.

I went to someone of those reputed to be wise, so that there, if anywhere, I would test the pronouncement, and show the oracle, "This man is wiser than I, but you declared me [wiser]." (21b8–c2)

"Test the pronouncement" (*elegxôn to manteion*, also translatable as "refute the oracle") does not mean "show the divination to be false." Socrates dismisses the possibility that the oracle spoke a falsehood (21b6–7). But Socrates might refute the surface meaning of the divination to approach accurate understanding of it.[9]

Socrates first examines the politicians. It is natural for Socrates first to examine politicians, as he searches for someone with bigger wisdom than his own, because politicians' reputed expertise – about how everyone in a city should conduct their lives – is certainly wisdom somehow big – either as widely encompassing, or as prestigious, or as life-guiding:

So I considered him thoroughly – I need not speak of him by name, but he was one of those in political life – and when I considered him and conversed with him . . . , I was affected something like this: it seemed to me that this man seemed to be wise, both to many other human beings and most of all to himself, but that he was not . . .

For my part, as I went away, I reasoned with regard to myself: I am wiser than this human being. For probably neither of us knows anything fine and good, but he supposes he knows something when he does not know, while I, just as I do not

---

[8] Lloyd (1989, 83):

In the classical period you can be called *sophos* in any one of the arts, painting or sculpting or fluteplaying, in athletic skills, wrestling or throwing the javelin or horsemanship, and in any of the crafts, not just in piloting a ship or healing the sick or farming, but, at the limit, in cobbling, or carpentry or cooking: all these examples can be illustrated from the Platonic corpus.

Lloyd cites *Laches* 194d–e; *Lysis* 210a, 214a; *Meno* 93d; *Euthydemus* 271d, 279e, 292c, 294e; *Protagoras* 312; *Hippias Minor* 368b; *Symposium* 175d–e; *Theages* 123b–126d; *Epinomis* 974eff.

[9] Burnet (1924) at 22a7 says:

Socrates set out with the idea of refuting the oracle . . . at least in its obvious sense; it was only when he had discovered its hidden meaning . . . that he felt disposed to champion the god of Delphi . . . The final clause is therefore ironical. This use of *hina* . . . to introduce an unexpected or undesired result ironically regarded as an end is as old as Homer.

Burnet's addition "at least in its obvious sense" is crucial. See Doyle (2004, 23) for controversy about whether Socrates attempts to show the oracle false. See Reeve (1989, 22–23).

know, do not even suppose that I do. I *do* seem likely to be a little bit (*smikrô(i) tini*: "by a little" or "in something small") wiser than he in this very thing: that whatever I do not know, I do not even suppose I know. (21c3–d7)

Socrates initially thinks the oracle's comparison has to do with knowledge of something "fine and good." The politician's reputed wisdom concerns the best life for the citizens of his city – obviously something "fine and good." That would be the topic of Socrates' conversation. When Socrates finds that the politician lacks the knowledge he is reputed to have and is unaware of his lack, Socrates for the first time considers himself wise in a way. He now counts his own contrasting condition – the mere lack of the false belief that he knows something fine and good – as a kind of wisdom. Since the time he first reacted to the oracle, he has changed his mind. He has corrected what he now sees to be a previous error, about not being wise even about any small thing.

Besides testing the reputed wisdom of the politician in order to under-stand the oracle, Socrates does something else not an obvious part of his clarifying project:

And then I tried to show him that he supposed he was wise, but he was not. So from this I became hateful both to him and to many of those present. (21c6–7)

We will return later to the question why Socrates undertakes the apparently extra project of trying to show to the politician his mistake about his seeming wisdom.

As Socrates investigates, he notices that those politicians most reputed wise seem peculiarly deficient compared to people considered more ordi-nary (*phauloteroi*: 22a5):

After this, I kept going to one after another, all the while perceiving with pain and fear that I was becoming hated. Nevertheless, it seemed to be necessary to regard the matter of the god as most important . . . I swear I was affected something like this: those with the best reputations (*hoi . . . malista eudokimountes*) seemed to me nearly the most deficient (*tou pleistou endeeis*), in my investigation in accordance with the god, while others who were reputed to be more ordinary seemed to be men more fit (*epieikesteroi*) in regard to being thoughtful (*phronimôs echein*). (21e3–22a8)

The "more ordinary" people Socrates refers to may be inconspicuous politi-cians, or they may simply be ordinary in the sense that they are not reputed to be wise about anything in particular. These more ordinary people seem to Socrates "more fit in regard to being thoughtful" (22a). That is, the smaller the reputation (for any kind of wisdom), the greater the fitness for being thoughtful. The greater the reputation, the less the fitness for being thoughtful.[10]

Socrates next examines some other claimants to the label "wise," the poets. The result is similar to his experience with the politicians, but with a difference. Not only do the poets show that they didn't know what they were talking about in their poems; they also make the mistake of thinking that their reputation for wisdom in poetry gives them a claim to being "wisest among human beings also about the other things." The "other things" are presumably the matters concerning which Socrates had examined the politicians, that is, matters concerning how people might best conduct their lives. The poets prove not wise about those other things (22a8–c).

Last, Socrates questions the craftsmen, who are certainly wiser than Socrates in their special expertises. The craftsmen also prove not wise about "the other things." "The other things" are clearly the "other things" of the examination of the poets, now described as "the biggest things":

> But . . . the good craftsmen also seemed to me to go wrong in the same way as the poets: because he performed his art in a fine way, each one deemed himself wisest also in the other things, the biggest things (22d7: *ta megista*). And this discordant note of theirs seemed to obscure that wisdom. (22d)

Socrates is then glad that he is not wise in the manner of the craft experts:

> So I asked myself on behalf of the oracle whether I would prefer to be as I am, being in no way wise in their wisdom or ignorant in their ignorance, or to have both things that they have. I answered myself and the oracle that it profits me to be just as I am. (22e)

Socrates' final point to explain how his examination of the reputedly wise earned him the name or label "wise," is this:

> Those present on each occasion suppose that I myself am wise in the things concerning which I refute someone else. (23b)

"The things concerning which I refute someone else" include the biggest things. On those matters, he has refuted all three groups he examined.

Socrates' preference not to be wise in the manner of the technical experts is one indication that he thinks the label a slander. Another indication is that he says the old accusers are "more terrible" (18b4) than the new. They accuse him "much more" (18e3) than the formal accusers:

---

[10]   de Stryker and Slings (1994, 68).

[The old accusers] got hold of you from childhood, and they accused me and persuaded you . . . that there is a certain Socrates, a wise man, a thinker on the things aloft, who has investigated all the things under the earth, and who makes the weaker speech the stronger. Those . . . are my terrible (*deinoi*) accusers. For their listeners hold that investigators of these things also do not believe in gods. (18b–c)

The vocabulary of the new or later accusers, as Socrates reports their charge, is this:

Socrates commits a crime[11] by corrupting the young and by not believing in the gods[12] in whom the city believes, but in other *daimonia* that are novel. (24b)

Although the word "wise" is not in the formal new accusation,[13] Socrates thinks that the old imputation of wisdom, the old "more terrible" accusation, lies behind the new one (19a8–b2). His summing up of the results of his questioning behavior also indicates that the label "wise" is the slander:

From this examination, Athenian men, many hatreds for me came to be – and the harshest and deepest sort – so that many slanders came to be from them, and being called this name, "wise." (22e6–23a3)[14]

The question now naturally arises: why is it so great a slander to be called wise concerning these "biggest things"? Part of the answer must be in Socrates' diagnosis of those he examined. His diagnosis was that their reputed wisdom was the source of their mistaken belief that they have wisdom about the biggest things. A mistake about the biggest things is one sort of big mistake. It is a slander to be classed with those who make a big mistake. Moreover, those most reputed for wisdom turned out to be

---

[11] The word *adikei* in an indictment is a legal term meaning "commits a crime" or "is guilty." See Burnet (1924) at 19b4d and at 24b9.
[12] The translation of the phrase "not believing in the gods" is controversial. Burnet at 18c prefers "not worshipping the gods" or "not acknowledging" (at 24c1) meaning "not conforming to customary observances." de Stryker and Slings (1994) at 18c3 and 24b9 argue for "not believing in."
[13] Socrates' imagined quotation of the old accusation at 19a ("the accusation from which has arisen the slander against me") doesn't use the word "wise," but uses a verb that gives the same effect, *periergazetai* (19b5). It can be translated "he is officious," "he is meddlesome," "he gets into what isn't his own business." And these have the effect of "he is impertinent," or "he is insolent," or "he is presumptuous." Burnet (1924) on 19b4 says that the clause "and he meddles"

is only added because . . . the old accusers had not said Socrates was legally "guilty" of anything, but only that he meddled with what did not concern him.

The slanderers had in mind that it is insolent to think about these extraordinary topics, topics that were perhaps in the domain of soothsayers.
[14] The last phrase would be more literally rendered "this name, 'being wise'." See Helm (1981) and Smyth (1920, §1615) for the phrasing. Edmunds (2006, 423) observes that although *sophos* "varied between positive and negative connotations," in Plato's *Apology* it is "distinctly derogatory."

less thoughtful than those with lesser or no reputation for wisdom. It is another slander to be classed with the less thoughtful.

We will learn more about the gravity of the slander implied in the label "wise," and more about what the biggest things that the reputed wise are reputedly wise about are if we look at some more types of reputedly wise people not among those whom Socrates examined in order to understand the oracle.

2.3 SOCRATES IS NEITHER AN INVESTIGATOR OF NATURE NOR A SOPHIST

Socrates does not report examining in reaction to the oracle two sorts of people that he recognizes as reputed wise and from whom he explicitly distinguishes himself in the *Apology*. These are the nature-theorists or physiologists and the sophists – though Socrates does not use the words "physiologists" or "sophists" in the *Apology*. Socrates says of the old accusers, who conflated Socrates with the nature-theorists:

[T]he slanderers slander, . . . "Socrates does injustice and is impertinent (*periergaze-tai*: 'is presumptuous') by investigating (*zêtôn*) the things under the earth and the heavenly things." . . . You yourselves have seen these things in the comedy of Aristophanes: a certain Socrates . . . claiming that he was walking on air and driveling much other drivel concerning matters about which I profess no expertise, either much or little. (19b–c)

The slanderers perhaps thought that since nature-theorists spoke about the realm of events considered signs from the gods, the nature-theorists were rivals to religion.[15] Popular opinion credited the nature-theorists with atheism (18c2–3).[16]

---

[15] Gomez-Lobo (1994, 16) explains the importance of Socrates' description:

> This way of specifying the domain of natural philosophy is highly significant, because it covers precisely the phenomena which had been traditionally taken to reveal the will of the gods. Soothsayers and prophets who were expected to provide members of the community with religious interpretations of these events were thus likely to regard the new physics as a threat to their craft and if adopted on a larger scale, as a threat to the religion of the state.

> Socrates' phrase, "things under the earth," also seems an allusion to Hades, the legendary underground realm of the dead.

[16] McPherran (1996, 92–116) explains how the strong implication of atheism came from the accusation that Socrates was like the nature-theoreticians and the sophists. In the *Laws* the Athenian Stranger perhaps represents the views of ordinary Athenians when he says that certain "wise men" (886d) say that sun, moon, and earth are simply earth and stone. At 889a–d he summarizes the explanations that "wise men" give of natural phenomena that eliminate reference to deities.

The nature-theorists Socrates probably had in mind, for example, Anaxagoras, seem to us today wildly speculative.[17] Yet the Socrates of the *Apology* is at least respectful of what they investigate. He says:

I do not say this to dishonor this sort of knowledge, if anyone is wise in such things – may I not in any way be the defendant against charges that large from Meletus – but in fact I, men of Athens, have no share in these things. (19c)

Socrates' qualification, "if anyone is wise in such things" expresses uncertainty that the practitioners are actually wise. His remark, "May I not . . . be the defendant against charges that large (*tosautas dikas*)" implies that he thought the charge of having no esteem for the knowledge that the nature-theorists professed was worse than the charge that he claimed that knowledge.[18] But the latter charge is bad enough.

Besides distinguishing himself from the inquirers into nature, Socrates distinguishes himself from the professional trainers in *aretê* or human achievement, the sophists, who sold their services to young men aiming at conspicuous success in competitive public life.[19] The sophists especially taught speaking skills. But Socrates believes the sophists claim a much larger sphere of expertise. The Socrates of the *Laches* says that the sophists

[17] Anaxagoras, mentioned at 26d, would be an example of the sort of theorist Socrates had in mind. Though Anaxagoras was no longer alive, presumably people who accepted his ideas were contemporary with Socrates. However wild these early speculators seem to us, we give them credit for taking the first step on a journey of genuine achievement in science. As Lloyd (1989, 336) says:

If many of the new wise men were short on delivery, they were long on aspiration, and the aspirations were of a kind that were, in time, to produce extraordinary delivery.

Lloyd concludes his book with this phrase, a gloss on the word "science": "The massive superstructures that have been erected on, or rather, built over, the foundations laid by some ancient visionaries."

There has been superstructure, but not obvious delivery, in the other area of interest – theology or atheology – of these early visionaries.

[18] Here I disagree somewhat with Burnet (1924). Burnet translates 19c7 "May Meletus never bring actions enough against me to make me do that." He comments:

Though he disclaims all competence in such matter for himself, Socrates is not to be frightened into expressing a contempt for science which he does not feel.

I think that rather than disclaiming potential fright, Socrates is simply making clear that his humility about the study of the natural universe is total.

[19] According to Griffith (1990, 188):

The pervasive Greek impulse toward competition, with its attendant psychological and social effects, has been well-documented and studied. Their "contest system," in its purest forms (e.g. war or athletics), is a "zero-sum" in which one person can win only if another, or several others, loses. Thus *aretê* amounts to "success, supremacy, being better" than others. Indeed, one of the main attractions, as well as dangers, of victory is the honor, envy, and even hatred that it elicits from one's rivals.

"alone claimed to be able to make me fine and good" (186c4). Socrates also does not disparage the wisdom and teaching skill the sophists are reputed to have. He simply denies having it:

If you have heard from anyone that I attempt to educate human beings and make money from it, that is not true either. Though this too seems to me to be fine, if one should be able to educate human beings like Gorgias[20] of Leontini and Prodicus of Ceos[21] and Hippias of Elis. (19d)

Socrates also mentions Evenus of Paros, "a wise man" (20b), reputed to be "knowledgeable (*epistêmôn*) in . . . virtue, that of human being and citizen." Socrates says:

I regarded Evenus as blessed if he should truly have this art . . . As for myself, I would be thinking myself very fine and priding myself indeed if I knew these things. But I do not know them. (20b–c)

It is significant that Socrates would regard Evenus as blessed if Evenus had the sort of wisdom that would enable him to teach people to be good human beings and citizens. "I regarded [him] as blessed" is *emakarisa*. Literally it means "I called him *makar*." *Makar* is most properly an epithet of the gods, although it can be used of supremely happy human beings.[22] Socrates thinks that someone who has this reputed wisdom of Evenus is god-like, for Socrates says:

Now those of whom I just spoke might perhaps be wise in some wisdom bigger than what is appropriate to a human being, or else I cannot say what [it is]. For I, at least, do not have knowledge of it, but whoever says so lies and speaks in order to slander me. (20d–e)

---

[20] Gorgias is classed as a sophist as a matter of tradition in that he was a traveling professional educator. Dodds (1959, 6–7) argues that Gorgias should not be classed as a sophist. Plato's *Gorgias* never depicts Gorgias as claiming to teach *aretê*. He teaches the specific skill of speaking (*Gorgias* 449a; 459d–460a). (See also *Meno* 95c.) Presumably his students hoped to use what Gorgias did teach to develop *aretê*. On the sophists as teachers of virtue, see Rowe (1983).

[21] Dover (1968, lv) says of Prodicus:

Prodicus was the most distinguished and respected intellectual of his day, and achieved in his lifetime . . . something like the "proverbial" status of Thales.

Burnyeat (1992, 63) observes that Prodicus is the sophist Plato names most often but discusses least.

[22] The Socrates of the *Hippias Major* speaks similarly to Hippias at 304b–c, using the related adjective *makarios*:

Friend Hippias, you are blessed (*makarios*) because you know what a human being (*anthrôpon*) ought to take up as a way of life (*epitêdeuein*) and you have taken up that way of life well enough, as you say.

Socrates is congratulating Hippias for Hippias' knowing what way of life any man should practice (*epitêdeuein*). See the LSJ entry for *makar*. The related adjective *makarios* is used for people with a secondary use for cities. The strong connection with the root word *makar* remains.

Socrates cannot seriously be considering the possibility that Evenus has this greater-than-human wisdom, since obviously Evenus and the others are not greater than human. Socrates is saying that the capacity to teach human virtue, to teach others what way of life to follow, is wisdom more than human. That is, it is fitting for a god.[23] And it is a lie and a slander to say that Socrates has this divine capacity to teach virtue.[24]

Since the sophists Evenus, Hippias, Gorgias, and Prodicus that Socrates mentions are professors of this bigger-than-human wisdom about how to conduct life, it may seem somewhat surprising that Socrates doesn't include them shortly thereafter when he mentions those that he examined to understand the pronouncement that no one was wiser than Socrates. In several of Plato's dialogues Socrates does in fact examine sophists, but the *Apology* does not tell us that he examined any sophists to understand the oracle.

Perhaps the oracle did not provoke Socrates to test sophists because Socrates assumes that the sophists are not to be counted among those "seeming wise" to his Athenian jurors and to the oracle. The sophists might seem wise to themselves and to those who hired them, but there was general Athenian distrust of the sophists, distrust that the oracle might be expected to share.[25]

2.4 SOCRATES IS NOT A SAGE

Socrates does not mention wise men of a third sort with whom we might expect him to contrast himself as he reacted to the oracle's pronouncement. They are the traditional sages. The unqualified term "wise" (*sophos*) is prominently a term of art for those traditional wise men. They were legendary for wisdom in various areas – technical expertise, political wisdom,

---

[23] Here I disagree with Benson (2000, 182). Benson thinks, first, that Socrates recognizes no conceptual problem with the thought that a human being might have greater than human wisdom and thinks, second, that Socrates is seriously allowing as a logical possibility that the sophists might be wise with a wisdom greater than human. Benson concedes that Socrates would not grant that this logical possibility is at all likely. I think the point is precisely that the ascription of superhuman wisdom to human beings is incoherent, but Socrates can't think of any other way but this obviously incoherent one to describe what the sophists claim for themselves ("or else I cannot say what [it is]" at 20d9–e2). (See also n. 35 below.)

[24] The Socrates of Aeschines Socraticus (*Alcibiades* fr. 11 Dittmar; *ssr* VI A 53,61) also disclaims knowledge of teaching virtue: "I had no knowledge I could teach the man to improve him, but I thought that by associating with him I could improve him through my love."

[25] *Meno* 91b–c gives evidence for Athenian distrust of sophists. Socrates has just referred to "those who profess to be teachers of virtue" as "those whom men call sophists." Anytus says:

May no one of my household or friends, whether citizen or stranger, be mad enough to go to these people and be harmed by them, for they clearly cause the ruin and corruption of their followers.

and great verbal skill, as displayed, for example, in the maxims or anecdotes of repartee associated with each sage reported in Diogenes Laertius.[26] Since there were no traditional sages around for Socrates to examine,[27] we don't ask why he didn't examine sages. But we can still ask why Socrates doesn't explicitly distinguish himself from the sages, for he would have been aware of traditional anecdotes that connected pronouncements by the Delphic oracle with the storied wise men, Anacharsis, Myson, Thales, and Solon.

In Diogenes Laertius'[28] version of a sixth-century anecdote (D.L. I, 108) the sage Anacharsis asked the Delphic oracle if anyone was wiser than Anacharsis. The oracle said that Myson was wiser. Anacharsis took an interest in his own reputation for wisdom, so he went to check out Myson. Diogenes Laertius relates that Anacharsis chided Myson because it was summer and Myson was repairing a plow. Anacharsis said, "This is not the season for the plow." Myson replied, "But it is the season to repair it." The anecdote invites us to infer that Myson's apt rejoinder establishes his superior wisdom.

The Delphic oracle made a pronouncement about wisdom in response to a slightly different question in the story of some fishermen who found a tripod tangled in their nets (D.L. I, 27–33). Asked by the fishermen who should get the tripod, the oracle answered, "Whoever is wisest." The fishermen made the judgment about wisdom, and gave the tripod to Thales. Thales delivered it to another sage, starting a sequence of deliveries that

---

[26] The reports of Diogenes Laertius (second century AD) are much later than the putative dates of the sages (early sixth century BC). But Diogenes Laertius' lore about the sages is still evidence of what was expected of sages in earlier antiquity.

Martin (1993, 113–116) identifies recurrent features of sages:

First, the sages are poets; second, they are involved in politics; and third, they are performers . . . By performance, I mean a public enactment, about important matters, in word or gesture employing conventions and open to scrutiny and criticism, especially criticism of style. Performance can include what we call art. But . . . it can also include such things as formalized greetings . . . rituals, insult duels, and the recitation of genealogies . . . [V]erbal skill is part and parcel of the sages' roles as poetic performers; . . . the function of the wise men as poets and actors come together in their production of proverbial sayings.

Goldman (2004, 6–8) links sages and aphorisms.

[27] All the traditional sages are dated at the early sixth century BC. There is some literary evidence that "the canon was forming . . . at the beginning of the fifth century; though the first explicit attestation of a Group of Seven is in Plato *Protagoras* 343a" (OCD *s.v.* "Seven Sages").

[28] D.L. (1991); Hicks (1925/1991); Parke and Wormell (1956, II s.n. 245 and I, 384–385). D.L. twice gives a direct quotation of the oracle's response in verse (D.L. I, 28 and I, 106). D.L. I, 30 reports that Chilon also asked the Pythian Apollo who was wiser than Chilon and also got the answer "Myson." Parke and Wormell (1956, I, 385) say that the response about Myson is one of a group of three legends "probably . . . all . . . produced at Delphi in the period when the oracle was at its height in the mid-sixth century." de Stryker and Slings (1994, 77–8, including n. 57) give references and history of the Myson story.

finally reached Solon. Solon sent the tripod to Delphi, saying that the god is wisest.[29] In the anecdote Solon did not deny that he was wise: he did not resist being put into a competition with the god.[30] Solon took his wisdom as comparable to, though less than, the wisdom of the gods.

Myson differs from Thales and Solon in the anecdotes in that the oracle herself deems Myson wise, while people, not the oracle, award the wisdom-prize to Thales or Solon. So the presumably actual wisdom of Myson, pronounced on by the oracle (who cannot mean anything false)[31] and displayed in Myson's repartee, may differ from the reputed wisdom of Thales and of Solon. Very little beyond the anecdote is known about Myson. Perhaps the oracle named Myson because he lived so obscurely. Myson was "famous for his very obscurity"[32] and lacks the reputation that Socrates diagnosed as causing the incapacity for thoughtfulness of the politicians and as causing the bad mistake of the poets and craftsmen.

The ancient stories are evidence that people would naturally understand the oracle about Socrates as a comparison to the reputed wisdom of the sages. The Socrates of Plato's depiction would have been aware of these stories. (The Socrates of the *Protagoras* lists Myson among the sages at 343a4.) Socrates would have seen that the oracle's answer to Chaerephon implied that Socrates was at least as wise as the traditional sage Myson.

Since Socrates decides, after examining his contemporaries, that he has the very small wisdom that consists in not believing himself wise, he might have credited himself with the wisdom of the obscure Myson, which also consisted in humility. But in front of his judges it would have been inadvisable and arrogant-seeming for Socrates to compare himself to any sage. The jurors might very well have taken the actual wisdom of Myson, named by the oracle, to be the same as the divine wisdom reputed of other sages, such as Solon. It seems a good strategy of Socrates not to mention

[29] Montuori (1981, 136) says the oracle to Chaerephon is "linked to the old legend of the tripod." But Montuori cites D.L. for the tripod anecdote, not an older source. This is part of Montuori's case that Plato invented the story of the oracle to Chaerephon.

[30] D.L. I, 28–29 gives a similar anecdote about the bowl of Bathycles, inscribed to whoever had done the most good by his wisdom. The bowl was given to Thales, passed around to all the sages, and returned to Thales, who then gave the bowl to the shrine of Apollo at Didyma. Unlike Solon, Thales doesn't claim that the god is wiser.

[31] Some evidence, though far from conclusive evidence, that the oracle was considered incapable of lying is in Euripides' *Iphigenia in Tauris*: 1247ff.: "Phoebus, . . . [you] now sit on the golden tripod, on an undeceiving throne" (*apseudei thronô(i)* 1254). Socrates evidently thinks that at least his audience believes the oracle cannot lie, since he introduces it as "a speaker trustworthy (*axiochreôn*) to you" (20e6).

[32] *Oxford Classical Dictionary*, 3rd edn., "Seven Sages" entry by Griffiths. D.L. credits only one life-guiding maxim to Myson. Solon, on the other hand, like other sages, has several.

in his defense any traditional sages, some of whom had reputations for near-divine wisdom.

2.5 THE THOUGHTFULNESS (*PHRONÊSIS*) THAT SOCRATES CONSIDERS SO IMPORTANT

We may now assemble pieces for an explanation of the magnitude of the slander involved in a reputation for being wise about the biggest things.

Socrates says that more important than honor, reputation, and money is care of the soul:

I will speak just the sorts of things I am accustomed to. "Best of men, you are an Athenian, from the city that is greatest and most reputed for wisdom and strength: are you not ashamed that you care for having as much money as possible, and reputation, and honor, but that you neither care for nor give thought to thoughtfulness (*phronêseôs*), and truth, and how your soul will be the best possible?" And if one of you disputes it and asserts that he does care, I will . . . examine and test him. And if he does not seem to me to possess virtue, but only says he does, I will reproach him, saying that he regards the things worth the most (*ta pleistou axia*) as the least important, and the paltrier things as most important . . .

No greater good has arisen for you . . . For I go around and do nothing but persuade you . . . not to care for bodies and money before, or as vehemently as, how your soul will be the best possible. (29d–30b)

Socrates' statement is worth several comments.

First, since he also says at 32d, "[M]y *whole* care is to practice nothing unjust or impious" (my emphasis), we have evidence that he simply identifies care of the soul with acting justly. The two different descriptions, "care of the soul" and "not practicing what is unjust and impious," describe exactly one concern. He thinks of the soul as the source of the way you act. Care for the soul to be the best possible is care about how best to conduct your life. I emphasize that care for the soul is a very practical matter of figuring out how you will conduct your life day to day. It is care for your dispositions and beliefs, your mental and emotional equipment out of which you act every day. (Socrates does not mean that care for the soul is concern for some separable item stuck in the body, the tending of which is separate from concern for the activities of daily life.)

Second, the passage indicates that the most important thing to care about – how to live – is the very thing that the reputed wise men claimed to know about. How to guide the lives of people in a city is what the politicians were reputed to be wise about and what the sophists offered to teach about.[33] The most important thing to care about then is the biggest thing someone could claim to know about.

Third, to care about how to live well (to care about your soul) requires having thoughtfulness. 29d9–e3 is evidence, as Socrates asks: "Are you not ashamed that you... neither care for (*epimelê(i)*) nor give thought to thoughtfulness (*phronêsis*) and truth, and how your soul will be the best possible?"

Fourth, Socrates reports that he initiates conversation with Athenians with a challenge: "Athenian... are you not ashamed that you... neither care?" And this seems odd. His challenge seems to assume that the person he is speaking to – apparently any Athenian – does not care for his soul. We need some explanation of why it would be appropriate to accost a random Athenian with that accusation. The most likely explanation is that Athens is "best reputed for wisdom."[34] Socrates' examination of reputedly wise people revealed that they were least thoughtful, so Socrates has reason to think it likely that any citizen of a city reputed for wisdom is also not thoughtful.

Fifth, the passage tells us that examination or testing can disclose that someone does not care about this most important matter, how he lives. Consider Socrates' examination of Meletus in the *Apology*:

You have sufficiently displayed that you never gave any thought (*ephrontisas*) to the young. And you are making your own lack of care (*ameleian*) plainly apparent, since you have cared nothing (*ouden soi memelêken*) about the things for which you bring me here. (25c)

---

33 At *Gorgias* 515c–d Socrates gets Callicles' assent to the proposal that a person active in politics has the object of making the citizens as good as possible. At 516b Callicles assents to the statement that Pericles was a "caretaker of men," and that he should have turned people out more just and not more unjust "if while he cared for them he really was good at politics" (516c). The assumption that the political art is the same as the knowledge of how to educate people in virtue would explain why in the *Meno* it is relevant for Socrates to elicit from his interlocutor, Anytus (who is also one of the formal accusers) the proposition that certain politicians can't even bring up their own children well (*Meno* 92e–94e). Anytus assumes that the politicians' reputed wisdom is the knowledge of how to educate people in virtue. *Meno* (91a–b) refers to "that wisdom and virtue which enables men to manage their households and their cities well, to take care of their parents, to know how to welcome and to send away both citizens and strangers as a good man should" in connection with the question whether virtue is teachable. At *Meno* 92e–94a Anytus thinks that anyone among Athenian gentlemen (*tôn kalôn kagathôn* 92e4) will make a young man a better man (i.e. educate him in virtue (92d)) than the sophists would. The examples concerning whom Socrates then goes on to ask whether they were "good teachers of their own virtue" are all of people prominent in public life ("good at public affairs" (*agathoi ta politika* 93a5–6)). The examples he considers are Themistocles, Aristides, Pericles, and the statesman Thucydides. *Meno* 99e–100a suggests that virtue in a statesman/citizen is without understanding unless the person who has it can make someone else into a statesman/citizen.

34 de Stryker and Slings (1994, 19–21, especially n. 36) think Plato could not realistically portray Socrates as speaking in 399 BC of Athens' great reputation, since it had suffered a severe decline. I think Socrates might reasonably refer to Athens' past glory.

Socrates reaches this assessment of Meletus after these steps in their conversation. Meletus, who claims that Socrates corrupts young people (24c)
and that it is most important that young people be made better (24d) is
at first unable to answer (24d) when Socrates asks him who does make
young people better. Meletus claims (25d) that only one person, Socrates,
corrupts young people. Meletus is unable to explain how this extraordinary
situation obtains with young people when it does not obtain with other
animals. Meletus shows that he has not bothered to examine his own views
in a minimal way. Even in his confused state he is confident enough to take
the measure of Socrates' life, and to deem that Socrates deserves execution
for corrupting others. As Socrates says, Meletus is "easily bringing human
beings to trial" (24c6).

The manner of Meletus' failure under examination displays his lack
of thoughtfulness and lack of care. Having brought legal charges against
Socrates for believing in half-divine (*daimonia*) beings different from the
gods of Athens, Meletus says at 26d–27 that Socrates does not believe
in gods at all. Meletus has not noticed his simply contradictory professions. When Socrates calls his attention to his contradiction, Meletus is
untroubled. He does not desist, in his ignorance, from confidently assessing
another's life.

Mere failure to survive examination is not what reveals Meletus' lack
of thoughtfulness and care. It is Meletus' not being puzzled or hesitant
when his immediate contradiction appears that reveals his thoughtlessness.
Indeed, your failure of a Socratic examination, if accompanied by a troubled
and humbled reaction, might be exactly what did reveal your care and
thoughtfulness.

2.6 THE "GREATEST THINGS"

Socrates has used the plural phrase "the greatest things" or "the biggest
things" (*ta megista*: 22d7). It clearly refers to the same items as the phrase
"the things concerning which I refute someone else" (23b). I understand
it to refer to matters involved in how people would best live their lives.
Considering these matters as a whole, I then speak of this as the (singular)
biggest thing: the question how one should live one's life. I think that is
the sole content of the phrase "the greatest things," as well as of the phrase
"the things worth the most" (30a1–2). In particular it does not mean "the
most advanced or complicated technical things" such as tripling the cube
or explaining the scientific problems of the day.

I also think that Socrates would not have in mind what awaits us after death as one of the "greatest things" to think about. He says that we should not think about death at all when deciding how to act: one should consider only whether we are doing just things or unjust things, that is, the actions of a good man or a bad one (28b).[35]

2.7 WHY THE LABEL "WISE" IS A TERRIBLE SLANDER

We may now draw some conclusions.

First, it has become clear that caring about the greatest or biggest thing, or the most important thing, is different from knowing about it. Care about how to live is thoughtfulness or *phronêsis*. Knowledge about how to live Socrates speaks of as wisdom (*sophia*). The sophists' reputed wisdom about "the greatest things," because it is (reputed) knowledge, implies the much larger capacity to teach others how to live.[36] But Socrates thinks that this knowledge or *sophia* that brings with it the capacity to educate others to live their lives well (20d–e) is in fact too big for people and, rather, fitting for a god.[37] And Socrates emphatically denies that he has that capacity, as when he says:[38]

---

[35] On the point that our fate after death is one of the greatest things that might be known about I disagree with Kahn (1996, 89) who includes several items among the greatest things:

> Socrates concludes that wisdom concerning "the greatest things" (how to make men better, what constitutes a good life, what awaits us after death, and the like) is not available to human beings at all, but is a possession of the gods alone. (1996, 89)

Kahn apparently does not (as I would not) count knowledge of the world of nature as one of the greatest things, because Socrates does not rule out the possibility that people might achieve that.

[36] See Reeve (1989, 37–45) on "the knowledge of virtue claimed by the professional sophist teachers of it – i.e. *expert knowledge* as we may call it" (Reeve 1989, 34). Reeve says:

> Expert knowledge of virtue enables someone to teach people to be virtuous. In Socrates' view, that is what the . . . sophists claimed to be able to do (*Grg.* 519c3–d1; *Hp. Ma.* 283c2–5; *La.* 186c2–5; *Prt.* 319a3–7). Gorgias, Prodicus, Hippias, and Evenus are mentioned precisely in regard to the question of who Callias should engage to teach his sons virtue. (1989, 37)

McPherran (1996, 198) also observes that expert knowledge implies teaching ability.

[37] Reeve (1989, 40) has an interesting argument that the craft-knowledge of virtue is god-like. Referring to *Apology* 30b3–4 which says that "virtue . . . makes wealth and everything else, both public and private, good for a man," he comments:

> [I]f virtue has the property of making life and its other components good, and if craft is luck-independent, anyone who has craft-knowledge of virtue surely has a god-like power. For it does seem reasonable to suppose that only a god-like being could both reliably make himself virtuous and insulate the good he would thereby achieve from the threatening effects of bad luck (cf. *Men.* 100b2–4; *Rep.* 497b7–c3).

[38] Compare *Theages*, which makes exactly this point. Socrates is speaking to Demodocus, who wants Socrates to teach his son, Theages (127b–c). Theages wants to lead (*archein*) citizens (126a) and would like Socrates to take him into his company (*suneinai*: (127a)). Socrates says:

I would be thinking myself very fine and priding myself if I had knowledge of these things . . . But I do not have knowledge of them . . . Those of whom I spoke might perhaps be wise in some wisdom greater than human . . . I . . . do not know it, but whoever says so lies and speaks for the purpose of slander against me. (20c1–e3)

Second, it has become clear that although Socrates does not consider himself wise, he evidently considers himself to care about how to live and to be thoughtful about how to live.[39] His rebuke of Athenians at 29d shows that.

Third, because Socrates found those reputedly wisest least fit for being thoughtful, we see that believing that you know about how to live is an obstacle to being thoughtful about how to live. Socrates' self-description in the *Apology* tells us that he practices thoughtfulness and care. That is, he actively tests himself by examining his and others' action-guiding beliefs.

[I]f Theages . . . is looking for some . . . persons who profess to be able to educate (*paideuein*) young people, we have here Prodicus of Ceos, Gorgias of Leontini, Polus of Acragas, and many more, who are so wise (*houtô sophoi*) that they go to our cities and persuade the noblest and wealthiest of our young men . . . to learn from them . . . Some of these persons might naturally have been chosen both by your son and by yourself; for I have no knowledge of those blessed (*makariôn*) and fine objects of study.

At this point Socrates says he knows nothing but love matters. This presumably includes how to treat a beloved. For the Socrates of the *Lysis*, that means to humble the beloved (*Lysis* 210e). That might suggest that the sophists don't love those they teach.

[39] Here I disagree with Benson (2000, 182). Benson cites 29d2–30b2 where, according to Benson, Socrates exhorts the people of Athens to care for the wisdom they lack.

Benson says of Socrates' exhortation: "This would be utter nonsense if Socrates believed that the wisdom they lacked was unattainable."

I would object that at 29e1 Socrates does not urge Athenians to get *sophia*; he urges them to get *phronêsis*, that is, thoughtfulness. Presumably a large component of thoughtfulness is the small and not divine wisdom that you don't know the big thing that the reputed wise men think they know. Benson is of course correct to say that Socrates' exhorting Athenians to strive for something unattainable would be unintelligible. But if, as I think, Socrates is exhorting them to care for thoughtfulness, which includes merely human wisdom, which is attainable, the exhortation is intelligible. Socrates is not urging them to go after the (purported) divine wisdom of the sophists that involves the capacity to educate human beings into virtue. Benson cites *Lysis* 218a4, where Socrates says that "the wise, gods or men" can't do philosophy (can't love wisdom). But that doesn't imply that any men are wise. It means that *if* anyone is wise – whether god or man, he can't love wisdom.

de Stryker and Slings (1994, 15–16)) take *phronêsis* and *sophia* to be the same ("perfect knowledge (*sophia, phronêsis*)" and "Only god possesses perfect knowledge"). They take *sophia* to be beyond human reach. It seems to me, on the contrary, that in the *Apology* Socrates uses the words *sophia* and *phronêsis* to maintain a deliberate distinction between the divine wisdom that humans cannot have (*sophia*) and the thoughtfulness that they can work at (*phronêsis*). In other dialogues he does not distinguish wisdom and thoughtfulness when it isn't necessary for his purposes in the particular discussion (e.g. *Euthydemus* 281b).

Benson's sound argument that Socrates thinks what he is exhorting people to get (as it happens, *phronêsis*) is accessible provides a solid reason to conclude that what he is urging them to get is distinct from *sophia*.

Forster (2007) discusses Socrates' lack of divine knowledge.

Acknowledging ignorance is necessary for constant examination. If, instead, one believes that one is knowledgeable, one will see no reason to test oneself. So one cannot possibly be thoughtful. One will be, as Socrates discovered in his examination of claimants to knowledge, the least fit for being thoughtful. One cannot desire to get one's soul into the best state possible if one thinks it is already in the best state.[40] One cannot then care about virtue.

We can now say more about the mistake that the politicians, poets, and craftsmen, who bear the label "wise," are making. Their mistake is to think that they have the god-like ability to teach people how best to live. It is a big mistake because it is a mistake about the most important thing for people to care about. It is then the biggest mistake possible for a human being. Moreover, because to bear the label "wise" causes the defect that those who bear it are least fit for being thoughtful, those reputed wise can transmit a very bad condition when they pretend to teach others their wisdom. Their students, now believing themselves wise about the biggest things, will themselves be less fit for being thoughtful about their lives than before being taught. To be less thoughtful is to be more foolish. To be foolish is the worst condition for one's soul.[41] These reputed wise men that can induce thoughtlessness in their students are therefore in a position to do the worst harm to others by preventing them from caring about the most important things.

At last, we have the explanation why the label "wise" is such a terrible slander. It implies that Socrates is making the biggest mistake possible for a human being. It implies that he is not thoughtful. It implies that he cannot care about the most important thing. And, finally, it implies that he is in a position to do the worst possible harm. So those who label him wise are, as Socrates says, the most terrible of his accusers (18b3, 4; 18e3). Socrates does

---

[40] Yonezawa (1995) identifies *phronêsis* (which he calls "prudence") with "the Socratic awareness of ignorance rather than expert knowledge . . . That is to say that prudence is human wisdom." I agree that, as Yonezawa says, there is a strong connection between awareness of ignorance and *phronêsis* (thoughtfulness), but I think *phronêsis* must go beyond the awareness of ignorance into an active search for possible self-contradiction. If thoughtfulness were simply identical with awareness of ignorance about the most important things, Socrates would not *gradually* have discovered that those who were most reputed for wisdom were not thoughtful. It would have been obvious. But Socrates seems surprised that the most reputedly wise were the least thoughtful: he says (22a): "I swear . . . I actually (*ê mên*) experienced some such thing." It required some further step to discover that those unaware of their ignorance made no active effort to avoid acting out of their ignorance.

[41] For the idea that the worst thing is to be thoughtless see also *Crito* 44d. Socrates says:

Would that the many could produce the greatest evils, Crito, so that they could also produce the greatest goods! That would indeed be fine. But as it is, they can do neither. For they aren't capable of making someone either thoughtful or thoughtless, but do whatever they happen on.

not mean that their accusation, "wise," is terrible in being most likely to bring the most repercussions from the public. He means that their charge is the worst and most shameful possible charge.[42] To say, then, that Socrates is wise perpetuates the slander that dismayed Socrates.[43]

2.8 SOCRATES IN THE *APOLOGY* SOMETIMES ECHOES HIS ACCUSERS

We have seen (20d; 21d; 22e–23b) that Socrates distinguished the superficial understanding of the oracle from the correct meaning that he finally assigned to it.

To understand the oracle superficially is to think that its comparison that no one is wiser than Socrates means that no person is wiser-in-Athenian-reputed-wisdom than Socrates. It is to suggest that Socrates thinks he has a kind of wisdom that actually only the gods could have (23a5–6: "Really, the god is wise").

Socrates decides that when properly understood, the word "wise," as it figures in the oracle, makes an ascription of a different kind of wisdom to Socrates. He is "wise in a human way" (21d). The oracle means that Socrates has the tiny wisdom of not supposing that he knows anything big. His wisdom has nothing to do with reputation, and it is merely about a small thing. Socrates now has a new use for the word "wise," a use in which it cannot correctly be applied to the gods.

Though Socrates and his slanderers use the word "wise" differently, it is not obvious how to express the difference. Shall we say that "wise" is ambiguous? Shall we say that it is a very incomplete predicate? Or shall we say the popular application of "wise" is a misuse? There seems to be some argument for saying the latter if the word, as popularly understood for "divinely knowledgeable," is false of all of the people to whom it is popularly applied. But the matter of what exactly to say about the word "wise" is worth more reflection.

---

[42] That it is the charge of being wise that repelled Socrates would explain why the oracle is not mentioned in other dialogues of Plato's besides the *Apology*. Once he understood the oracle, Socrates would not have been inclined to spread about the news of the oracle, which would be so easily misunderstood to be giving him the slanderous label, "wise." Socrates' calling Chaerephon's brother (21a) as witness for the oracle story seems evidence that the pronouncement of the oracle was not widely known even near the end of Socrates' life. Plato, in not mentioning the oracle in other dialogues, would be reproducing Socrates' silence about it.

[43] I would thus very much resist the formulation of Goldman (2004, 14):

Plato casts Socrates as also the heir of that earlier philosophical tradition, which spoke in maxims and aphorisms, and which makes the platonic Socrates not only a figure to whom primarily a "method" and an attitude can be attributed, but also a sage.

To select a manner of expression that is accurate about the role of the word "wise" in Socrates' defense, I'll look at some other locutions that Socrates uses differently from his accusers.

For example, Socrates says explicitly that he doesn't use the phrase "terrific at speaking" in the same way as his accusers:

[The accusers] said that . . . I am terrific at speaking (*deinou ontos legein*). They are not ashamed that they will immediately be refuted by me in deed, since I will show myself as in no way terrific at speaking . . . unless of course they call terrific at speaking the one who speaks the truth.[44] For if they mean this, I would agree that I am an orator – but not in their way. (17a)

Socrates explains a terrific speaker as one who says what is true. Presumably his accusers do not mean, when they say that Socrates is a terrific speaker, that a terrific speaker tells the truth. They mean that a terrific speaker can sway an audience in the direction he chooses. When Socrates says, "if they mean this," he raises the possibility that the accusers might mean exactly what he means. But he does not seriously think so, since he goes on to say that he is an orator, but not in their way.[45] He means by "terrific speaker" and "orator" something different from what his accusers mean.

Socrates says (35d) that he believes (*nomizô*)[46] in gods as none of his accusers do. Since his accusers say that he does not believe in gods (26c7), and would obviously say that they themselves do believe in gods, Socrates applies the phrase "believes in gods" differently from his accusers.

He says (40e) that he correctly calls "judges" those who voted for his acquittal. He implies that it is incorrect to call the others "judges," as he

---

[44] de Stryker and Slings (1994) comment on "unless of course they call terrific at speaking one who speaks the truth" at 17b 4–6:

The hyperbaton, by which Socrates disjoins the elements of the standing phrase *deinos legein*, emphasizes his paradoxical suggestion that his opponents are giving the expression a meaning of their own, not in accordance with normal usage,

I would say, more neutrally, that Socrates is giving the expression a meaning different from the meaning his accusers give it. Whether his accusers are speaking with normal usage would depend upon whether ordinary language users more admire persuasive speakers than they admire truth-telling speakers. We don't know what normal usage is until we have a good grasp of the tastes of most Athenian speakers. But the distinction between Socrates' usage and his opponents' usage is firm.

[45] Burnet (1924) at 17b6 explains *ou kata toutous*, which I understand as "not in their way" as meaning "not on the same level as them," "not to be compared with them." He says: "Accordingly [it] . . . is equivalent to . . . 'too good an orator to be compared with them'."

Helm (1981) cites Smyth (1920, §1690 2b), which gives *Apology* 17b6 as meaning "an orator after their style." My understanding is closer to Smyth's than to Burnet's.

[46] Burnet (1924) in his note on d6 says that the verb practically means "I fear god." I wouldn't expect Socrates to be alluding to fear here. "I genuinely acknowledge" seems to me a more likely sense. (See LSJ: the verb seems to refer to a disposition of acknowledging, rather than to temporary lip-service.)

understands the word "judge." He has previously said (18a) that a judge (*dikastês*) considers whether what is said (at a trial) is just or not. He is using the word "judges" differently from most of Athens, who apply the word "judges" simply to those in a certain judicial role. (Throughout his speech Socrates avoids addressing the jurors as "judges," although that is a standard form of address for a party in a trial to use. Meletus calls them "judges" at 26d.)[47]

In the case of another important word, "philosophize," we can deduce that Socrates uses it differently from others. He says:

> They [the accusers] say that Socrates is someone most disgusting, and that he corrupts the young. And whenever someone asks them, "By doing what and teaching what?" they have nothing to say, but are ignorant. So in order not to seem to be at a loss, they say the things that are ready at hand against all who philosophize: "the things aloft and under the earth" and "not believing in gods" and "making the weaker speech the stronger." (23d)

His accusers use "to philosophize" to cover lecturing about things Socrates never talks about (19d) – the heavens, the underworld and afterlife, not believing in the gods, and making the weaker speech the stronger (23d). His audience will recognize the accusers' use. Socrates might have said of the old accusers, "they say the things that are ready to hand against all those who, *as they would say*, philosophize."[48]

Socrates uses "philosophize" in a way that contrasts with the popular use and his accusers' use:

---

[47] De Stryker and Slings (1994, 35) say: "Socrates never in the course of his defence addresses them as a body with the phrase *ô andres dikastai*."

De Stryker and Slings reserves that phrase for those who voted for his acquittal (40a2–3). De Stryker and Slings (1994, 35, n. 25) cite *Gorgias* 522c1–2, where Socrates

speaks of the helplessness which will befall him if he is ever brought before a court; for then he will not be able to speak the truth and . . . to use *your* words for them, "*ô andres dikastai.*"

This is an example of how Socrates calls attention to the way someone else speaks when he wants to indicate that it differs from the way he would himself speak.

[48] Though Socrates uses only the verb "philosophize" and doesn't use the noun "philosopher" in his defense speech, it is relevant, to understand the use of "philosophize" that he expects from his accusers, to look at how some other people in Socrates' time used the related noun, "philosopher." For example, Gorgias, reputedly the best speaker–competitor of his time, mentions in his *Encomium of Helen* (7.13):

Contests of philosophers' accounts (*logoi*) in which is revealed how easily the swiftness of thought makes our confidence in our opinion change (trans. Richard D. McKirahan from McKirahan (1994, 377)).

His phrase, "[c]ontests of philosophers" shows that he thought of philosophers as contestants engaged in verbal competitions of persuasion.

If you would say to me . . . "Socrates, . . . we will let you go, but on this condition: that you no longer spend time in this investigation or philosophize; and if you are caught doing this, you will die" – if you would let me go . . . on these conditions, I would say to you, "I, men of Athens, salute you and love you, but I will obey the god rather than you; and as long as I breathe and am able to, I will certainly not stop philosophizing; and I will exhort and show you, saying to whomever of you I happen to meet just the sorts of things I am accustomed to: . . . are you not ashamed that you care for having as much money as possible, and reputation, and honor, but that you neither care for (*epimelê(i)*) nor give thought to (*phrontizeis*) thoughtfulness (*phronêseôs*), and truth, and how your soul will be the best possible?" And if one of you disputes it and asserts that he does care, I will question him and examine and test him. And if he does not seem to me to possess virtue, but only says he does, I will reproach him, saying that he regards the things worth the most as the least important and the paltrier things as most important. (29d)

When he says, "I will certainly not stop philosophizing," and then goes on to explain that he will not stop examining and reproaching, he shows that he is using "philosophize" for examining and reproaching. At 28e5–6 philosophizing is glossed as "examining myself and others."

Socrates' activity that he calls "philosophizing" here is quite different from the activity to which his accusers apply the verb "philosophize." His accusers say that theorizing about nature or the gods (or absence thereof), for example, is philosophizing. To make pronouncements about the nature or nonexistence of gods would be incompatible with Socrates' awareness of his ignorance.[49] For Socrates philosophizing involves examining people who claim they care, reproaching those who under examination reveal that they do not care, and urging people to care for the most important things.[50]

In saying (23d) that not believing in the gods is held against "all who philosophize," Socrates uses "philosophize" in a popular way that contrasts very strongly with his self-descriptive use. Given Socrates' understanding of "philosophize" as he uses it of himself (explained at 29d–e), it would be

---

[49] Compare Socrates in the *Phaedrus* (229–230): "It seems to me ridiculous to investigate things that belong to others (*ta allotria*) when I am ignorant of this," where "this" refers to himself, i.e. the best conduct of his life.

[50] If you claim that you care, and claim that you possess virtue, and prove not to, you show that you do not care.

Weiss (2001, 182) comments:

In the *Apology* a sign that one lacks or has failed to acquire virtue seems to be one's *caring* about the wrong things: "And if one of you . . . asserts that he does care . . . And if he does not seem to me to possess . . . virtue, but only says he does, I will reproach him, saying that he regards the things worth the most as the least important, and the paltrier things as more important." (*Apology* 29e–30a2)

Weiss observes that some readers take this passage to show that virtue requires some important, perhaps definitional, knowledge. Weiss (1991, 182, n. 27) cites Irwin (1977, 90).

false to say, "The nature-theorists philosophize." Speaking at 23d, Socrates is echoing his accusers.

He echoes an accuser comparably when he says:

Meletus, the good and city-loving, as he says. (24b4–6)

Socrates' addition, "as he says," tells us that in calling Meletus "good and city-loving," Socrates speaks as Meletus speaks. In translating, we might put quotation marks around "good and city-loving," to indicate that the phrase is a direct quotation from Meletus, presumably from Meletus' presentation of his case to the jury.[51] Socrates is not endorsing Meletus' self-assessment. Speaking to himself, Socrates would not say that Meletus is good and city-loving. But here Socrates is not speaking as he would ordinarily speak. He is echoing Meletus.

Similarly at 24d4 Socrates says to Meletus:

Tell these men, who makes [young people] better? For it is clear that you know – because you care (*melon ge soi*).[52]

Later Socrates shows that Meletus neither knows nor cares. Yet here Socrates mirrors what Meletus would say about himself. (Perhaps in speaking to the judges, Meletus has claimed that he cares, or perhaps Socrates is making wordplay.)

Although Socrates speaks as Meletus speaks, and although Socrates does not himself think that Meletus is city-loving or patriotic, or knows or cares, we don't yet have evidence that Socrates means something different by the words "city-loving," "patriotic," "knows," or "cares" from what Meletus means. We do have evidence that when speaking for himself, expressing his own convictions, Socrates applies these words to different people. We have

---

[51] West and West (1998) translate with quotation marks, not used in ancient Greek: "But against Meletus, the 'good and patriotic,' as he says, and the later accusers, I will try to speak next" (24b).

West and West (1998) may be indicating that the phrase is a direct quote from Meletus, or may be using the quotation marks as so-called "scare-quotes," or "sneer-quotes," or "irony quotes" to show that Socrates is not endorsing what he says.

de Stryker and Slings (1994) at 24b point out that it would have been the usual practice for parties in a lawsuit to "extol their own ethical and civic merits."

Socrates attributes what he is saying to his interlocutor also at *Hippias Major* 304b–c: "Hippias, you are blessed, because you know what a man ought to take up as a way of life, and you have taken up that way of life well enough, as you say."

[52] de Stryker and Slings (1994, xiii and 299) differ from Reeve on the effect of the particle *ge* with the participle. Reeve (1989, 87) thinks that the participial clause cannot be supplied with "because" since then Socrates would be making the silly claim that if you care about something you know about it. De Stryker and Slings say that the particle in a participial clause often has the force of "because." I would not dispute de Stryker and Slings on the translation. Reeve is of course right that the inferential sequence looks odd. But here in suggesting a weak inference, Socrates might be echoing what Meletus would say: that because he cares so much, he does know about these matters.

evidence that when speaking as his accusers speak, he may say something that he thinks is false, although others would say that it is true.

For such locutions as the phrase "terrific speaker" and the verb "philosophize," however, it seems more correct to say that Socrates not only applies these locutions differently, but that he also means by them something different from what his accusers mean. For he explains the sense of his words differently from the way he would explain the sense of his accusers' words.

We have now a short list of locutions, each of which Socrates explicitly acknowledges that he uses differently from the way his accusers and his Athenian audience use them: "wise," "terrific speaker," "orator," "believes in the gods," and "judges." In fact each of these satisfies a test for ambiguity, in that it is true and false of the same things. It is both true (given one explanation of what the words mean) and false (given another explanation of what the words mean) to say: "Socrates is a terrific speaker," "Socrates is an orator," "Socrates is wise," "Those who are on Socrates' jury and who voted against him are not judges," "Socrates believes in gods," and "Socrates' accusers do not believe in gods." We can also infer that the verb "philosophizes" is ambiguous. For Socrates holds that it is false to say that he philosophizes as his accusers understand what doing philosophy is; but it is true that he philosophizes as he describes it at 29d.

To be thorough, we should also consider the possibility that the words that seem ambiguous are not actually ambiguous, but that one or other of Socrates or his accusers uses them incorrectly and simply misapplies them.[53] However, if the words are established parts of ordinary Athenian language, that is some reason to say that ordinary Athenians know how to use those words. If lots of ordinary Athenians declare that someone is a judge, that person is a judge, for example. If ordinary Athenians say they believe in gods, then they do believe in gods. Yet Socrates also has some claim to know how to talk, so we can also grant him his uses of the familiar words. However, anyone who is not sensitive to the ambiguities, as Socrates is, is likely to misunderstand others.

The verb "philosophize," in contrast to the other locutions, is less ordinary and familiar.[54] However, it has the accusers' use that Socrates' audience will recognize. (My chapters 7 and 9 will explore how other people use it.)

---

[53] Gallie (1964b) is relevant to the question of who, if anyone, is using the differently applied locutions correctly.

[54] Nightingale (1995, 14–15) lists the very few early occurrences of words from the "philosophy" word group. Chapter 7, section 7.3 (pp. 202–204) discusses some of these.

I mention here another important word that there is so far no reason to think Socrates uses differently from his accusers, and no reason to think ambiguous. That is the verb "know." The next sections will make clearer why I think so.[55]

2.9 WHILE KNOWING NOTHING BIG, SOCRATES DOES KNOW SOME THINGS

Socrates denies that he knows anything big: "I am conscious (*sunoida emautô(i)*) that I am wise, neither in something big nor in something small" (21b4–5) and "I was conscious (*sunê(i)dê emautô(i)*) that I knew (*epistamenô(i)*) almost[56] nothing" (22c9–d1).[57]

We have seen that Socrates changes his mind about his not knowing anything small (21d). He decides that his not supposing that he knows what he doesn't know is a small bit of wisdom. That may seem an odd thing for Socrates to count as wisdom. Wisdom – a kind of knowledge – should have some definite content. *Not* to suppose something does not seem a grasp of some specific content. Socrates clearly implies, however, that he has the knowledge whose content is: that he doesn't know the biggest things. The implication is clear because his saying that he is conscious that he knows almost nothing comes close to saying, "I know that I know almost nothing." If we grant that the proposition that one knows almost nothing is itself almost nothing, Socrates is in no danger of contradiction.

Similarly at 23b3–4 he knows (*egnôken*: West and West (1998): "has become cognizant") that he is worth nothing with respect to wisdom. That is just a reaffirmation that he doesn't know anything important. It is a restatement of the one small thing he knows (as at 22c9–d1).

Given that Socrates so strongly professes his ignorance, it might seem to threaten his consistency that Socrates also professes knowledge of certain

---

[55] Vlastos (1994a, 39–67) thinks that Socrates himself uses "know" with two different senses. Vlastos thinks that when Socrates claims not to know anything, he is speaking of certain infallible knowledge, but when Socrates claims to know something, he is speaking of elenctic knowledge, that is confidence based on a claim's surviving the elenchus. In the following sections that consider Socrates' claims of knowledge, I will not find any evidence that Socrates is using "know" with two different senses.

[56] "Almost" translates *hôs epos epein* (literally, "so to speak"). Burnet's note (Burnet 1924) on the same phrase at 17a4 explains that the effect is of "practically"; the phrase restricts a too sweeping claim. "Practically" = "for all practical purposes" or "you might as well say."

[57] Socrates says he does not know several specific things. For example, at 29a6–b1 he says, "No one knows whether death may not be the greatest of goods for a man." At 29b5 he says, "I do not know sufficiently about the things in Hades." At 37b6–7 he says he does not know whether death is good or bad. That is also implied by 42a. At 19c4–5 he professes no expertise (*epaïô*), big or small, about the things the Socrates of Aristophanes' play drivels on about.

other things.[58] However, if nothing that he claims to know is big, then he can consistently say also that he knows that he knows nothing big.

I will now argue that nothing Socrates claims to know counts as big knowledge. It would be an instructive project to consider every instance in which Socrates claims to know something, but it would take me too far away from my main project here. So I will give my argument for three examples. They will indicate how I would argue that other matters of which Socrates claims to know do not count as big knowledge. I will omit to consider how Socrates has arrived at certain very strong convictions that he stops short of calling knowledge.

One example of Socrates' claiming to know is this:

To do injustice and to fail to be persuaded (*apeithein:* also translatable as "to disobey") by one who is better, god or man, that it is a bad and shameful thing (*kakon kai aischron*) I do know. (29b)[59]

This appears initially not compatible with Socrates' assertion that he has no big wisdom.[60]

[58] Several of his assertions of knowledge I'll put aside for my present purpose of seeing if any of them is incompatible with Socrates' assertion that he doesn't know anything important. For example, at 20d he enjoins the jurors, "Know well that I will tell you the whole truth." Since he is telling the jurors to know it, presumably he himself knows that he is telling the whole truth. At 22d he knew something about the craftsmen: "I knew that I would discover that they, at least, knew many fine things." At 24a6 he says, "I know rather well that I incur hatred." At 28a he enjoins the jurors to know that he is hated for examining people, which implies that he knows that himself. If these assertions are consistent with his claim that he knows nothing important, all the objects of his knowledge mentioned in these statements have to be relatively unimportant. That is, they are not life-guiding insights. I believe that the first two can count as small-scale personal knowledge. The second is simply a consequence of the analysis of what a craftsman is. It will be evident from my discussion in the main text that no obvious or near-definitional claim by itself is life-guiding. So no definitional claim by itself would count as big knowledge.

Forster (2007) outlines the apparent conflict between Socrates' belief in "universal human ignorance" and "perfectly confident beliefs about ethical matters which he considers of the utmost importance" (2007, 5). Forster has a different resolution of the apparent conflict than mine.

[59] The verb *apeithein*, "to disobey" by etymology means "to fail to be persuaded." Burnet (1924) at 29b6 says that it is a solemn verb, usually used with reference to the laws of God or man.

[60] Brickhouse and Smith (1989, 129) comment on the initial appearance of incompatibility:

[S]omething new seems to have crept in: whereas before he said that he was aware of having no wisdom great or small (21b4–50), he now tells us that he does in fact know one thing: that one ought never to disobey one's superior.

They refer (1989, 130) to 29b6–7 as the expression of "such substantive and general convictions." They consider the possibility, but do not finally accept as an explanation, that Socrates asserts this as knowledge grounded in divination, a message from the gods. They decide that divination would not be required, since everyone thinks, presumably without benefit of special messages from the gods, that one ought not to disobey one's superiors:

[What] is explicitly stated (that one ought not to disobey one's superiors) would in fact almost certainly be accepted as uncontroversial by Socrates' jurors. (1989, 130)

They eventually decide that 29b6–7 is not substantive and hence wouldn't count as important knowledge.

The apparent incompatibility disappears, however, once we realize that this is not big wisdom. First, *beltioni*, "the one who is better," I take to mean the one who actually is better: that is to say, the one who actually does know or who is better placed to know.[61] Second, the exact phrasing of 29b6–7 tells us that not being persuaded by the one who is better is identified with, is the very same thing as, doing injustice. Socrates' phrase "to do injustice and to fail to be persuaded by one who is better" means "to do injustice, that is, to fail to be persuaded by one who is better." That the "and" is explicative or epexegetic is made clear by the singular adjective forms of "bad" and "shameful." It is a bad and shameful thing (not things) to do injustice and to fail to be persuaded by one who is better. It is one bad thing Socrates is talking about, not two separable things.[62]

If we understand "the one who is better" to indicate the one who knows better, then the statement that it is bad and shameful to do wrong and not to be persuaded by the one who is better – who has better understanding of the matter – is entirely obvious. It is, as we might say, an analytic or obviously necessary truth. It isn't, however, anything explanatory. It is in the genre of truths such as "Everyone wants to do well," and "If we had plenty of good things, we would do well," which Socrates says at *Euthydemus* 278e are "stupid" or (279a) "indisputably so." Things of this genre are perhaps among the many "unimportant" things Socrates says he knows at *Euthydemus* 293e. The statement that it is bad not to be persuaded by the one who knows better repeats itself. It is like saying "It is bad and shameful to do what is known to be wrong" or simply, "It is wrong to do wrong." Because it is analytic, it has no action-directing force. It does not help one to avoid doing injustice, just as any definition by itself does not recommend particular actions.[63] It would not count as big knowledge. So

---

[61] Weiss (2001, 172) glosses *beltioni* as "the one who is an expert, whether god or man."

[62] Brickhouse and Smith (1989), quoted in n. 60, take *beltioni*, literally "the better one," to mean "one's superiors." An example of disobeying one's superiors is failing to follow the orders of one's officer in wartime. This is a possible example, but not the only example; it is a good example of following one's betters if we assume that the commanding officers actually do know better than the people they command. The rendering "superiors" suggests a superior or commander within some institutionalized or familiar hierarchy. Given that translation, the clause with epexegetic *kai* would imply that every action of wrongdoing was within a hierarchy of superiors who give orders. In the human sphere of course that is not so. We can do wrong without disobeying any person who is in charge – unless we assume that gods in charge implicitly give orders at every point in everyone's life. If so, then we could identify wrongdoing with disobeying a superior officer. There's no evidence in this passage that Socrates has that picture of human action.

[63] Brickhouse and Smith (1989, 134) say it has no action-guiding force also because of the difficulty of telling who one's superiors are in nonmilitary settings.

Socrates' assertion of this knowledge at 29b6–7 does not conflict with his saying that he knows nothing important.[64]

Brickhouse and Smith propose a different resolution of any apparent inconsistency between Socrates' asserting that he knows he must obey his superior and asserting that he knows nothing big:

> The difference between knowledge *that* something is the case and knowledge *how* it is...(or why it is) is one feature of the difference between what we might call "ordinary" knowledge and the kind of knowledge that scholars have come to call "expert" knowledge... [T]he kind of knowledge Socrates claims to lack [in *Gorgias* 508e–509a]...is knowing *how* his result is the way it is. Socrates claims not to be wise, in other words, he is no expert.[65]

> [At *Apology* 29b] he knows (i) *that* it is wrong to disobey one's superior...He is not claiming to know (ii) *how it is* that disobeying one's superior is evil.[66]

I accept the worthwhile distinction between knowing that something is so and knowing how it is so that Brickhouse and Smith make. I believe, as they do, that it plays an important role elsewhere (*Gorgias* 509). But I would say that in the case of the wrongness of not being persuaded by one who knows better there is in fact an answer to the question: "How is it?" The answer, in this case, is simply, "It just is. Of course you are doing wrong if you are not persuaded by the one who knows what is right." That is the same as the sort of answer that would be given to "Why is it that a

---

[64] Nehamas (1999a, 44) says of 29b6–7:

> The central idea is that at 29b6–7 Socrates is saying that it would be bad and shameful to fail to be convinced or persuaded by either a human or a divine moral expert.

> The possibility of translating *apeithein* as "not being convinced by" may now suggest that this is not after all a substantive moral principle. (1999a, 47)

> Even if we insist on translating *apeithein* as "to disobey," Socrates is not making a substantive point. Once you have recognized that someone is better than you are, you have become convinced by that person's views. And on Socratic grounds, it is impossible to fail to act on these views. (1999a, 57, n. 53)

> Sedley (2007, 274) says of the passage:

> Socrates takes it as guaranteed true by the meaning of its own terms: if someone is better than you, it goes without saying that that person's judgment as to how you should conduct yourself outweighs your own.

[65] Brickhouse and Smith (2000, 109).

[66] Brickhouse and Smith (2000, 111). I have added numerals to separate two of their points in the quotation that follows. The explanation quoted in the text is in addition to and perhaps replaces the explanation of theirs cited in n. 63 from Brickhouse and Smith (1989).

square has four sides?" The answer is, "It just does. That is what it is to be a square."[67]

Granted, there are still the further and so far unanswered questions, "What exactly is right or wrong?" or "How is it that anything whatsoever is good or evil?" or "What is it for something to be good?" And it is possible, as Brickhouse and Smith think, that Socrates has in mind at *Apology* 29b that he doesn't have the answer to those larger questions. But what Socrates says at 29b doesn't compel their interpretation. The resolution I propose is simpler.

Some of Socrates' other claims to knowledge mention harm or benefit. Here is one example.

At 30c he tells his audience, "Know well that if you kill me, being the sort of man that I say I am, you will not harm me more than yourselves." He could hardly urge his audience to know in this instance without believing that he knows that same thing. So here he claims to know that harm will come to his audience from a particular course of action. This knowledge seems of action-guiding importance. And it is not merely personal. It verges on a profession of the ability to teach others how best to live, which of course is exactly the wisdom that Socrates disavows. Is it then big knowledge?

I would say not. If Socrates assumes (as obvious or axiomatic) that the greatest harm is to become more foolish, it is clear how the Athenians will harm themselves if they kill him. When the Athenians kill Socrates, whose role was to make them more (humanly) wise by his questioning, they will lose the benefit he provides them when he questions the reputation for wisdom that Socrates diagnosed as the cause of the most deplorable ignorance. As citizens of "the city . . . best reputed for wisdom" (*eudokimôtatês eis sophian*: 29d8) Athenians are then especially at risk of making the biggest mistake. They are likely to think mistakenly that they are wise about the biggest things, and they are least likely to be thoughtful. To kill Socrates will be to decrease the likelihood that they will be cured of their foolishness. They will do themselves, but not Socrates, maximal harm. (At 31a Socrates says that if the city were to kill him, "you would spend the rest of your lives asleep.") The proposition that by decreasing the opportunities to be rendered less foolish you harm yourself is in Socrates' view obvious, and hence not big. It is teachable by reflection on the connection between the

---

[67] Weiss (1991, 172) comments:

> The . . . claim may seem like a substantive moral belief, but it is really just a corollary of . . . [recognition of one's own ignorance]: only one who recognizes his own ignorance would admit the importance of obeying the one who does know; it is those who lack awareness of their own ignorance who recoil from seeking the guidance of experts.

notions of the soul and of foolishness, as reflection on the notion of square will establish a connection between being square and having four sides. We must grant, however, that by itself that proposition is not enough to reach the conclusion that killing Socrates will decrease those opportunities. For that conclusion there is need of an empirical premise that Socrates' examinations do render people less foolish. Apparently Socrates thinks that his audience can know that premise, perhaps as a matter of experience. (The fact that many in the audience do not believe it does not imply that they could not come to know it.) If so, he can urge his audience to know that his execution will harm them, though not him.

2.10 SOCRATES' KNOWLEDGE THAT THE GOD ORDERS HIM TO TEST PEOPLE IS NOT BIG

The third and last claim of knowledge that I consider I give more extended treatment. After Socrates explains that he will not stop philosophizing, that is, examining people and reproaching those who show they don't care for thoughtfulness about how they are to live, he says:

I will do this to whomever, younger or older, I happen to meet, both foreigner and townsman, but more so to the townsmen, inasmuch as you are closer to me in kin. The god orders these things, know well. (30a)

Since Socrates is urging his audience to know that the god orders him to examine and then to reproach those who don't care about thoughtfulness, Socrates implies that he himself knows that the god orders what Socrates is doing. Several questions now arise:

(i) Is this putative knowledge, which seems to be about a specific kind of life conduct, not big?

(ii) Since knowledge implies teachableness, is Socrates attempting to teach in making the assertion that the god orders Socrates to examine and reproach people for their lack of care?

(iii) His claim that the god orders these things suggests that Socrates knows that there is a god. Is not that, or anything else involving the gods, not momentous knowledge?

(iv) What is the ground for Socrates' knowledge that the god orders this? If his ground is a message uniquely to Socrates from the god, it is not obvious that he can give the audience reason to believe it. A revelation uniquely for Socrates is not a likely ground for his audience to know something.

I'll begin by discussing question (iv). My discussion will answer the other questions also.

Some apparent evidence that the oracle was the source of Socrates' knowledge that the god orders his behavior is Socrates' reaction to the oracle:

> It seemed to be necessary to regard the matter of the god as most important (*to tou theou peri pleistou poieisthai*). (21e)

This certainly tells us that Socrates took the oracle as provocation to start examining people. Only after learning of the oracle's answer to Chaerephon's impetuous (21a) question did he begin the examining and then reproaching that earned him his slanderous name, "wise." But no doubt long before Chaerephon posed his question to the oracle, Socrates had impressed Chaerephon by his conversational skills. (In Plato's depiction the "keenness for argument" and the "noble and divine" impulse for argument of the adolescent Socrates impressed even the venerable Parmenides of the *Parmenides* (130b, 135d).) Socrates' verbal skills must have seemed to Chaerephon to resemble the legendary verbal skills of the traditional wise men, such as Thales and Solon, whom the fishermen who found the tripod considered as contestants for a wise-prize. Socrates must have seemed to Chaerephon to be a kind of victor in exchanges that Chaerephon witnessed. Once Chaerephon had thought of the sages, it would have been natural for Chaerephon to ask the oracle about Socrates the very question that the sage Anacharsis had posed about himself.

Socrates' questioning behavior after hearing of the oracle would then have been a kind of continuation of his behavior before the oracle – but a continuation with a difference. Before the oracle Socrates might just have been conversing with his friends or with anyone else that he for some reason enjoyed talking with.[68] In his youth he may have enjoyed stylized

---

[68] Hitchcock (2000, 62–63) argues that Socrates invented the question-and-answer technique, which eventually was corrupted into eristic by people such as Euthydemus and Dionysodorus:

> There is no reliable evidence of any predecessor or independent contemporary of Socrates having taken the role of questioner in a question-and-answer discussion directed at determining whether the answerer's thesis can be refuted. The most probable origin of professional eristic, then, is Socrates himself. This is not to say that the brothers got their repertoire of fallacious tricks from Socrates, but that they practiced the type of refutation in which Socrates engaged, and inserted into it the trickery which subsequently earned the name "sophistry."

> This is of course a large historical claim worth reflecting on. I find it implausible because, for example, Xenophon *Memorabilia* 1, 2, 46 is some evidence that question-and-answer conversation was a practice in Pericles' youth. See also Lloyd (1979, 86) who sees the elenchus as having grown out of practices in the assembly and courtroom.

question-and-answer exchanges, just as his young friends now enjoyed them (23c4; 33b9–c4). After the oracle, Socrates saw himself as testing presumed authorities, those reputed wise, in order to understand the oracle. And after the oracle, Socrates added to his questioning the annoying element of reproach. His questioning, now altered in scope and, combined with reproach, annoyed people and got Socrates hated.

Even though it must be granted that the oracle *prompted* Socrates' enlarged activity, it does not now follow that the oracle *provides grounds* for his knowledge that the god orders him to examine and reproach. Nor, therefore, does it follow that the oracle provides grounds unique to Socrates. There are, moreover, some positive reasons to conclude that the oracle does not provide a basis unique to Socrates to know that the god orders him to reproach and examine.

A first point to consider is that the message of the oracle is not a special message to or about Socrates. Chaerephon's question, "Is anyone wiser than Socrates?" is no more a question about Socrates than it is about anyone else. The answer, "No," is equally about everyone.[69] If no one is wiser than Socrates, then everyone is not wiser than Socrates. Socrates would have seen the implication immediately.[70]

A second point is that the oracular utterance by itself does not ascribe wisdom of any kind to Socrates. Socrates, as depicted, would also have been quite capable of the logical observation that the dictum "no one is wiser than Socrates" does not imply that Socrates is wiser than someone.

---

[69] The question then is equally about Chaerephon. That is partly an answer to Montuori's claim (1981, 70) that the oracle could not have been given in the presence of other people. Montuori says:

> We are in fact well aware that whenever the question addressed to the oracle concerned a person other than the questioner, the question had to be submitted and recorded in writing . . . We also know that the written reply was sealed and handed to the questioner, and the Suda tells us that if anyone other than the person concerned directly got to know the contents, he risked losing his eyes, hands, or tongue.

Montuori counts this against Xenophon's report (*Apology* 14) that many people were present at the oracle to Chaerephon. Other authors say that there were cheap sessions, at which several people might be present, where answers were given by lot.

Montuori (1981, 64) says: "Socrates tells his judges of the special favour shown him by the Delphic god."

I resist the phrase "special favour." Socrates did not take the pronouncement as an honor. Instead, he was immediately puzzled and resistant to the surface meaning. The surface meaning of the similar pronouncements did seem to the traditional sages in our anecdotes honorific. (Anacharsis expected the honor; Solon and Thales mildly resisted the honor, but not in the same way Socrates did.)

[70] de Stryker and Slings (1994, 80) think Socrates reached it as a conclusion that he gradually discovered. I think Socrates could have seen it immediately and could have still been puzzled by the oracle. His puzzlement is not merely because he knows that he has no remarkable wisdom, but because he apparently expects, or at least at this stage entertains the hope, that someone else somewhere has some substantial (if not divine) wisdom.

The oracle is consistent with everyone's being perfectly foolish. Socrates rephrases the oracle at 21b5–6 with "declaring me wisest." This also, as Socrates would have seen, is not yet an affirmation of wisdom. Even if Socrates was massively ignorant, he might be wisest among human beings who were all equally massively ignorant. All who are as wise as people ever get to be are the wisest people. So the oracle is not necessarily conferring an honor. The pronouncement that no one is wiser than you are, or that you are wisest, is praise only if someone somewhere is somewhat wise. If others are completely confused or foolish, then it is no compliment.

Moreover, the oracle could be interpreted entirely negatively as saying that no one has divine wisdom more than Socrates, who in fact has zero divine wisdom. The oracle would of course need no information about Socrates to pronounce that no one was wiser than he if she was speaking of divine wisdom. To pronounce that everyone has zero divine wisdom is simply to repeat the advice of one inscription at the oracle's site at Delphi.[71] The inscription, "Know yourself," in its most prominent or traditional meaning is telling the viewer to be humbly aware of his own limitations and his nondivine status. It says in effect, "Don't think you are as wise as the gods." Though the impulsive Chaerephon, when he asked his batty question, probably had in mind the specific skill in question-and-answer discussion that he had observed in Socrates, there is no reason to think that the Pythia was aware of Socrates' specific skill. The Solon anecdote shows that it was natural to interpret her as speaking of divine wisdom. On the other hand, the Myson anecdote is some reason to think that she was pronouncing on the humblest human wisdom. To assess Socrates' human wisdom reasonably, her evidence – if she had any – might have been that

---

[71] Here I disagree with Brickhouse and Smith (1989, 95). They say:

> Even if the Pythia and the priests at Delphi were generally inclined to give the suppliant the answer he wanted to hear, it is unlikely they would have given the answer they did in this case if Socrates had not already had a considerable reputation as a wise man. Otherwise they would have risked discrediting themselves.

I'd say on the contrary that Delphi took no risk in saying what amounted to, "No human being has divine wisdom and any human being who realizes that he does not have divine wisdom is wiser than any human being who doesn't realize that."

Montuori (1981, 650) says: "One wonders what the priests of Delphi knew about the wisdom of Socrates to enable them to answer."

Again, the possibility should also be considered that the oracle did not need to know much, or anything, about Socrates, to answer. Given one ordinary sense of "wise," which amounts to "divinely wise," no human being is wiser than any other, because all are equally not wise.

de Stryker and Slings (1994, 78) think that either Socrates' simple social status or his (putative) criticism of democracy or both would have recommended Socrates to Delphi for a favorable pronouncement.

My explanation of the oracle's answer is simpler.

she had never heard of Socrates. If his reputation had not reached her, she had no reason to think he made pretensions to wisdom.[72]

No matter what she meant, however, the fact remains that her pronouncement was not more about Socrates than about everyone else. So Socrates could not base his confidence that he in particular was doing what the god orders on being singled out by the oracle.[73]

And clearly Socrates does not finally believe that the oracle had singled him out. Socrates comes to think that the oracle is treating him as a mere example:

> In the oracle [the god] is saying that human wisdom is worth little or nothing. And he appears to say this of Socrates and to have made use of my name in order to make me an example (*paradeigma*) as if he would say, "That one of you, O human beings, is wisest who, like Socrates, has become cognizant that in truth he is worth nothing with respect to wisdom." (23a6–b4)

While investigating, Socrates discovers that he knows something that many other people do not know – that he is "worth nothing with respect to (divine) wisdom." The oracle plus that new discovery leads him to the conclusion that Socrates is wisest, which is now at last a positive ascription of wisdom. As Socrates recognizes at 23b, his being wisest is consistent with there being several people who are, equally, wisest.

Happily, since we have found out that the oracle cannot be the basis for Socrates' knowledge that he is ordered to examine and reproach, it turns out that Socrates does not need that basis either. There is a straightforward and short argument not mentioning the oracle and available to anyone,

---

[72] Montuori (1981, 65) asks about Chaerephon's question:

> Were not such a question and answer . . . a negation in themselves of the morality professed at Delphi, which in opposition to the insolence of *hubris*, counseled a humble awareness of human limitations?

The answer seems to me to be that although Chaerephon asked his question prompted by his admiration for a specific skill Socrates had displayed, the Pythia took the question as though it were the sort of question that had been asked about the sages. And she could have answered the question on the basis of her permanent stance about human wisdom. See also Reeve (1989, 30–31).

[73] Here I partly disagree with de Stryker and Slings (1994, 80–82). They make two points: (a) The oracle's actual utterance does not explicitly say that a god is giving Socrates a mission. Plato makes a gradual transformation of Socrates' first mention of the oracle into "the notion of a divine mission." That is Plato's invention. (b) If Plato thought that the oracle was the origin of Socrates' activity, it would be unintelligible why Plato does not allude to it in his other writings.

I would disagree with point (b). What could explain Plato's failure to make an allusion to the oracle in other works might be that Socrates did not mention it in ordinary conversation. And what could explain that would be that Socrates saw that the oracle would probably be misunderstood as saying something alarmingly elective.

not just to Socrates, to the conclusion that any gods there may be wish for Socrates to examine and reproach.

The argument is as follows. It begins with the assumption that the gods wish benefit for human beings. (More on that assumption later.) If the gods wish benefit for human beings, then, since the best thing for a person is to be thoughtful (*phronimos*) (29d–30a), the gods want human beings to be thoughtful. Being thoughtful requires human wisdom – that is, avoidance of the biggest mistake of thinking that you know something big that you don't know. (For the people who most lack human wisdom, that is, who most think they know something big, are least fit with regard to being thoughtful (22a3–6).) Hence the gods want all people to have human wisdom. Further, people get human wisdom by being made aware of their ignorance. Examination and reproach can make them aware of their ignorance and can thus remove the mistake that is an obstacle to thoughtfulness. So the gods want people to be examined and reproached. Socrates is then doing what the gods wish, a good thing. Granted the assumptions I've mentioned, anyone could reach this conclusion quickly. So it should count as teachable knowledge. That is the first part of the straightforward argument.

Someone might object here – relevantly to question (iii) above – whether the knowledge that Socrates is doing what the gods want is not pretty big knowledge. Someone might object that the assumption that the gods wish benefit for human beings is not a straightforward assumption to be easily granted. It shouldn't have looked obvious to Socrates. He was aware that there was controversy about whether the gods exist. He could not reasonably have counted, and hence wouldn't have counted, the proposition that the gods exist as obvious, even though he himself believes it. I would answer that I expect that what he assumes as foundational is the conditional proposition that if anything is a god, it is good (and hence wishes benefit for human beings). And that proposition is all we need for the argument. Socrates apparently believes that any god is good as strongly as he believes that any square has four sides.[74] Socrates does not directly state in the

---

[74] Vlastos (1991b, 165) gives this argument on behalf of Socrates that the gods are good (The argument uses a premise that the gods are wise; Vlastos apparently takes it as more obvious that the gods are wise than that they are good):

Socrates would reason that if knowledge of good and evil entails moral goodness in a man, it would entail the same in a god. And since the god's wisdom surpasses greatly that of the wisest man, god's goodness must surpass no less greatly that of the most virtuous man. And since he holds that goodness in a man can never cause evil to anyone [Vlastos cites *Crito* 49c and *Republic* 335d] he is

Apology that the gods wish benefit for human beings, but perhaps we can see the assumption behind some remarks. He says:

> You should think this one thing to be true: that there is nothing bad for a good man, living or dead, and that the gods are not without care for his affairs.[75] (41c)

He says that if the Athenians kill him, they'll suffer the harm of not being examined, "unless the god sends someone else in his concern for you" (31a6–7). That suggests that he thinks that the gods care for, or wish benefit for, human beings.[76]

I emphasize that for Socrates to believe in the gods, and for him to take as axiomatic or foundational that if anything is a god, it is good, is not inconsistent with Socrates' famous agnosticism. Socrates is agnostic, but not without conviction. Socrates has beliefs he lives by; he just does not offer them as teachings coming from an expert.

It is no objection that the point that every person benefits from confronting his own ignorance apparently didn't occur to Socrates until after the oracle. The distinction between the oracle's being a provocation and its being a basis stands firm. Socrates, in this respect like anyone else, did not think of every possible argument at all times. The oracle occasioned the examination that showed him that being labeled "wise" in the slanderer's sense was a sign of being not thoughtful. The oracle thus called Socrates' attention to his human wisdom and to its value of decreasing the likelihood of thoughtlessness (22a; 22d–e). After thus discovering the value of human wisdom, Socrates becomes appreciative, if not quite celebratory, of his avowed ignorance (22e). In calling Socrates' attention to the value of human wisdom, the oracle called Socrates' attention to the argument that human wisdom was among the benefits the gods wish for human beings. But only the argument, which is within everyone's reach, and not the oracle that prompted it, can provide the reasons for Socrates' knowledge that the gods wish him to examine and reproach.

It might be objected that although the argument so far establishes that the gods, if any, wish people to be examined and reproached, the argument

bound to hold that *a fortiori* neither can goodness in a god: since God can be only good, never evil, God can only cause good, can never be the cause of evil to anyone, man or god.

I am not sure that Socrates would have felt the need to find prior reasons why a god could not be a malevolent genius.

[75] "Affairs" is *pragmata*, also translatable as "troubles."

[76] At the end of *Republic* book 2 Socrates extracts from Adeimantus the view that the gods can do no harm, but provide only benefit. That is evidence that at least some other people held it. The assumption that the gods do not wish bad for human beings appears at *Tht.* 151d. (It does not count as special wisdom, since Socrates in the *Theaetetus* says he does not have wisdom (150d; 210c).)

does not establish that the gods want Socrates in particular to examine and reproach. Only the oracle could be Socrates' source of his particular mission. So our argument needs a second part.

This is the second part and the answer to the objection. Socrates has the further information (learned by experience) that most other (and perhaps all other) Athenians do not engage in examining and reproaching ("Another such will not easily arise for you" (31a2).) So the argument that the gods wish someone to examine and reproach plus the extra information that no other, or not enough other, Athenians do it would have been reason enough for Socrates to conclude that the gods wish him to examine and reproach. The ground for Socrates' knowledge is the straightforward first part of the argument just sketched plus his experience of other people.

If we accept that Socrates knows that the gods wish him to examine and reproach, then we should expect to find that Socrates could teach what he knows, since he holds that what is known can be taught. The straightforward argument just set out is clearly teachable. It also seems that others could fairly easily learn, if they are not already aware, that most other Athenians do not engage in Socrates' sort of examination. That is not to say that there is a high probability that many others will put together the various pieces to reach the conclusion that Socrates knows that any gods there may be wish him, in particular, though not exclusively him, to examine others.

A final objection is that we have not reached our intended conclusion about what Socrates meant. Socrates says not merely that he knows that the gods *wish* him to examine and reproach, but that the gods *order* it. To get the further conclusion that the gods order this to Socrates, we need some more premises. It would suffice to add the premise that the gods' wish is the gods' command. It seems likely that his audience assumes that the gods' wish is the gods' command. If so, they have the material for a simple argument to the conclusion that the gods order Socrates to examine and reproach.

Now that we understand tentatively how Socrates and his audience can know that the god orders him to examine and reproach, that is, to promote the benefit of human wisdom, there still remains the question whether Socrates' knowledge of this is big knowledge. I think not. The knowledge that any god orders him to promote human wisdom, or equivalently, the (safely conditional) knowledge that if anything is a god, it orders the benefit of promoting human wisdom, a very small wisdom, is also small knowledge because it is almost definitional.

Naturally Socrates, at his trial on a charge of impiety, doesn't highlight or emphasize the condition, "*If* anything is a god." He is speaking to an audience many of whom believe in gods. He is showing what gods as he understands them would order. Here he doesn't dwell on differences between himself and his audience on the topic of gods. He alludes to differences briefly when he says, "I acknowledge [the gods] as none of you do" (35d). A difference he has in mind may be that members of his audience may think that the gods can do harm or don't care about human beings generally: the mythology with which his audience was familiar is evidence of such a conception of the gods.[77]

My verdict on the implied claim that Socrates knows that the god has ordered that he examine and reproach is that it does not count as big. It does not approach the divine knowledge of how to educate human beings that Socrates does count as big, and that he disclaims. Socrates' knowledge is something available to anyone, so he can urge that his audience know it.

My conclusion concerning Socrates' assertions that he knows some things is that nothing he knows is big. Either what he knows has the emptiness of analytic claims or definitions which by themselves do not lead to actions, like my examples from 29b and from 30c in my previous section, or it is as small as his small human wisdom, like the example from 29e–30a just discussed. Such claims to know are then consistent with his assertion that he knows nothing big.

I observe that there is so far no reason to distinguish different senses of "know." Whatever Socrates knows, he knows it in the same sense of "know" as he doesn't know what he doesn't know. He consistently uses the word "know" to label only what can be taught to others.[78] His basis for

---

[77] Following the argument sketched above in n. 74 Vlastos (1991b, 165–166) observes of Socrates' belief that gods are good:

> To heirs of Hebraic and Christian tradition this will hardly seem a bold conclusion. For those bred on Greek beliefs about the gods it would be shattering. It would obliterate that whole range of divine activity which torments and destroys the innocent no less than the guilty... careless of the moral havoc it creates... What would be left of... the... Olympians if they were required to observe the stringent norms of Socratic virtue which require every moral agent... to act only to cause good to others...? Required to meet these austere standards, the city's gods would have become unrecognizable.

> On the assumption that any god must be wise and good see Parker (1988, 267): "Philosophers could not accept the riotous Olympians of mythology, since it was now axiomatic that any god must be wholly wise and good."

[78] I note, in disagreement, that Benson (2000, 236) says this of these passages in which Socrates claims to know something:

> In the end, I must confess to a certain amount of ambivalence toward these passages in which Socrates professes knowledge. On the one hand, these professions appear careless, vernacular, and unconsidered. He is not professing to know a truth in what we might call the strict and philosophical sense of knowledge but rather only professing to know in a loose and ordinary way. He is, we might say, speaking with the vulgar.

everything he knows is not a divine source available only to Socrates. It is entirely available to others.

2.II THE SOCRATES OF THE *APOLOGY*

I select for our recollection here some important things that we learn from the *Apology* about its Socrates.[79]

Socrates thinks that the greatest or biggest thing a human being could claim to know would be how to conduct his own life well. To know or to be wise about that biggest thing would imply the capacity to teach other people how to conduct their lives well.

Socrates thinks that the capacity to teach other people how to live their lives well would be a divine capacity. No human being has that divine wisdom.[80] Socrates is thus not wise in the popular or traditional sense of

> In n. 46 to this passage Benson says:
>
> Socrates indicates that he is susceptible to making knowledge professions when he should not at *Charmides*. In reply to Critias' criticisms of his method, Socrates explains that he refutes (*elegxô*) for "no other reason than that because of which I would examine myself what I say, fearing lest I am unaware that I think I know something when I do not" (166c8–d2). See also perhaps *Hippias Major* 286c5–d7 and 304d5–e3.

The passages Benson cites as evidence for a tendency to make knowledge professions when he should not might simply be Socrates' reiteration of the moral danger of false pretension.

    Socrates distinguishes as at *Gorgias* 509 (Brickhouse and Smith (1994, 38–41)) between knowing *that* something is true, and knowing *how* it is that something is true. Socrates can know that p, for example, if he has reduced its denial to absurdity. But his knowing that p doesn't give him the knowledge of how it is that p is true, or what is the full explanation of why it is that p. Benson takes that to be a distinction between types of knowledge or senses of "know." I take it that the sense of "know" is exactly the same, but the objects of the instances of knowledge mentioned are different items – that p and how it is that p. So far as I can tell, Socrates always speaks with the vulgar in his use of "know," although he disagrees with some others about what is or can be known.

[79] My account of the Socrates of the *Apology* is very close to that of Kahn (1996) in §5 of his chapter 3, which takes the *Apology* as our strongest evidence for the historical Socrates. My slight disagreements with Kahn are:

    (1) I would rephrase slightly Kahn's point that philosophy is the search for wisdom (*sophia*). Since, as Kahn agrees, Socrates thinks *sophia* is not possible for humans, I wouldn't say Socrates is searching for it, although he is of course engaged in philosophy, as he says.

    (2) I do not believe a Socrates who pursued definitions of courage and the like is "formally incompatible with the epistemic stance of Socrates in the *Apology*" and "does not fit the picture of the questioner who knows only his own ignorance and who is not in search of an explanatory science of nature" (1996, 95). Asking such definitional questions seems to me an excellent way for the ignorant Socrates to reveal the ignorance of people who purport to teach *aretê*, or one of the particular virtues.

    My larger disagreement with Kahn will emerge later in this book.

[80] Nor, *contra* Benson (2000), does he seek this divine wisdom. Benson (2000, 183, n. 71) says:

> If we look at the context of the passages I have cited for Socrates' desire and exhortation to obtain the knowledge he and his interlocutors lack [Benson refers to *Euthyphro* 15c11–12; *Laches* 101a2–7;

the word "wise" in which ordinary people apply it to sages, and in which sophists or politicians apply it to themselves.

Socrates considers it a terrible slander to be labeled "wise" in its ordinary use because the label implies that he is reputed wise about the biggest things and thus is in a position to do the worst harm to others.

Socrates has a small amount of human wisdom in that he has the distinctively human knowledge that he does not know about the biggest things. In this he is unlike a number of other people he has talked to who are unaware of their ignorance. Without human wisdom a person cannot live thoughtfully (with *phronêsis*). To live thoughtfully is continually to test or examine yourself. If you fail an examination and find contradiction in your beliefs, that doesn't establish that you are not thoughtful. What establishes that you are not thoughtful is your not caring when you contradict yourself, your not acknowledging your ignorance, and your not keeping on testing yourself with the goal of discovering and eliminating any unsustainable beliefs. Lacking human wisdom, you cannot care about the most important thing to care about, how to live your life well.

Socrates recognizes that other people use certain key words or phrases differently from the way he uses them when talking to himself or in his preferred use. He acknowledges explicitly his different understanding of the locutions, "terrific speaker," "orator," "judge," "wise," and "believes in the gods." He sometimes speaks as those to whom or about whom he is

and *Gorgias* 505e4–5 plus 506a3–5] it is reasonable to think that the knowledge he seeks is precisely the knowledge he disavows in the Delphic oracle story. In the *Euthyphro* and *Laches*, it is definitional knowledge that he disclaims and urges the acquisition of, while the exhortation in the *Gorgias* is followed by his reminder that he has no more knowledge than Callicles [506a3–5], just the kind of disclaimer we would expect in light of the Delphic oracle story.

Benson thinks that there is no good reason to suppose in the *Gorgias* passage that it is one kind of knowledge he looks for and another kind he lacks. I'd object, for these reasons. The knowledge Socrates disavows in the *Apology* – knowledge of how to teach human virtue – is knowledge the ascription of which is a "slander." The ascription would simply be a mistake, rather than a slander, if Socrates thought there was some chance of obtaining such wisdom. The search for what turns out to be divine knowledge (how to educate people in virtue including having the definitions that are a necessary possession for a teacher) is, however, useful. That search leads you to the crucial discovery of your own incapacity and everyone else's incapacity. The knowledge that you know nothing important is a prerequisite for caring. The knowledge that you are not in a position to teach others and that you are in a position to do them the worst harm by acting like a teacher of virtue perhaps needs constant reinforcement.

I note that in the *Gorgias* passage at 506c Socrates says that if Callicles refutes Socrates, Callicles will be written up (*anagegrapsê(i)* – a surprising word in the light of Socrates' nonauthorship) by Socrates as his "greatest benefactor" (*megistês euergetês*). So being refuted is better than or at least as good as being given a definitive answer or being applauded for one's own answer. As is clear from the main text, I would resist speaking of different kinds of knowledge, rather than just different objects of knowledge.

speaking, speak, and not as he would speak if he were talking to himself. And when he speaks as others do, what he says often would not be true if he were speaking to himself about his own convictions. When Socrates is speaking as someone else speaks, the reader might add some clause such as "as you say," or "as others say," if Socrates doesn't add such a clause himself.

In particular, what Socrates means by saying that he philosophizes is different from what his accusers mean when they say, "he philosophizes."

Socrates knows a few things, but his knowing them is consistent with his not knowing anything big.

My understanding of the Socrates of the *Apology* is a starting point for testing my hypothesis that the Socrates of the other dialogues of Plato is the same in all these respects. My hypothesis predicts that the *Apology*'s description of what Socrates did with his life holds true of the Socrates that Plato depicts in other dialogues at other times in that life. Chapters 3–6 will look at the Socrates of some other dialogues.

CHAPTER 3

Socrates in the digression of the Theaetetus: *extraction by declaration*

3.1 THE DIGRESSION AND ITS SETTING

A famous passage in the *Theaetetus* presents a challenge for my thesis that the Socrates of any of Plato's dialogues is profoundly the same as the Socrates of the *Apology*. Socrates, the main speaker of the passage (172–177), labels it a "digression" (*parerga*: "by-work") at 177b8. Not only does the Socrates of the digression seem different from the Socrates of the *Apology*, he also seems different from the Socrates of the rest of the *Theaetetus*. In the surrounding dialogue Socrates deploys argument, analysis, and critical reflection of the greatest interest as he considers the theme question: "What is knowledge?"[1] The digression has no argument, analysis, or critical reflection. It has both dismayed and fascinated readers. Gilbert Ryle calls it "the philosophically quite pointless digression."[2] On the other hand, Myles Burnyeat credits the passage with "impassioned otherworldliness."[3] He says:

Plato puts the full power of his rhetoric into an extreme expression of his own vision of the human condition.

However, Burnyeat also recognizes the two faces of the passage. He says that today's readers

are . . . likely to find [it] alien and repellent, even as we are gripped (despite ourselves) by the sweep and force of the rhetoric.

I will admit immediately that I do not at all have the experience that Burnyeat describes of being gripped despite myself by the sweep and force of its rhetoric.

This chapter will pursue Ryle's insight that the passage is philosophically pointless. But I will find that the pointlessness has a point. I will argue

---

[1] The dialogue's analytic excellence continues to inspire much careful reflection. Some examples, from a field of many, are the essays of Fine (1979a, 1994, 1998), now all reprinted in Fine (2003).
[2] Ryle (1966, 158).   [3] Burnyeat (1990, 35–36).

59

that the initially repellent digression fits perfectly into its brilliant setting
of analysis and critical examination: despite initial appearances its Socrates
is the avowedly ignorant Socrates of the *Apology*.

The setting of the digression within the larger framework of the *Theaetetus* is that the digression immediately follows Socrates' announcement that
a larger argument (*logon*) or statement is arising from a lesser one. The lesser
is Protagoras' claim that in certain cases seeming coincides with being. For
example, to say that something is sweet or hot or pleasant amounts to
nothing more than to say that something seems sweet or hot or pleasant
to someone. These examples illustrate Protagoras' dictum, "Man is the
measure of all things," which Socrates and Theaetetus have rephrased at
152 as: "Every thing is, for me, the way it appears to me, and is, for you,
the way it appears to you." Socrates asks:

Shouldn't we say . . . that the theory stands up best in the version in which we
sketched it while we were supporting Protagoras? It goes like this. Most things
actually are, for each person, the way they seem to him, for instance, hot, dry,
sweet, or anything of that sort . . . (171d)[4]

The larger thesis has it that we can reduce what is to what seems also in the
area of justice: to say that something is just or fine for a state is to say no
more than that it seems just or fine to that state, though it might appear
the opposite to some other state or at some other time. Socrates formulates
the larger thesis thus:

And about matters that concern the state, too – things which are fine, shameful,
just and unjust, pious and not – it will hold that whatever sort of thing any state
thinks to be and lays down as legitimate for itself actually is, in truth, legitimate
for it . . . in the case of what's just or unjust, pious or not, they're prepared to insist
that none of them has by nature being of its own; but that what is according to
common belief – this becomes true whenever it seems so and for as much time as
it seems so. (172a)[5]

---

[4] I use several translations with an occasional change: McDowell (1973); Benardete (1984);
Levett/Burnyeat (1990).
[5] Socrates gives an earlier statement of the larger thesis when he is acting out the part of Protagoras:
"If any sort of thing seems just and fine to any state, then it actually is just and fine for it, as long as
that state accepts it" (167c4–6).
   Sedley (1999, 312–313) usefully describes the context of the digression:

   Socrates is proceeding effectively with his task of debunking Protagoras' relativist doctrine, "Man is
   the measure of all things," and has shown how it cannot be held to apply universally . . . However,
   there is a more restricted form of relativism which Socrates concedes may survive the critique so far,
   and which has many adherents, and that is a relativism of values: many will insist that such properties
   as "just," "lawful," "beautiful," and "holy" are purely human impositions on the world, so that here
   at least Protagoras' relativism must stand: Man *is* the measure of such things.

The digression passage will reject this larger thesis. The digression will retain a firm distinction between what seems just and what is just. This chapter will ask how exactly the digression does that.

The digression has two quite separable parts: first Socrates gives a sketch of the philosopher; then Socrates gives advice about how to conduct one's life. I will briefly describe and comment on the sketch of the philosopher to make clear that it presents some problems of interpretation. Then I will develop a strategy for interpreting it. Then I will describe the remainder of the digression. My description of the remainder will provide reason to apply to the remainder of the digression the strategy I developed for interpreting the digression's sketch of the philosopher. I will then be able to offer an overall comment about the role of the digression within the *Theaetetus.*

3.2 THE FIRST PART OF THE DIGRESSION

In the *Theaetetus* Socrates mostly converses with Theaetetus, a remarkable sixteen-year-old very talented in mathematics, a serious and eager student. A secondary interlocutor is Theodorus, a distinguished elder mathematician, the teacher of Theaetetus. It is to Theodorus that Socrates addresses his digressive speech.

Socrates launches into the speech at 172c when Theodorus comments that they have plenty of time for discussion. Socrates then extensively contrasts philosophers, who have plenty of time for discussion, with people habitually engaged in lawsuits, who are bound by the time limits in Athenian courts. Among many claims that Socrates makes or implies about philosophers, I select these, which create an initial puzzle for my thesis that the digression's Socrates is the same as the Socrates of the *Apology*:

(1) The philosopher doesn't know his way to the marketplace or where the law-courts are (173d).
(2) The philosopher never sees or hears the laws (173d).
(3) The philosopher doesn't know that he doesn't know these things (173e).
(4) Only the philosopher's body lives and sleeps in the city, while his mind has come to the conclusion that matters in the city are of no account (173e).
(5) The philosopher's mind pursues reflection on things within the depths of the earth or in the heavens, and never condescends to things at hand (173e–174a).
(6) The philosopher doesn't notice what the man who lives next door is doing: the philosopher only asks. "What is man?"(174b).

(7) The philosopher induces people to abandon the question: "What injustice might I be doing to you or you to me?" and instead to examine justice itself and injustice itself (175b–c).

(8) The philosopher is, as it were, suspended at a height and gazing down from his place in the clouds (175d).

Theodorus whole-heartedly accepts Socrates' portrait of the philosopher. He says:

Socrates, if your words convinced everyone of what you are saying as they do me, there would be more peace and fewer bad things among men. (176a)

The secondary literature has long noticed that in dialogues closely linked to the *Theaetetus* Plato denies of Socrates every one of the descriptions (1)–(8) listed above.[6] Against (1), Socrates spends lots of time in the marketplace (*Apology* 17c); he can find his way to a law-court (*Euthyphro, Apology, Theaetetus* (210d). Against (2), he refused to support the mass trial of seven generals because he knew that would break a law (*Apology* 32b), and he will soon vividly imagine the laws speaking to him (*Crito*). Against (3), he is quite aware of what he doesn't know (*Apology* 21d). Against (4), he constantly inquires about how the people in his city are conducting themselves (*Apology* 29d–30b). He thinks that how people conduct their lives is the greatest or most important thing, not "of no account" (*Apology* 29e). Against (5), he does not investigate things below ground or in the heavens (*Apology* 19b–d). Against (6), the *Theaetetus* itself shows us that he is very interested in particular people (143d–e; 144c5). Against (7), he never abandons the question: "Might I be doing injustice?" His whole life is concerned with that question (*Apology* 32d). He will consider it shortly in the *Crito*. And against (8), he explicitly objects to Aristophanes' portrait of him as someone carried around aloft (*Apology* 19c).[7]

3.3 AN ACUTE INTERPRETATIVE PROBLEM

That the *Euthyphro, Apology*, and *Crito* specifically deny of Socrates these descriptions he gives of the philosopher in the digression creates an acute interpretative problem. First, there is a problem because Plato closely links these three dialogues to the *Theaetetus*. And, second, in Socrates' defense speech at his trial that Plato recreates in the *Apology* Socrates clearly identifies himself as a philosopher (29d).

---

[6] For example, Annas (1999, 55–56). Blondell (2002, 298–301) notes differences and similarities between Socrates and the philosopher of the digression.

[7] On these details and others, see Waymack (1985) and Rue (1993).

Readers have almost without exception taken the Socrates of the dialogues *Euthyphro*, *Apology*, and *Crito* to be entirely one and the same
character.[8] But they have not always seen the equally obvious continuity
with the *Theaetetus*.[9] I will dwell on the link between these three dialogues
and the *Theaetetus* because it is going to be part of my reason for inferring
that Socrates does not accept the picture of the philosopher that he draws
in the digression.

Plato's second-to-last sentence of the *Theaetetus* especially creates a strong
link to the *Euthyphro*. Socrates says that he must now go to court to
acknowledge a charge against him. The *Euthyphro*, in Plato's fiction, takes
place a short time after the conversation of the *Theaetetus*, the time it would
have taken Socrates to walk from the location of the *Theaetetus* in Athens
to the relevant court building in Athens. He encounters Euthyphro on
the doorstep of the court and has the conversation of the *Euthyphro* there.
Plato could hardly have made it plainer that the Socrates of the *Theaetetus*
and the Socrates of the *Euthyphro* (and hence of the *Apology* and *Crito*) are
the same.

Taking it, therefore, that the Socrates of the *Theaetetus* is the same as the
character in the *Apology*, I note that in the *Apology* Socrates says he won't
stop philosophizing while he breathes and is able (29d4–5). That would
mean that he philosophizes pretty constantly. The *Apology* describes what
he won't stop doing, that is, what he counts as philosophizing. Socrates
says:

While I breathe and am able to, I certainly will not stop philosophizing, and I will
exhort you and explain this to whomever of you I happen to meet, and I will speak
just the sorts of things I am accustomed to: "Best of men, you are an Athenian,
from the city that is greatest and best reputed for wisdom and strength: are you
not ashamed that you care for having as much money as possible, and reputation,
and honor, but that you neither care for nor give thought to thoughtfulness
(*phronêseôs*), and truth, and how your soul will be the best possible? And if one of
you disputes it and asserts that he does care, I will . . . examine (*exetasô*) and test
(*elegxô*) him. And if he does not seem to me to possess virtue, but only says he
does, I will reproach him, saying that he regards the things worth the most as the
least important, and the paltrier things as more important. (29d)

---

[8] An exception is Kahn (1996, 93–95), who regards the Socrates of the *Euthyphro* as importantly
different from the Socrates of the *Apology*. He thinks the ignorant Socrates of the *Apology* could not
consistently search for definitions as the Socrates of the *Euthyphro* does. However, Kahn (1996, 88)
acknowledges a strong link between *Apology* and *Crito*.

[9] Long (1998) finds the *Theaetetus* evocative of the *Apology*, but then draws a conclusion completely
different from mine. Sedley (2004, 85–86) finds similarities between the Socrates of the *Apology*
and the Socrates of the *Theaetetus*, but reaches an understanding of the digression also completely
different from mine.

As Socrates thus describes it, his philosophizing is a multi-part activity. Socrates initially questions an interlocutor whether he is ashamed of not caring. When an interlocutor responds that he does care, Socrates examines the interlocutor. Then Socrates reproaches, if the interlocutor does not seem to possess virtue. Examining someone is itself a three-part activity. Its first step is to extract a statement that reveals the convictions the examined person lives by[10] (41b). The second step of examining is for Socrates to explore the consequences of the convictions he has revealed. Often the exploration finds contradictions. In the *Theaetetus* Theodorus describes these first two stages of Socrates' examining:

> You don't let go of anyone who comes up to you until you have forced him to strip and wrestle with you in argument. (169b)

I take it that what Theodorus' metaphor calls "stripping" is Socrates' revealing his interlocutor's life-guiding beliefs. "Wrestling" is drawing consequences from those beliefs.[11] The third step in Socrates' examining, if he finds that someone's life-guiding convictions do imply a contradiction, is to observe whether the interlocutor cares about that. He speaks of his concern for whether people care in the *Apology*:

> [W]hen my sons grow up, punish them, paining them with regard to these very same things with which I pained you, if they seem to you to care for money or else before virtue, and if they are reputed to be something when they are nothing, reproach them just as I did you that they do not care for what one ought, and they think they are something when they are worth nothing. (41e)

So thinking you are something when you are nothing is either the same as or implies not caring for virtue. Caring for the most important things is

---

[10] Some evidence is 39c: Socrates says that some people think that by killing him they will be released from having to give a testing of their lives.

[11] Nicias in *Laches* describes Socrates' constant practice:

> Whoever comes into close contact with Socrates and associates with him in conversation, even if he began by conversing about something quite different in the first place, keeps on being led about by the man's arguments until he submits to answering questions about himself concerning his present manner of life and the life he has lived hitherto. And when he does submit to questioning, . . . Socrates will not let him go before he has well and truly tested every last detail. (187e)

Socrates' examination of Meletus in the *Apology* is a good example of the first two steps of examining (27a: "[Meletus] appears to me to be contradicting himself"; 27b: "I am doing my discussions in my customary way").

Charmides informs us that one undresses a soul by discussion:

> Why don't we undress (*apedusamen*) this part of him? . . . Surely he has reached the age when he is willing to discuss (*dialegesthai*) things.? (154d)

See *Protagoras* 352a: "uncover."

either the same as or necessary for having virtue (29d0–e). And reproaching for not caring for the most important things is an important part of what Socrates counts as philosophizing.

As previously observed, Meletus' behavior under questioning in the *Apology* is an illuminating example of what not caring is. Socrates says several times that Meletus shows that he doesn't care (24c; 25b; 26b). Our evidence is that Meletus isn't puzzled or troubled by contradiction, and that Meletus continues in his course of action despite having incoherent reasons for it. In contrast, the youngster Theaetetus in the *Theaetetus* expresses puzzlement over contradictions (155) and gives up with equanimity proposals that prove unsustainable (210b); Socrates praises him for the unlikelihood that he will be burdensome to his associates by thinking that he knows what he doesn't know (210). So Socrates does not reproach Theaetetus for not caring. Socrates proceeds to the stage of reproaching when and only when the interlocutor shows that he doesn't care. Socrates' reproach is to say that the person untroubled by his contradictory views doesn't care about the most important thing.[12]

We may sum up by saying that for the Socrates of the *Apology* philosophizing is constant examining (that three-part activity of extraction, exploration, and observation) plus conditional reproaching.

Our problem for interpreting this first half of the digression, then, is complex. It is not only that Socrates' account of philosophizing in the *Apology* is inconsistent with his description of the philosopher in the digression and that much of the description of the digression philosopher is false of Socrates himself, who claims in the *Apology* to philosophize. There is also the problem that Socrates' act of putting forward the description of the philosopher in the digression seems to be a counter-example to Socrates' claim in the *Apology* that he constantly philosophizes – that is, constantly examines and conditionally reproaches his interlocutor.

Although I take the explicit linking of the *Theaetetus* with the *Apology* as an important datum for interpreting them, some scholars do not. Instead they take the later date of composition of the *Theaetetus*, which is widely agreed on, to fit in with their view that the later Plato created a character Socrates who was a different sort from the Socrates of the *Apology*. My view is that because Plato so evidently deliberately links the *Theaetetus*

---

[12] Weiss (2006) thinks the dialogues give no instances of Socrates' exhorting (including reproaching) or preaching: the "didactic-dressings down of people that are recounted in the *Apology* are not to be taken as literal representations of what Socrates did" Weiss (2006, 248–249). Rather, she finds that reproach is implicit in the elenctic exchanges that show that an interlocutor does not know what he claims to know.

with the *Euthyphro* and hence the *Apology*, he gives very strong indication that the reader should take Socrates as the same sort of character, not just a homonym, in that group of dialogues.

Although many people have noticed the discrepancies between Socrates' description of the philosopher in the *Theaetetus* and Plato's depiction of Socrates in the closely linked dialogues, we don't yet have a satisfactory explanation for the discrepancies. I propose to give one.

3.4 THEODORUS

To understand why Socrates addresses this discordant description of philosophers to Theodorus, I'll consider what the *Theaetetus* says about Theodorus. It tells us that he is a traveling educator from Cyrene whose renown as an expert in geometry and astronomy has attracted many students (143d; 168a).[13] Theodorus would call himself a philosopher (173b; 175c1).[14] Theodorus considers himself expert at educational matters generally (145a6). He considers himself able to assess the good character or virtue and the wisdom of young people (145a6–9). What he selects to praise about the youngster Theaetetus is Theaetetus' quickness at learning, his excellent memory, his courage, and his focus and progress in his lessons (144a–b). Theodorus accepts being described as a wise man (146c). Despite his reputation as wise, he expresses much reluctance to enter into the kind of conversation that he thinks typifies Socrates. Several times (at 146, 162, and 165) he begs off answering Socrates' questions because of his age. (His plea is not very convincing, because he is close in age to the sixty-nine-year-old Socrates, who still wants to engage in question-and-answer conversation.) Theodorus says, for example:

It had better be the younger one who gives the answers, because it won't be so disfiguring (*aschêmonêsei*: a geometrical pun?) if he trips up. (165b)

---

[13] There was another Theodorus of Cyrene, an atheist, who was a hundred years later than the geometer of the *Theaetetus* but since antiquity persistently confused with our geometer (Nails 2002 *s.v.* "Theodorus").

[14] In his opening address to Theodorus Socrates says:

If I cared more about those in Cyrene, Theodorus, I'd be asking you about things there and concerning those people, whether any at your place are active with a concern for geometry or any other philosophy (*tina allên philosophian*). (143d)

In addressing Theodorus with the phrase "any other philosophy," Socrates speaks as Theodorus would speak. He is recognizing that Theodorus would call geometry "a philosophy." More reasons for my interpretation of this passage in the *Theaetetus* will emerge later.

Though Theodorus is reluctant, Socrates eventually manages to draw Theodorus into answering questions as a surrogate for his deceased friend, Protagoras. Theodorus answers on behalf of Protagoras for about twelve pages of dialogue (169c–183a). Answering on behalf of someone else and getting refuted is perhaps less disfiguring than answering for yourself.

Theodorus' surrogate answers partly display his conception of philosophers. His assent to the description (including (1)–(8)) that Socrates gives in the first part of the digression is further partial display. Theodorus shows more of his conception of philosophers when he says at 173c that philosophers are not attendants on their arguments but the arguments are the slaves of the philosophers: each argument waits around to get finished whenever philosophers think best. In addition, in another dialogue that Plato has linked very closely to the *Theaetetus*, the *Sophist* (its conversation occurring the day after the *Theaetetus*), Theodorus says that he thinks all philosophers are divine (216a ff.). He doesn't explain what he means by that. I store it up as another hint of Theodorus' conception of philosophy.[15]

3.5 EXTRACTION BY DECLARATION

I now want to compare Theodorus to Socrates, as the *Theaetetus* depicts Socrates.

A first point is that Socrates (169b) has what he calls "so terrible a lust," for examination discussions, whether as examiner or examinee. He thinks they benefit both him and his interlocutor. He says:

Countless numbers of Heracleses and Theseuses, mighty in arguing, have met me and hammered me quite well, but that doesn't make me give up; so terrible a lust (*erôs deinos*) for exercise (*gumnasias*) about these matters has got into me. So don't you refuse to benefit both yourself and me, while you get rubbed up against me. (169b–c)[16]

---

[15] Possibly Socrates is acknowledging Theodorus' picture of the status of philosophers when Socrates addresses Theodorus at the beginning of the digression (172c3) with *daimonie*, "you semi-divine fellow."

[16] Socrates' mention of his *erôs* for exercise evokes both the *Symposium* and the *Parmenides*. The latter's Parmenides advises the adolescent Socrates to exercise a lot. (In his seventieth year Socrates recalls the conversation with Parmenides with admiration (*Theaetetus* 183–184).) In the *Symposium* (177c) Socrates says he knows nothing except erotic matters – *ta erôtika*. *Ta erôtika* is perhaps a little pun, conveying both that Socrates understands what it is to desire consumingly (*eran*), and also that Socrates knows how to ask questions (*erôtan*). *Erôtikê* is derivative from *eran*, with the ending *tikê*. Officially, the adjective derived from *erôtan* is *erôtêtikê*, with an additional tau. But at the level of a pun, *erôtikê* could be derived from *erôtan*, as *skutikê* is from *skutos* or *skuteuô*, without the additional tau. The perfect "I have asked" is *êrôtêka*. My fanciful etymology for a pun is somewhat supported by *Cratylus* 398d, where Socrates relates "hero" to *erôs* and *erôtan* because heroes were dialecticians and skilled questioners.

Further, Socrates is prepared for the argument to get the better of him. In that case, he says:

If we can't find any way out of our difficulty, then I suppose we'll be humbled, and submit to our argument like seasick passengers, letting it trample on us and treat us as it likes. (190b)

Similarly in the *Euthyphro* at 11d Socrates will express lack of control over the arguments; he wishes that his statements would stay put (*menein*), but they don't.

The end of the *Theaetetus* (210b11–d) is evocative of statements in the *Apology* though its allusions to midwifery do not occur in the *Apology*:

If you try to become pregnant with other things after these and if you become so, you will be full of better things because of the present examination. And if you should be empty, you will be less burdensome to your associates and gentler, because you will sensibly not be thinking that you know what you do not know. This much my art is capable of, but no more. And I don't know any of the things that others know, as many great and wondrous men as there are and have been. (210b–c)

When Theaetetus wonders whether Socrates really believes what he is saying, or is just trying Theaetetus out, Socrates replies:

I neither know nor claim as my own anything of that kind, . . . I'm . . . offering you bits to taste from the products of each group of wise men until I can help to bring what you think out to light. (157c–d)

It is of interest that Socrates thinks that by giving Theaetetus a taste of the views produced by wise men, Socrates can bring to light Theaetetus' own beliefs (157d2).

When Theodorus asks Socrates to tell him an answer. Socrates says:

You are simply and honestly a speech-lover, Theodorus. You think that I am a sort of sack of speeches and can easily draw one out that will say how these things are not so. You aren't bearing in mind what's happening. Not one of the arguments comes from me but always from the one that is having the discussion with me. I know nothing more, apart from a tiny bit, enough to be able to get a statement from someone else who is wise, and to take its measure (*apodexasthai metriôs*: to accept it in a measured way). That's what I'm going to do now: I'm going to try to get an argument from Theaetetus, not to say anything myself. (161a7 ff.)

Socrates' self-description seems extreme: he gives *no* statements or accounts of his own. He *always* gets what he says from the one conversing with him. Similarly Socrates gives an extreme description when he reports that many people correctly reproach him because

I always ask others, and I myself profess nothing about anything on account of having nothing wise [to say]. (150c4–7)[17]

Socrates' extreme self-description occurs within Socrates' questioning of Theaetetus, but there is no reason to suppose that it does not continue to apply throughout the dialogue, and hence to the conversation that Socrates will have with Theodorus in the digression. If so, Socrates implies that the statements of the digression addressed *to* Theodorus come *from* Theodorus, and do not come from Socrates. Since this point is very important to my argument, I'll dwell on it.

The reader of the *Theaetetus*, or of any of Plato's dialogues with Socrates as speaker, may resist Socrates' claim that his arguments and statements come from the person he is talking with.[18] The reader is inclined to say instead that when a proposition is contained in some wildly creative question of Socrates to which an interlocutor assents, the proposition has not really been extracted from the interlocutor. Rather, Socrates has supplied something that the interlocutor would never have come up with by himself. In what sense, then, can Socrates claim in the first place that Socrates' wildly creative proposals do not belong to Socrates and in the second place that they do belong to the interlocutor?[19]

Socrates' statement that his arguments *always* come from the person he is talking with forces on us this answer: the interlocutor's assent to a hitherto undreamt-of proposal in a question counts for Socrates as getting a proposition from his interlocutor. What count as your views for the purposes of an examination discussion are not only views adopted formally long ago and proclaimed ever since; your views also include proposals that appeal to you to which you assent when you are first asked about them. That is why Socrates is entitled to say that he always gets the contents of his surprising novel questions from his interlocutors.

In the digression addressed to Theodorus Socrates does not ask questions and get assents. Rather, he enunciates declarations that Theodorus praises.

---

[17] Reading *apophainomai*. For a summary of some textual issues and a defense of *apophainomai*, see Cooper (2007, 34).

[18] For example, *Euthyphro* 11c5: "The statements are yours." (See also *Alcibiades* I 112d–113c.) See Frede (1992).

[19] Benardete (1997, 34) refers to "Socrates' Heraclitean–Protagorean thesis, which he simply foists on Theaetetus." Blondell (2002, 265) similarly cites 184e as "drawing attention to the fact that it is actually Socrates who is producing the ideas."

But Socrates' adverb, "always," implies that he counts even this sequence of declarations as extracted from his interlocutor.[20]

The sense in which these declarations do not come from Socrates is that Socrates is not presenting himself as endorsing or recommending them, because he has already said that he knows nothing, except how to get a statement from someone else who is wise, and to take its measure. That is to say, Socrates has told us that he merely tests candidate wise statements. He does not offer them as doctrines or teaching, even though he may be the first to utter them.

The sense in which even Socrates' declarative sentences do come from his interlocutor is that the interlocutor has accepted and not challenged them. Socrates may fairly count both interrogation and declaration as extraction of beliefs from an interlocutor because it is always open to an interlocutor under Socratic examination to distance himself from Socrates' proposals: it is open to the interlocutor to dissent or to ask for clarification. Interlocutors sometimes do resist or challenge, though perhaps not as often as we would like or expect. In contrast with Socrates' mode of discussion, which allows for request for clarification, there was among Socrates' contemporaries a stylized question-and-answer contest whose rules permit only a "yes" or "no" response (as in the *Euthydemus*[21]). But that is not the kind of discussion that Socrates is having in the *Theaetetus*.

We must conclude from Socrates' self-description plus his behavior in the digression that he has a mode of extraction by declaration as well as a mode of extraction by interrogation.

We get some information about Socrates from the way Socrates praises Theaetetus. Early on Socrates praises Theaetetus for the reaction of wondering that Socrates says belongs to a philosopher and is the only starting point of philosophy (155d2–4). Socrates' concluding praise (210) is to say that because of the present examination Theaetetus will not be a burden to his associates in the way that people who think they know what they don't know are burdensome.

---

[20] At 184e Socrates says to Theaetetus: "But perhaps it would be better for you to say these things while being the answerer (*apokrinomenon*) rather than for me to interfere (*polupragmonein*) on your behalf (*huper sou*)." In contrast to Blondell (2002, 265) I take 184e to imply that Socrates' mode of presenting an assertion to which the interlocutor assents and Socrates' mode of asking explicit questions to which the respondent answers "yes" are equivalent modes of arriving at the interlocutor's beliefs. Whether Theaetetus answers questions or assents to assertions, nevertheless Theaetetus is still the one to "say these things." But Socrates thinks it better to ask questions in Theaetetus' case. (In other cases, as will turn out to be so with Theodorus, asking questions won't work, so Socrates will choose another mode of examination.)

[21] At 295b the brothers rebuke Socrates for asking for clarification.

We can now contrast Socrates and Theodorus.

Theodorus is a wise man, a *sophos*, with a range of expertise, someone who can make assessment of wisdom and virtue as well as teach geometry. In contrast, Socrates is not wise. (In the *Apology*, as shown earlier, he is horrified by the reputation of being wise.) He knows nothing more than the person he is talking to, except how to get a statement from someone who is wise and to take its measure. He only claims expertise in craving and questioning. All of Socrates' arguments, statements, or theses (*logoi*) come from the person he is talking with.

Theodorus has an elevated view of philosophers. Theodorus thinks that philosophers have their arguments totally under their control, like slaves, and that philosophers are divine. In contrast, Socrates is prepared for the argument to trample and humble him, and he thinks that philosophers are in the first place puzzled.

Theodorus praises Theaetetus for his quick learning and his steady progress. In contrast, Socrates praises Theaetetus for his puzzlement, and Socrates expects that Theaetetus will not be burdensome to his friends because he won't think that he knows what he doesn't know.

Theodorus doesn't like examination–discussion. But Socrates is wild about it.

3.6 REFLECTIONS ON THE EXTRACTION FROM THEODORUS

I revisit now our interpretative problems about the description of the philosopher in the first part of the digression. First, Plato takes care to tell us that the Socrates of the *Theaetetus* is the same as the Socrates of the *Euthyphro*, who is obviously the same Socrates as in the *Apology*. So we may infer that the Socrates of the *Theaetetus* is the same as the Socrates of the *Apology*. The Socrates of the *Apology* tells us that he is a philosopher, so the Socrates of the *Theaetetus* is that same philosopher. Yet in the digression he gives a number of descriptions of the philosopher that are false of him. Second, in the *Apology* Socrates explains his philosophizing as constant examination and (conditional) reproach. Yet to enunciate the description of the philosopher in the digression seems to be neither to examine nor to conditionally reproach.

To solve the first problem I say that the description of the philosopher in the digression is being extracted from Theodorus. It is Theodorus' conception of the philosopher, as Theodorus' hearty assent shows. It is not Socrates' conception. That it is false of Socrates who will not long afterwards at his trial declare himself one who constantly philosophizes is thus not a problem.[22] For the second problem, I say that by giving his speech, Socrates reveals Theodorus. So Socrates' speechifying is the first part of an examination. It is a confirming instance of, rather than a counter-example to, Socrates' claim in the *Apology* that he constantly philosophizes.

Socrates' emphatic claim that he *always* gets his statements from the wise person he is talking to together with Theodorus' enthusiastic assent (176a2–4) to Socrates' declarations are two straightforward reasons to say that the digression's description of the philosopher represents Theodorus' views. Some details of phrasing in this first part of the digression confirm the impression that its description of the philosopher represents what Theodorus believes, and suggest that Socrates cannot believe it.

A first detail is (173b) that having commented unfavorably on the litigious person, Socrates asks Theodorus if he would like the discussion to be about "those from our own chorus" (*tous de tou hêmeterou chorou*), that is, as is clear a few lines later, those who spend time in philosophy. Theodorus echoes Socrates' phrasing with "we who are choristers in this sort of thing" at 173c. The image of philosophers as a chorus, a group of people who recite in unison something composed by someone else, is grotesque, and entirely at odds with the Socrates who has appeared up to now in the *Theaetetus*, not to mention the Socrates of the *Apology*.[23] Theodorus explicitly includes himself as a chorister.

Another detail is that Socrates ends his description of the philosopher, before he moves on to the second part of the digression (which will present our second set of problems) by saying:

The one, whom you call a philosopher, has really been brought up in freedom and leisure. (175e)

---

[22] I thus disagree as much as possible with Sedley (2004, 67–68), who says:

The philosopher's interest in broad definitional questions about justice and man ... makes him relatively indifferent to practical questions about actual justice between actual human beings. It is a mistake to try to explain away this prominent feature of the Digression. That a life of pure intellectual endeavor, or "contemplation," as it came to be known, is superior to one devoted to civic virtue, more god-like, and for these reasons more worthy of the philosopher, was [a] doctrine which Plato would enunciate at the climax of the *Timaeus* (89d2–90d7) and which his pupil Aristotle would advocate in largely similar terms at the end of the *Nicomachean Ethics*. It is important that we should try to understand and contextualize this recurrent thesis of ancient ethics, rather than seek ways of reading the texts that will save our philosophical heroes from saying it in the first place.

I judge it equally important to place this occurrence of the recurrent thesis in the context of the plain indications that Plato gives us that the Socrates of the *Euthyphro*, *Apology*, and *Crito*, of whom the description of the digression philosopher is decidedly false, is identical with the Socrates of the *Theaetetus* who articulates it. There is no interpretative problem about why the Pythagorean narrator of the *Timaeus* would articulate the thesis.

[23] Blondell (1998, 234) comments that a chorus is a grotesque metaphor for imitators of Socrates.

The phrase, "whom you call a philosopher" (175e1)[24] is a concluding signal that Socrates is speaking here as Theodorus speaks. He is using the word "philosopher" as Theodorus uses it.[25]

A last detail, belonging to the structure of the dialogue, suggests that the digression belongs to Theodorus. When, despite his reluctance (146b; 162b; 165b), Theodorus makes the limited agreement to answer certain questions as a stand-in for his deceased friend Protagoras (169c6–7), Theodorus serves as formal answerer in two passages. The digression, and nothing else, occurs between those two passages. So Plato has placed the digression exactly within Theodorus' official contribution to the discussion as answerer. That seems another sign that what Socrates says in the digression belongs to Theodorus.

It is, moreover, straightforward to explain why in the particular case of Theodorus Socrates does not engage in the sort of extraction via questioning that we are familiar with from dialogues such as the *Euthyphro*. Socrates cannot first question Theodorus to extract his views and then explore their consequences, being on the lookout for contradiction, because Theodorus refuses to be questioned (at 146b, 162b, and 165b). However, when at 169b Theodorus says that Socrates doesn't let anyone get away without forcing him to strip and wrestle, Theodorus unknowingly gives a half-accurate prediction of his own fate. By assenting vigorously to both the first and second parts of the digression-speech (176a2–4 and 177c2–4), Theodorus strips and reveals himself as much as he would have by answering questions.[26]

Although we now understand why only an apparent lecture from Socrates will uncover Theodorus' views, the question arises why Socrates is interested in getting Theodorus' views out into the open at all. We might naturally ask: what is the good of doing just part of an examination, just the extraction part, and not going on to the next part, the exploration of the consequences of the extracted views?

A possible though partial answer is that Socrates may hope to proceed to exploring consequences on the next day, since with the last sentence of the *Theaetetus* Socrates arranges to meet with Theodorus the next morning. A more likely answer seems to me to be that Socrates is uncovering these self-congratulatory beliefs of Theodorus so that the young Theaetetus can

---

[24] One manuscript has *kaloumen*. I'd conjecture a copyist who thinks that Socrates is endorsing his speech.

[25] Compare *Apology* 24b: Socrates describes Meletus as "the good and patriotic, as he says."

[26] At 173c Theodorus says that they can go on discussing, with the arguments as their slaves, because "neither judge, nor, as for the poets, spectator, presides over us who will be in charge of us and make a judgment about us." It doesn't occur to Theodorus that Theaetetus at least might make a judgment of his own about the conversation afterwards. (I am grateful to Christopher Moore for calling this passage to my attention.)

examine them for himself later. It is important for Theaetetus to examine Theodorus' views because Theaetetus has chosen Theodorus as a wise guide. Socrates is often interested in the examination of people who act as guides or teachers to the young. He gives extensive examinations of teachers in *Protagoras, Laches, Hippias Major, Hippias Minor, Gorgias*, and *Euthydemus*.

3.7 THE SECOND HALF OF THE DIGRESSION: *HOMOIÔSIS THEÔ(I)*

Now I turn to the second half of the digression. I am going to apply to it the same strategy that I have just proposed for the first half. I'll propose that Socrates is not enunciating doctrine. He is in no way committed to the statements he puts into his address to Theodorus. He is instead conducting an extraction-by-declaration of Theodorus' beliefs.

A main reason to say that the second part of the digression is an extraction by declaration of Theodorus' views and not an expression of Socrates' convictions will be that the declarations of the second half are life-guiding recommendations that are unexamined, even though they cry out for examination. That is, to recommend a way of life without examining it is out of step with the Socrates of the *Euthyphro, Apology*, and *Crito*. And Plato has taken care to signal that the Socrates of the *Theaetetus* is identical with that Socrates of the *Apology*. To recommend a way of life without examining it is also out of step with Socrates' disclaimers of knowledge in the *Theaetetus* (as in his very last speech at 210c5–6). Given the signals of the identity of this Socrates with the Socrates of the *Apology*, and given Socrates' strong disclaimers of knowledge or wisdom in the *Theaetetus*, we must be suspicious of the digression's apparent recommendations that need examination and do not get it. The Socrates Plato depicts here would not hold, and would certainly not proclaim to others, life-guiding views that he has not examined. (In the *Euthyphro*, for example, Socrates and Euthyphro agree at 9e that we should not just accept what a speaker says: we must consider it (*skepteon*).)

For my purpose of arguing that certain statements of the second half of the digression do not represent claims that Socrates is endorsing it would be enough merely to make plausible that they deserve examination and do not get it. I don't have to prove that they could not survive Socratic examination.[27] But in fact, I'll suggest that, so far as I can see, they would

---

[27] I am grateful to Tim O'Keefe for emphasizing the distinction between showing that a directive is sufficiently unclear that it needs examination and showing that it is decidedly unacceptable.

not survive examination. My way of figuring that out will be to do my own examination of them. No doubt my own examination of them is not as incisive as Socrates' would be, but I have to work with what is available to me. Of course I acknowledge that the results of my examination are not final.

I will select from the second half several of seventeen claims into which the second half naturally divides. To support my point it will not be necessary to discuss every one. They are a mixture of acceptable and objectionable claims. I will grant a few claims that seem to me harmless, but discuss in more detail only some of those I find most questionable, even after I have attempted to give them a sympathetic reading.

This second part of the digression, called the *homoiôsis theô(i)* or "likeness to God" passage in the secondary literature, offers as a life-guiding principle that you make yourself like god. Readers of Plato in antiquity believed that it was a straightforward statement of Plato's mature ethical theory.[28] It has received much attention lately as part of a revival of interest in what we can learn from the ancient interpreters.[29] As much as I recognize the merits of the ancient thinkers, I believe that they made a mistake, a bad one, about this passage, and that the current scholars who are attempting to put it in the position of being Plato's considered statement of his ethical theory are mistaken to follow the ancients on this point.[30]

Theodorus responds to the first half of the digression with its description of the philosopher and his contrast with the litigious man, with warm appreciation:

Socrates, if you convinced everyone of what you are saying as you do me, there would be more peace and fewer bad things among men. (176a)

Socrates takes up the phrase "bad things" in the first three statements of his reply to Theodorus at 176:

(1) It isn't possible that bad things should be destroyed because there must always be something opposite to the good.
(2) And it isn't possible for them to become established among the gods.
(3) Of necessity they make the rounds of (*peripolei*) our mortal nature (*thnêtên phusin*) and this region here.

Although someone might object to some of these first claims, I am going to take them as acceptable. It seems to me not immediately

---

[28] Annas (1999, 52–53) mentions the first-to-second-century AD Alcinous and the first-century BC Arius Didymus.

[29] For example, Annas (1999) and Sedley (1999, 2004).

[30] An older discussion that takes it as a straightforward recommendation of Plato's is Rutenber (1946).

implausible – though of course the point could be further explored – that if anything is good, something is bad. There admittedly isn't some kind of general logical truth of that sort about all pairs of opposites. But there might be something special about good and bad. I forgo thinking about that unresolved point in order to work through the second half of the digression. So I grant Socrates' claim (1). I do, however, acknowledge that it deserves more discussion, especially if considered as a claim about human practices, institutions, and actions. If it is so considered, the difference between accepting it and rejecting it might be the difference between resignation and hope.

I'll also grant claim (2). Even without committing to the existence of gods, one can agree initially (though of course again there could be discussion) that if there are gods, bad things don't get instituted among them – that is, they don't suffer or do bad things.

And I'll also grant claim (3). The three claims together might seem at first glance to imply that gods have a region distinct from our own. But in the interest of a sympathetic reading, I'll understand the implication to be simply that gods are different from people. That understanding allows for the possibility, which seems an important one, that gods could be in whatever region they wanted to be in. So, so far, so good.

Socrates now continues:

(4) That's why one ought to try to escape from here to there as quickly as one can. (176a)

(5) Flight is becoming like God (*homoiôsis theô(i)*) as far as possible (*kata dunaton*). (176a–b)

(6) Becoming like is becoming just (*dikaion*) and pious (*hosion*) with thoughtfulness (*meta phronêseôs*). (176b)

The recommendation to become like God by becoming just, pious, and thoughtful seems strongly to imply that the gods *are* just, pious, and thoughtful. Socrates continues the theme of the justice of God in two later statements:

(7) Let us state the truth in this way. God is in no way unjust at all, but is as just as possible. (176b–c)

(8) There's nothing more like a god than one of us who has become as just as possible. (176c)

The suggestion that the gods are just, pious, and thoughtful is puzzling and merits reflection.[31] To start with, it is not obvious that the gods can

---

[31] Rue (1993, 89–91) says, "Justice and piety are not properly attributes of gods, or at least of Greek gods," citing the *Euthyphro*'s suggestions that piety has to do with what human beings owe to the gods, while justice has to do with what people owe to each other and to the gods.

be pious. Toward whom would the gods be pious?[32] Certainly not toward us. And it is not part of the ancient lore about gods that plural gods have piety toward one another. The Liddell–Scott dictionary (Liddell and Scott 1843/1961) doesn't give us any encouragement to apply the word "pious" ("disposed to obey divine law" is one translation) to gods.[33] Moreover, later in the same day the Socrates of the *Euthyphro*, charged with impiety (12e) who, I am emphasizing, is identical with the Socrates of the *Theaetetus*, will be at a loss as he investigates with Euthyphro what it is for an action to be pious. The Socrates of the *Apology* who knows nothing important and who is not a teacher would not be making a life-guiding recommendation using a predicate he admittedly is not an authority on.

There is also a question what it would be for the gods to have thoughtfulness. The Greek word is *phronêsis*. *Phronêsis* in the *Apology* is what human beings should aim at. In the *Apology* it prominently involved acknowledgment that one did not know about the greatest things. People who had the greatest reputations for being wise turned out to be least likely to be thoughtful. It involves exercising care to avoid the sorts of contradictory life-plans that Socrates' examination reveals. Such care would seem unnecessary for gods. Thoughtfulness is different from the divine wisdom that Socrates reserves for the gods. One would expect their wisdom to preclude their having contradictory views. One thinks of Aristotle's account (in *Nicomachean Ethics* VI, ch. 5), where *phronêsis* is a particularly human kind of thoughtfulness involving deliberating in conditions of uncertainty and steering appropriately through possible affective hazards. It seems as inappropriately deflating to say that gods are thoughtful as it would be inflated to advocate divine wisdom for humans.[34]

The implication that the gods are just also merits examination.[35] The traditional conception of the divine justice of Zeus involves his allotting

---

[32] *Euthyphro* 12e–15a discusses piety as tending for and service to the gods, and knowledge of sacrificing and praying, with no suggestion that the gods enact it toward one another. Weiss (1996) argues that as Socrates understands holiness (or piety), a pious person cannot have expertise about the good and bad. If so, it would seem impossible, not just odd, for gods to be pious. For different support, see Rue (1993, 90).

See Wildberg (2003) for an opposing view of piety.

[33] Sedley (2004, 84) says that it would be contrary to usual Greek practice to call gods "pious." Some translators seem to recognize the oddity here, by resisting the most natural rendering of the Greek word (*hosion*). One translator renders it by "pure." Another renders it "religious" (which to me sounds every bit as odd as it does to say the gods are pious).

[34] Plotinus *Ennead* I, 2 in Armstrong (1966) wonders whether the god mentioned in this passage of the *Theaetetus* could have the "so-called civic virtues," including practical wisdom (*phronêsis*) and justice.

[35] Rue (1993) goes somewhat too far in saying that the Greek gods were not just. The ancient Greeks did speak of the justice of Zeus. *Euthyphro* at 6a says that Zeus is "best and most just of the gods." Lloyd-Jones (1983) emphasizes the justice of Zeus as related to the order of the universe. Rue's

punishment to wrongdoers and rewards to the worthy.[36] A recommendation that people should aspire to enact justice like Zeus the enforcer[37] would not appeal to the Socrates of the *Euthyphro*. Plato depicts Socrates as quite surprised by Euthyphro's officious eagerness to see that an injustice committed by his father gets punished.[38] Euthyphro, on the other hand (at 2b), is confident that Socrates would not bring an indictment against anyone.

Socrates is probably not thinking of the traditional gods of myth, anyway, since the gods of the myths are not portrayed as especially fair to anyone.[39] (Glaucon's opinion of gods comes out at *Republic* 360b, where the person with the ring of Gyges could do whatever bad things he wished, "being equal to a god (*isotheon*) among humans.") So leaving aside Zeus the avenger and other gods of the myths, let us imagine gods who do no injustice, and ask how exactly they might do positive acts of justice. The kind of justice of which we human beings have some experience often involves the sharing of scarce or limited goods to which we have equal claim, and it often involves the giving to others of what we owe to them. It is not obvious that that sort of justice would be appropriate to the gods. What exactly would be the limited resources that gods should share or that they would owe to anyone? My doubts about the applicability of the description "just" to gods are somewhat supported by Aristotle's sarcasms in book x of the *Nicomachean Ethics* when he considers in what sense gods might do well. Aristotle asks:

What sorts of actions must we assign to [the gods]? Acts of justice? Will not the gods seem absurd if they make contracts and pay back deposits and so on?'[40] (1178b8–12)

> comment, though too strong, usefully calls attention to the need for examination of the claim that the gods are just.
>   Plutarch, *Moralia*, "The Divine Vengeance" (550a) cites Pindar as describing the god who rules the world as "the demiurge of justice." Plutarch takes that to mean that god knows how to dispense punishment. Socrates' view of the gods is discussed in several of the essays in Smith and Woodruff (2000).
>
> [36] For this thread in the ancient Platonists and their locating it in Plato, see Annas (1999, 56–57). Other authors who see the need for a distinction are Plotinus and Aquinas. If justice is defined as in the *Republic*, it isn't clear how the gods would instantiate it, as Plotinus observes in *Ennead* I, 2. Aquinas in *Summa Theologica* Question xx–xxi distinguishes human justice and the justice of God.
> [37] See Lloyd-Jones (1983) for Zeus as the preserver of *dikê*.
> [38] *Euthyphro* 4b7–c3; 5d8–6a5; 7b7–9. Irwin (1998, 42) comments that Euthyphro "simply argues that if an injustice has been committed, the gods demand punishment for it."
> [39] Euthyphro points out at 6a, apparently in support of the claim that gods are interested in justice, that Cronos castrated Ouranos because Cronos thought Ouranos had done injustice and Zeus bound Cronos because of what Zeus took to be an injustice of Cronos. This seems a double-edged example, since it apparently also is evidence that gods do injustice.
> [40] This and the following quotations are in the translation of Ross, rev. Ackrill and Urmson (1980).

It seems necessary at least to clarify the recommendation to become like the gods in justice by making some distinction between human justice and divine justice. For example, it might be claimed that divine justice involves allotting punishment to wrongdoers and rewards to the worthy, as in the myth of the *Gorgias*. But then we seem to have the proposal that the highest aspiration of people would be to enact justice like Zeus the enforcer – a most unappealing recommendation – and presumably of no interest to the Socrates who would bring no indictments (*Euthyphro* 2b).

Other ancients besides Aristotle recognized a need to clarify any claim that the gods are just. For one example, the Platonist Alcinous (of the early centuries AD) resolves the difficulty he sees with the claim that gods are just by taking it as a claim about a secondary deity who maintains the order of the heavens, and not about the supreme deity in Alcinous' scheme, who is too superior to have virtue.[41] The directive that we should become just in the manner of the gods then becomes for Alcinous the somewhat metaphorical directive to become as orderly in our own lives as the heavens are. Understood as a recommendation to approach the unfailing predictability of certain astronomical events, that directive is not clearly a plausible guide for human beings.

Another possible way to interpret the directive to become like God in being just is to take it to mean simply that people should become good in their own human way. To become good in the way appropriate to people is arguably to become just.[42] In becoming good in the human way, people will then become like God, who is good in the way appropriate to gods. So understood, the recommendation now is to become good in the usual human way, which is at least familiar. But now the reference to God is idle. It isn't clear why the recommendation to be good in the human way is explained or strengthened by the thought that insofar as we are good in our human way, we will be resembling God, who is good in whatever

[41] Alcinous in Dillon (1993) says in ch. 28:

> [W]e mean, obviously, the god *in* the heavens, not of course, the God above the heavens, who does not possess virtue, being superior to this.

Dillon (1993, xxiii) comments:

> The "god in the Heavens" is necessarily the Demiurge or "intellect of the whole heaven," A's second god in the scheme presented in chapter 10. To bring the supreme deity of chapter 10 into a relationship of "likeness" to man would be to compromise his transcendence, presumably, apart from the absurdity of imputing to him virtues in any ordinary meaning of the word.

[42] In an extended discussion of the question Plotinus proposes (*Ennead* 1, 2): "There is nothing to prevent us, even if we are not made like in regard to virtues, being made like by our own virtues to that which does not possess virtue." That is, we might be good in our way, via the virtues, and thus be like to something else that is good in a different way, not via the human virtues.

way is appropriate to gods. (It would be no less, and no more helpful, to be instructed to become as good as gold, or as good as hollyhocks, or dolphins, or geometry proofs.)

Another possibility for understanding the suggestion to become good or just like God is to think of Plato's depiction of the creator-God in the *Timaeus*. He is good in that he ungrudgingly brings goodness, a likeness to himself, into the world (*Timaeus* 29d–e).[43] That suggestion seems worth considering, although there is the natural immediate objection to it that it seems odd to call the ungrudging but completely gratuitous creation of good an act of justice, as though it met a requirement. It would seem to be a gift rather than an act of justice.

But leaving aside that oddity, suppose Socrates *is* recommending that we imitate God the creator by ungrudgingly and gratuitously creating good. That would be appealing advice. But then, again, the reference to God seems to add no useful content. The advice, "Be an ungrudging creator of good things," stands on its own pretty well. The addition, "Be like God," does not add clarification. As something to think about while acting, the directive is not as helpful as the simpler, "Be an ungrudging creator of good things."

Actually, the addition might be somewhat distracting. An agent having it in mind might be in danger of focusing on himself, not on his project of creating good things. If he has in mind the directive: "Ungrudgingly create good in order to be like god," his project becomes a project of accessorizing. The addition, "like God," then seems slightly pernicious. The directive seems to have "one thought too many," to borrow a phrase from Bernard Williams.[44]

Socrates doesn't mention any other human virtues such as courage and temperance. But again there springs to mind Aristotle's comment in *Nicomachean Ethics* x as he considers whether the gods are supposed to be temperate. He says:

Is not such praise tasteless (*phortikôs*)? . . . [It would be] trivial and unworthy of gods. (1178b15–18)

---

[43] I am grateful to Julia Annas for pointing out a glaring omission in an early version of this paper – that I did not consider the creator-God, depicted, for example, in Plato's *Timaeus*, who is quite different from Aristotle's god. We must include the creator-god of ancient thought also to understand the *Theaetetus* notion of likeness to God.

[44] Williams (1981, 18), imagines a person who thinks, as he chooses to rescue his wife instead of someone else also in need, not simply "This is my wife" but "This is my wife and in situations like this it is morally permissible to rescue my wife."

And there is a logical oddity. It can't quite be true that there's nothing more like a god than one of us who has become as just as possible, unless we qualify by adding the phrase, "except for God himself." Since even the dimmest conception of God seems to involve great power and self-certifying superiority or authority, our becoming as just as possible wouldn't seem obviously to elevate us from our present relative lack of power or cosmic status to maximal god-likeness.[45]

A further oddity is an inconsistency between the first part of the digression and what is stated here. At 175c the philosopher has given up asking the question, "What injustice am I doing to you?" 176c now recommends that a person become as just as possible. It seems impossible for a human being to become just without asking of his particular actions "What injustice might I be doing?" The Socrates of the *Crito* (clearly identified with the Socrates of the *Theaetetus*) asks it about himself at 48c–d. So if Socrates were proposing the digression as his own endorsements, he would be an obviously inconsistent Socrates.[46]

Moreover, the Socrates of the *Euthyphro* (also clearly identified with the figure of the *Theaetetus*) says that he knows nothing (6a–b) about the gods.[47] The Socrates of the *Euthyphro* wishes for knowledge about what divine things are. He doesn't already have it (4e–5a; 15e). That it would obviously not be consistent for a Socrates avowedly ignorant of the divine to give a life-directive of imitating god is strong reason to think that Socrates is not giving such a life-directive.

I conclude that the proposal to become like God is so far unclear. Even if the proposal can ultimately be understood in some perfectly reasonable way, it cannot be so understood immediately. It cries out for examination. I don't feel in a position to declare that it is definitely absurd. But on our minimal examination of the possibilities, it at the moment seems either

---

[45] Mitchell Miller has made the interesting suggestion to me that in the digression we have a radical application of Protagoras' *homo mensura* view: Man is the measure even of the divine.

[46] Paul Woodruff has suggested that the verb at 175, which is *ekbênai*, means "go beyond" rather than "give up." If we understand the verb to mean "go beyond," then the description of the philosopher here would have him asking both what injustice he might be doing and also what injustice itself is. That is a possible reading but the more drastic one that I have taken seems more natural to me. The literal meaning of *ekbênai*, "step out of," seems to me to suggest a real departure, as does the repetition of the prefix "out of" at 175c4.

[47] Similarly in the *Cratylus* Socrates says:

The first and finest line of investigation, which as intelligent people we must acknowledge, is this, that we admit that we know nothing about the gods themselves or about the names they call themselves – although it is clear that they call themselves by true ones. The second best line on the correctness of names is to say, as is customary in our prayers, that we hope the gods are pleased by the names we give them, since we know no others. (400d)

tasteless, or unappealingly officious, or implausibly astronomical, or idle, or (as having one thought too many) verging on pernicious. The Socrates we know from the *Euthyphro*, *Apology*, and *Crito* would not let pass without examination a claim so unclear.

I will indulge in a personal reaction to the recommendation to become like God. It reminds me of an argument in Nietzsche's *Thus Spoke Zarathustra*. Nietzsche's speaker says:

> If there were no gods, how could I stand not to be a god! Therefore there are no gods. (§24; Nietzsche 2006, 65)

The recommendation to be like God strikes me as amounting to a different but similarly ridiculous train of thought: if there were gods, how could I endure not to be one? Therefore I declare that I can be as like to one as possible!

So I am very resistant to the thought (pending, of course, further exploration) that one should adopt as a life-guiding plan to become like any god. In fact, I'll go out on a limb here, and say that (pending, of course, further exploration) the recommendation to aim at becoming like God strikes me as the worst idea I have ever heard in philosophy. I can't think of any other errors that are even in the same league.[48]

Socrates later makes these observations. If I understand them, they are a direct rejection of Protagoras' larger thesis, from which the digression began:

(9) [T]hey're ignorant of the damage from injustice, which is the last thing one should be ignorant of. It isn't what they think, beatings and executions: people sometimes behave unjustly and suffer none of those things. No, it's one which it's impossible to escape. (176d–e)

(10) If there are patterns (*paradeigmatôn*) set up in reality (*en tô(i) onti hestôtôn*), one divine (*theiou*) happiest one, the other most miserable godless (*atheou*) one, and if they don't see that that is so, they don't notice, because of their foolishness and utter lack of understanding (*eschatês anoias*), that through their unjust actions they are becoming like the one and unlike the other, for which they pay the penalty (*tinousi dikên*) of living the life which is like the one they become like. (176e–177a)[49]

---

[48] Theages in Plato's *Theages* shares Nietzsche's wish to be a god (*Theages* 126a). Walt Whitman has the opposite thought. He thinks that if he were anything special – he does not consider the possibility of being a god – he couldn't stand for anyone else not to be so. Whitman says: "By God! I will accept nothing which all cannot have their counterpart of on the same terms!" (Whitman (1993), *Song of Myself*, §24, verse 507).

[49] The clause that I have translated as beginning "if there are patterns" could also be translated as "since there are patterns." (The construction is a genitive absolute, *paradeigmatôn hestôtôn*. The reader

(11) If we say that if they do not get rid of their cleverness (*deinotêtos*), and that when they die that place that is pure of bad things will not receive them, but that here they will always have the way of life that is a likeness (*homoiotêta*), bad men associating with bad things, they, as clever and unscrupulous men, will hear these things entirely as coming from some fools. (177a)

The last two of these statements have been subject to different interpretations. A mild interpretation is to take the patterns set up in reality (literally: "in what is" – *tô(i) onti*) – simply to be such things as what divine happiness is, and what godless misery is, as opposed to what they seem to someone to be.[50] Patterns so understood are the contents described in the answer to such questions as: "What is real happiness?" On this mild interpretation Socrates is saying that if there is content to the notions of what is divine and most happy, and of what is most miserable, as opposed to what seems so to someone or other, then the person who does injustice will resemble what is most miserable, and that will be a bad thing. The penalty for the person who does unjust things will be that he becomes unjust and bad and his life becomes miserable and bad, because there really is such a thing as what unjust is that is the pattern for whatever is unjust. It is distinct from what seems unjust to some or other group. If there is such a thing as what unjust is, then the person who does injustice is living a bad life.

Possibly Theodorus interprets Socrates' statements more extravagantly to refer to paradigmatic forms that are items of some special theory, as some commentators do. But there is no ground for that in Socrates' words here.

Socrates is probably correct at (11) that the damage he cites won't seem very impressive to the systematically unscrupulous person. We can well imagine that the systematically unscrupulous person will scoff when told about such alleged damage.

Socrates' apparent allusion at (11) to being shut out of a good afterlife is uncontroversial because it is conditional – "*If* we say . . ." And Socrates seems right that the tough characters[51] he is imagining will think that those who reproach them are foolish.

---

must supply the appropriate adverb for the clause.) Some translations treat the opening clause as an assertion. Those translations are possible, and I am not attached to "if" as opposed to "since," but I think it noteworthy that (10) does not begin with a flat assertion.

[50] Sedley (1999, 312) and Sedley (2004, 78–79) says, on the contrary, that it is clear that the pattern of divine happiness is God. He doesn't indicate what the pattern of godless misery would be.

[51] I borrow the phrase "tough characters" from Burnyeat (1990, 33): "tough guys," "tough-minded characters."

For full understanding of (9)–(11) more examination would be in order. But given my mild interpretation, I do not see any immediate objection to them. I will accept them in order to go on.

Before looking at the last of the statements of Socrates' speech in the second half of the digression that I have selected to discuss, I take stock of progress so far. First, among Socrates' claims there are some that cry out for examination. When they are subjected to our minimal examination, they do not withstand it. Second, with the three statements just discussed, Socrates has extracted from Theodorus that Theodorus firmly rejects Protagoras' larger thesis that what is just simply is what seems just.

Rejection of Protagoras' larger thesis that what is just amounts to what seems just might look like a good thing. But there is reason to think that blunt rejection of Protagoras' larger thesis is not genuinely what the Socrates of the *Theaetetus* would advocate. Even if Protagoras' larger thesis is as wrong as it can be, it is not adequately dealt with in a digression that merely preaches its negation at us. Simple negation is completely unhelpful. It is unequal to the task of helping us understand how it is possible to talk about what is when our only way to approach what is is via the way things seem to us. Socrates recognizes that the latter is our only approach just before the digression, when he says:

We have to make do with ourselves as we are, I think, and always say what seems (*ta dokounta*) [to be so]. (171d3–5)

The Socrates of the *Crito* illustrates his reliance on what seems to him:

I not only now, but always, am such as to obey nothing else of mine than that argument which appears best (*beltistos phainêtai*) to me upon reasoning. (46b6)

(Other relevant occurrences of "appear" or "seem" in *Crito* are at 46c1; 46d6; 48b3; 48c1; 48d3.)

Protagoras' larger thesis, his identification of what is with what seems in the area of value, also admits that we rely on what seems to us to figure out what is. Protagoras uses that admission to reach an unacceptable conclusion. Yet his thesis points to a genuine philosophical puzzle. The easy unexamined denial of the thesis that Socrates extracts from Theodorus is not a worthy response. It is an unexamined position and therefore something that would not be endorsed or proclaimed either by the Socrates of the *Apology* who says that the unexamined life is not worth living or by the Socrates of the *Euthyphro* who elicits from Euthyphro agreement that one ought to consider what a speaker says, not just to accept it (*Euthyphro* 9e).

Some commentators on the digression do think that the digression is an appropriate serious response to Protagoras' larger thesis. One commentator says, for example:

The long digression . . . (172b–177c) is Socrates' rejoinder, his declaration of faith that even for these values there are objective standards. He achieves it by a portrayal of the philosopher as essentially unworldly, unconcerned with the here-and-now thanks to the breadth of his intellectual horizons and his preoccupation with universal, objective values instead of localized ones.[52]

To me attempts to read the digression in this way as Socrates' serious response to the larger thesis of Protagoras seem unconvincing in the extreme. The Socrates of the *Apology* – who, as we have established, is identical with the Socrates of the *Theaetetus* – is not unworldly and not the sort of person to advocate unexamined views that stand in need of examination.

3.8 THE SOLUTION TO OUR PROBLEMS ABOUT THE DIGRESSION

It is now clear what is the promised solution to our problems about the digression: Socrates is not giving a lecture that includes pronouncements that are inconsistent with his assertions that he has no wisdom of his own, many of which pronouncements do not withstand our own minimal examination. Socrates' apparent lecture is an extraction by declaration of

---

[52] Sedley (1999, 313). Polansky (1992, 135) thinks that the digression is Socrates' own seriously meant response to Protagoras: "The digression defends the philosophical life based on absolute standards." Blondell (2002, 303) says: "Here Socrates provides an inspiring synoptic vision of the place of human beings in an intellectual and moral cosmos, which underlines the insoluble paradox of our place at the crossroads of particularity and abstraction." Guthrie (1978, vol. v, 92) speaks of "The other-worldly, religious spirit of the Digression" which "transports us momentarily away from the prevailing analytical tenor of the *Theaetetus*." I am not transported.

Bradshaw (1998, 67) has a more complex account of how, as he thinks, the digression is intended as a serious response to Protagoras. He says:

I would suggest that the best way to understand Socrates' argument is as an inference to the best explanation. Socrates envisages two serious possibilities for governing action in accordance with a reasoned view of morality . . . Socrates' argument is thus not solely that the pursuit of justice considered as an absolute is more noble than that of the excellences involved in political rule and the manual arts. It is that only this pursuit can ultimately attain fulfillment, and that that fact in turn shows something important about its relationship to reality.

Without going into more details I'll say only that I find this interesting interpretation less plausible than my view that because the assertions of the digression are not examined, they are not represented as serious responses. Benardete (1984, 133) finds what Socrates says ridiculous: "Socrates thus looks even more ridiculous than Theodorus, for without a shred of proof or the shadow of a doubt he proclaims what god is, while saying the philosopher has trouble finding out what man is." Benardete doesn't seem to draw a conclusion about Socrates' or Plato's intentions.

views that belong to Theodorus. It articulates Theodorus' inclinations. Socrates' sequence of apparent pronouncements is Socrates' invitation to the young Theaetetus, and Plato's invitation to the reader, to examine those pronouncements. The digression fits perfectly into its setting of examination.

That the digression's advice needs examination, and does not withstand our minimal one, so far as I can see, and of course pending further examination, is an additional very strong reason not to take it as an expression of Socrates' own convictions and recommendations. We have of course already the reason against attaching it to Socrates and for attaching it to Theodorus that Socrates says, "Not one of the statements comes from me but always from the one having the discussion with me" (161a).

I've now carried out my plan to make the same proposal for the advice-giving portion of the digression as the one I made for the digression's description of the philosopher, so it's now obvious what is my solution to the interpretative problems about the digression. The digression is not a departure from the central project of the *Theaetetus*, which is to examine someone. Although the digression does indeed lack any of the argument or critical reflection of the rest of the dialogue, it nevertheless takes a step in the direction of examination. It reveals the sort of life-guiding advice that appeals to the teacher Theodorus. It is the stripping part of an examination. It just doesn't get to the wrestling part. As in the rest of the *Theaetetus* and its companion dialogues, in the digression Socrates shows that he philosophizes with every breath. The point of the otherwise pointless digression is to create an opportunity or invitation for the young Theaetetus to wrestle with the life-guiding thoughts of his teacher. If Theaetetus cannot get a better outcome than I could – and I leave open the possibility that he could – he shouldn't trust the unreflective Theodorus as a life-guide.

3.9 CONCLUSION: THEODORUS AGAIN, AND THEAETETUS

With the solution to our problems of interpretation in hand I now turn to Socrates' final statements in the digression. They describe an effect of examination on the unscrupulous characters who advocate being cleverly unjust as a life-way. Socrates says:

(12) But there's something that happens to them. Whenever in private there is a need to give and receive argument (*logon dounai te kai dexasthai*), about the things they find fault with, and when they are willing to endure it manfully for much time, and don't unmanfully flee it, then, oddly, when they finish

up, they are not satisfied with themselves concerning what they are saying, and that rhetoric withers away somehow, so that they seem no different from children. (177b)

Since there are not present in the *Theaetetus* any advocates of systematic injustice who submit to examination and then are not satisfied with themselves as their rhetoric withers away, the question arises to whom, if anyone, Socrates' description applies. I suggest that we begin to answer the question by reflecting that there can be empty or undefended rhetoric for any position, wrong or right. We can remind ourselves that refusal to submit to examination at all is equivalent to the failure of empty rhetoric. We can then apply Socrates' description even to amiable characters who judge that some people and their lives are bad, but don't make the serious effort that Socrates constantly makes to try to understand and explain such judgments. We can in fact apply Socrates' concluding comment that rhetoric dries up and its owners look like children to the rhetoric that is closest by in the *Theaetetus*. That is the rhetoric of the digression that Socrates has extracted by declaration from Theodorus, the *philologos*, the speech-lover and wise man who resists examination and who thinks that philosophers, among whom he counts himself, are divine.[53]

Although Theodorus resembles the sophists in making claim to wisdom, Theodorus is very different from other professed wise men that Socrates examines in other dialogues. Theodorus seems the most innocuous educator and wise man with whom we see Socrates in conversation. Theodorus doesn't seem to be trying to use other people to his advantage. Theodorus has a genuine subject to teach to young people. Theodorus doesn't brag to Socrates. Theodorus shows by his appreciative assent to the digression that he believes, unlike his late friend Protagoras, that justice is not simply identical with what seems just to some collection of people.

But Theodorus' assent to the digression is flawed because it is unexamined. It does not face up to a genuine philosophical puzzle. Under our minimal scrutiny above the digression that Theodorus so much appreciates seemed to be partly inadequate, partly empty, partly confused, and partly inconsistent. The rhetoric of the digression, too, would dry up under examination, if Theodorus submitted to examination. So, so far, we have

---

[53] Several commentators characterize the digression as rhetoric – but not as empty. Burnyeat (1990, 31), for example, speaks of "extraordinarily bitter eloquence"; he says Socrates "launches into rhetoric" (1990, 34), and that "Plato puts the full power of his rhetoric into an extreme interpretation of his own vision of the human condition" (1990, 36). Waterfield (1987, 177) speaks of "glorious, impassioned writing" and "a rhetorical passage" and asks "Is the irony of using rhetoric to denigrate its usual practitioners intentional?" Ryle (1966,158), quoted earlier, reacted differently.

no reason to think that the unexaminable Theodorus is any different from children.

Despite Theodorus' apparent decency, Theodorus' unwillingness to be examined indicates his complacency and self-satisfaction, his lack of puzzlement on a most puzzling point. In his complacency he reminds me of Cephalus in the *Republic*, who leaves after only a preliminary examination by Socrates.[54] As an educator specializing in geometry, Theodorus is different from Cephalus, the arms manufacturer. Theodorus doesn't seem to be in a position to make a prominent contribution to large-scale political injustice. The *Theaetetus* doesn't tell us much about Theodorus' influence on his world. We only see Theodorus ("God-gift") presented as the guide of the most talented and promising young Theaetetus ("God-asked-for"). Theodorus makes the telling comment that "young people are capable of progress in anything" (149b).

The introductory framing dialogue (142a–b) tells us that Theaetetus died from his wounds and dysentery after fighting courageously at Corinth. He was twenty-four at his death, only eight years away from his conversation with Socrates.[55]

Though we don't have many details about Theaetetus and Theodorus, we have enough to see at least that the *Theaetetus*, behind its dazzling array of argument and exploration, has a profound and pervasive sadness. Socrates addresses the young Theaetetus affectionately – eight times with the vocative, "child."[56] After the information from the dialogue's introduction, these vocatives come off the page like a cry.

---

[54] The reader of Plato's book 1 can himself examine Cephalus' life, though it requires following out some clues that are unobvious to us but might have been obvious to Plato's contemporaries. Gifford (2002) shows how Plato provides the material for the reader to make a damning critical assessment of Cephalus' life.

[55] Nails (2002) entry on "Theaetetus" and her references convincingly establish that the battle of Corinth referred to is a battle that occurred in 391 BC. Nails also calls attention to Eucleides' saying:

how prophetically Socrates had spoken about him . . . he said that Theaetetus was absolutely bound to become worth telling about if he arrived at adulthood. (142c5)

The conditional qualification, "if he arrived at adulthood," has point if Theaetetus died before the age of thirty. Presumably Plato had some reason for mentioning, in addition to Theaetetus' wounds, what at first seems an unnecessary detail – the specific illness (*dusenteria* – internal disorder) that had arisen in the army.

[56] Halliwell (1995, 97): "with marked affection." Seven addresses are at 145d4; 151e4; 156a2; 158a5; 162d3; 184d1; 200c7. An eighth is to both Theaetetus and young Socrates at 148b3. Halliwell comments on the repetitions of Socrates' form of address:

[T]heir dramatic function is not so much to highlight specific points as to serve as reminders of the age of the respondents and of Socrates' mindful awareness of this fact. They therefore play a general part in the presentation of Socrates' qualities as someone who, if not a formal teacher of the young, is at any rate keenly interested in fostering their capacities for intellectual and moral reflection.

Theodorus addresses Theaetetus twice by his name.

So Plato's mention of Theaetetus' promise cut short by early death in war together with the portrayal of Theaetetus' acceptance of guidance by the wise man Theodorus is troubling. We can apply here the argument we constructed from the data in the *Apology* that the people with the greatest reputations for being wise were in a position to do the most harm. I don't suggest that we immediately blame Theodorus' guidance because Theaetetus didn't live to fulfill his full promise. Although we cannot but count Theaetetus' early death a terrible thing, Socrates perhaps would have thought that the only really bad thing that could happen to Theaetetus would be for him to do injustice (*Apology* 29b; 30d). Did Theaetetus do injustice? We don't know. Whatever was the injustice of the Athenian action at Corinth in which Theaetetus was part in 391 BC, perhaps Theaetetus' intention was simply to stand with his young friends-in-arms. Nevertheless, Theaetetus' life is clearly diminished.[57] The association of Theodorus with that diminished life raises for me the question whether Theodorus, with his reputation as a wise man and his unexamined views, might not have been "burdensome to his associates" (in Socrates' phrase at 210c). In contrast, Socrates thinks Theaetetus, who has had the experience of being delivered of some misconceptions, will not be burdensome to his associates (210c).

The *Theaetetus* gives us the strong impression that Theaetetus, or any of those young people "capable of progress in anything" (146b5–6) would fare better by taking up Socrates' practice of examining, instead of trusting, the elders they presume to be wiser.

---

[57] Chapter 4 of Sharp (2006) studies the exchange between Terpsion and Eucleides in the frame of the *Theaetetus*. Sharp observes Plato's "positioning the question of the title character's personal qualities as the most rhetorically prominent theme in the work's introduction." Sharp concludes convincingly, "The subject matter of the *Theaetetus*, according to Plato's rhetoric, is Theaetetus." Sharp's observation resolves a question I had for about fifty years about the poignant frame of the dialogue.

CHAPTER 4

Socrates in the Republic, *part 1: speech and counter-speech*

The *Republic* is an interesting case for my hypothesis that the Socrates of all of Plato's dialogues is the same questioning character as the Socrates of the *Apology*. It has seemed to many readers, on the contrary, that there are two different Socrateses even within the *Republic*. That is one of two interpretative problems about the *Republic* with which I begin.

4.I STRANGENESS AND DISCONTINUITY

There is wide agreement among readers of the *Republic* that in the last nine of its ten books Socrates proposes many views that are in various ways strange. One or another very careful and very sympathetic commentator has called one or another of these views "curious," "altogether peculiar," "philosophically frustrating," "seriously flawed," "very ugly," "risible absurdity," "too hasty and too crude," "embarrassingly bad," "botched," "outlandish," "a mistake," "shocking," "truly bizarre," "preposterous," "hysterical," "utterly grotesque," "repellent," "inhuman," "incoherent," "nearly unintelligible," or has said that they "rightly move us to horror."[1] The

---

[1] "Curious entity": Cooper (1997b, 23); "altogether peculiar": Roochnik (2003, 114); "philosophically frustrating": Annas (1981, 256); "seriously flawed": Heinaman (2004, 393); "very ugly": Annas (1981, 269); "risible absurdity" and "botched": Smith (2000, 124); "too hasty and too crude" and "embarrassingly bad": Annas (1981, 330 and 345); "outlandish": Blondell (2002, 199); "a mistake": (Annas 1981, 322–323); "shocking" and "truly bizarre": Blondell (2002, 209 and 249); "preposterous": Bloom (1968, 380); "hysterical,": "utterly grotesque," "repellent," "inhuman," and "incoherent" (Annas 1981, 344, 275, 330, 333, and 141); "nearly unintelligible": White (1979, 3). White also (1979, 3) refers to "Uncounted objections . . . against Plato's arguments and formulations at almost every stage." Guthrie (1978, vol. IV, 1975, vol. IV, 560) comments that some proposals of the *Republic* "rightly move us to horror." Milder expressions of discomfort are in Reeve (2004, ix): "likely to find abhorrent" and Reeve (2004, xxiii): "may not appeal to us," "things that are likely to estrange us most from the *Republic*," "unattractive direction," and "It is difficult not to see the cure as at least as bad as – if not worse than – the disease". Brown (1998, 25) votes that for the producing class: "the only *eudaimonia* conceivable for members of this class would be, in effect, their playing their part like good cogs in the great machine."

In contrast, see Burnyeat (1992, 185).

strangeness of Socrates' proposals in the *Republic* needs explanation: can the Socrates of the *Republic* possibly mean what he says?

A second feature of the *Republic* that needs explanation is the much-noticed feature that the Socrates of book 1 seems very different from the Socrates of books 2–10. In book 1 Socrates questions several interlocutors and reduces their answers to absurdity. He claims that he is ignorant about justice. He is the examining and ignorant Socrates of the *Apology*. But the Socrates of books 2–10, far from avowing his own ignorance, seems to enunciate doctrine confidently.[2] He gives a blueprint for a just city-state and an account of justice in the individual person. One commentator says that there is a "fracture line in [Socrates'] character between book 1 and book 2" in that the Socrates of book 1 is elenctic and the Socrates of books 2–10 is constructive.[3] Another commentator says that anyone who held the beliefs of Socrates in book 1 and also the beliefs of Socrates in 2–10 would have to be schizophrenic.[4] The question naturally arises why Plato presents a character in books 2–10 that is so different from the character of the same name in book 1. Is the *Republic* comparable to a book whose first chapter depicts Santa Claus in his sled delivering gifts at Christmas and whose next nine chapters depict Santa on a broomstick frightening children on Halloween? Is Plato an inept author?[5]

Moreover, for many readers the transformation of the questioning, avowedly ignorant Socrates of book 1, who is evocative of the Socrates of the *Apology*, into the apparently authoritative purveyor of an "elitist program"[6] in books 2–10, is disturbing. The transformation of the profound Socrates who thought an unexamined life was not worth living for any human being into a Socrates who judges that many people would be better off living unexamined lives as quasi-slaves of cleverer people (590cd) seems worse than inept: it seems positively distasteful and ugly.

Various explanations have been proposed for the strangeness and the discontinuity. I mention some for contrast with the explanation I will offer.

---

[2] See Annas (1981, 57); Bloom (1968, 337); Grote (1867, 240).   [3] Blondell (2002, 165, 199–200).

[4] Vlastos (1991a, 45–46). Vlastos (1991a, 46–47) counts *Republic* book 1 as giving us one Socrates and *Republic* books 2–10 as giving us another.

[5] Some interpreters (Wolfsdorf (2008)) would deem the question inappropriate because ancient Greeks took no interest in the consistency of characters. It seems unlikely to me that Plato was not interested in that. Other characters that recur in different dialogues are quite recognizably the same persons (Alcibiades, Crito, Hippias, Chaerephon). Certainly no other character within a single work changes dramatically. Later I will mention some other evidence of Plato's care for depicting Socrates as the same.

[6] Blondell (2002, 203) refers to "the elitist program that Socrates will put forward."

One proposed explanation for the strangeness is that when Socrates states something outrageous, he is being ironic, and perhaps meaning the opposite of what he says in order to be thought-provoking.[7] Another proposed explanation is that in books 8–10 Socrates revises and takes back some of the startling proposals for the Kallipolis, the city constructed in books 2–7.[8] By the end of the *Republic* they are not to be ascribed to Socrates because he revises them out of the picture.[9] Another proposal is that the *Republic* is a deliberate though implicit reduction to absurdity of the possibility of an entirely just city.[10]

One proposed explanation for the apparent discontinuity is that in book 1 Plato uses Socrates as a vehicle for beliefs and methods Plato endorsed early in his writing career while in 2–10 Plato uses Socrates as a vehicle for beliefs and methods Plato endorsed later.[11] This explanation of the discontinuity of course does not explain the strangeness of books 2–10. It only transfers the strangeness to Plato, and it has Plato making lots of blunders in reasoning. It still leaves the problems of ineptitude and distastefulness.

That these explanations are offered indicates the felt need for explanation. The *Republic*, despite its status as a classic of literature, philosophy, and political commentary, is a profoundly weird book.

I will give a new explanation for the apparent discontinuity and the admittedly real strangeness of books 2–10. This will be part of my argument

---

[7] Smith (2000, 124) offers as explanation for the strangeness that it can provoke thought in the reader.

[8] Roochnik (2003, 69).

[9] A particular consequence of Roochnik's treatment is this. I quote his summary of a conclusion for which he argues in some detail (2003, 69):

> Kallipolis requires philosophers to become rulers. But as the tripartite psychology itself suggests, Socrates' city in speech cannot in fact sustain the development of philosophers . . . : philosophy is essentially erotic, and this erotic energy would be choked by the tight regulations of books 2–4. Furthermore . . . the exclusively mathematical curriculum proposed for the guardians in book 7 . . . is too one-sided to nourish the philosophical soul. As Socrates makes clear in books 8–10, a life of freedom and exposure to human diversity is needed for that.

> Schofield (1999b, 80) also suggests that the *Republic* is self-revising.

[10] Bloom (1968, 409). So apparently Strauss (1978b, 75):

> Since the city as city is a society which from time to time must wage war, and war is inseparable from harming innocent people (471a–b), the unqualified condemnation of harming human beings [which Socrates arrives at in book 1] is tantamount to the condemnation of even the justest city.

> That is, as I understand it, Strauss takes a main lesson of the *Republic* to be that no one who lives in a society can avoid having injustice as a life-policy.

[11] Vlastos (1991a, 50, 53):

> As Plato changes, the philosophical persona of his Socrates is made to change, absorbing the writer's new convictions, arguing for them with the same zest with which the Socrates of the previous dialogues had argued for the views the writer had shared with the original of that figure earlier on.

that the Socrates of books 2–10 is the same consistently avowedly ignorant, nondoctrinal, and examining character as the Socrates of book 1. The Socrates of the whole *Republic* is then the Socrates of the *Apology*. There will remain no grounds to charge the author of the *Republic* with ineptitude or tastelessness. And we will have another piece of support for my thesis that the Socrates of any of Plato's dialogues is the same person as the Socrates of the *Apology*.

4.2 QUESTION AND ANSWER DISCUSSION IN BOOK 1

Socrates' questioning manner in book 1 provokes Thrasymachus famously to complain. After listening to Socrates and Polemarchus, Thrasymachus says:

What nonsense have you two been talking, Socrates? Why do you act like idiots by giving way to one another? If you truly want to know what justice is, don't just ask questions and then refute the answers simply to satisfy your competitiveness or love of honor. You know very well that it is easier to ask questions than to answer them. Give an answer yourself, and tell us what you say the just is. And don't tell me that it's the right, the beneficial, the profitable, the gainful, or the advantageous, but tell me clearly and exactly what you mean; for I won't accept such nonsense from you.[12] (336c)

Socrates replies that he is serious, but simply incapable of giving such an answer. Thrasymachus then accuses Socrates of being deceptive (*eirôneia*).[13] Socrates says in return:

No one could answer a question framed like that . . . I'm amazed. Do you want me to say something other than the truth? . . . Do you think [a person who is asked] any less likely to give the answer that seems right to him, whether we forbid him or not? (337b–c)

Thrasymachus asks, "Is that what you're going to do, give one of the forbidden answers?" Socrates responds:

I wouldn't be surprised – provided that it's the one that seems right to me after I've investigated . . . How can someone give answer . . . when he doesn't know it and doesn't claim to know it, and when an eminent man forbids him to express the opinion he has? It's much more appropriate for you to answer, since you say you know and can tell us. (337c–e)

---

[12] Translations from the *Republic* (text Slings 2003) are my own with consultation of Shorey (1963); Bloom (1968); Griffith (2000); Waterfield (1993); and Reeve (2004).

[13] Vlastos (1991a, 24) says: "Thrasymachus is charging that Socrates lies in saying that he has no answer of his own to the question he is putting to others."

The words "question" and "answer" that occur in Thrasymachus' complaint and Socrates' response are of course entirely familiar ordinary words. But they also serve there as signs or prompts for a certain kind of convention-guided or stylized conversation, as they do in other dialogues of Plato.[14] It is a kind of competition of Socrates' time that young men especially took up as a pastime or recreation. As depicted by Plato, Socrates often engages in these stylized conversations but to serve his serious purpose of questioning people about how they live their lives. The characteristic prompting vocabulary, "question" and "answer," indicates that one person is taking on the formal role of questioner, while another is taking on the formal role of answerer. The answerer's assigned role is to submit to questioning under which he tries to maintain a position that he has chosen without contradicting himself. The questioner's role is to test whether the answerer can do that. The questioner conducts his test by asking mostly questions with only "yes" or "no" answers. The answerer must answer "yes" or "no."

The roles of questioner and answerer within the conventions of this stylized conversation are distinct roles. Compare in baseball the distinct roles of a pitcher and a hitter. The pitcher cannot bat the ball at the batter. The batter cannot pick up a dropped ball and throw it.

For example *Alcibiades Major* 112d–113c alludes to some conventions of question-and-answer conversation.[15] Socrates says that he was certainly not

---

[14] *Protagoras* 338d–e; 348a. A much more rule-governed activity of question and answer than occurs in Plato's dialogues is codified in Aristotle's *Topics*, which is our best source for argumentative exercises that went on in Plato's Academy (Smith (1997, xiv)). Brunschwig (1986, 33) says:

The *Topics*...are restricted to organized, codified, almost ritualized debates...The questioner must put only questions which can be answered by "yes" or "no," and the answerer must say either yes or no, except in a few specified cases when he is allowed to say, "What do you mean?" or "Do you mean this or that?" These regulations are obviously meant...to ensure that if the questioner succeeds in proving [the denial of the answerer's original proposal] on the basis of premises explicitly accepted by the answerer, the latter has no reason to complain of the former: the conclusion has not been imposed on him or extorted from him.

Question-and-answer conversations in Plato's dialogues only approximate this totally codified form to a greater or less extent. The abrupt opening of the *Meno*, where Meno asks whether virtue is teachable or not, shows Meno using the disjunctive challenge that would open a formal question-and-answer conversation. Socrates immediately rejects the challenge on the grounds that he is incompetent to answer. School debates required an umpire, while Socrates emphasizes that it is an advantage of the sort of question-and-answer conversations that he has in mind that no judge is needed (*Republic* 348b). For the impression of an evolution in the manner of question-and-answer conversations in Plato's dialogues, see Brisson (2001).

[15] I take the *Alcibiades Major* to be by Plato. On its authenticity see discussion and bibliography in Denyer (2001, 14–15). See also Clark (1955, 231–240) for issues relevant to authenticity and Gordon (2003) for the dialogue's worth.

saying, that is, affirming, what came up in the conversation in which he was questioner. This exchange ensues:

SOC. Come then, tell me in one word: When questioning and answering occurs, which is the one saying (*ho legôn*), the one questioning or the one answering?
ALC. The answerer, it seems to me, Socrates.
SOC. And just now through the whole argument, I was the one questioning?
ALC. Yes.
SOC. And you the one answering?
ALC. Entirely.
SOC. Well then, which of us has spoken (*eirêken*) what was said (*ta lechthenta*)?
ALC. I appear to, Socrates, from what was agreed on . . .
SOC. Then, it turns out . . . you run the risk of having heard these things from yourself, not me, and I am not the one saying these things (*ho tauta legôn*), but you [are], and you hold me responsible *(eme de aitia(i))* in vain *(matên)*. (113a–c)

This exchange concisely confirms that in a convention-bound question-and-answer conversation the answerer, and not the questioner, has ownership of the answerer's answers.[16] The questioner is not committed to any of the answers he elicits. But the answerer counts as saying or asserting for the purposes of the discussion whatever he assents to, even if the answerer has never before contemplated the propositions the questioner puts forward in his questions. What the answerer assents to now belongs to the answerer.

Thrasymachus clearly thinks of question-and-answer conversation as a kind of competition in which only the answerer takes the risk of looking like the foolish loser. Thrasymachus complains because he thinks Socrates never takes that risk. Socrates, on the other hand, doesn't answer others because he does not claim to know; he thinks that a person who claims to know or to have answers is the most appropriate person to be an answerer.[17]

Thrasymachus may be in error that Socrates never serves as answerer, though perhaps not in error in a way that would interest Thrasymachus. In the *Hippias Major*, where the words "question" and "answer" again serve as prompts for a convention-governed conversation, Socrates says he has some experience as answerer (287a). That is why he would like Hippias to be the answerer, so that Socrates can get practice questioning. In speaking of his experience as answerer, Socrates must be alluding to his conversations with himself, where he has been refuted and been angry with himself for being unable to answer himself adequately (286d–e).

---

[16] For emphasis on the questioner's detachment from the answers, see Frede (1992).
[17] Brunschwig (1986, 35) connects Socratic ignorance with his inability to serve as answerer.

In that they can be used as prompts for a certain type of conversation the words "question" and "answer" that are the signs of the sort of convention-governed conversation Socrates has with Alcibiades and with Hippias may be compared to our utterance, "Knock-knock," which serves as a prompt to get the response "Who's there?," which in turn serves as another prompt. Similarly in our time in certain subcultures of the United States the phrase "Yo' Mama" is a prompt for a kind of competitive conversation governed by its own conventions.[18]

At *Republic* 348 Socrates contrasts the question-and-answer sort of conversation that he has been having up to that point in book 1 with a different sort of conversation governed by different conventions. Socrates gives Glaucon a choice between two different modes of conversation to try to persuade Thrasymachus out of Thrasymachus' thesis that the unjust life is better than the just life. Socrates says to Glaucon:

Do you want us to persuade him, if we're able to find a way, that what he says isn't true? . . . If we should speak to him setting in contrast (*antikatateinantes*) a speech against a speech (*logon para logon*) about what good things being just has in store, and then he replies, and then we do, we'd have to count and measure the good things on each side, and we'd need a jury (*dikastôn tinôn*) to decide the case (*tôn diakrinountôn*). But if, on the other hand, we investigate the question, as just now [we were doing], by agreeing with each other, we ourselves can be both jury and advocates (*rhêtores*: public speakers, pleaders, rhetoricians) at once . . . Which pleases you?[19] (348a)

Glaucon replies, "This one." Here he prefers the question-and-answer mode of persuasion. Socrates describes such question-and-answer talk as "agreeing with each other" (*anomologoumenoi pros allêlous*).

---

[18] For any readers unfamiliar with "Knock-knock" jokes, here are a couple of samples. The punch line is, so far as I know, always some kind of pun or wordplay. "Knock-knock." "Who's there?" "Toucan." "Toucan who?" "Toucan live as cheaply as one."; "Knock-knock." "Who's there?" "Alaska." "Alaska who?" "Alaska you to be my valentine." For readers unfamiliar with "Yo' Mama" exchanges, they are also called "the Dozens" or "Slippin'." They belong to a verbal competition that began in African American slave culture as training for males especially to endure abuse. Majors and Billson (1992, ch. 8) gives a helpful discussion. Each participant responds to an insult from the other participant with his own insult. Here are some contemporary printable sample insults: "Yo' mama so ugly her parents hired the neighbor kid to play her in home videos." "Yo' mama so ugly the neighbors chipped in to buy curtains for her windows." Defeat in slave culture consisted in getting angry. Today victory can be measured by audience applause. A number of websites collect sample insults. An early article is Dollard (1939). Hesk (2007, 126, n. 9; 156, n. 75) compares antiquity's contest exchanges with ours.

[19] The context, with its reference to the need for judges, makes clear that the meaning of *para* is "opposed to." Riddell (1877/1973, §124) lists *para* meaning "contrasted with." *Republic* 603a1 exemplifies the meaning "opposed."

Socrates' claim that to engage in question-and-answer is to agree with each other bears reflection. If question-and-answer conversation can also seem to be a competition – even if Socrates doesn't see it that way, aren't the conversationalists in disagreement with one another, rather than in agreement? No, not entirely, for there are several areas of agreement. For one thing, it may be agreed at the end of such a conversation that the answerer's starting thesis has been refuted. For another thing, during the conversation it will be agreed that certain things follow from certain other things. But still, cannot answerer and questioner disagree on the answerer's answers, since the questioner is in no way committed to them? Yes, but both questioner and answerer agree in the minimal sense that both agree to use the answerer's replies as premises that drive the discussion.[20] So there is in fact quite a bit of agreement during question-and-answer discussion. And at the end there is the important agreement that both answerer and questioner have learned something from the discussion about the consequences and consistency of the claims being tested.[21]

That Socrates offers Glaucon a choice between the two types of conversation is instructive. It shows that although Socrates in book 1 engages only as questioner in question-and-answer conversation, the Socrates of book 1 would also be willing to engage in the different sort of conversation that Socrates calls "speech against speech" (*logon para logon*). Glaucon, not Socrates, makes the choice of question and answer at that point in book 1.[22]

---

[20] There is this illustrative use of "agree" in *Laches* 190b–c:

SOCRATES: We must begin by knowing what virtue is, for if we had no idea what virtue is, then how could we serve as counselors on how best to acquire it?
LACHES: We couldn't by any means.
SOCRATES: Then we agree that we know what it is.
LACHES: Yes, we agree.

Socrates is not here declaring that he is personally committed to the claim that he knows what virtue is. He is agreeing only that the claim that the conversationalists know what virtue is will have a role in the ongoing discussion. If anything, he is committed only to the conditional claim that *if* someone didn't know what virtue is, that person would have no business teaching virtue. Contrast Wolfsdorf (2004, 102), who says this passage indicates that the Socrates of the *Laches* assumes that Laches and he know what excellence (virtue) is.

[21] Blondell (2002, 202) calls book 1 agonistic and books 2–10 cooperative. But here Socrates says the opposite: question-and-answer conversation is a cooperative search. A *logon para logon* exchange is a contest that needs an external judge.

[22] Contrastingly, the Socrates of the *Hippias Minor* wants to question Hippias, though Hippias wants speech-against-speech (369c6: *antiparaballe logon para logon*). The audience is apparently to judge between them ("these will know"; *eisontai houtoi*) which is better.

4.3 A DIFFERENT KIND OF CONVERSATION IN BOOKS 2–10:
SPEECH AGAINST SPEECH

By book 2, Glaucon has changed his mind. He asks for a speech-against-speech conversation. In so asking, he structures the rest of the *Republic*. Glaucon says:

> I have yet to hear anyone defending justice in the way I want, proving that it is better than injustice. I want to hear it praised (*enkomiazomenon akousai*) by itself, and I think that I'm most likely to hear this from you. Therefore, I'm going to speak at length in praise of the unjust life, and in doing so, I'll show you the way I want to hear you praising (*epainountos*) justice and denouncing injustice. (358c–d)

Socrates consents to that way of continuing, saying:

> For what would a man of sense more enjoy speaking and hearing (*legôn kai akouôn*) about often? (358e)

Glaucon does not refer back to the distinction that Socrates made previously in book 1 between question-and-answer and speech-against-speech conversation, but nevertheless it is clear that Glaucon now wants speech-against-speech discussion. Socrates' answer, with the simple terms "speak" (*legein*) and "listen" (*akouein*), which can be perfectly ordinary vocabulary, here serve as terms of art or prompting language that goes along with the speech-against-speech convention, just as the ordinary terms "ask" and "answer" go with the question-and-answer convention.[23]

According to Socrates' distinction from book 1 (348), it is an important feature of speech-against-speech discussion that there is need for a jury to decide which was the better speech. The jury must count and measure the good things on each side. Speaker and counter-speaker do not or cannot reach agreement by themselves which one gave the more effective – that is, persuasive – speech. Audience appeal decides it.

A typical setting for speech and counter-speech is the courtroom. In the courtroom someone other than the speakers decides between the speakers. People who give persuasive speeches in the courtroom are not reaching agreement with one another. They are trying to state a case in such a way as to persuade a jury. The jury decision in favor of one speech is perhaps simply equivalent to the jury's pronouncing that the speech has persuaded the jury, but the jury decision of course has more status and effect: the jury

---

[23] Shorey's (1963) note on 348b explains the speech-against-speech mode with references.

verdict serves as the judgment that the speech was persuasive, that anyone ought to be persuaded by it. Speaker and counter-speaker, however, need not be, and usually are not, persuaded by one another. They do not agree on the jury's verdict.

So Glaucon at the beginning of book 2 has got Socrates to agree to give a counter-speech, like a speaker at a trial. Socrates' response uses some language of the courtroom. Socrates thinks it might be not pious to fail (368c) "to come to the aid of justice when it is being slandered (*kakêgoroumenê(i)*)." Slander can be a legal category.

In the earlier passage and here speech-making is taken to be a way of persuading. Glaucon previously wanted Socrates to persuade by questioning. Now Glaucon wants Socrates to persuade by a speech. Glaucon says:

Do you want to seem to have persuaded us or truly to persuade us that in every way it is better to be just than to be unjust? (357a)

Socrates replies, "Truly, if I should choose, if it were up to me."

Socrates' reply to Glaucon at 357a that Socrates would prefer truly to persuade has some ambiguity. "Truly persuade" can mean "successfully bring about a listener's belief" or also, and not equivalently, "persuade of the truth," or more complexly, "persuade of the truth for the right reasons." Successful persuasion is not necessarily persuasion of the truth, as some of Glaucon's later uses of "persuade" in the *Republic* show.[24] But provisionally I would assume that Glaucon wants to be persuaded to believe something true.

When Socrates says that he would prefer to persuade truly, but with the qualification, "if it were up to me," Socrates suggests that persuading someone truly is not entirely up to Socrates. Why so? One reason is that to persuade someone genuinely rests very much with the potential persuadee. Even if a speaker who actually is an authority recites correct reasons that lead inevitably to a conclusion, the recitation will not effect a listener's persuasion unless the listener understands and genuinely accepts what he has heard.

The *Alcibiades* I illustrates this obvious point that persuasion is interior to the persuadee. At 114d Socrates predicts that he will persuade Alcibiades that the just is expedient:

---

[24] Glaucon will soon speak of persuasion and clearly mean that the persuader is getting the person persuaded to believe something false. At 361b: the unjust person is able to speak persuasively to avoid consequences if his misdeeds are revealed. At 365d: teachers of persuasion help those who take advantage of others to get skilled at persuading. At 365e–366a: the gods can be persuaded so that the unjust citizens can escape penalties. Citizens are later to be persuaded of the noble lie.

ALC. Speak then.

SOC. Just answer my questions.

ALC. No, you yourself must be the speaker.

SOC. What? Do you not wish to be persuaded the most?

ALC. Entirely, indeed.

SOC. And you would best be persuaded if you should say that these things hold thus.

ALC. It seems to me.

SOC. Then answer; and if you do not hear from your very self that the just is expedient, don't trust anyone else who says [so]. (114d)

To be persuaded that the just is expedient Alcibiades must hear himself say that the just is expedient. Only Alcibiades' answering questions and revealing his assumptions, not Socrates' being a speaker, will have the maximum persuasive effect. If we have here the prompting vocabulary of question-and-answer conversation contrasted with that of speech-against-speech conversation, Alcibiades first asks for a speech to persuade him. Socrates then elicits Alcibiades' belief that question and answer will best effect persuasion. Socrates then turns the conversation to question and answer. Socrates' last comment suggests that the only speaker that can "the most" – i.e. genuinely – persuade Alcibiades of something is Alcibiades speaking to himself. That would be because a successful persuasive speaker has to build on the beliefs of the hearer. Socrates' advice to Alcibiades not to trust anyone but himself on the topic of whether the just is expedient is striking.

If we apply the *Alcibiades Major*'s lesson about persuasion to the *Republic*, we'll conclude that Glaucon's being persuaded truly won't come about, if it does come about, simply as a result of any speech Glaucon hears from Socrates. It will come about only if Glaucon assents because he has understood what follows from what he accepts.

Having indicated that persuasion is not entirely up to him at 357a, Socrates will nevertheless aid justice in whatever way he can (368c). Socrates will attempt persuasion, so far as he is capable of it. However, as a matter of fact, he thinks that he is entirely incapable. Socrates says to Glaucon:

The more I trust you, the more I'm at a loss as to what I should do. On the one hand, I can't help out. For in my opinion, I'm not capable of it. (368b)

Socrates explains why he is willing to take on this impossible project:

I fear lest it not be pious for one who is present to stand idly by (*apagoreuein*: to give up: literally, to hold off from public speaking) and not aid justice when it is being accused, if one is still breathing and capable of speaking. The best thing is to help in whatever way I can.[25] (368b–c)

4.4 A QUESTION ABOUT GLAUCON AND A TEMPORARY PUZZLE ABOUT SOCRATES

It is natural to wonder why Glaucon has changed from preferring question-and-answer conversation in book 1 to wishing speech and counter-speech in book 2. The explanation may be this: we may safely assume that Glaucon, as a companion of the Socrates of book 1, has answered Socrates' questions often before. The *Republic* early on sketches Socrates as one who engages in conversation: Polemarchus invites Socrates to come to talk (*dialexometha* (328b)); Cephalus recognizes Socrates as someone who can offer the pleasures of talk (*tous logous* (328d)). Socrates likes conversing (*dialegomenos*) with the very old to learn from them, and immediately begins questioning Cephalus. After Polemarchus takes up the conversation, Thrasymachus complains because Socrates always questions and never answers; Thrasymachus thought the conversation was a stylized question-and-answer exchange. So the opening of book 1 gives a brief character-sketch of Socrates as a well-known questioning conversationalist, and the rest of book 1 confirms it.

We also have the information that Glaucon has just spent a good part of the day with Socrates. We can easily imagine that Glaucon was subjected to many questions already earlier in the very same day, not to mention during his prior acquaintance with Socrates. Possibly Glaucon is now weary or wary of answering Socrates' questions for himself, though Glaucon is interested in hearing Thrasymachus answer. I speculate about Glaucon's weariness, but there are some later signs of his wariness to answer Socrates' questions (e.g. 595–596).

It is even more natural to wonder why the ignorant Socrates of book 1 is now willing to engage in speech and counter-speech in book 2. We even have a temporary puzzle. Socrates in book 1 was willing to engage in speech and counter-speech, and Glaucon turned down his offer; now in book 2 Socrates actually agrees to give a counter-speech. Our puzzle is: why is the ignorant Socrates of book 1 willing to engage in counter-speech at all? After all, the Socrates of book 1 didn't want to answer Thrasymachus' questions because Socrates didn't have answers. But giving a speech looks a lot like making a long answer. Is Socrates being inconsistent?

---

[25] I am indebted to Betty Belfiore for discussion of *apagoreuein*.

I'd say not. To give a persuasive speech is quite different from giving an answer. An answerer who offers a proposal to be tested is in the position of an authority who claims to know something and who should accordingly be able to cope with questions about it. Hence Socrates doesn't like to answer others because he makes no claims to authority. A speech-maker, however, does not necessarily present himself as an authority in the same way as an answerer does. A counter-speaker's task is persuasion, as a speaker before a jury aims at persuasion. It is not necessary that the speakers in such a speech-and-counter-speech setting know, or even believe, what they are talking about. Glaucon, for example, says he does not believe the conclusion for which his speech argues (358c). Certainly, in a courtroom setting at least one speaker does not know what he is propounding, since the courtroom speakers argue for opposite conclusions. Here we expect that Socrates, as depicted, believes the conclusion that Glaucon and Adeimantus have asked him to defend – that justice is better than injustice. But nevertheless, because Socrates is in the speech-and-counter-speech setting, we cannot assume that he will believe all the reasons he gives to persuade his listeners. That is one way in which he does not present himself as an authority as he gives his speech.

It is after all consistent then for the Socrates of book 1 who dislikes taking the role of answerer or putative authority to take the role of speech-maker according to the conventions of speech and counter-speech. He is not thereby claiming to be an authority. So far, then, we haven't yet found a difference between the Socrates of book 1 and the Socrates of book 2.

And I would like to call attention to an important similarity. Though by giving a persuasive speech, Socrates does something different from questioning, there is this similarity to questioning: both speech-making and questioning reveal something about the person Socrates is talking to. A speech-maker who persuades a listener reveals what at the moment appeals to the listener to believe. A questioner who makes proposals in questions to which an answerer assents also reveals what appeals to the answerer at the moment of questioning. However, an important difference between speech-maker and questioner is that a speech-maker does not pursue what persuaded the listener into the further stage of critical examination.

My explanation how speech-making in book 2 would be in character for the Socrates of book 1 differs from Socrates' explanation why he will give a counter-speech. He says (368c) that although he believes himself incapable, he nevertheless thinks it might be terribly wrong to hold off from public speaking when justice is being slandered, as in the speeches of Glaucon and Adeimantus. So Socrates has a serious reason to undertake his persuasive task. Glaucon reminds Socrates of that reason at 427e:

You promised you would look for [justice] because it's not pious for you not to bring help to justice in every way in your power.

Glaucon evidently takes Socrates as having a serious reason for making a courtroom-style defense of justice.

But we now have a new question about Socrates' speech in books 2–10. What serious pious purpose can Socrates hope to accomplish by giving an outrageous, though persuasive, speech? I'll return to that question later.

4.5 JOSTLING CONVENTIONS: QUESTION-AND-ANSWER CONVERSATION WITHIN PERSUASIVE SPEECH

Grote sees the courtroom cast of the discussion starting in book 2. Describing the speeches of the two brothers, Grote says:[26]

In the second Book we find two examples of continuous or Ciceronian pleading . . . , which are surpassed by nothing in ancient literature for acuteness and ability in the statement of a case.

Grote doesn't mention that Socrates' response to the brothers in *Republic* books 2–10 is also a speech that pleads a case.

Socrates' plea-speech that goes on for eight-and-a-half books of the *Republic* is admittedly an unconventional one. For one thing, it is not continuous, since it is broken by many questions from Socrates and by answers from the brothers. Socrates moves his promised speech as much in the direction of his usual question-and-answer conversation as he can. So Socrates does not follow exactly the pattern that the brothers give Socrates in their speeches. Glaucon and Adeimantus do not ask any questions or get Socrates' agreement to anything in their persuasive speeches. (Hence Socrates is unpersuaded, for the brothers make many assertions that Socrates, were he in a question-and-answer conversation, would surely have explored. I am thinking especially of assertions about human behavior and motives to which Socrates himself is a counter-example (e.g. 359b; 359e; 360d; 366b–d).) Socrates merely interrupts Glaucon once at 361d to praise Glaucon's skill by saying, using a phrase that evokes a competitive setting: "How vigorously you clean off each of the two men – just like an image of a man (*andrianta*: statue) – for their judgment (*epi tên krisin*)."

Plato sometimes reminds us, by using vocabulary that belongs to the speech-and-counter-speech or speaker-and-hearer convention, that that is the convention under which the conversation in books 2–10 is proceeding.

---

[26] Grote (1867, vol. III, 122). Blondell (2002, 192): "courtroom atmosphere."

Just before Socrates gives his account of justice in the individual, there is this exchange:

I said, "In my opinion we have for a long time been speaking and hearing about it without understanding of ourselves that we were speaking of it in a way."

"A long prelude," he said, " for one who is eager to hear." (432e)

At 450b Thrasymachus asks if they are going to be wasting time or listening to speeches. Glaucon takes up the phrase, "listening to speeches" (*logôn akouein*), in his next comment. At 450d-e Socrates expresses his hesitation about making speeches at the same time as he is searching, when he doesn't trust himself (or perhaps isn't trustworthy or lacks conviction):

If I trusted myself to know what I was speaking about, encouragement would be fine. For one who knows, to speak to people both wise and dear about the greatest matters that are also dear is safe and heartening. But for one who lacks trust and is searching, at the same time to make speeches – what I am indeed doing – is fearful and risky. (450d–e)

Socrates is hesitant because he doesn't want to mislead his friends about such important matters. Socrates is uncomfortable with the role he has piously – and politely, as a guest – agreed to take in the conversation. At 489e Socrates says, "Let's speak and listen." And at 536c Glaucon calls himself a "listener" or "hearer" (*akroatê(i)*) while Socrates calls himself an "orator" or "pleader" (*rhêtôr*). LSJ gives that occurrence of "hearer" as said "of persons who come to hear a public speaker." In using the term "orator," Socrates emphasizes his role as one who is giving a plea-speech.

Socrates signals his combining the two conventions of speaking-and-listening on the one hand and questioning-and-answering on the other at 595c when Socrates says to Glaucon, "Listen then, or rather answer." I take it that "Listen" is a verbal reminder that they are supposed to be in a speech-and-counter-speech contest, while, "or rather, answer," is Socrates' signal that he has as much as possible turned the conversation into a question-and-answer conversation. Glaucon replies here, "Ask on," but soon after he is too deferential to want to answer (596a); and he turns the speaking task back to Socrates (who continues to ask questions anyway). "Listen" and "speak" also occur at 608d. But again Socrates goes on to ask questions, as though he were in a question-and-answer discussion. 583b is a particularly interesting example of how Socrates discovers what Socrates needs for his speech within his interlocutor. Socrates says that he has heard from some wise men that certain pleasures are like shadow-drawings. Glaucon at first doesn't understand, and wants to know what Socrates is saying. Socrates says "I will discover" if Glaucon answers while Socrates searches. Glaucon agrees to that procedure here: "Do the asking, then." It is striking that Socrates says he will find out from Glaucon's answers what he, Socrates, means.

Although Socrates strays from the speech-making mode modeled by the brothers to the extent that Socrates asks many questions to elicit the brothers' opinions, Socrates does not stray entirely into the question-and-answer type of discussion. He stays within the speech-and-counter-speech convention in an important way in that when Socrates gets answers from the brothers, Socrates does not subject those answers to further examination or rethinking in the way we might expect from book 1. Rather, Socrates simply builds on the brothers' answers to get further results.

The initial staging of the discussion early in book 2 provides the explanation why Socrates simply builds on the brothers' responses, and does not examine what he has built. That initial staging tells readers that we are witnessing speech and counter-speech, which will result in a judgment (*eis tên krisin* 361d). We are not witnessing an occasion for elenctic examination. Just as Socrates did not question the brothers during their speeches, the brothers also mostly do not question Socrates during his long speech of books 2–10, except for clarification. That is because questioning or resisting would not be an appropriate response from the audience during a speech under the conventions for speech and counter-speech. (Similarly, in *Hippias Minor* (364b) Socrates did not want to hinder Hippias' display speech by raising questions.) In a persuasive speech it might be appropriate, though nonstandard, for the speaker to ask questions of his audience to elicit the premises on which he will build his persuasion, as Socrates asks questions of Glaucon and Adeimantus. It would not be appropriate, however, on the occasion of competitive persuasion, to subject the hearers' premises to examination. Within the speech-and-counter-speech convention, examining assertions of the speech in mid-speech would be as incongruous as responding to the challenge, "Yo' mama," with the question, "Who's there?"

4.6 GLAUCON AND ADEIMANTUS REQUIRE OF SOCRATES A MADE-TO-ORDER SPEECH

The project to which Socrates agrees in book 2 and undertakes to the end of book 10 is not only persuasion; it is persuasion under a number of constraints that the brothers impose. The brothers order up from Socrates a speech of a very definite kind with a very definite result. They get from Socrates their made-to-order speech.[27]

Glaucon has placed his order first at 358d. Glaucon wants Socrates to tell him "what justice and injustice are and what power each itself has when it's by itself in the soul" (358b). Glaucon's own speech against justice is a model to show what Glaucon wants from Socrates: "I'll show you the way I want to hear you praising justice and denouncing injustice" (358d). Praising is a persuasive project, not a critical or analytic one.

Similarly Adeimantus has his requirements:

None of you has ever condemned injustice or recommended justice except in terms of the reputation, prestige, and rewards they bring. Nobody has ever yet . . . given a sufficiently detailed account of each of them in itself, when it is present with its own force in the soul of the person possessing it, undetected by gods or by men. No one has shown that injustice is the greatest of the evils the soul has within it, or that justice is the greatest good. (366a)

What Adeimantus says isn't quite accurate, since the arguments Socrates extracted in book 1 did not mention reputation, prestige, and rewards. Adeimantus will also prove to be a forgetful listener elsewhere.

Adeimantus wants Socrates (367e) to show "what effect each has because of itself on the person who has it – the one for good and the other for bad – whether it remains hidden from gods and human beings or not." Adeimantus knows Socrates has been spending his whole life considering justice:

I could endure other men's praising justice and blaming injustice in this way, extolling and abusing them in terms of reputation and wages, but from you I couldn't, unless you were to order me to, because you have spent your whole life considering nothing other than this. So don't only show us by the speech that justice is stronger than injustice, but show what each in itself does to the man who has it. (367d–e)

---

[27] In a useful and complex study that reaches conclusions different from mine Long (2007, 229–230) says that Glaucon "sets . . . a specific project" for Socrates:

Socrates does not . . . stumble upon the correct approach by himself; the agenda is set for him by Glaucon, who says that he will show Socrates the *way* in which he wants him to praise justice and criticize injustice. In 358b he has specified that Socrates should settle the nature of justice and injustice and the effect they have in themselves on the *soul* . . . Adeimantus repeats Glaucon's prescription.

This seems to me an accurate account of the brothers' demands. But the brothers' demands do not seem a good plan to me. In a serious discussion of how best to live it is not obvious that one should set agendas and make prescriptions. It seems better to start talking, ask questions, and see what happens.

Glaucon and Adeimantus both want Socrates to talk about justice strictly in the soul of the just person, not at all about justice as it relates to other people. It is a consequence of what Glaucon and Adeimantus require that Socrates is forbidden to mention as a benefit of justice for the agent that it accords other people their due and that it doesn't treat others shamefully. Those points do not fall within the class of internal benefits that Socrates is allowed to extol. The requirement that Socrates must speak of the benefits of justice as some kind of internal psychic matter leads Socrates eventually to propose that justice for each person is for each part of that person's soul to be doing its own work (441d–e; 443b). Glaucon's and Adeimantus' requirements shape what Socrates offers as a description of personal justice.

There are occasional reminders that books 2–10 are a made-to-order production, a command performance, constrained or compelled by Glaucon and Adeimantus. Just after hearing comparison of the sun and the good, for example, Glaucon expresses amusement at what seems to him a somewhat mysterious pronouncement. Socrates says:

It's your own fault (*su . . . aitios*) for forcing me (*anagkazôn*) to say what seems best to me (*ta emoi dokounta*) about it. (509c)

I take "seems best to me" to mean "seems best to me for the purposes of this particular conversation," a conversation in which, I've argued, Socrates gives a speech to persuade Glaucon of what Glaucon asked for. Socrates also reminds Glaucon in book 10 at 612c–d of some of the conditions under which Socrates' counter-speech was given: "Will you grant back to me what you borrowed from me in the speech?" In several other places Socrates attaches the content of books 2–10 to Glaucon and Adeimantus: 403b ("you will establish as law in the city being founded"); 409e ("Will you not establish as a law for the city . . . ?"); 421 a–b ("if we are making genuine guardians"); 463c ("your laws" – speaking of the breeding arrangements).

4.7 THE CITY OF BOOKS 2–10 IS GLAUCON'S, BUILT UNDER A CONDITION HE IMPOSES

When any speech persuades its audience, it reveals something about the audience. Socrates' speech is especially revelatory of Glaucon and Adeimantus because they have given some requirements for the sort of speech they want to hear. There is an even stronger component of audience revelation because at 372 Glaucon spontaneously provides another important condition on Socrates' speech.

Socrates is starting his plan to look for justice on a large scale in a city, a preliminary to looking for justice on the smaller and harder-to-see scale in the soul of the individual. Socrates begins to describe the city in which he'll look for justice. One interesting feature of the community he describes is that its members are concerned to avoid poverty and war (372c). Socrates summarizes:

Their life will pass in peace and good health, and at their death in old age they will pass on a similar way of life to their offspring. (372d)

But Glaucon rejects this city that Socrates describes first. Glaucon calls it a "city of pigs." Glaucon wants furniture and more complex food – *opsa* or relishes – in the diet of the people in the city-under-construction. "*Opsa*" has a wide application to anything that accompanies bread or grain foods. At Glaucon's request for *opsa* Socrates mentions olives and cheese. Glaucon wants more conventional *opsa*. Socrates includes some, and then lists many other apparently implied additions.

Some of the additions that Socrates gets Glaucon to agree ensue upon *opsa* and furniture are surprising. For example, my students ask, when they reach the addition, "prostitutes and pastries," "Where did that come from?" But I want to focus only on Glaucon's agreement to a particular result: that the additional items mean that the conversation should be about a city that will require new land and an army to defend its wealth.[28]

Socrates' description of the city newly provided with furniture and more varied food is this:

All right, I understand. It isn't merely the origin of a city that we're considering, it seems, but the origin of a *luxurious* (*truphôsan*: living softly) city... Then we must enlarge our city, for the healthy one is no longer adequate. We must increase it in size and fill it with a multitude of things that go beyond what is necessary for a city... And the land, I suppose, that used to be adequate to feed the population we had then will cease to be adequate and become too small... Then we'll have to seize some of our neighbors' land... And won't our neighbors want to seize part of ours as well, if they too have surrendered themselves to the endless acquisition of money and have overstepped the limit of their necessities?... Then our next step will be war... Then the city must be further enlarged... by a whole army, which

---

[28] See Davidson (1997, 3–35) for discussion of *opsa*. Adam (1963) says that Glaucon uses *opson* "in its narrower sense of animal food (whether fish or flesh). Socrates on the other hand uses the word in its wider sense of anything eaten in addition to, or along with, bread, e.g. vegetables." The ancient Athenian diet did not include much meat. Meat was an item associated with religious festivals and sacrifices. The addition of meat as a regular item at the table is a significant one. I don't wish to dwell on the interesting topic of the economics of meat production. For my purposes here I dwell only on Glaucon's ready assent to a city that requires warfare, which contrasts with Socrates' initial inclination to discuss a city that deliberately avoided warfare.

will do battle with the invaders in defense of the city's substantial wealth and all the other things we mentioned ... Warfare is a profession ... Now isn't it of the greatest importance that matters having to do with war be practiced well? ... Then to the degree that the work of the guardians is most important, it requires most freedom from other things and the greatest skill and devotion ... and ... a person whose nature is suited to that way of life. (372e–373)

Glaucon assents, sometimes very strongly, to each question and each proposal or implicit question of Socrates. So here, even as in a question-and-answer conversation, Glaucon decidedly assumes ownership of the proposals. Glaucon's demand for the luxurious city, thus spelled out by Socrates, is now an antecedent condition for the city in which Socrates will look for justice. Socrates will build on this antecedent condition, by using it and other premises that Glaucon and Adeimantus accept by assenting. But I wish to emphasize this conspicuous intervention by Glaucon, which subordinates Socrates' search for justice to the new condition that Socrates is considering a luxurious city for which it is "of the greatest importance that matters having to do with war be practiced well" (374c3–4).[29]

I'll mention something that might be considered to affect our understanding of Glaucon's new condition, but that actually doesn't affect it. It is a later passage surrounding 399e up to 410. In a discussion of some types of music and instrument and craftsman that will be forbidden in the city under construction Socrates says:

By the dog, without being aware of it, we've been purging the city we recently said was luxurious ... Come then, and let's purge the rest. (399e)

---

[29] The transition from the simple city to the luxurious city strikes commentators differently. Clay (2002, 27) in Griswold (2002) finds it important and sinister.

   Vlastos (1995b, 78–79) contrastingly, takes the transition to the luxurious city to be necessary to move the discussion to talking about people who have sufficiently complex lives to be useful to discuss:

   Man's goal here is nothing higher than material well-being, and at its lowest level ... Yet even so, ... all the participants benefit reciprocally ... But all this happens without the planned foresight of the common good and hence with no possibility of extending the area of mutually beneficent give-and-take in to the higher reaches of well-being.

   I object strongly to that description. It leaves out the socializing implied in these activities of the inhabitants of the simple city: feasting with their children, appreciating their lives (as is implied by the description "crowned with wreaths, [they] sing of the gods" (372b)) and it underestimates the thoughtfulness required to "live out their lives in peace with health" and "to hand down other similar lives to their offspring," as well as their deliberate avoidance of war.

   Alcinous in Dillon (1993, 34.1) notices the importance of the freedom from war of the first city. He says of the *Republic*: "In this work he first sketched out the state free from war, and secondly that which is 'fevered' and involved in war."

Some commentators take this to mean that the purged city that will be the focus of discussion for the rest of the *Republic* is now no longer luxurious.[30] I think not.

Socrates specifically mentions purging the city of rather few things. He eliminates certain things that have to do with the arts – certain kinds of music (398e; 399a) and the instruments that produce the music (399c) and the craftsmen that produce the instruments (399d), certain rhythms (399e) and unsuitable images whether poetic or visual and the craftsmen that produce them (401b). There will be a law (403b) that a lover may go no further than kissing or embracing his boyfriend in a fatherly way. Apparently fish will not be a permitted food (404c) nor boiled meat, but roasted meat will be allowed and apparently required for the army (404c). There won't be sweets (404c), elaborate foods (404d), Corinthian girls (404d), or Attic cakes (404d). Certain kinds of medical treatment will apparently be eliminated (407d). Though the details of the purging are not entirely clear, it is clear that what is eliminated will not affect the need for extra territory that brought on the need for an army in the first place. The chief cause of the need for territory was the extra population and the need for more food, especially herded animals (373c). Those do not get eliminated in the purging process. And certainly the army remains. The purged city has a warrior class devoted to territorial protection and expansion. The simple city that Glaucon was scornful of deliberately chose a way of life that would avoid war (372c). The war apparatus remains central in the purged city.

Given the proposal of the luxurious city with its ensuing army at 372–374, much of Socrates' persuasive speech in 2–10 now has the status of a conditional or "if . . . then" claim.[31] The antecedent of the conditional is:

---

[30] West (2004, 2–3), for example, says:

> In Plato's *Republic*, Socrates advocates a war of imperial expansion in order to acquire the territory needed to sustain the city's material needs. By the time Socrates has finished purging the city of luxuries, its territorial needs are likely to be quite small. This expansionist war, then, is not likely to amount to much.

> I disagree: I do not see evidence that purging has any important effect on the military needs and the focus on an aggressive army for the city. I am indebted to Betty Belfiore for suggesting that I consider the effect of purging the city.

[31] The new condition seems to me so important that it severely works against the assessment of Blondell (2002, 208):

> [Sokrates] is still limited by his respondents, but only in the sense that they never present him with a serious challenge of a kind that might force him to modify his views in any fundamental way . . . Instead they leave him free to develop his argument however he chooses.

"if we are designing a city a very important part of which is a military force to serve a population that desires soft living." The consequent of the conditional, what follows the "then," is the description of the city in which justice will be sought. This consequent amounts to a large conjunction of many results, all agreed upon by Glaucon and Adeimantus.

Keeping in mind that an outcome of Glaucon's condition is that it is most important (374c4, e1) for the city under construction to have an effective military force, I list some sample results just in the dimension of its military readiness. There must be supervision and censorship of stories told to the people who are going to grow up to be fighters (*machimois*) (386c). The rulers of the city must be the best soldiers – those among the military with the best skill at guarding the city (412c). There must be a noble lie that all the citizens of the city have common ancestry as descendants of the very earth on which they live (414b–415d).[32] There must be a breeding program to assure the quality of the children (459d–e: "The best men must have sex with the best women as frequently as possible"). Children who are to be part of the military must see warfare from an early age (466e–467c): "this must be laid down first (*huparkteon*): making the children spectators (*theôrous*) of war," so "children must be led to war on horseback as spectators, and if it's safe anywhere, they must be led up near and taste blood, like . . . puppies" (537a). This last proposal is reminiscent of some Spartan practices. If you find these recommendations shocking, as many readers have found them, that is probably because you are taking them unconditionally. The proposal that very young children should watch their parents and other relatives, with whom they have a "community of pain and pleasure" (464a), killing and being killed, is shocking – "a child development nightmare," to quote one of my Minnesota undergraduates. But on the condition that you are trying to produce maximally effective warriors, it may very well be just the thing.

Socrates gives very frequent reminders that an initial assumption of the discussion is that the city is carefully prepared for warfare. Explicit mentions of the capacity for warfare are at 378b; 386a; 386c; 387b; 387d; 388a; 395d–c; 399a; 404a; 404b; 415b; 415d; 416a–c; 416d; 451–453; 456a; 458b

---

Since the rest of the *Republic* is enormously creative, it is to an extent true that Socrates can develop his argument however he chooses. But there is the important limit to his creativity that Socrates must exercise it in finding things that will appeal to his particular interlocutors so that they will have reason to continue to reflect on them afterwards. They'll then be reflecting on where their own presuppositions have led them.

[32] West (2004, 3) suggests interestingly that this fictitious story about their ancestry makes it unnecessary for the citizens to consider whether they are living on unjustly gotten land.

("Consider... whether [these arrangements]... would be most advantageous of all for both the city and its guardians"); 503c–d; 521d; 522e; 525b
("Our guardian is both warrior and philosopher"); 525c; 527c; 537c ("consider who is most steadfast in studies and steadfast in war").[33] For example,
Socrates says of those who are thirty-five years old who have met the tests
for being guardians:

Now after this they'll have to go down into that cave again for you, and they must
be compelled to rule in the affairs of war (*ta peri tôn polemôn*) and all the offices
suitable for the young. (539d–e)

There are recurrent signals of the conditional status of the proposals that
Socrates makes about the city, although some of these do not specifically
mention war. One is a qualifying phrase at 541. Socrates proposes that true
philosophers who have come to power in the city will send everyone over
the age of ten into the countryside and will then bring up the children
under the arrangements described previously. Glaucon readily assents when
Socrates asks:

Is this the quickest and easiest way for the city and constitution we've discussed to
be established, become happy, and bring most benefit to the people among whom
it's established? (541a–b)

Socrates' qualifying phrases, "for the city and constitution we've discussed"
and "to the people among whom it's established," are reminders of the
conditional status of his proposal. He is talking about a city and a group of
people under Glaucon's condition – the luxurious city with its specialized
warrior class to maintain the territory they needed to satisfy the citizens'
superfluous needs, the city that has been described up to this point. *If* these
people are the ones under consideration, *then* the quickest way to create
their city is to do what Socrates proposes – to build it from the beginning
starting with the very young.

Other such indications of the conditionality of Socrates' proposals are,
e.g., at 398c ("Couldn't everyone by now discover what we have to say about
how [the manner of song and melody] must be if we're going to remain

---

[33] Annas (1981, 184) objects that Plato is confused because he talks about the Guardians' capacity
for fighting when he should be talking about their superior reasoning capacity as what suits them
to be in charge of the city. The project of creating a militarily effective city would be of course
an extremely complex practical project that would be beset with contingencies, so I am uncertain
whether or not Socrates' proposals would actually be the most effective means toward that end. But
despite the admitted uncertainty, I would say, in contrast to Annas, that the proposals that Plato
has Socrates make are not irrelevant but are rather plausible if Socrates is building on Glaucon's
condition of a highly effective military force.

in accord with what has already been said?"); 410a (best "for the city" if judges let people with inferior bodies die and kill those whose souls are incurable); 454d–e ("with respect to what we're talking about"). At 474a, after Glaucon has predicted a violent critical reaction to Socrates' proposal that philosophers must be rulers, Socrates reminds Glaucon that they are speaking under Glaucon's condition. Socrates says, "You're the one that brought this on me."

Glaucon refers back to his condition, I believe, at 544. Socrates has just completed the description of the city, having filled in with the digression of books 5–7 details about women and children – another audience request (449b–450a). Glaucon describes the point at which the discussion broke off and to which they will return:

> You were doing pretty much as now, as though you had gone all the way through the statements about the city, saying that you would propose a city such as you then described as good and a man like it [as good], and you seemed to be saying these things although you were able to talk about a yet finer man and city. (543c7–544a1)

Glaucon is remembering that Socrates' speech is not about Socrates' first choice of city. Socrates' first choice was the healthy city, the true city of 372e. (Socrates didn't mention a true and healthy man at 372e, but that would naturally ensue upon his plan to find justice in a man by first looking at a city.) But now at 544 Socrates is speaking under Glaucon's condition of the luxurious city.[34]

Because Socrates' construction of the city is under the condition of its being an efficient war machine, Socrates' references to the city as "best" or "good" must be understood as themselves conditional or qualified. "Best city" means "best-city-under-certain-conditions," where the prominent condition is that the city aims to be skilled at warfare. The several passages in which Socrates speaks of the city as best or good should all be made relative to the appropriate condition. These passages are examples: 423 ("greatest" (or possibly "biggest")); 427e ("good at last" (*teleôs agathên*)); 434e ("we founded [a city] best as we could"); 439 ("good" and "correct"); 472e ("we were trying to produce in an account a paradigm (*paradeigma*) of a good city"). For a last example, Socrates says:

---

[34] Adam (1963) and Reeve (1988, 170–171) think it refers to the difference between on the one hand the luxurious city of books 2–4 before philosopher-kings are introduced, and on the other hand the city of books 5–7. Annas (1981, 296) argues against that and so concludes that Glaucon's comment is an "unexplained oddity." If, as I believe, Glaucon refers back to the simple healthy city, the comment isn't odd.

Well then, Glaucon, these things were agreed on: that for a city that is going to be situated at the top (*akrôs oikein*), women are in common, children are in common, and all [their] education, while in the same way [their] pursuits (*epitêdeumata*) both in war and in peace, are in common, and their kings are those who have become (*gegonotas*: have been produced) best both in philosophy and with respect to war. (543a)

"A city...at the top" should be understood as "a city at the top given Glaucon's condition of military effectiveness." The kings of such a city should of course be those who are best at war. (I'll consider later the point that the kings should also be best at philosophy.)

Having in mind the conditionality of Socrates' proposals for the best city-under-Glaucon's-initial-conditions, I'd translate the word *Kallipolis*, which occurs only once in the *Republic* at 527c but which has captivated commentators so that they use it often, as "Finetown" or "Prettycity." Such translation hints at the alliteration and metrical flavor in the Greek, as the alternate and equally literal translation "Beautiful City," does not. Adam (1963) following Jowett and Campbell (1894, 335) thinks the word carries tenderness and affection. I would say that the alliterative or jingly quality has an equally good chance of carrying a trivializing or disparaging tone. I would compare "Tricky Dick" or "Flip Flop." The context in which Socrates uses the word is this exchange:

"Then to the greatest extent possible," I said, "the men in your Prettycity must be enjoined in no way to abstain from geometry. For even its by-products aren't slight."

"What are they?" he said.

"What you said about war, of course," I said... (527c)

Socrates continues, "and in addition, with respect to finer reception of all studies, we surely know there is a general and complete difference between the man who has been devoted to geometry and the one who has not." Though Socrates' addition should not be omitted, clearly we should also notice that the first thing Socrates mentions as a by-product of geometry is the uses in war activities that Glaucon mentioned (526d).

The phrase "ideal city" which commentators often use of the city Socrates has imagined, seems to me odd, though perhaps it is an attempt to capture Socrates' reference at 472 to the city as a "paradigm" or the reference at 592b to a "paradigm of it in heaven." I understand "paradigm" to mean "paradigm of a city established under the condition of its having as a main goal an effective military." A better phrase, if one were going to use the word "ideal," which so far as I know doesn't correspond to any adjective Plato uses, would be the phrase "the ideal city-under-the-conditions-provided-by-the-interlocutors-in-this-conversation."[35]

4.8 THE "BEST" CITY SOCRATES DESCRIBES IN THE *TIMAEUS*

In Plato's *Timaeus* in conversation with the interlocutors Timaeus, Critias, and Hermocrates, Socrates describes a city that has many similarities to the city of the *Republic*. The dramatic setting of the *Timaeus* is not connected to the setting of the *Republic*. This is very clear because Plato gives us a completely different set of interlocutors. Some commentators ignore that and declare that the *Timaeus* conversation is a sequel to the *Republic* conversation.[36] To so declare is unfortunate: it means we remove the possibility of asking the question why Plato would give us two strikingly similar conversations with different interlocutors. I can answer that. People who don't ask it don't.

In the *Timaeus* Socrates summarizes what he said to Timaeus, Critias, Hermocrates, and one other, now absent, in a conversation of the previous day. Timaeus, Critias, and Hermocrates are now to reciprocate for Socrates' speech and "entertain in return" (*antaphestian*: 17b). Socrates says that on the previous day he described

The kind of constitution which seemed to me likely to prove the best and the character of its citizens.[37] (17c)

---

[35] In the light of Glaucon's initial condition under which the city is established it seems to me slightly askew to ask, as does Ackrill (2001, 231):

[W]ho would not wish to live in a city or state ... in which the wisest and best governed, not in their own interest but as servants of the city, promoting the happiness of all its members ... ?

One answer would be: someone who did not admire what made the members of the city happy (as they thought).

[36] Rowe (2007, 5), says:

Plato himself takes care to link *Timaeus* with *Republic*, making the conversation represented (fictionally "recorded") in the former take place on the day after the conversation "reported" by Socrates that constitutes the latter.

This discounts Plato's care to tell us that the day before the *Timaeus* Socrates had a conversation on a topic similar to the theme of the *Republic* with a completely different set of interlocutors. That shows how important Plato thought that sort of conversation was for Socrates. Cornford (1957a, 4–5 and 11) has it right.

[37] I use the translations of Zeyl (2000), Bury (1966), and Cornford (1957a) with an occasional change.

I take it that "best" here in the *Timaeus* also should be qualified by "given that I am entertaining particular sorts of interlocutors." Socrates' interlocutors say that they appreciated Socrates' description of the city:

The one you described was very much to all of our minds (*mala hêmin . . . pasi kata noun*). (17c)

The *Timaeus* does not say whether Socrates gave an uninterrupted speech or elicited the description of the city from his interlocutors by questioning them. We do know that the category of the *Timaeus* conversation is mutual entertainment (17b). Entertainment differs from competitive *logon para logon* conversation and also from examining-conversation that proceeds by question and answer. Most of what Socrates summarizes as his entertaining speech of the previous day is talked of as a joint product ("Didn't we begin" (17e); "we said" (17d); "we ordained" (18c); and the like). That Socrates treats his entertaining speech as a joint product seems a sign that this offering is also very sensitively addressed to his particular audience.

When Socrates summarizes his contribution of the previous day, he mentions a number of things very similar to parts of the city of the *Republic*. (i) There was separation of the farmers and craftsmen from the defense forces (17c). (ii) Each class was assigned a single appropriate occupation, so that the defenders solely defend (17d). (iii) The guardians are gentle in administering justice to their friends and tough in fighting battles against external enemies (18a). (iv) To ensure gentleness and toughness the guardians must combine the spirited and the philosophic to a rare degree (18a). (v) They are trained physically and mentally in all studies suitable for the purpose (18a). (vi) They have no gold or silver or other private property (18b). (vii) The characters of the women are to be molded in a similar way to the men's, and the women share the same occupation both in war and in the rest of life (18c). (viii) Marriages and children should be shared in common by all (18c–d) (no one recognizes his own children and regards everyone as related to everyone else). (ix) The men and women in authority should secretly arrange that the best women mate with the best men and the bad with the bad (18d–e). (x) Children of the good are to be brought up and cared for. The children of the bad are to be secretly distributed elsewhere (19a: Zeyl: "to another city"). (xi) As children grow up, any in the wrong place will be promoted or demoted accordingly (19a).

Socrates asks if that is an adequate summary of the previous day's discussion and Timaeus says that Socrates has "not at all" omitted anything (19b). If we compare the list above to a list of features of the city of the *Republic*, we find that the *Timaeus* city description lacks the *Republic*'s account of the soul that helps to create the correspondence of the parts of the soul to the classes in the *Republic*'s city. It's unclear whether there are philosopher-kings in the *Timaeus*, though there are certainly philosopher-guardians. I believe that the reason the account of the soul is missing is that the guests whom Socrates entertains on this occasion have not constrained him to describe justice "by itself" and "in the soul" of the individual, as Glaucon and Adeimantus did.

For the rest of the conversation, Socrates says he wants to see the people of the city he described engaging in some activity. He feels as he would if he saw some fine animals in art or in repose and wanted

To see them moving and going for a prize in the contest in a [pursuit] among those that seem suited to their bodies. (19b–c)

In the case of the city he described he says:

I'd love to listen to someone give a speech depicting our city in a contest with other cities, competing for those prizes that cities typically compete for, fittingly going into war and in engaging in war (*en tô(i) polemein*) displaying what is fitting to its education and upbringing, both in deeds . . . and words. (19c)

That is to say, Socrates thinks the city is especially suited for war. But Socrates (19d) is incapable of offering the kind of account he would like to hear from Timaeus. Even poets and sophists can't do it:

Because they have traveled so much and never had a home of their own, they may fail to grasp the true qualities which those who are philosophers and statesmen would show in action and in negotiation in the conduct of war and battles (*en polemô(i) kai machais*)[38] . . . Thus there remains only that class which is of your disposition – a class which both by nature and nurture, shares the qualities of both the others. For Timaeus here is a native of a most well-governed state, Italian Locris, and inferior to none of its citizens either in property or in rank; and not only has he occupied the highest offices and posts of honor in his state, but he has also attained, in my opinion, the very summit of eminence in all branches of philosophy (*philosophias d'au kat'emên doxan ep'akron hapasês elêluthe*). (19e–20a)

Socrates says to Timaeus, Critias, and Hermocrates, "You alone, of men now living, could show our state engaged in a suitable war" (*polemon preponta*: 20b).

This is not the place to discuss the *Timaeus*. The *Timaeus* does not in fact ever get around to a description of the city in war, because Timaeus'

---

[38] Lee (1977) oddly, translates "in peace and war" instead of "in war and battles, " though peace isn't mentioned.

speech is given over to describing the creation of the world. The description of the city in battle remains an unwritten plan of Plato's. But it is relevant for my purposes to mention the *Timaeus* because it shows that Socrates' interlocutors in the *Timaeus* are another audience interested in a city most suited to the activity of war. His interlocutors are appropriate people to be entertained by a description of such a city, and they think that philosophy equips one especially to describe a city at war. I believe that what Socrates contributes to the *Timaeus* conversation has a great deal to do with his interlocutors' interests, and is neutral on Socrates' unconditioned opinions. Rather, it shows what he thought was appropriate to relate under the condition that he was to entertain these particular interlocutors. And because it gives us an additional audience for a description of a similar state, it shows us that Glaucon and Adeimantus were not singular in their interest in a state focused on the military.

4.9 THREE REASONS AGAINST FINDING SOCRATES COMMITTED TO HIS PROPOSALS IN BOOKS 2–10

We now have three reasons to forbear from saying that the Socrates of books 2–10 is committed to the proposals in his speech and instead to attach the proposals to Glaucon and Adeimantus. First, Socrates, as the speaker of a persuasive speech, need not be articulating his own convictions, but must be building on the beliefs of his hearer. As Socrates says in the *Gorgias*:

Each group of people takes delight in speeches spoken in its own character, and is disgusted by those given in an alien one. (513b–c)

Second, despite his agreement to give a speech, Socrates reverts to his familiar questioning mode as much as possible. When he does that, Glaucon and Adeimantus are doubly committed to what Socrates proposes: they are committed as persuaded listeners; and they are committed as answerers within Socrates' nonstandard speech who have responsibility for what they assent to.

Our consideration of Glaucon's new condition now gives us a third reason, applicable especially to books 2–7, to say that Socrates is not committed to the features of the city constructed in words there. Socrates' proposals about the city have the status of conditional, or "if...then" claims built on the requirements of his audience, and importantly on Glaucon's condition of the luxurious city. Since it is Glaucon, not Socrates, who has provided the antecedent condition, even though both Socrates and Glaucon may agree on the conditional, Socrates is not committed to the consequents. The brothers, who have accepted both antecedent and conditional, are also committed to the consequents.

Although all of Glaucon's and Adeimantus' responses serve as conditions of the discussion, conditions for which they, and not Socrates, have ownership, I selected the condition of the luxurious city for special emphasis because Glaucon spontaneously interrupts Socrates to introduce it, rather than waiting to be prompted by a question. It is even more closely attached to Glaucon than the statements of which Glaucon takes ownership when he assents to novel proposals that originate in Socrates' questions.

We might compare the question: Does Socrates mean or believe or make a commitment to what he says in the *Republic*? to the question: If someone says "If it is raining, then I will take my umbrella," does she mean or believe or make a commitment that she will take her umbrella? Under the perfectly ordinary circumstances I am imagining, the most natural answer to the latter question is: No, she does not mean or make a commitment that she will take her umbrella. She means and makes a commitment that she will take her umbrella *if* it rains. It would be misleading to leave out the condition and to report that she meant or said or made a commitment that she would take her umbrella. Similarly, the most accurate answer to the question: Does Socrates mean or endorse his proposals about the city in which justice is to be sought in the *Republic*? is that Socrates means and says something conditional: if certain conditions hold, then there are a number of consequences. For example, if certain conditions hold, then the city constructed in words is the best city. Socrates has not told us that he embraces the conditions under which he is constructing the city.

CHAPTER 5

Socrates in the Republic, part II: philosophers, forms, Glaucon, and Adeimantus

5.1 WHEN CAN WE SAY THAT SOCRATES DOES NOT BELIEVE PROPOSALS HE MAKES IN BOOKS 2–10?

I have argued that the brothers' assent to Socrates' proposals in the *Republic* commits them to those proposals. Socrates, as persuasive speech-maker, so far commits himself to nothing that he says in his speech. His not committing himself, however, does not imply that he rejects any of the novel proposals to which he gets the brothers' assent. Only his explicit examination and his discovery of absurdity would imply that Socrates as depicted rejects what led to absurdity. And in *Republic* 2–10 he does not examine.

In the absence of Socrates' examination we readers may of course ourselves examine Socrates' proposals. We may after reflection reach the strong judgment that the lives of most of the people in the city constructed in imagination are not worth living: the philosophical ruling class is required to spend much of its life on military planning for this state that maintains its ill-gotten territory to meet excess desires of the manufacturing class that the military class fights for; all three classes have their lives largely organized around the maintenance of the shallow goal of the militarily efficient city that Glaucon set when he restricted discussion to the luxurious city; the arts are censored severely; the reproductive and childrearing arrangements seem inhuman; many of the citizens are, like slaves, unable to choose their ways of life (590).

In short, upon examination we may find Prettycity in many ways quite unacceptable. The several authors quoted at the beginning of chapter 4 did exactly that.

Nevertheless, though we find these results unacceptable, we may not say that Socrates has in effect reduced Glaucon's assumptions to absurdity though Glaucon does not recognize this. The judgment of absurdity is our own external finding about what Socrates says.[1]

We may, however, say something more tentative but still interesting about Socrates as depicted. Plato leaves readers free to believe, as I in fact do, that Socrates, as depicted in the *Republic*, is as capable as the Socrates of any other dialogue would be of revealing absurdity, if there is any, in Glaucon's city.[2] He is certainly as capable as we are. Comparing our own capacities with the depicted Socrates', we have a test for what the depicted Socrates *would* reject if he *were* in examination mode. Our test is that if we can see an absurdity, he certainly could. So though we cannot say that Socrates *does* reject much of what he proposes, we can reasonably estimate what he *would* reject if he were in examination mode.

Accepting that test, we can use the work of the authors quoted at the beginning of chapter 4 to say that yes, Socrates, were he in examination mode, would find the very features they found unacceptable equally unacceptable.

5.2 SOCRATES' DEPICTION OF THE PHILOSOPHER

For my purposes here I will briefly consider as a theme that does not survive our examination the account of the philosopher that emerges from discussion with Glaucon. Our own minimal scrutiny will give us reason to say that Socrates, as depicted, would not endorse that account.

A passage in book 2 first mentions philosophers. It is just after Socrates has declared, on the basis of Glaucon's suggestions and agreements, that the city under construction needs an army of warriors or guardians who are spirited, swift, and strong. Socrates makes a comparison between a guardian and a puppy. There is some muted play on the similarity of the words in Greek for guardian (*phulax*) and puppy (*skulax*). The English translations "warrior" and "terrier" might gesture at the wordplay:[3]

Do you think, I said, that for guarding (*eis phulakēn*) the nature of a purebred puppy (*skulakos*) differs from [that of] a well-bred young man? (375a)

---

[1] I do not go quite as far as de Lacy (1976, 66). His article, which is in many ways quite congenial to my overall picture, concludes, after listing some of the distasteful features of the city that Socrates constructs, "It is tempting to suppose that by means of these paradoxes Plato is telling us that the initial hypothesis about the origin of cities is not entirely satisfactory."

[2] Blondell (2002, 209).

[3] The nominatives are *phulax* (guardian) and *skulax* (puppy). Forms of the word for guardian occur at 374e1, 375b4, 375d1, 375e1, and 375e6. The sole form of the word for puppy in the passage is *skulakos* at 375a2.

Socrates then raises the concern that the guardians' spiritedness will lead them to be savage to their fellow citizens, instead of gentle (375c). But Socrates quickly suggests an answer to this concern:

We didn't notice that there are, after all, natures such as we thought impossible, possessing these opposites... One could see it in other animals too, especially however in the one we compared to the guardian. You know, of course, that by nature the disposition of purebred dogs is to be as gentle as can be with their familiars and people they know and the opposite with those they don't know (*agnôtas*)...

In your opinion, then, does a man who will be a fit guardian need, in addition to spiritedness, also to be a philosopher (*philosophos*: literally, "lover of wisdom") by nature? (375d–e)

Glaucon asks for an explanation. Socrates explains:

This too, you'll observe in dogs, I said, and it's a thing in the beast worthy of our wonder...

When it sees someone it doesn't know, it's angry, although it has never had any bad experience with him. And when it sees someone it knows, it greets him warmly, even if it never had a good experience with him... Well, this does look like a pretty affection of its nature and truly philosophic...

In that it distinguishes a friendly from a hostile look by nothing other than by having learned the one and being ignorant of the other, I said. And so, how can it be anything but a lover of learning since it defines what's its own and what's alien by knowledge and ignorance?... Well, I said, but aren't love of learning (*to... philomathes*) and love of wisdom (*philosophon*) the same?... Then the man who's going to be a fine and good guardian of the city for us will in his nature be philosophic, spirited, swift, and strong. (376a–376c)

Glaucon agrees readily. Many commentators find this comparison somewhat odd, but look for redeeming features.[4] Some explain its oddness by saying that Plato is being not serious.[5] I think it better to acknowledge that this sketch of what it is to be philosophical proves under scrutiny to be outright wrong and irredeemable, and to reflect on that.

---

[4] Some readers e.g. Reeve (1988, 179) object only mildly to the account of philosophers as lovers of what they have learned.

It seems to me quite doubtful that Plato was ignorant of the rather basic fact about dogs that dogs can hate the familiar or that Plato would depict Socrates as ignorant of it.

See also Annas (1981, 80), who objects but tries to salvage redeeming content.

[5] Bloom (1968, 350) comments that the comparison is wrong but doesn't explain why Socrates would make an erroneous comparison. My reaction, rather than to take this as a nonserious preparation for a better account of philosophers later, is to take the unacceptable comparison here as a suggestion that the later description of philosophers is also unacceptable.

Glaucon does not question Socrates' proposal that the love of the learned, the attachment to the familiar, is the same as the love of learning. But Glaucon should not have assented to that: the two are decidedly not the same. Love of the familiar or known is different from love of learning. The latter requires receptivity to the currently unfamiliar. Glaucon is not agreeing that a philosophical nature wishes for the unknown to become known. Glaucon is instead accepting the thought that a philosophical nature is hostile to the unknown. Glaucon does not recognize the incoherence of saying that the love of the learned plus rejection of the unfamiliar is the love of learning. That Socrates is giving a persuasive speech explains why he does not go on to the stage of testing the proposal that would bring out its mistakenness.[6]

The implication that philosophy is love of learning occurs in other dialogues. In *Symposium* (204) and *Lysis* (218) philosophy or love of wisdom requires acknowledged ignorance or lack of wisdom: learning may approach the wisdom that philosophers love. If philosophy is love of learning, it is certainly not exclusive affection for what has been learned, the familiar.

To understand this introduction of the philosophers in book 2, it would be helpful to know if Glaucon considers himself or Socrates a philosopher. We aren't told at this point in the dialogue. If Glaucon does think Socrates is a philosopher, then Glaucon for the moment is committed to the totally unacceptable result that the philosopher Socrates is fond of the familiar and resists what he does not know. Simply from reading the *Republic* up to this point, we know different: we know that Socrates was interested in the new goddess whose honoring events he went to the Piraeus to see; we know that Socrates liked the procession of the alien Thracians.

---

[6] The guardian is compared to the dog in that "when it sees someone it knows, it greets him warmly, even if it has never had a good experience with him." That suggests the absurdity that if a guardian has fought often (or even only once) with an enemy, the enemy, who is now known and familiar, is someone to be greeted warmly.

On the behavior of dogs with familiar people, there is this in Mark Twain's *Huckleberry Finn*, chapter 40, where dogs have been set on the trail of suspected robbers, who are in fact, Huck, Tom, and Jim:

They'd had all the dogs shut up, so they wouldn't scare off the robbers; but by this time somebody had let them loose, and here they come, making powwow enough for a million; but they was our dogs; so we stayed in our tracks till they catched up; and when they see it warn't nobody but us, and no excitement to offer them, they only just said howdy, and tore right ahead towards the shouting and clattering.

The picture of philosophers to which Glaucon attaches himself in book 2 has some similarities and some differences to Twain's dogs. A difference is that Twain's dogs are at least eager for the unfamiliar. I am grateful to John Wallace for the reference to Twain.

Because the thought that the guardian–philosopher loves only the familiar and resists the unfamiliar is simply inconsistent with the thought that the guardian–philosopher loves learning, it seems to me not useful to pursue the question: What reasonable or at least salvageable thing could Socrates possibly mean by this unacceptable sketch of philosophers? It seems more fruitful to ask: What could Glaucon learn about himself if, later, he reflected on these claims he has accepted?

Socrates treats the theme of the philosopher in conversation with Glaucon for a second time in books 5 and 6 (474b–486). Socrates has proposed "the smallest change" that would turn a city into a city of the sort he has described up to that point. This is how Socrates describes this "smallest change:"

Until philosophers rule as kings in their cities, or those who are nowadays called kings and powers become genuine and adequate philosophers, so that political power and philosophy become thoroughly blended together, while the many natures that now pursue either one exclusively are prevented from doing so, cities will have no rest from evils, my dear Glaucon nor, I think, will the human race. And until this happens, the same constitution we have now described in our discussion will never be born to the extent possible. (473c–e)

Glaucon says that people will attack Socrates for this speech. Socrates responds, tellingly:

But aren't you the one who is responsible for this happening to me? (474a)

Glaucon promises to defend Socrates in any way he can:

What I can do is provide good will and encouragement and maybe I would answer you more suitably than someone else. So with the promise of this sort of assistance, try to demonstrate to the unbelievers that things are as you claim. (474a)

Socrates responds:

It seems to me necessary if we are going to escape from the people you mention, to define (*diorisasthai*) for them who the philosophers are that we dare to say should rule, so that when they are clear, one can defend oneself (*amunesthai*), showing that for some it is fitting by nature to touch philosophy and to lead in a city, but for others not to touch it and to follow the leader. (474b–c)

Glaucon agrees that this is the right time to define (*horizesthai*). He seems quite enthusiastic about demonstrating that philosophers should rule.

Socrates gets Glaucon's agreement (474c–485b) that the philosopher loves certain types of learning. Glaucon, in assenting, is again inconsistent, since he has not given up his initial agreement in book 2 that the philosopher loves the familiar and is hostile to the unknown. If Socrates were engaging in a standard examination, Socrates might ask some different questions to move Glaucon to see that Glaucon is inconsistent.

At 485d–e Glaucon agrees that "true philosophers" would abandon any pleasures that come through the body. Again it would be interesting to know if Glaucon considers himself a philosopher. If he does, his agreement about true philosophers fits ill with his concern at 372c–d for not just relishes, but proper up-to-date relishes.

5.3 GLAUCON'S AGREEMENTS ABOUT FORMS IN BOOKS 5–7 DO NOT SURVIVE EXAMINATION

The second stage of the discussion with Glaucon (475–480) further explains what the philosopher is by setting out what the philosopher knows. It leads at 487a to the desired outcome that what he knows fits him uniquely to rule the imagined city. I quote some parts of relevant passages, separating bits that make different points, and then comment.

(i) "Since beautiful is the opposite of ugly, they are two . . . Since they are two, isn't each also one? . . . The same argument also applies then to justice and injustice, good and bad, and all the forms (*eidôn*); each is itself one." (476a)

(ii) "On the one side I put those of whom you were just speaking, the lovers of sights, the lovers of arts, and the practical men; on the other, those whom the discussion is about, whom alone one could rightly call philosophers . . . The lovers of hearing and the lovers of sights, on the one hand," I said, "surely delight in beautiful sounds and colors and shapes . . . but their thought is unable to see and delight in the nature of the beautiful itself . . . " (476a–b)

(iii) "Wouldn't, on the other hand, those who are able to approach the beautiful itself and see it by itself be rare?" "Indeed they would." (476b)

(iv) "The man who holds that there are beautiful things (*kala . . . pragmata*), but doesn't hold that there is beauty itself (*auto . . . kallos*) and who, if someone leads him to the knowledge (*gnôsin*) of it, isn't able to follow . . . is he living a dream? . . . Doesn't dreaming . . . consist in believing something to be not a likeness but rather the thing itself to which it is like? . . . " (476c)

(v) "What about the man who, contrary to this, believes that there is something beautiful itself and is able to catch sight both of it and of what shares in it and doesn't believe that what shares is it itself, nor that it itself is what shares? . . . Wouldn't we be right in saying that this man's thought, because he knows, is knowledge, while the other's is belief, since he believes?" (476d)

(vi) "It is not possible that the object of knowledge and the object of belief are the same." (478b)

(vii) "The majority of people's many conventional views about beauty and the rest are somehow rolling around between what is not and what purely is . . . And we have agreed earlier that if anything turned out to be of that sort, it would have to be called an object of belief, not an object of knowledge." (476d)

(viii) "What about those who in each case look at the things themselves that are always the same in every respect? Won't we say that they have knowledge, not mere belief?" (479e)

Remark 1

Commentators say that 476a is the first introduction of Plato's theory of forms in the *Republic*, and that Glaucon shows that he is already familiar with it.[7] I agree of course that Glaucon is presented as being very receptive to what Socrates says. But there is no reason to think that here Socrates is assuming a full-fledged technical theory of forms including propositions articulated explicitly only in other dialogues.

There is, in the first place, not sufficient reason to say that the phrase "the beautiful itself" and the word "forms" introduce anything new, surprising, or technical. The word "itself" here may very well be simply the familiar topic-focusing device that has turned up in the *Republic* previously without attracting any comment.[8] In book 1 Socrates mentions "this itself, justice" at 331a, and his audience, and readers, understand what he is talking about. Socrates treats the topic he calls "this itself, justice" as equivalent to what he calls "the just, what it is" at 354a. The latter phrase is equivalent to "what just is." Some evidence of the equivalence of such phrases is that in book 10 the phrase "that itself which a bed is" (*autên ekeinên ho estin klinê*: 597c3) is treated as equivalent to "what a bed is" (*ho estin klinê*: 597c9). The phrase, "what just is" has a perfectly ordinary use in English, as in the sentence, "If that wasn't a just decision, I don't know what just is."

Book 4 gives another example of how Socrates uses "itself" as a topic-focusing device:

Insofar as it's thirst, would it be a desire in the soul for something more than that of which we say it is a desire? For example, is thirst thirst for hot drink or cold, or much or little, or in a word for any particular kind of drink? Or isn't it rather that in the case where heat is present in addition to the thirst, the heat would cause

---

[7] Annas (1981, 195). Adam (1963) comments at 476a:

This is the first appearance of the Theory of "Ideas" properly so called in the *Republic*. It should be carefully noted that Plato is not attempting to prove the theory; Glaucon, in fact, admits it from the first.

[8] Stokes (1986, 267) observes:

It is simplest to think of "itself" in this passage as meaning "by itself." That such expressions are at this stage of the dialogue already technical terms seems an unnecessary assumption based on a very uncertain view of what Socrates says to Glaucon at 475e6.

the desire to be also for something cold as well; and where coldness, something hot; and where the thirst is much on account of the presence of muchness, it will cause the desire to be for much, and where it's little, for little? But thirsting itself (*auto . . . to dipsên*) will never be a desire for anything other than that of which it naturally is a desire – for drink . . . (437d–e)

Of all the things that are such as to be related to something, those that are of a certain kind are related to a thing of a certain kind, as it seems to me, while those that are severally themselves (*ta d'auta hekasta* 438b1–2)[9] are related only to a thing that is itself . . . Knowledge itself (*epistemê . . . auto*) is knowledge of learning itself (*mathêmatos autou*) or of whatever it is to which knowledge should be related; while a particular kind of knowledge is of a particular kind of thing . . . (438a–c)

So a particular sort of thirst is for a particular kind of drink, but thirst itself (*dipsos . . . auto*) is neither for much nor little, good or bad, nor, in a word, for any particular kind, but thirst itself is naturally only for drink itself (*autou pômatos*) . . . Therefore the soul of the man who's thirsty, insofar as it thirsts, wishes nothing other than to drink. (439a–b)

Here the phrase "thirst itself" means "thirst considered by itself without any additional description." The phrase focuses on the bare topic of thirst, as opposed to some specific type of thirst. "Itself" is a topic-focusing device; that at least should be our first way of understanding it. Glaucon may in book 5 take the phrase to do more than focus a topic; but we have no reason to believe that Socrates, as depicted, is recommending that, especially if Glaucon's understanding turns out to be obscure or incoherent.

Remark 2

Similarly, the word "forms" (*eidôn*) at 476a is not inevitably a technical term. An ordinary speaker could agree to what Socrates says. The literal meaning of *eidos* is "that which is seen" or "appearance." It is what is presented to the viewer. Similarly for *idea*, which occurs at 479a. "Aspect" seems to me an approximate equivalent in English. Proposing to have a conversation about an aspect of things seems to me a natural and ordinary thing to do. The use of a phrase such as "the beautiful itself" or "the beautiful, by itself" is a natural way to start a conversation about a specific aspect of something. One might naturally in conversation want to focus on

---

[9] At 438b Adam (1963) comments:

auta is *ipsa*, i.e. by themselves alone, without qualification: cf. [438d] and 437e . . . The phraseology of this passage . . . is no doubt interesting for the light which it throws on the origin of the terminology adopted in the Theory of Ideas . . . but we could make no greater mistake than to suppose that Plato is here speaking of hypostatized Ideas.

a single aspect such as beauty that many beautiful things share. Similarly, there is no reason to take "share" (476d) to be some mysterious technical term. To say in ordinary discussion that several things share beauty is simply to say that they are all beautiful.

Remark 3

In passage (i) above (476a), Socrates concludes that beautiful and ugly are each one thing from the premise that beautiful and ugly are two (two items or two things). He gets that premise from the prior datum that beautiful is the opposite of ugly. (Book 10 (596b) argues for the conclusion that the couch and the table are each one from the simpler premise that a couch and a table are two different things. Socrates says that there are many couches and tables, but the forms concerning these furnishings are two, one of couch and one of table.) Obviously it is straightforward to deduce that if you have two things, each of them is one.

The statements in this sort of inference are perfectly ordinary and natural: beautiful is the opposite of ugly. Hence beautiful and ugly are two – two items, or two things. Hence beautiful is one (or one thing) and ugly is one (other or different thing). We might not have expected the predicate adjectives, "beautiful" and "ugly," to be used (as opposed to mentioned) in subject position in a sentence, but they obviously can be thus used, quite naturally. So far Glaucon has agreed to nothing out of the ordinary.

Remark 4

In passage (ii) above (467a–b) Socrates distinguishes a group of people who delight in beautiful colors and shapes, but whose thought is unable to see and delight in the beautiful itself. It's not immediately clear what "see" amounts to here. Taken literally, it seems correct that thought can't see the beautiful itself, since it is people with eyes or vision that see things, not thought. But then the group of people who delight in colors and shapes wouldn't be distinguished from anyone else on the grounds that their thought can't see the beautiful itself. No one's thought can literally see the beautiful itself, by itself. When we do literally see anything beautiful, what we literally see is always a beautiful something or other. Passage (iii) above (476b), that those who are able to see the beautiful itself by itself are rare, would then be true in the extreme: there would be no such people.

But that literal interpretation of "see" doesn't give the right sense to the passage: it seems clear that Socrates is suggesting and Glaucon agrees that there are such people who "approach" and "see" the beautiful itself. It seems more likely that the talk of approaching and seeing is a way of saying that certain people acknowledge that there is such a thing as the beautiful, considered by itself – or, equivalently, beauty or what beautiful is. There are, according to Glaucon, some people who acknowledge that. And Glaucon thinks that these people are rare.

Remark 5

Glaucon isn't invited to explain why he thinks that people who can approach the beautiful itself and acknowledge it by itself are rare. Given our ordinary topic-focusing use of "itself," I would say that they are not rare. Anyone who understands the ordinary topic-focusing use of "itself" can do what Glaucon thinks is rare. Anyone who accepts that distinctions can be made in speech at all between beautiful and ugly acknowledges the existence of the beautiful itself, i.e. what beautiful is.

Remark 6

At 476c (in passage (iv) above) Glaucon accepts that there are also some people who, in contrast, do not acknowledge the beautiful itself. Such a person "believes in beautiful things but does not believe in the beautiful itself." I would have liked to hear more about that person, because to me he sounds an impossible fiction. He would be someone who believed that there are beautiful things but who also believed there is no such thing as what beautiful is. Compare the person Glaucon envisages with the perfectly sensible person who believes that there is no such thing as what slithy is and hence that there are no slithy toves. But if someone believed that there is no such thing as what beautiful is, how could he recognize anything as beautiful or be devoted to beautiful things in the first place? I don't understand why Glaucon agrees that there is such a person. So far as I can see, if the sight-lover says there are many beautiful things in distinction from ugly things, he thereby acknowledges that there is such a thing as what beautiful is, that is, the beautiful itself.

But perhaps Glaucon is not envisaging someone with this impossible combination of beliefs. Perhaps instead Glaucon's agreement that there are people who believe in beautiful things but do not believe in the beautiful itself is evidence that Glaucon does not understand the phrase "the beautiful itself" in the ordinary topic-focusing sense in which it is equivalent to the phrase "what beautiful is." If so, we still would not have evidence that

Socrates endorses understanding the phrase in some extraordinary way, since Socrates gives no explanation of a new meaning. It would be more likely that Socrates is revealing Glaucon by mirroring Glaucon and showing what appeals to Glaucon.

Remark 7

At 479 Glaucon agrees also that the lover of sights "can in no way endure it if anyone asserts that the beautiful is one and the just is one and so on with the rest." It follows by *modus tollens* (given the claim at 476a that if beautiful and ugly are two, then each is one) that the lover of sights also can't say that the beautiful and the ugly are two. Hence, he can't say that they are opposites. It looks as though he is unable to make some very important distinctions – if he is able to make any at all. Again, so far as I can see, anyone who thinks that beautiful is the opposite of ugly, thinks that beautiful is one thing and ugly is a second thing. Again, it seems unlikely in the extreme that there is any such person who loves beautiful sights but does not think that beautiful is one thing and ugly is another.

Remark 8

The philosopher is said to be awake. He contrasts with the sight-lover, who is said to be dreaming. Dreaming consists in believing something to be that which it is like. Glaucon then seems to be agreeing that the sight-lover believes that the many beautiful things are (all there is to) the beautiful itself. But the thought (from Remark 6) that there is no such thing as the beautiful itself is obviously not compatible with the thought that the beautiful itself is the many beautiful things. Again, the sight-lover, as described, is an unlikely figure.

Remark 9

Glaucon agrees that (a) the philosopher doesn't believe that what shares (in something itself) is that item itself. For example, the philosopher would not agree that the many beautiful things are beauty itself. Glaucon also agrees that (b) the philosopher has knowledge. (The philosopher's thought is knowledge (476d4: *gnômên*). At 480e Glaucon will agree that the objects of the philosopher's knowledge are things themselves (i.e. items such as the beautiful itself).)

It is natural to ask in what the philosopher's knowledge at 476d4 consists. Partly it will involve his believing that there is such a thing as the beautiful itself. But 476d4 suggests that he has knowledge because of not having the belief that the beautiful itself is the many beautiful things. Yet the mere lack of the mistaken belief that the beautiful things are beauty itself doesn't seem enough to count as knowledge. We expect knowledge to be the presence of some thought-content, not a mere absence. A likely candidate for a thought with content would be the thought that the beautiful itself is not the same as the many beautiful things. (Here the phrase "the beautiful itself" is to be understood in its ordinary way as equivalent to "what beautiful is.") So a part of the philosopher's knowledge consists in the thought that what beautiful is is not the same as the many beautiful things. And that seems a perfectly reasonable thought. (See remark 12 (pp. 133–134) for an argument for it from the material that Socrates supplies Glaucon.)

That implication, however, does not fit well with Glaucon's agreements at 477–479. There he agrees that the knowable – what we know – and objects of belief – what we have beliefs about – are not the same. 479 (passage (vii) above) seems evidence that the many beautiful things are objects of belief but not knowable. So the philosopher's thought that the beautiful itself is not the same as the many beautiful things – since that thought is as much about the many beautiful things as it is about the beautiful itself – cannot, according to 479, count as knowledge, contrary to what 476 suggests. Further, the thought that the beautiful itself is not the same as the many beautiful things also can't count as belief, since it is about the beautiful itself as much as it is about the many beautiful things. So there is an unexplored puzzle in what Glaucon agrees to. The philosopher can neither know nor believe that the many beautiful things are not what beautiful is.

Remark 10

Glaucon agrees at 479e-480a to Socrates' proposal that those who in each case "look at each of the things themselves (*auta hekasta*) that are always the same in every respect (*aei kata tauta hôsautôs onta*)" have knowledge. Socrates has previously referred to the beautiful itself in a way that suggests that it is the same in every respect. At 479a he refers to "beautiful itself and a certain idea of beauty itself... always holding in the same way in the same respects" (*auto... kalon kai idean tina autou kallous... aei kata tauta hôsautôs echousan*). At 484b "philosophers are those who are able to grasp what is always the same in all respects, while those who are not able to do so but wander among what is many and varies in all ways are not philosophers."

The thought that the beautiful itself (= what beautiful is) is always the same in every respect is a separate point from the point that the addition "itself" is a topic-focusing device, so I will dwell on this new point. For variety and clarity and possibly to create a challenge, consider the topic of mud itself. We can obviously talk about mud itself as distinct from landslide mud and shoe mud, and other varieties of mud. Mud itself = what mud is = the aspect or form of mud.

Since mud itself is included under each of the things themselves, 479 (passage (viii) above) implies that mud itself (as distinguished from muds of such and such kinds) is always the same in all respects. Is that an unfamiliar and odd thing to say, so that it would be evidence that we have an entirely new technical topic of forms here, or does it fit with the ordinary topic-focusing use of "itself"? I would vote that it fits with the topic-focusing use. Mud itself, what mud is, is always earth mixed with water.[10] The particular mud on my particular shoe, however, is equally not mud (if its water evaporates and merely dust remains). If so, then the many bits of mud are as changeable as the many beautiful things. But when the mud on my shoe goes out of existence, that doesn't change what mud is.

So I would object to Glaucon's assent that nonphilosophers do not think that there is some aspect, beautiful itself, always the same in all respects (479). I would say on the contrary that it is an ordinary or familiar claim accepted by anyone who considers it.

Remark 11

Book 5 concludes with Glaucon's agreement when Socrates asks:

Must we therefore call philosophers but not lovers of opinion those who delight in each thing that is itself? (*auto . . . hekaston to on*). (480a11)

Glaucon agrees to something similar in book 6:

SOCRATES. Let this be agreed by us concerning the natures of philosophers that they always love the learning that makes clear to them [something of] that being that always is and does not wander around subject to coming-to-be

---

[10] In the *Parmenides* a young Socrates is doubtful that there is a separate form for mud. In the *Theaetetus* the seventy-year-old Socrates asks, "What is clay (*pêlos*: mud)?" Socrates rejects the answer, "Potter's clay, oven-maker's clay, brickmaker's clay." The "short and commonplace" thing to say would be: it is earth mixed with water (147c). Socrates gives this example in the *Theaetetus* because he wants to illustrate how to answer the question, "What is knowledge itself?" (146d).

and decaying . . . And indeed . . . [let it be agreed] that [they love] all of it and are not willing to give up any part, whether small or bigger, more held in honor or more dishonored. (485a–b)

Glaucon's agreement seems to me either a clear mistake or, more likely, unclear, and a revelation that he is in some confusion. In our ordinary topic-focusing use of "itself," there is an item that is itself for pretty much any single noun or adjective we use. (That is in fact agreed to at 596a–597 in book 10.) But we have no evidence that the philosophers Glaucon has in mind have interests that range so widely as to include every item itself. They would not be interested in mud itself and housecleaning itself, or even the bed itself, so far as we can tell. So if Glaucon had in mind our ordinary topic-focusing "itself" he would be saying something obviously wrong here in agreeing that philosophers are interested in "each thing that is itself." He is perhaps revealing that he does not have that ordinary use of "itself" in mind. But even if Glaucon has in mind something extraordinary, we readers need not ascribe anything extraordinary to Socrates as Socrates' own conviction here. Socrates is giving a persuasive speech, and Socrates has just got Glaucon's explicit agreement to part of it.

Remark 12

Here is the argument promised in Remark 9 to the conclusion that the beautiful itself is different from the many beautiful things. That is to say, the conclusion is that what beautiful is is different from what is beautiful.

This is an argument with which, I've said, any ordinary person should agree. Or, since the argument is so obvious, any ordinary person in effect does agree to it, even if he hasn't considered it, just as any ordinary person in effect agrees that or understands that the moon is not in his refrigerator, although that topic has never entered his head. We can arrive at this argument mostly by putting together what Socrates says and what Glaucon accepts into a three-part argument.

(a) The first part of the argument for this is supplied at 475e–476a:

   (a1) What beautiful is is the opposite of what ugly is.

   (a2) Therefore what beautiful is is different from what ugly is. (There is a basic assumption that opposites can't be identical: they are two, rather than one.)

(b) The second part of the argument comes from 479a–b:

   (b1) Any things that are beautiful (in some way) are also ugly (in some way).

(b2) Therefore, the many things that are beautiful are identical with the many things that are ugly. That is, the collection of the many beautiful things is identical with the collection of the many ugly things. That is, what is beautiful is identical with what is ugly. Evidence for this point is what Glaucon agrees to at 479b. Socrates imagines that even a person who maintains that there is no such thing as the beautiful itself will have to concur when Socrates asks:

> Of all the many beautiful things, is there one that won't also seem ugly? Or any just one that won't seem unjust? . . . Then is each of the many things any more what one says it is than it is not what one says it is? (479a)

This first says that anything beautiful will also *appear* ugly. But it then goes on to say that each of the many things *is* not any more what one says it is than what one says it isn't. It would be worthwhile to consider why Socrates moves from appearing to being. But I will take it for my purposes here that Socrates wants to make a general point that any of the many things that has one of a pair of opposites (from a certain range of pairs of opposites) also has the other. (My qualification "from a certain range" alludes to the circumstance that the argument won't work for certain pairs of opposites, such as odd and even or male and female. That might be worth exploring elsewhere.)

(c) The third part of the argument that I claim anyone would agree to is this. Nothing in the text corresponds to it:

(c1) Suppose, for reduction to absurdity, that the many beautiful things (i.e. what is beautiful) were identical with the beautiful itself (what beautiful is).

(c2) By the same principle, what is ugly would be identical with what ugly is.

(c3) But since, as shown just above at (b), what is beautiful is identical with what is ugly, it would then follow that what beautiful is is what ugly is.

(c4) And that would be impossible, as observed at (a) above, because it would mean that two opposites are one.

Remark 13

Book 6 opens with Socrates' report of this exchange:

> "And so, Glaucon," I said, "through a somewhat lengthy speech who the philosophers are and who the nonphilosophers has, with considerable effort, somehow been brought to light."

"Perhaps," he said, "that's because it could not easily have been done through a short one." (484a)

Adam (1963) notes that the word "lengthy" has troubled some commentators, since the discussion extends only over six Stephanus pages. Adam decides that is long enough to count as long. The qualification "with considerable effort" (*mogis*) also seems somewhat inappropriate, since there hasn't been any particular effort. Glaucon has mostly agreed readily. For example, Glaucon accepts that Socrates has spoken correctly (475e4) even though Glaucon also says he doesn't know what Socrates means.

Socrates says (475e) that it wouldn't be easy to explain about philosophers to someone else, but he expects that Glaucon would agree. Socrates' very next point is that since beautiful and ugly are two, each is one. Since I think that is obvious, I think, contrary to what Socrates says, that it would be easy to say to anyone else. Why would Socrates say that it wouldn't be easy with others, and why would Glaucon then later agree (484a) that the discussion took effort? I consider that question later.

Remark 14

At 485c Glaucon agrees that the philosophers, those most fit to rule the city under construction, must have this feature:

[Their] being willing in no way to accept what's false, but to hate it, and to cherish the truth. (485c3–4)

This seems inconsistent with Glaucon's earlier agreement (414–415) that at least the first generation of rulers of his city will perpetuate a "noble lie" about the citizens' ancestry.[11]

From these remarks I draw some conclusions about the passage at 474–485. First, it reveals again that Glaucon has an inconsistent view of philosophers: they love learning but are hostile to the unfamiliar; they hate falsehood, but are willing to support a foundational lie. Second, it does not clearly present a difficult technical theory of forms. Taken at face value, the

---

[11] At 531d–534e in book 7 in conversation with Glaucon we glean more information about the philosopher. There the spectator of being is the one most skilled at the art of conversation, the dialectician (*dialektikos* – a word apparently coined by Plato – literally, the master of cross-talking). This passage about dialectic does not much mention philosophy, but we can deduce that since the spectator of being of book 5 is the philosopher, the master of *dialegesthai* of book 7 is the philosopher. Book 7's account of mastery of *dialegesthai* implies that the dialectician assumes as little as possible, questions and tests assumptions, arrives at something that does not have the status of an assumption that needs to be tested, is able to survive the testing of any assumptions in question and answer, and also is over fifty years old.

statements that Glaucon thinks only rare people would accept are state-ments that any ordinary speaker should, or in effect does, agree to. That Glaucon says only rare people accept them suggests that he takes them to have a sense different from their face or ordinary sense. What sense that is is not clarified. It seems unlikely that the Socrates who accepts what he has considered and clarified (337c; 338c) now is depicted as accepting these statements in some extraordinary unexamined sense. Third, Glaucon agrees to some claims that need examination. Again, Socrates, as depicted, would not be endorsing them.

5.4 WHAT ADEIMANTUS ACCEPTS CONCERNING PHILOSOPHERS DOES NOT SURVIVE EXAMINATION

Socrates concludes his explanation for Glaucon of whom Socrates means by philosophers:

Do we not seem to you to have gone through each of the things necessary and fol-lowing upon one another for the soul that is going to get hold of being sufficiently and completely? . . . Is it possible you will criticize in any way a practice which one would not become such as sufficiently to practice it if one were not by nature of good memory, quick to learn, suited for greatness, gracious, a friend and kin-dred to truth, justice, courage, temperance . . . To such people only, when they are perfected in education and age, would you not turn over the city? (486e1–487a8).

Adeimantus now responds with an objection that leads to Socrates' further explanation of philosophers for Adeimantus:

One might say that in discussion he cannot oppose you on each point that is questioned, but that he can see in fact that of those who start out in philosophy, not merely touching upon it for the sake of getting educated and then leaving it behind when still young, but spending a longer time occupied in it, most become altogether weird – so that we don't say totally wicked – and those who seem the most decent suffer this by reason of the pursuit you praise: becoming useless for their cities . . . How can you be speaking well when you say that cities will have no rest from evils before the philosophers rule in them, whom we agree to be useless to them? (487c4–e)

Adeimantus doesn't know if these objections are true, but (487d) "would gladly hear" Socrates' opinion. Adeimantus wants to be a hearer. Socrates replies: "You would hear that they appear to me to speak the truth." Socrates is about to grant Adeimantus' wish to be a hearer.

Adeimantus, representing the objectors, clearly already has in mind a group of people whom he considers to be engaging in philosophy past their youth. Representing the objectors, he doesn't mention any details of the philosophers as spectators-of-unchangeable-being-and-knowables that Socrates described in book 5. Nor does he mention any particular figures, including Socrates. And the *Republic* hasn't shown us Socrates as a philosopher of the type described in book 5, who spectates things themselves (479–480) in preference to changeable things. Mostly our Socrates has been discussing practical arrangements about specific matters.[12] Although Adeimantus does not ever call Socrates a philosopher, Adeimantus apparently thinks of Socrates as a philosopher: he accepts Socrates' including himself as one of the small group of philosophers that "keep company with philosophy as fits [its] worth" (496b). That Adeimantus thinks that Socrates arrived at his proposal that philosophers should rule by a process of irresistible questions to Glaucon is evidence that Adeimantus thinks that at least Socrates' philosophical practice involves question-and-answer conversation plus deduction. Question-and-answer is also more likely to be the sort of philosophy that the people Adeimantus thinks have gone on in philosophy too long would have been doing in their youth, rather than spectating beauty itself like the philosophers of Socrates' account for Glaucon in book 5. Book 5's account mentions only spectating forms (479e6: *theômenous*), not questioning and answering. At 537d–e Glaucon still has in mind that philosophy as understood by some people involves question-and-answer conversation. Glaucon agrees that the practice of dialectic has a bad effect, because when young people get their first taste of refuting and getting refuted, they start to distrust everything: "they themselves and the whole activity of philosophy become the objects of slander among the rest of men" (539c).

So Adeimantus' objection at 487 seems to be ignoring the conception of philosophers that Socrates so deliberately set out in book 5. Despite Socrates' having given the supposedly clarifying account of philosophy of book 5, Adeimantus still has fixed in mind his own conception of current philosophers who do question-and-answer deduction and refutation, the conception that apparently coincides with what the ridiculers and the many think of as philosophers.

I select a few parts of the discussion with Adeimantus from 487 to 495 for remark.

---

[12] Scott (2008, 380) asks if what Socrates is doing in the *Republic* is "philosophy in the true sense of the word," that is, philosophy as Socrates explains it in books 5–7. Scott decides not. But Schofield (2006, 9) says that "a lot of the philosophy in the dialogue" is on political questions.

Remark 1

At 487e–488a Socrates chides Adeimantus for making fun of Socrates after throwing Socrates into "the ill-provable (*dusapodeikton* (488a1)) argument." This seems most likely to be an allusion to the large task the brothers set Socrates in book 2. However, it could be an allusion to the task of the immediate context: to defend the proposal that philosophers should rule. In either case the word "ill-provable" raises the suspicion that whatever Socrates will come up with will not actually convince him.

Remark 2

Socrates next (488a–489c) undertakes to explain why people think philosophers are useless: he offers the image of a skilled ship pilot, one who pays attention to the seasons, the heaven, the stars, and the winds (488d), who is scorned by the group of sailors on board who take over the ship. Socrates compares the sailors to statesmen in power, and the true pilot to the philosopher (489b–c). The hard-of-hearing and short-sighted ship owner chained up by the sailors stands for the rest of the city, the *dêmos*. The statesmen are apparently the ones who say that philosophers are useless (489c). Socrates says to Adeimantus:

I do not think you need the image examined (*exetazomenên*) to see that it is like the cities with regard to their disposition toward the true philosophers. (489a4–6)

Adeimantus agrees. But we can disagree strongly: Adeimantus does need the image examined. In what way is study of stars and winds comparable to the study of justice itself and beauty itself? The skilled pilot who knows about wind itself and stars themselves but doesn't recognize a particular wind and a particular star would be in trouble.

Remark 3

Socrates previously described the knowledge that was the outcome of the guardians' education thus:

Then . . . [is] what I say so? – that we will not be educated before (nor those whom we say must be educated as guardians) until we know (*gnôrizômen*) the different forms of temperance and bravery and liberality and suitability for greatness and such things as are kindred to these, and again their opposites, everywhere they turn up, and we perceive them being in the things in which they are, both them and their images, and we do not disdain them in small things or in great, but we think that [they are the object] of the same skill (*technês*) and care (*meletês*)? (402b9–c)

That sort of particular knowledge would not be possible for the philosophers as described in book 5 who have knowledge only about such items as justice itself.

The image of the ship pilot needs explanation even if we grant that there is a rather vague point about the image applicable to many spheres: sometimes in order to do a certain task, you need to undertake some preliminary studies that are not obviously connected with it. One might want to build a bridge and be surprised that a first step would be to learn some mathematics and physics. But the usefulness of the preliminary study can be explained to hopeful bridge-builders, and is confirmed by the existence of operating bridges designed by people who did the preliminary study. Adeimantus has not yet seen a convincing explanation of how spectating justice itself and the like will lead to skill at governing cities. And Socrates only speculates later (499c–d) that there might have been actual governments that would confirm it. Adeimantus should have asked for some clarification.

Remark 4

Let us grant that some people say that the philosopher (as they conceive of philosophers) is one who looks on things above (*meteôroskopon*) and an idle talker (*adoleschên*) (489a). But the philosophers Socrates described in book 5 are not looking at the heavens. Nor have we been told that the philosophers of book 5 might be called idle talkers or that they talk much at all. The idle talkers or chatterers we hear about in other dialogues are mostly not talking about beauty itself. At *Sophist* 225d disputation that is done because a person enjoys eristic and earns no money from it is idle chatter. At *Theaetetus* 195d Socrates is annoyed at his own idle chatter – "dragging arguments up and down" and not dropping any argument. At *Phaedo* 70c no one would say Socrates is talking idly when on his death day he discusses whether a person's soul exists after the person has died. The suggestion is that some people might say that to discuss that when death was not imminent was idle chatter. (See also *Phaedrus* 269e for idle chatter.) The going conception of idle chatter seems to be general enough to cover any speculation or discussion of topics that are controversial, not standardly resolvable, and not about to have practical results. Again Adeimantus, as he agrees that the philosopher would be accused of idle chatter, seems to have in mind his preconception of philosophers as conversationalists of a certain kind, rather than the new conception of philosophers as spectators of being just outlined in book 5.

Remark 5

Adeimantus agrees at 493d–494a that the multitude can't accept that there is the fine itself, as distinct from the many fine things. We saw in the discussion with Glaucon that it is implausible that the multitude can't accept that. Either Adeimantus is not thinking clearly about the multitude or he has an inflated view, not required by what Socrates has actually said so far, of what the fine itself is.

Remark 6

Adeimantus believes that the majority are not capable of being philosophers (494a3). Therefore (*ara anagkê*), they blame people who do philosophize (494a5–6). The "therefore" is not explained.

Remark 7

Socrates next explains how talented young people – those for whom it is easy to learn, who have good memories, courage, and generosity and suitability for greatness (494b) – are turned away from philosophy. Socrates is expanding on Adeimantus' claim that some who start out in philosophy become bad, as distinct from useless (487d; 489d–e; 490d). People who want to make use of a talented young person will flatter him:

Won't such a one be first among all in everything, straight from the beginning, especially if his body matches his soul? . . . Kinsmen and fellow-citizens will surely want to make use of him when he is older for their own affairs . . . They will, therefore, lie at his feet begging and honoring him, taking possession of and flattering beforehand the power that is going to be his . . . What do you suppose . . . such a young man will do in such circumstances, especially if he chances to be from a big city, is rich and noble in it, and is, further, good-looking and tall? Won't he be overflowing with unbounded hope, believing he will be competent to mind the business of both Greeks and barbarians, and won't he, as a result, exalt himself to the heights, mindlessly full of pretension and empty conceit? . . . Now if someone were gently to approach the young man in this condition and tell him the truth – that there is no sense (*nous*) in him although he needs it, and that it's not to be acquired except by slaving for its acquisition – do you think it will be easy for him to hear through a wall of so many evils? . . . But if . . . thanks to his good nature and his kinship to such speeches, one young man were to apprehend something and be turned and drawn toward philosophy, what do we suppose those will do who believe they are losing his use and comradeship? Is there any deed they won't do or word they won't say, concerning him, so that he won't be persuaded, and concerning the man who's doing the persuading, so that he won't be able to persuade, and won't they organize private plots and public trials? . . . Is it possible that such a man will philosophize? (494b–495a)

Adeimantus agrees that this initially talented person won't philosophize ("Not at all" (*ou panu:* 495a)).

Again it would have been helpful if Adeimantus had asked for some examination of several parts of the extreme position that he agrees to:

(a) He might have asked: if this talented young person philosophizes "not at all," how did he ever get identified as a philosopher by the ordinary people who think philosophers are bad? Perhaps we are to assume that at least in his youth he engaged in the question-and-answer conversation that Adeimantus' imagined objector thought of as included in philosophy. Then after having done this minimal philosophizing in his youth, this wonderful young person philosophizes not at all in the manner of the philosophers described in book 5. If that is what Adeimantus meant, his "Not at all" should then have been qualified.

(b) Adeimantus might have asked if Socrates is talking about people who have the nature suitable for a philosopher (492a) – people who *would* be good at philosophy (spectating the forms) if they took it up, but who never get a chance to do that and instead get corrupted and do the greatest harm to cities (495b). Adeimantus' reply "Not at all" is then appropriate, but we want to ask: how then, since these people do not ever actually do what counts as philosophy, do they contribute to the reputation that philosophers become vicious?

(c) Some readers think that Glaucon and Adeimantus display the nature of a philosopher that Socrates outlines at 485b–487a, 491a–492a, and 494b.[13] If so, then we want to ask if the young Glaucon and Adeimantus are not the very people who are most likely to be flattered into thinking they are competent to mind the business of both Greeks and barbarians. They are after all advising Socrates on the plans for the construction of an entire civic structure for the best city. If they are these flatterable young people, then they fit the description that Adeimantus agrees to: that if someone told the young person in this condition the truth – that he has no sense (*nous*) in him, but he needs it and won't get it unless he slaves for it (494d5–9) – it would not be easy for him to hear.

---

[13] For example, Blondell (2002, 211).

And then they are most likely to be those turned away from philosophy (494e–495a).

(d) We might also ask if Adeimantus thinks Socrates has a nature less suited for philosophy than the philosophic nature Socrates refers to (492). There is no evidence that Socrates was "first in everything" (494b) – for example, presumably, athletics and studies such as mathematics and music. (*Euthydemus* 272c tells us that Socrates took up harp-playing, laughably, late in life.) We know Socrates wasn't especially tall, good-looking, or well-connected in family. He would luckily have been able to escape the flatterers. But could he still do philosophy with his less-than-perfectly-suited nature?

Remark 8

Socrates next explains how unworthy practitioners take up philosophy to fill the spaces left empty by the absence of the people most suited for philosophy who have been led away from it by flatterers. It seems likely that he means that these unworthy practitioners take up what some people call philosophy, perhaps refutation or some practice of "idle chatter." It doesn't seem likely that he means that they take up philosophy as the spectating of being as in book 5. According to Socrates these unworthy people take up philosophy (of some sort) because of its prestige. They then give philosophy a bad reputation:

Unworthy men come to her – like an orphan bereft of relatives – and disgrace her. These are the ones who attach to her reproaches such as even you say are alleged by the men who reproach her – namely, that of those who have intercourse with her, some are worthless and the many worthy of many bad things . . . For other little men see that the place has become empty although full of fine names and pretensions; and just like those who run away from prisons to temples, those men too who are cleverest at their own little arts are overjoyed to skip from their arts into philosophy. For even though philosophy is faring thus, its prestige (*axiôma*) remains more magnificent (*megaloprepesteron*: more fitting for greatness) compared to the other arts. (495c–d)

This statement about prestige deserves some reflection.

According to what Adeimantus has agreed to earlier, most people think philosophy is idle chatter or star-gazing: philosophy nevertheless has prestige (Allen (2006): "prestige"; Reeve (2004): "reputation"; Bloom (1968): "magnificent station"). We want to ask: prestige from whom? Prestige or esteem of course comes from being admired – by someone who has some credentials for making a judgment of admiration. If someone that lacks understanding of your admirable accomplishment admires you, then such admiration lends you no prestige. If only the people who practice philosophy unworthily grant it prestige, then those who scorn them would have no reason to think it prestigious. So we naturally wonder who is conferring this prestige on philosophy and what would be the best way to express the thought to which Adeimantus agrees. Perhaps we can unfold his thought into a number of implicit claims:

(a) There is an activity that some people call "philosophy" (perhaps idle chatter).
(b) Certain people – ((i) other than the people who practice idle chatter? or (ii) the very people who practice the activity of (a)?) – admire the activity of (a).
(c) So yet other people take up the activity in (a).
(d) There is another activity (spectating forms) that we (as in book 5) are calling "philosophy."
(e) People not involved in (a), (b), (c), or (d) think that the people who are doing (a) are worthless.
(f) The people of (e) therefore think that the people who do activity (d) are worthless (because the people of (e) don't realize that "philosophy" is used for rather different things).

Since most people (consider the insane majority at 496c) have been excluded as not having good judgment, and since the opinion of the few people who understand what philosophy (as described in book 5) is will not matter to the people who scorn philosophers, it is still difficult to see where the philosophy of type (a) is getting its prestige from. Does it have prestige only for its practitioners? But they should not be able to confer prestige in the eyes of scornful nonpractitioners. We wish Adeimantus had asked for more clarification on this point.

Remark 9

Adeimantus assents to these questions:

When men unworthy of education come near her [philosophy] and keep her company not according to [her] worth (*kat' axian*), what sort of notions and opinions will we say they beget? Won't they be truly fit to be called sophisms, connected with nothing genuine or worthy of true thoughtfulness (*phronêseôs*)? (496a)

Here we naturally ask: what is it to keep company with philosophy not according to its worth? Perhaps it is to say that one is a philosopher when one has in mind some conception of philosophy other than the one that Socrates sketched in book 5 – the conception that Adeimantus doesn't seem firmly to have in mind anyway. We also want to ask: what are the ill-begotten sophisms? Book 5 precludes there being sophisms about the fine itself and the just itself: they are the objects of knowledge, never of opinion (477a2–3; 478a11–13). So the ill-begotten sophisms must be on some other topic. If so, then they wouldn't be instances of philosophy as described in book 5. So again Adeimantus must have in mind his own conception of philosophy. What Adeimantus is assenting to here seems to amount to: there is some activity someone calls "philosophy" that produces bad arguments and is not what Socrates was describing as philosophy in book 5; people who practice it unworthily – but "unworthily" now seems superfluous, since it is an unworthy practice to begin with – give whatever is called "philosophy" a bad name.

Remark 10

Socrates then describes a very small group "of those who keep company with philosophy according to [her] worth (*kat' axian*: as it deserves)" (496a11–12). He lists persons of five different sorts that might be in this group: (a) someone who is in exile away from corrupting influences; (b) a great soul living in a small city that stays out of the city's affairs; (c) some few people who come to philosophy from some other art they disdain; (d) some like Theages whose sickness keeps them away from political affairs; (e) and "not worth mentioning" – "our case (*to hêmeteron*)," the divine sign. (The divine sign is not worth mentioning because it has perhaps occurred in few or no people before.) Adeimantus presumably takes Socrates to mean that Socrates is one of this small group that keeps company with philosophy worthily because of his divine sign.

Does Adeimantus think that he and Glaucon are in this small group that escaped corruption along with Socrates? If so, into which of the five groups do they fall?

Remark 11

Socrates says that if there were a suitable city for the nature of a philosopher to grow up in it will make plain that it really was divine and the rest are human, in terms of both their natures and their practices. (497b–c)

"[W]as" suggests that this was a point that came up earlier. Whatever Socrates is referring to, he repeats the point that philosophers are close to divine later at 500b–e when he is still speaking to Adeimantus:

A man who has his understanding truly turned toward the things that are has no leisure to look down toward the affairs of human beings and to be filled with envy . . . But rather, because he sees and contemplates things that are in a regular arrangement and are always in the same condition, things that neither do injustice to one another nor suffer it at one another's hands, but remain all in order according to reason – he imitates them and, as much as possible, makes himself like them. Or do you suppose there is any way of keeping someone from imitating that which he admires and therefore keeps company with? . . . Then it's the philosopher, keeping company with the divine and the orderly, who becomes orderly and divine, to the extent that is possible for a human being. (500d)

Here we want to ask: how does contemplating the orderly and divine make one closer to being orderly and divine? In any number of cases contemplating and thus keeping company with something that one admires has no tendency whatsoever to make one similar to the thing one admires and contemplates.

Remark 12

At 499d Socrates suspects that Adeimantus would still say that the many would think it impossible for philosophers to be rulers. Socrates says:

Don't make such a severe accusation against the many. They will no doubt have another sort of opinion if instead of indulging yourself in quarreling with them, you soothe them and do away with the slander against the love of learning (*philomath-ias*) by pointing out whom you mean by the philosophers, and by distinguishing, as was just done, their nature and the character of their practice so the many won't believe you mean those whom they believe to be philosophers. (499e–500a)

Socrates' reply again recognizes that there are different views of what counts as a philosopher. The philosophers that he described in book 5 are evidently not what the many currently think of as philosophers.

Remark 13

Adeimantus agrees when Socrates asks:

Then don't you also agree that the harshness of the masses toward philosophy is caused by those outsiders who do not belong and who have burst in . . . abusing one another, being disposed to love envy (*philapechthêmonôs*), and always making statements about human beings – doing what is least appropriate to philosophy? (500b)

Here we want to ask whether, as he agrees to this, Adeimantus thinks that the philosophy that outsiders burst into is philosophy understood via his preconception of philosophy as involving inescapable questioning or whether he is thinking of outsiders bursting into the activity that Socrates described in book 5. The latter seems unlikely. Whatever he has in mind, he is agreeing that something "least appropriate to philosophy" is talking about individual people.[14] Also, he agrees that it is people who love envy – that is, I take it, people who love to be envied, who have made the many harsh toward philosophy.

5.5 WHAT CAN WE CONCLUDE FROM THE DESCRIPTION OF THE PHILOSOPHER FOR ADEIMANTUS?

The account Socrates gives of philosophers for Adeimantus (487–495) expands on the account of book 5 for Glaucon. Adeimantus seems to have trouble keeping the latter in mind instead of his preconceived notion of philosophers. On Socrates' account for Adeimantus philosophers have rare natural capacities (491b); they accept some views that the many can't accept (493e–494a); people unable to philosophize (because of being unable to accept that the fine itself is, rather than the many fine things) blame philosophers (494a); philosophers are not honored by the many (488–9); yet philosophers have enough prestige to attract hangers on or imitators who associate with philosophy unworthily (495d–e). Philosophers think about what is changeless and divine; they therefore approach closer to being divine themselves (497b–c; 500c–d). It is least appropriate for philosophers to talk about human beings (individual people) (500b). People who love envy have made most people dislike philosophy (500b).

We don't know if Adeimantus thinks that he has the nature of a philosopher. We can tell that he finds most ordinary people to be inadequate. If Adeimantus does think of himself as a philosopher, he thinks he is quite special. If so, then he has also agreed to the implication for special young

---

[14] Shorey (1963, 68), note a suggests this refers to gossip. Telling anecdotes or name-dropping seem other possible references.

people (494d5–9) that he needs someone to tell him he has no sense in him and that he should slave to get it.

We cannot say, as we could for Glaucon, that the account Adeimantus accepts of philosophers is plainly inconsistent. So we do not have, as we had for the account that Glaucon accepts, the strongest reason to say that the account could not possibly express Socrates' own convictions about the practice he engages in. However, we do have the point that Socrates says it is an "ill-provable argument" that Adeimantus has "thrown" him into. We have the important but explicitly unexamined metaphor of the ship pilot to start off the discussion. We have many confused details for which Adeimantus should have asked clarification. These things are reasons to say Socrates does not believe his account of philosophers here.

5.6 THE EFFECT OF DISTANCING SOCRATES FROM THE CONTENT OF HIS SPEECH IN BOOKS 2–10

Chapter 4, section 4.9 (pp. 118–119) claimed that for three main reasons Glaucon and Adeimantus have ownership of the city constructed in imagination in the *Republic*.

In addition to those reasons, there are many indications throughout the dialogue that Socrates sees his speech as something that the brothers have ownership of. For example, at 470e4 Socrates refers to "the city you are founding," and at 473b to "all you have prescribed." At 474 he asks if Glaucon is not responsible for any ridicule Socrates will get for his proposal that philosophers rule; Glaucon agrees that he is responsible. We have seen that at 487e7–488a1 Socrates comments that Adeimantus has "thrown" him into an ill-demonstrable argument. At 458c6 he says to Glaucon, "Now, you are their lawgiver, and in just the way you selected the men, you will select the women." At 517b5–6 Socrates says, speaking to Glaucon of the image of the cave-prison and the upward journey to the light, "you long (*epithumeis:* you have an appetite) to hear of this – but god knows if it is true." Socrates indicates that the cave simile with its distinction of most people from some one or few enlightened or elite is especially the sort of thing that Glaucon wants to hear. The phrasing "you long to hear" is perhaps a reminder of the phrasing, using the same verb, with which Glaucon and Adeimantus prompted Socrates' speech (358b: Glaucon says, "I long to hear"; 367b: Adeimantus says "longing to hear").

My thesis that Glaucon and Adeimantus have ownership of the *Republic* does not entail my thesis that Socrates does not. Rather, my separate evidence that Socrates does not himself accept everything he proposes is that much that Socrates proposes and that the brothers accept does not survive examination. Although we do not discover that it is unacceptable in the same way as we discover that proposals in other dialogues are unacceptable – by watching Socrates examine them – we can discover its unacceptability by doing our own examining. To find from our own examination that a proposal is inconsistent or very unclear is as good as finding that Socrates, as depicted, cannot endorse it.

If we accept that what Socrates says need not express his own convictions but instead reveals the thoughts of his interlocutors, what difference does that make? If we say that a great deal of the *Republic* represents insupportable inclinations and assumptions of Glaucon and Adeimantus, do we imply that we have less reason to work at interpreting or understanding the *Republic* than if we think that its many puzzling statements represent the convictions of Socrates, as depicted, or of Plato? Do we then make it too easy to interpret the *Republic?* Whenever a passage seems confused, instead of trying to understand, do we have a good excuse to give up and to declare that it represents a hopeless confusion of one of the brothers?

I think not: in fact, not at all. I will say more about that later. My proposed interpretation does, however, have some effects on my own reading. One effect is that I can welcome it when commentators' examinations discover that bits of the *Republic* are incoherent or flawed. Such discoveries are entirely consistent with my view that the *Republic* is designed to draw attention to the confusion of the interlocutors. A second effect is that because I have distanced Socrates from his proposals in the *Republic*, I do not have the worry that I must say that Socrates, as depicted, or Plato is oddly inconsistent or careless or confused or that certain passages are not to be pressed too hard or taken too seriously. I do not have to account for the unlikelihood that Socrates, as depicted, was inconsistent or careless, because so far I have no evidence that he was. Insofar as Socrates is not depicted as inconsistent or careless, I have no evidence that Plato was.

The question "Why does Plato depict Socrates as endorsing outrageous and unsustainable proposals?" then becomes unnecessary. But another question becomes of interest: What sort of people are Glaucon and Adeimantus that Socrates as depicted would think them an appropriate audience for the sort of speech he addresses to them?

5.7 THE CHARACTERS OF GLAUCON AND ADEIMANTUS

I do not have a solid or complete answer to that question. A clear possibility is that the brothers are so eager for passive instruction from Socrates.[15] They are so hopeful about the possibility of an utterly compelling, brief – day-long, rather than life-long – speech for a life-determining conclusion (596a; 608d; 614b) that they are willing to suspend their critical powers and to be receptive to novel proposals unexamined on this occasion.[16]

Beyond the brothers' obvious eagerness, does the *Republic* tell us more about them to help us answer more fully our question why they assent to proposals of Socrates that do not withstand examination? So far as I can see, the dialogue does not give us much independent evidence about them. By "independent evidence" I mean evidence that does not consist simply in their assent to what Socrates puts to them.[17] It is unfortunate for me that there isn't much independent evidence, because independent evidence would provide a clear way of testing – possibly confirming or possibly falsifying – my interpretation. But just the recognition that there is conceivably falsifying data is important. It is important to me that I should be able to at least imagine something that would falsify my hypothesis about the *Republic*.[18] The conceivability of such potentially falsifying data

---

[15] Blondell (2002, 201) points out usefully that the respondents don't have pretensions of the sort that other interlocutors do and comments that Socrates has then no reason to "provoke or deflate" them. I would object that because the brothers are overeager to be told what to believe, Socrates has much reason to examine them. Evidence of overeagerness is this exchange. Glaucon says: "Don't hesitate . . . Your hearers won't be hard-hearted, or distrustful, or ill-willed" (450d).

Socrates doesn't take that as encouragement:

Best of men, presumably you're saying that because you wish to encourage me . . . Well, you're doing exactly the opposite . . . To make speeches (*tous logous poieisthai*) at a time when one is in doubt and seeking . . . is frightening . . . It's not because I'm afraid of being laughed at – that's childish – but because I'm afraid that . . . I'll not only fall myself but drag my friends down with me . . . I expect that it's a lesser fault to prove to be an unwilling murderer of someone than a deceiver about fine, good, and just things in laws. (450e–451b)

[16] As Penner (2005, 1) says of Socrates' account of justice:

What Socrates does . . . is to introduce a *new* conception of justice – one which would not have occurred to Thrasymachus, Glaucon, or Adeimantus in a million years unless Socrates had proposed it.

An example of Glaucon's extreme receptivity is at 530b where Socrates asks a question and Glaucon answers, "It certainly seems so to me, now when I hear it from you."

[17] For what we know about Glaucon and Adeimantus, see Nails (2002).

[18] I am indebted to Ellen Wagner for the important question concerning what I would count as evidence against my hypothesis that the brothers, and not Socrates, have ownership of *Republic* 2–10.

implies that my interpretation is not unfalsifiable. If it were unfalsifiable, it would be an entirely worthless interpretative effort.

For example, one thing that would independently falsify my claim would be the brothers' dissenting deliberately from something Socrates proposes and then goes on to develop. That would be evidence that the *Republic* does not reveal the brothers' assumptions and inclinations. But there is no such development-despite-dissent. A second, more indirect kind of falsifying evidence, falling short of the brothers' directly denying some statement of Socrates', would be some sign that they are not really the sort of people to accept Socrates' proposals. For example, if there were evidence that Glaucon was well known to be a pacifist, or that Adeimantus, who censors the arts severely, had a long-standing side career as an actor, that kind of inconsistency would raise doubts that they have ownership of the *Republic*. But so far as I know, there is no such evidence inside or outside the *Republic*.

Here I will simply give the short collection of what I have noticed so far, mostly about Glaucon, that seems to me somewhat independent evidence about the brothers.

Socrates says to the brothers:

You are the sons of a great man, and Glaucon's lover began his elegy well when he wrote celebrating your achievements at the battle of Megara. (368a)

This tells us that Glaucon was at least twenty at the time of the *Republic* and probably not more than twenty[19] and that Glaucon has distinguished himself in battle.

An important piece of independent evidence is Glaucon's spontaneous intervention to call the first city a "city of pigs." That entirely spontaneous contribution – not something directly elicited by a declaration or question from Socrates – tells us that Glaucon is not satisfied with the simple city and, very importantly, it tells us that he was not impressed by its deliberate project of avoiding war.

Another of Glaucon's spontaneous interventions is to add something to Socrates' hesitant suggestion (468b) that someone who has distinguished himself in battle should while on campaign kiss and be kissed by each of the adolescents and children who are with the army: Glaucon volunteers the addition that "while they are still on campaign, no one he [the distinguished warrior] wants to kiss (*philein*) shall be allowed to refuse, so that if he

---

[19] Nails (2002) at the entries for Glaucon, Adeimantus, and Plato gives the likely birthdates: Adeimantus 432; Glaucon 429, and Plato 424.

passionately loves another, whether male or female, he will try harder to win the prize for bravery." (Glaucon has not provided for the possibility that a second warrior equally distinguished for bravery with the first, might not want to be kissed by the first.) That tells us that Glaucon is erotic (for which see also 475d) and somewhat self-centered.

Glaucon likes enumerations. Glaucon's first spontaneous contribution to book 2 is his three-fold distinction of kinds of goods. He contributes another enumeration at 400a. Another spontaneous contribution tells us that Glaucon is a fan of solid geometry (528d: "outstandingly appealing").[20]

According to Adeimantus, Glaucon is ambitious, and a lover of honor (548d–e).

Glaucon is evidently a regular associate of Socrates. He has spent the day in company with Socrates.

Socrates knows that Glaucon breeds birds and dogs (459a). If Glaucon is experienced with dogs, his agreement (at 376) that dogs welcome familiar people from whom they have "never experienced anything good" – i.e. by whom they have been mistreated – should make us suspicious about how much he is retaining his critical faculties as he listens to Socrates. It is odd that Socrates' statements about dogs didn't inspire Glaucon's dissent as immediately as did Socrates' proposal of a city without standard relishes (372).

Outside the *Republic* we read that Adeimantus, but apparently not Glaucon, was present at Socrates' trial (*Apology* 34a). Neither brother was at his execution. Glaucon is a silent auditor in the frame dialogue of the *Parmenides*, while Adeimantus has a few welcoming words there. And we perhaps learn that Glaucon developed a distaste for philosophy, if the Glaucon addressed in the *Symposium* (173a) is the same as the Glaucon of the *Republic*.[21]

From outside Plato's writings we read in Xenophon's depiction (*Memorabilia* III, vi) that Glaucon had political ambitions when about twenty years old, and Socrates took an interest in Glaucon because of Plato. By Nails' (2002) chronology Plato is then about fifteen. Xenophon portrays Glaucon as unable coherently to answer Socrates' questions about how Glaucon will help the city in which he wants to be politically prominent.

That is all I can produce as somewhat independent evidence about the brothers from the *Republic* and elsewhere.

Slightly less independent evidence is some of Glaucon's responses to Socrates' prompts. Socrates alludes to mathematical practice and

---

[20] Blondell (2002, 204 and 200) notices this.   [21] As Nails (2002) thinks. See under "Glaucon."

mathematicians in talking with Glaucon (510c–e; 525d: "You surely know what people who are clever in these matters are like"; 526a: "Now have you ever noticed that those who are naturally good at calculation are also naturally acute in practically all subjects?"): Socrates apparently assumes that Glaucon is familiar with mathematical practice, or at least has opinions about it. Glaucon agrees with the Pythagoreans that the sciences of astronomy and harmonics are akin. Socrates seems rather careful to attach the Pythagorean view to Glaucon (the question he asks uses the word "we"; I take it to be the questioner's way of signaling that he will use the answers his answerer supplies, not to imply that what is extracted is also a conviction of the questioner):

"They say, and we, Glaucon, agree. Or how do we react?" "Just so," he said. (530d8)

So we know that Glaucon has some acquaintance with Pythagorean ideas. The reference to Pythagoreans seems important, as the sole explicit mention of Pythagoreans in Plato's dialogues. Socrates goes on to say, apparently about the Pythagoreans he has referred to, that they look for numbers but they do not ascend to problems and to asking why (*dia ti*) certain numbers are concordant. Glaucon agrees with that, too. Here at least he shows that even if he has some agreement with the Pythagoreans, he is willing to accept Socrates' invitation to criticize them and go beyond them.

Glaucon refers to himself and Adeimantus, and perhaps others, as *akousmenoi*, hearers (450d). This may be an allusion to Pythagoreanism, since the followers of Pythagoras were his "hearers."

Glaucon is familiar with talk of forms. At 475e–476d Socrates says it would not be easy to explain what he is about to say to someone other than Glaucon. Socrates then talks about forms for the first time in the *Republic*.[22]

Something else that might shed light on Glaucon is that in speaking to Glaucon at certain major points in the *Republic* Socrates uses the vocative, "dear Glaucon": this occurs when Socrates introduces philosopher-rulers (473d5–6), when he marks the relationship between the image of the cave and the earlier images of the sun and line (517a8), when he says Glaucon would be unable to follow if he talked about the power of dialectic (532e–533a), when he says that the contest that concerns becoming good or bad is a great one (608b), and when, relating the myth of Er, he speaks of the risk involved in a choice of life (618b). Halliwell says:[23]

---

[22] Adam (1963) on 476a.   [23] Halliwell, quoted from (1995, 93–94).

[T]he emphasis of the vocative contributes to the parainetic seriousness, or even portentousness, of Socrates' tenor, at the same time as it locates his utterances on the level not of public statement (despite the presence of an audience) but of a deeply personal communication of beliefs with one young friend.

I would take the affectionate vocative at these interesting points in the *Republic* also to indicate how important these particular sites in the conversation are for the revelation of Glaucon's character.

I will now use that small amount of information, together with our impression of the brothers from their conversation with Socrates, as a basis for some tentative proposals about the brothers.

Glaucon's interest in mathematical studies makes him a likely audience for Socrates' proposals about the mathematical education of the guardians in book 7. Glaucon's interest in mathematics and no distaste for war makes Glaucon a naturally receptive audience to Socrates' several mentions that mathematics and geometry are especially studies for warriors (522e; 525b; 526d; 527c). That Glaucon likes to enumerate and likes mathematics could explain why Socrates addresses most of the enumerative or mathematical points to Glaucon. For example, when Glaucon re-enters the conversation at 398d Socrates addresses him with an enumeration.

It's interesting to speculate, but is of course no more than a speculation triggered by the mention of Glaucon's agreement with the Pythagoreans on the one point that astronomy and harmonics are akin, that Glaucon has some interest in and perhaps sympathy to some Pythagorean thought. I emphasize "some." I certainly do not claim that Glaucon is sympathetic to every Pythagorean idea, especially since it is difficult to say when a particular idea should be called "Pythagorean." (And there was a strand of Pythagorean thought that was not interested in mathematics, but only in *akousmata*, the sayings of Pythagoras.) If Glaucon was attracted to certain Pythagorean ideas, that attraction could explain a number of details of the *Republic*. (i) It would explain why Socrates thinks it appropriate to address two extravagant numerological proposals to Glaucon and could expect Glaucon's assent. One extravagant proposal is the imagined account of the Muses (546a–d) that there is a nuptial number – perhaps 12, 960,000 – that it is crucial to calculate correctly to determine appropriate breeding dates for the guardian class. Another extravagant proposal is the calculation that the just man's life is 729 times more pleasant than the unjust man's (587b–588a). Since one group of Pythagoreans had numerological views, someone sympathetic to that thread in Pythagorean thought might be sympathetic to these extravagant proposals about the power of calculation.[24] Socrates introduces the proof that the just man's life is 729 times more pleasant than the unjust man's life by reporting what Socrates has heard from some "wise men" (583b): that pleasures other than those of the knowledge-able person are like shadow-drawings or illusory paintings. Glaucon after some discussion accepts that as a part of the proof. Adam (1963) believes the wise men referred to are Orphic or Pythagorean ascetics. (ii) Glaucon's eagerness for war and his interest in the military relates to Pythagoreans. Pythagoreans were prominently involved in the practical application of mathematics to warfare.[25] (iii) Another Pythagorean strand in what Socrates addresses to Glaucon is the story of the transfer of souls from one species to another in a long cycle of lives after death (618a–620d).[26] (iv) Sympathy with some Pythagorean distinctions would explain why Glaucon is recep-tive to hearing that some people are "true philosophers" and others are not. The Pythagoreans had intra-sect distinctions. The *mathêmatikoi* thought the *akousmatikoi* were insufficiently Pythagorean.[27] That is relevant to the topic of philosophers because ancient reports had it that Pythagoras invented the word "philosopher" to label himself. (See the discussion of Pythagoras in chapter 6, p. 167.) A sect that rejected others as Pythagore-ans was likely to be rejecting them also as philosophers. (v) Sympathy

---

[24] Burkert (1972, 481) finds a probable relation of the nuptial number with Pythagoreanism. Burkert (1972, 477–481) discusses interest in numerical correspondences. See also Burkert (1972, 429).

[25] Kingsley (1995, 145) says:

[T]he early stages of innovation in the design of weaponry depended heavily on the practical applica-tion of mathematics, and Pythagoreans are known to have been pioneers in this very field; . . . During the late fifth and early fourth centuries southern Italy and Syracuse, which were centers of Pythagore-anism at the time, were also at the forefront in the innovative design and production of machines of war. Second, and more specifically, . . . the one person who during this period was associated most closely with applied mathematics, and in particular with breakthroughs in the field of mechanics, was . . . Archytas . . . Ancient sources link the Pythagorean school of Archytas – who was himself elected by Tarentum seven times as its military general – not only with general advances in mechan-ical science but also with innovations in warfare and the design of weaponry . . . According to Pythagoreans, war is a harmony when correctly conducted.

[26] There is much evidence that Pythagoras and Pythagoreans believed that the souls of the dead transmigrated into other species. E.g. Xenophanes makes fun of that belief. See McKirahan (1994, 81–84).

[27] Iamblichus VP 81, 82 (DK58C4). Burkert (1972, 192–208) discusses the distinction between *mathêmatikoi* and *akousmatikoi* and Iamblichus' report. Burkert (1972, 205) says of developments in Pythagorean thought:

Since the "mathematical" tradition, in its Platonic metamorphosis, became completely dominant in the literary realm, the contention of the *mathêmatici* also won out, that the *akousmatici* were not genuine, but only imperfect Pythagoreans.

But Burkert (1972, 278) also says: "[S]ince the *acousmatici*, later on, did not recognize the *mathematici* as Pythagorean."

with Pythagorean thought would explain why Glaucon agrees that the best guardians are (469a) "god-like" people and why Adeimantus agrees that the guardians are to be as "god-like" (383c) as they can be. Adeimantus thinks that philosophers are "really divine" and that others are merely human (497b). Divine or near-divine status was ascribed to Pythagoras.[28] He was in fact deemed so divine that people avoided speaking his name but referred to him as "that man."[29] (vi) Pythagorean ascription of a kind of divinity to Pythagoras together with Socrates' awareness that the brothers have some sympathy with Pythagoreanism might explain a turn of phrase that scholars have puzzled over. Socrates addresses the brothers with the phrase, "children of that man" at 368a (*paides ekeinou tou andros*). There are a couple of possibilities for the reference of the phrase, "that man." The phrase "that man" is a conventional way to refer to someone deceased or notable, for example, possibly the deceased Ariston.[30] Adam (1963) thought that Socrates was referring to Thrasymachus as the ancestor of the position that Glaucon and Adeimantus want to explore.[31] But since the phrase is also a conventional way of referring to Pythagoras, the phrase "children of that man" could be a conventional way of referring to sympathizers with Pythagorean ideas. Socrates could here be using it to address the brothers as sympathizers with Pythagoreanism.[32] (vii) Adeimantus has some inclination toward another strand of Pythagorean thought. At 500c–d Socrates says to Adeimantus that the philosopher, who thinks of what is orderly and divine, becomes so.[33] As Richard McKirahan puts it:

The numerical basis of the *kosmos* implies that the *kosmos* is comprehensible to humans, and the knowledge of it which benefits our soul demands thought and understanding. Our soul becomes orderly (*kosmios*) when it understands the order in the universe. This is the inspiration that underlay the developments in Pythagorean thought.[34]

---

[28] Iamblichus *VP* 31, 53, 143–144.   [29] Iamblichus *VP* 88–89, 53.
[30] Shorey (1917, 436).   [31] Burnyeat (2004) sides with Adam.
[32] Burnyeat (2004, 84) says, "Shorey's Pythagorean allusion is much less suited to the dramatic context," and notes "not to mention that the *Republic*'s allusions to Pythagoras (600b) and Pythagoreans (530d–e and 531b–c) are somewhat distanced and critical." Even if we take the *Republic*'s actual references to Pythagoras and Pythagoreans as critical, that does not preclude Socrates' speaking of Glaucon and Adeimantus as followers of Pythagoras.
   The phrase "child of that man" is also used in the *Philebus* (36d 6–7). Again scholars have been puzzled, and again it might be a way of referring to Pythagoras, since the interlocutor of the *Philebus* is also addressed as though he has Pythagorean sympathies.
   Iamblichus *VP* 250 says that the Pythagorean Aristoxenus says that Epaminondas called the Pythagorean Lysis, who was his teacher, "father." That might be a trace of a practice going back to Pythagoras.
[33] Iamblichus *VP* 86: "Their whole way of life is arranged for following the god."
[34] McKirahan (1994, 114).

McKirahan cites *Republic* 6 500c–d, where Socrates speaks to Adeimantus. (viii) Glaucon is astonished at 608d that Socrates says that it is "not difficult" to say that the soul is immortal, and that it would be not difficult for Glaucon also. The Pythagorean view that the soul was immortal was itself a new way of bridging the gap between the divine and human.[35] Glaucon is surprised that there is a proof, but accepts it at 611. (ix) That Adeimantus has heard Pythagorean views and is troubled by them might mean that Pythagoreans are included among those people of whom Adeimantus said at 366 that they praise justice and blame injustice by mentioning the rewards or punishments that are their consequences in the afterlife.[36] (x) Socrates addresses Glaucon as someone who is aware that Pythagoras passed on a way of life to his followers (600b). This is the unique mention of Pythagoras by name in Plato's dialogues. (xi) Iamblichus, who wrote much later than Pythagoras, but who is nevertheless a source for Pythagorean lore, tells of the concern to preserve the way of life and not innovate:

> The philosophy of the *akousmatikoi* consists in unargued *akousmata* without proof to the effect that one must act in this way, and the other things that were spoken by that one, these things they guard closely as divine decrees. These people do not profess to say anything for themselves. (*VP* 82)

If Adeimantus had some sympathy for Pythagorean avoidance of innovation, that would help explain why he agrees at 424b that there can be "no innovation in musical or physical training that goes against the established order" in the city under construction. (xii) The inclusion of females among the guardian class is also evocative of Pythagorean practice.[37] Sympathy for Pythagorean treatment of women would explain Glaucon's and Adeimantus' acceptance of Socrates' proposal of the role of women in the *Republic*. (xiii) Pythagoreans held property in common, as do the philosopher-kings.[38] (xiv) Pythagoreans may have used the word "itself," which Socrates uses in discussing forms in books 5 and 6, as a technical

---

[35] McKirahan (1994, 85).

[36] McKirahan (1994, 86–87):

> The Pythagorean way of life . . . aimed to improve the soul and attain for it the best possible destiny, which consists either in attaining the best of reincarnations or in complete freedom from the necessity of continued rebirth.

> As Vegetti (1998, vol. II, 221–229) observes, Adeimantus is familiar with ritual practices and formulas (364b; 364e; 365e–366a) to ward off punishment after death.

[37] Kingsley (1995, 162) observes that the ancient sources emphasize that both men and women were Pythagoreans.

[38] Iamblichus *VP* 81. There is some problem with using Iamblichus as evidence here, because later Pythagoreans may have been ascribing to older Pythagoreans the way of life of the *Republic*.

locution.[39] If Glaucon and Adeimantus were familiar with and sympathetic to what Pythagoreans said about things themselves, we would have a partial explanation why the brothers accept what Socrates says. (Another part of the explanation is that, as I've said, most of what Socrates says on the topic of forms in the passage from books 5 and 6 discussed above is entirely natural and acceptable, despite Glaucon's agreement that it was difficult.)

It is admittedly speculative to connect the brothers' receptivity to many of the things that Socrates proposes with the brothers' prior sympathy to Pythagorean ideas. However, it is not speculation to suppose that there were Pythagorean views in the air at the time of the depicted Socrates, and to suppose that Pythagorean ideas might have had some attraction for people looking for a framework in which to think about how they might live their lives.

Our impression of what were the Pythagorean ideas in the air at the time is dim because we do not have texts for Pythagorean thought until after the time of Plato and because in the later reports we cannot well distinguish what are later accretions and what are genuine early elements possibly traceable to Pythagoras. Walter Burkert thinks that the survival of an interest in Pythagoreanism is partly due to the very lack of texts. Instead of texts, Burkert says, there was

a "name," which somehow corresponds to the persistent human longing for something which will serve to combine the hypnotic spell of the religious with the certainty of exact knowledge – an ideal which appeals, in ever-changing forms, to each successive generation.[40]

The "hypnotic spell of the religious" and the equally hypnotic spell of "the certainty of exact knowledge" are, however, safe to attach to Pythagorean lore at any time. And that is all I need to make reasonable, though of course not entirely firm, my proposal that an interest in Pythagorean ideas, as well as "the persistent human longing," would help to explain Glaucon's and Adeimantus' receptivity to many of Socrates' suggestions.

---

[39] Burnet (1930/1971, 308–309) thinks the *Phaedo* represents talk of forms, imitation of forms, and the use of "itself" as Pythagorean.

[40] Burkert (1972, 10–11). What precedes the passage quoted in the main text is this:

[T]he special difficulty in the study of Pythagoreanism comes from the fact that it was never so dead as, for example, the system of Anaxagoras or even that of Parmenides. When their systems had been superseded and lost all but their philological and historical interest, there still seemed to be in the spell of Pythagoras' name an invitation to further adaptation, reinterpretation, and extension. And at the source of this continuously changing stream lay not a book, an authoritative text which might be constructed and interpreted, nor authenticated acts of a historical person which might be put down as historical facts.

I will dwell on the point, which seems to me especially significant, that Glaucon likes enumerations and correspondences and that Socrates very often addresses to Glaucon proposals that have a mathematical flavor. In contrast, Socrates' addresses to Adeimantus very seldom involve any enumeration and never any more complicated moves. As previously mentioned, Glaucon's first contribution to the conversation in book 2 (357a–d) is an enumeration. Socrates addresses to Glaucon the division of the soul into three parts (439–441) and the mapping of the parts of the city onto the parts of the individual's soul (441). And as previously mentioned, Socrates addresses to Glaucon the proposal for marriage lotteries and the calculation of the "nuptial number." Socrates addresses to Glaucon the image of the divided line with its division of the four types that can be objects of belief or knowledge and the mapping of those onto four types of mental condition (509d–511e). Glaucon produces the serial listing of the first through fifth happiest types of people (580b). Socrates addresses to Glaucon the proof that the just man's life is 729 times more pleasant than the unjust man's life (588e). Socrates addresses to Glaucon an argument known as the third bed argument (597b–c). He addresses to Glaucon the proposal that the creations of artists are three steps removed from reality (602c). He addresses to Glaucon the one question about Pythagoras (600b) and the one question about Pythagoreans (530d8), mentioning that Pythagoreans find music and astronomy akin. We of course credit Pythagoreans for discovering the amazing applications of mathematics to music. However, on the less bright side, it seems, given the little we know about Pythagoreans, that they were overconfident that mathematical schemes give a useful approach to every problem. According to Aristotle, Pythagoreans thought that justice was a condition (*pathos*) of numbers (*Metaphysics* 985b27). Aristotle grumbles:

Pythagoras first attempted to speak about virtue, but not successfully. For by referring the virtues to numbers he submitted the virtues to a treatment that was not proper to them. Justice is not a square number. (*Magna Moralia* 1182a)

All the counting and mapping and measuring and numerology that appeal to Glaucon would be explained if Glaucon had that same overconfidence. Although that is hypothesis, not definite information, nevertheless, Socrates' addressing the mathematical or numerological proposals to Glaucon, and not to Adeimantus, illustrates how Socrates is tailoring his persuasive speech to his particular interlocutor. Socrates is acknowledging Glaucon's special receptivity to these proposals. It seems to me more likely that Plato is depicting Socrates humoring Glaucon and getting revealing reaction from Glaucon than that Plato is depicting what Socrates accepts because Plato now accepts it.

The regularity with which in addressing Glaucon Socrates either counts some items, or orders items in a sequence, or maps some number of items onto an equal number of items invites the question whether the reader is supposed to find this deep or comical.

That Glaucon seems to be a regular associate of Socrates here would at first incline me to think very positively about Glaucon as another promising young man. But Glaucon's expectation that he will hear an instructive lecture from the Socrates of book 1 seems a warning sign. It suggests to me that perhaps Glaucon has not been paying enough attention to Socrates, and isn't as familiar with him as one might expect from regular association. Glaucon, who has already spent a whole day with the Socrates who at the end of book 1 is still baffled about what justice is, should not have expected instruction on that topic in book 2.

Glaucon's absence from Socrates' trial and execution might mean that Glaucon was no longer living, or might be evidence that Glaucon was eventually dissociated from Socrates' philosophizing. So the *Symposium* suggests if it is Plato's brother Glaucon to whom Apollodorus says,

[Before meeting Socrates] – I was more miserable than anyone, no less than you now: thinking I ought to do anything rather than philosophizing. (172e–173a)

To consider Adeimantus briefly: in the *Republic*, as I have mentioned, Adeimantus shows awareness of Orphic ritual and certain Pythagorean ideas. Adeimantus is the interlocutor for most of Socrates' suggestions about the arts and drama. Presenting Adeimantus as the interlocutor for conversation about stories, Plato shows that Socrates tailors his speech to his particular audience, since in book 2 Adeimantus was concerned about stories about justice. As evidence of Adeimantus' imperfect consistency I note that Adeimantus agrees without examination (387) to Socrates' proposal, "a good person is distinguished from other people by having the least need of anyone or anything else." But Adeimantus had previously agreed in book 2 that the city comes into being because people need each other (369b).

The point of Socrates' detailed speech in books 2–10, I've proposed, is to reveal its audience. A speech that persuades, as this one persuades the brothers, shows the assumptions and inclinations of its audience. In the case of Socrates' speech, which is on the fundamental life-influencing topic of what is just or right, the speech reveals assumptions that Plato's brothers live by. That is to say, it reveals what is most in need of examination.

In the *Gorgias* Socrates describes speech-making as a kind of flattery: that is, a successful speech relies on, and hence reveals, what the audience thinks is flattering to it. Socrates says in the *Menexenus* that it is easy to praise Athens to Athenians. Similarly, it is easy to praise the Kallipolis to potential Kallipolitans. An application of this thought that a successful persuasive speech flatters its audience is to raise the possibility that Glaucon, for example, assents to some of Socrates' proposals because he finds them flattering. Glaucon is flattered by the suggestion present in the metaphor of the cave that only a few people, among whom he counts himself, are able to distinguish appearance from reality while most cannot. The difficult sun and line metaphors are addressed to Glaucon. Glaucon seems charmed by the difficulty of the metaphor of the sun. He says (509b), "what a semi-divine overstatement!" Socrates replies that Glaucon forced him to say it (509c). Possibly in listening to Socrates talk about forms and true philosophers, Glaucon is flattered that, as he supposes, Socrates is imparting somewhat mysterious doctrine that only a special few can understand.

5.8 THE SOCRATES OF THE *REPUBLIC*

I conclude that the difference between Socrates' questioning manner of book 1 and his courtroom pleading-speech mode (with a questioning twist) of books 2–10 is not sufficient reason to say that Socrates is not one consistent nonauthoritative character throughout the *Republic*.[41] A better explanation for the change in Socrates' mode of speaking in book 2 is that Socrates has agreed to enter into the speech-against-speech convention. Since in book 1 he made an offer, declined by Glaucon, to employ the speech-against-speech convention, his agreement to do so in book 2 is not out of character. The rhetorical Socrates of books 2–10, still professedly ignorant, is a continuation of the Socrates of book 1, too professedly ignorant to be an answerer in a question-and-answer conversation but nevertheless willing to enter a speech contest. There is no sign that Socrates has retracted his stance that he assents to something if (and we expect only if) he has examined it and it survives the examination (337c–339b).

Nor is there any sign that Socrates is not still a most skilled examiner, though he does not exercise his examining skills in the usual way in books 2–10. Since Socrates does not examine his proposals in books 2–10, we must do so. If we find that some of his proposals to which the brothers

---

[41] Aune (1997) offers a completely different argument, mostly not compatible with mine, to say that book 1 fits with the rest of the *Republic*.

assent do not withstand our examination, that is important reason to think that they would not be acceptable to Socrates, as depicted, if he examined them.

Although any expressions of doubt by Socrates that are firmly within his persuasive speech can be used only with caution as hints of his genuine convictions, I note that there are many of these. At 433a as Socrates is about to give the account of justice in the city as everyone doing his own task, Socrates prefaces his account with, "Listen, whether I'm talking sense" (literally: "whether I'm saying anything"). That is, Socrates asks Glaucon to reflect on and figure out whether Socrates is saying something worthwhile, not just to receive it as from an authority. Socrates seems still tentative and exploratory, not authoritative. Socrates' invitation to Glaucon to consider whether Socrates is making sense departs in the minimal way Socrates allows himself from the speech-and-counter-speech convention. Glaucon does not seriously take up the invitation.

This expression of hesitation is striking:

It could be doubted that the things said are possible; and even if, in the best possible conditions they could come into being, that they would be best will also be doubted. So that there is a certain hesitation to fasten onto these things, lest the speech might seem to be a wishful prayer (*euchê*), my dear comrade. (450cd)

Commentators take this as Socrates' expressing a fear that the city as described might be a mere imaginative construction rather than something practically realizable. Even given its status as part of a speech to appeal to Glaucon and Adeimantus, it serves as a hint that Socrates fears lest his interlocutors think the city as described is what he actually wishes for, and will not in fact doubt it and examine it because they are so eager to be instructed by him.[42]

---

[42] Other examples of his claiming ignorance and incapacity or implying it after Book 1 are: 368b–c (Socrates doesn't have the capacity to help); 416b–c (Socrates doesn't think it is worth insisting that the guardians have been well educated for gentleness according to the scheme he's proposed; it's only worthwhile to say that the guardians have to encounter the right education, whatever it is, if they are to be gentle). Socrates doesn't know something or other at 429a, 430e, 432c, and 435c–d.

Some more expressions of doubt cited by Blondell (2002, 209) are: 414c; 452a; 453b; 457b–c; 472a; 473e; 474b; 497de; 499ab. She cites these as passages in which Socrates fears that his novel proposals will be ridiculed. I have a different impression: I don't think Socrates as depicted cares about being doubted, ridiculed, or disliked. He says it would be childish to worry about being laughed at (451a). He's willing to be ridiculed in several dialogues (*Gorgias, Euthydemus*) without being bothered by it. I think it more likely that what Socrates fears is his interlocutors' simply accepting unexamined ideas.

Blondell (2002, 210) also cites these expressions of doubt: 506c–507a (Socrates isn't able to say even what seems to him on the topic of what the good is, itself); 595c (Socrates isn't quite able to say what imitation means).

I am inclined to take Socrates' professions of ignorance and incapacity as sincere, even when – or especially when – his interlocutors dismiss them. In book 1 Thrasymachus thinks that Socrates' regular mode of asking questions and not answering, which Socrates says is due to ignorance, is instead an indulgence of Socrates' "love of honor" (336c). But there is no evidence that Socrates has any interest in being honored.

Socrates' introduction to his speech in book 2, addressed to the reader, not to Glaucon or Adeimantus, says he is saying what seems or appears to him:

I said then what seemed fitting to me (*eipon oun hoper emoi edoxen*). (368c8)

This introductory sentence implies the personal cast of all that follows. As I understand it, Socrates is saying what seems to him the best sort of a persuasive speech for these interlocutors. Socrates' just previous expression (368b) of his incapacity to do what the brothers ask seems to me to cast a decisively long shadow over his entire production.

It will be obvious that my interpretation differs from the several I mentioned at the beginning of chapter 4. (i) I don't think Socrates is ever being ironic and meaning the opposite of what he says. (ii) I wouldn't say Socrates is revising 2–7 in 8–10. I'd say he is continuing to elicit Glaucon's and Adeimantus' perhaps confused beliefs and to uncover what the brothers are receptive to. As it turns out, Socrates elicits some different beliefs in 8–10 than he elicits in 2–7.[43] (iii) I certainly don't think Socrates is reducing to absurdity the possibility of an entirely just city,[44] since he doesn't come anywhere close to describing an entirely just city. If he had in fact reduced to absurdity the claim that a just city is possible, Socrates would have shown that none of our lives is worth living. That seems to me an unlikely message for Socrates, as depicted, to wish to convey. We may of course make our own judgment that he has in effect reduced to absurdity the thought that Prettycity is desirable. But that is our own projection – and I think a likely one – of what Socrates would have said if he had gone on to examine Prettycity.

Blondell (2002, 217) says of the elenctic Socrates: "Socrates does sometimes speak at length, but such speeches are usually hedged with disclaimers or other evasion of personal authority." She cites in her n. 18 *Crito* 50a, *Gorgias* 465d–466a and 519de. I'd cite also these passages in the long speech of the *Republic*.

[43] Roochnik (2003). See n. 9 of chapter 4 (p. 92).   [44] Bloom (1968, 409).

5.9 THE PIETY OF SOCRATES' SPEECH TO PLATO'S BROTHERS AND ITS WORTH FOR PLATO'S READERS

I now return to a question raised earlier: what serious pious purpose can the admittedly ignorant Socrates hope to achieve by proposing some outrageous things as he discusses justice with Glaucon and Adeimantus? This is, after all, as I claim, the very same Socrates as the one who says in book 1 that justice is more precious than gold (336e), and who implies that the determination of which course of life would be most fulfilling for each of us is not a small matter:

Do you think to be determining a small matter, and not a way of conducting life (*biou diagôgên*) by which each of us who conducts himself that way would live a most fulfilling (*lusitelestatên*) life?[45] (344e)

What can that Socrates hope to achieve by sketching a state in which most people's lives are not worth living, if he wants to persuade the brothers that justice is better than injustice?

The most likely answer to our question seems to me to be that Socrates, as usual, has in mind the ultimate goal of inspiring examination. When Socrates utters what appeals to the brothers concerning justice in books 2–10, he thereby reveals assumptions they live by. He thereby takes the first step toward an examination of what is in them. Although Socrates is not allowed to conduct an examination on this occasion, the further stage of usefulness will come when and if the brothers actually do examine what they have assented to.

Some evidence of the expectation that the day's discussion is not the last word on the topics treated is at 388e, where Socrates says to Adeimantus that the argument has indicated that young people shouldn't lament at the slightest sufferings. Socrates then comments:

We ought to be persuaded by it until someone should persuade us by another better one.[46] (388e)

We readers do not see that further stage of useful examination and looking for better arguments within the *Republic*, but Socrates looks ahead to more occasions of discussion in Book 6 when he says:

---

[45] The adjective comes from an idiom, *luein telê*, meaning "pay off," as a debt. "A life with the most payoff" would be the most literal translation of the phrase.

[46] At 434c ff. Socrates says that the discussion is at a tentative point and suggests testing (he does not specify a definite future point) the account of justice in the city against the upcoming account of justice in the individual.

We won't relax our efforts until we convince him [Thrasymachus] and the others – or at least do something that may benefit them in that life, when, having come to be again, they encounter such speeches. (498d)

Some interpreters take Socrates to refer to reincarnation here. If Socrates' interlocutors have Pythagorean sympathies, they may well understand it so.[47]

Glaucon also expects that there will be more conversation on the same topics as in the *Republic*. He says:

Since the present occasion is not our only opportunity to hear these things, but we will get to return to them often in the future, let's assume that what you said about them just now is true. (532d)

In an argument that a soul cannot be destroyed by anything but its own peculiar sort of badness, Socrates says:

Let's refute (*exelegxômen*: let's thoroughly test) these arguments and show that what we said was not right. Or so long as they remain unrefuted (*anelegkta*: untested) let's never say that the soul even comes close to being destroyed by a fever or any other disease or by killing. (610a–b)

Socrates leaves open the possibility of future testing.

In giving his unusual speech, Socrates can have the serious and truth-seeking purpose of revealing assumptions that need to be examined in the future.

My distancing Socrates from what he says and my giving ownership of the *Republic* to the brothers gives rise, however, to a new question. Why is it worthwhile for us, the readers, to be presented with these elaborate constructions? After all, they are, to quote again some of the authors I quoted at the beginning of chapter 4, "curious," "philosophically frustrating," "very ugly," "too hasty and too crude," "embarrassingly bad," "preposterous," "hysterical," "utterly grotesque," and "repellent." In Plato's depiction Socrates reveals what appeals to the overeager Glaucon and Adeimantus. But why should what appeals to them interest us? Why is it worthwhile for us to see and to struggle to interpret, not the thoughts of Plato or Socrates, who already command our interest and respect, but rather what is at the moment in the possibly confused psyches of Glaucon and Adeimantus?

---

[47] Adam (1963, vol. II, 36, n. 24) says:

It is from casual allusions like the present, made in all seriousness, that we can best understand how profound and practical was Plato's belief in immortality. The seed sown here may bear its fruit in another life, so that the educator need not despair.

The answer I'd suggest is that while Socrates' speech gives the brothers a reflection of themselves that they can examine on some later occasion, it also gives us, the readers, a reflection of ourselves to examine. We can learn from asking, first, what more precisely the statements to which the brothers are so receptive mean and asking second, whether those statements appeal to us. If what Socrates says in the *Republic* about justice has as much appeal to us as it did to the depicted Glaucon and Adeimantus, we have an opportunity to learn something about the assumptions and inclinations we live by. We can ask, as Plutarch reports that Plato asked, "Can I possibly be like that?"[48]

[48] For details, see chapter 1, n. 34.

CHAPTER 6

Socrates in the Phaedo: another persuasion assignment

6.1 THE FAMOUS PROPOSALS OF THE SOCRATES OF THE PHAEDO

The Socrates of the *Phaedo* apparently differs from the Socrates of the *Apology* in two conspicuous ways. He offers arguments for the immortality of the soul. He famously enunciates that philosophy is the practice of dying and of being dead (64a). In contrast, the Socrates of the *Apology* did not know what happens after death (29a; 42a); and the philosophizing he claimed to do consisted of challenging, elenchizing, and reproaching his fellows (29d–e, discussed in detail in chapter 2).

I'll argue that for two reasons the apparent differences are merely apparent. First, the *Phaedo* gives us no reason to think its Socrates is not the same agnostic about death as the character Socrates of the *Apology*. Second, the *Phaedo* gives us strong reason to think that Socrates as depicted in the *Phaedo* does not endorse the conception of philosophy that he articulates there.

6.2 SETTING AND PARTICIPANTS

Phaedo narrates the *Phaedo*, an account of Socrates' conversation that Phaedo witnessed in prison on the day of Socrates' execution. Phaedo's narration occurs at Phlius, a locus of Pythagoreanism.[1] Phaedo's audience is Echecrates,[2] a member of the Pythagorean community at Phlius. The

---

[1] Aristoxenus' enumeration of Pythagoreans according to D.L. VIII, 46 (= Aristoxenus fr. 18–19 Wehrli) has four from Phlius. (Aristoxenus, born about 370 BC, is nevertheless one of our sources for information about Pythagoreans.) Similarly the list of the last Pythagoreans in Iamblichus (245–325 AD) VP 267 has four from Phlius. Burkert (1972, 105 n. 40) thinks Iamblichus' list goes back to Aristoxenus. Translations from the *Phaedo* are from Gallop (1975) with occasional changes.

[2] Nails (2002) s.v. "Echecrates." Echecrates was student of Philolaus and Eurytus. Echecrates appears in Aristoxenus' list (D.L. VIII, 46) and also in Iamblichus VP 267. Burkert (1972, 237) observes that Philolaus and Eurytus were "constantly" associated in the tradition. According to Aristotle *Metaphysics* 1092b10ff Eurytus was one who would assign numbers to man or horse by making a picture with pebbles. Theophrastus praised Eurytus "because he went farther than anyone else – into absurdity!" (Burkert (1972, 47, n. 107)).

166

main interlocutors of the conversation that Phaedo narrates are Simmias and Cebes. We learn at 61d that they have been studying with Philolaus, the renowned Pythagorean. Though the dialogue never mentions Pythagoras – perhaps partly because it was Pythagorean practice not to speak the name of the master,[3] Plato's readers of his era would have known Phlius as a Pythagorean locale and, moreover, as the location – in a current story – of an early use of Pythagoras' newly invented word "philosopher."

Cicero in the first century BC gives this version of the story. Cicero's report is of course much later than Pythagoras' putative dates in the sixth century BC:

Pythagoras, according to Heraclides of Pontus, the pupil of Plato . . . came . . . to Phlius, and with a wealth of learning discussed certain subjects with Leon the ruler . . . And Leon, after being amazed at his talent and eloquence, asked him to name the art in which he had most reliance; but Pythagoras said that for his part he had no acquaintance with any art, but was a philosopher. Leon was astonished at the novelty of the term and asked who philosophers were and in what they differed from the rest of the world. Pythagoras . . . replied that the life of man seemed to him to resemble the festival . . . celebrated with most magnificent games before a gathering collected from the whole of Greece; for at this festival some men whose bodies had been trained sought to win the glorious distinction of a crown; others were attracted by the prospect of making gain by buying or selling, whilst there was on the other hand a certain group, and that quite the best kind of free-born men, who looked neither for applause nor gain, but came for the sake of the spectacle and closely watched what was done and how it was done. Some were slaves of ambition, some of money; there were a special few who, counting all else as nothing, closely scanned the nature of things; these men gave themselves the name of lovers of wisdom – for that is the meaning of the word "philosopher." (*Tusculan Disputations* v, 3, 8)[4]

The conception of philosophy enters the *Phaedo* when Phaedo says of the last day that there wasn't any pleasure, even though pleasure would have been expected, since

we were in philosophy, as was our habit – for our discussions were some of that sort. (59a)

---

[3] Iamblichus *VP* 255.

[4] There is controversy about the story's historical accuracy. For my purposes its availability in Plato's time is all that matters. Burkert (1972, 65, 1977) and Hadot (2002, 15 and n. 1) find the story that Pythagoras invented the word implausible. Hadot thinks Heraclides' story projects the Platonic notion of philosophy upon Pythagoras. Guthrie (1962, vol. 1, 204) grants the story some historical accuracy.

　　D.L. (VIII, 8; I, 12) also tells the story, citing Heraclides, but with some different details. Iamblichus *VP* 58–59 has a yet more elaborate version.

According to Phaedo philosophy is usually a pleasure, and the conversation that Phaedo is about to relate is an example of philosophy as Phaedo understands it. Since Phaedo is attempting to communicate with Echecrates, Phaedo obviously expects that Echecrates understands philosophy in some way similar to the way Phaedo understands it. Our only evidence of what Phaedo thought philosophy was is his narration. Socrates will later say (61e and 70b) that they are spending his last day "mythologizing." So what Socrates calls "mythologizing" is an example of what Phaedo and Echecrates would call philosophy. (Socrates also says that he is not a mythologizer himself (61b5), though he knows myths by others, such as Aesop's fables (61b6).) Cebes' and Simmias' view of philosophy will emerge from their conversation.

Cebes first contributes to the prison discussion to ask why, as he has heard (60d), Socrates has been composing verses. Cebes wants an answer on behalf of his associate Evenus. Socrates explains (60e–61b) that he had had a recurrent dream message: "Work away and make music" (*mousikên*: activity in the sphere of the Muses). He had long thought that the dream was encouraging him to do what he was already doing throughout his life, because philosophy is the greatest music (*hôs philosophias . . . ousês megistês mousikês*: 61a3–4) and he was doing that. To Pythagoreans, who are intrigued by musical phenomena, Socrates' words may have a distinctively Pythagorean resonance.[5] But Socrates does not mention Pythagoreanism here. He at least has in mind the more ordinary thought that "philosophy" refers to an activity under the Muses' protection. Even a non Pythagorean might believe that.[6] As the mission to Delos delayed his execution, it occurred to Socrates that maybe the dream meant "music in the popular sense" (61a) – something with tunes or meter. So now he composes verse. He tells Cebes to give that message to Evenus, to bid Evenus farewell, and to "tell him, if he is sensible, to follow me as fast as possible."

Socrates clearly is advising that Evenus should die as soon as possible. Simmias is surprised at this advice to Evenus (61c), and says that Evenus is not the sort of person who would be willing to do that. Socrates replies:

Why, . . . isn't Evenus a philosopher? . . . Then Evenus will be willing, and so will everyone who has a share worthily (*axiôs*) in this business. But equally, he won't do violence to himself: they say it's forbidden (*ou . . . themiton*). (61c)

---

[5] Burnet (1911) takes the remark that philosophy is the highest music as the expression of a Pythagorean doctrine.

[6] Despite the ending *-ikê* of *mousikê*, which indicates an implicit occurrence of *technê*, not everything under the sphere of the Muses is necessarily a fully teachable *technê* (as Ion discovers in the *Ion*). The Muses were often invoked just because the would-be creator had no adequate *technê*.

Here Socrates employs a conception of the philosopher that implies that a philosopher would be willing to die, subject to the restriction that one should not commit suicide.[7] Socrates' advice to Evenus alludes to Evenus' reputation or self-description as a philosopher under that conception.[8] As such a philosopher, Evenus should be eager to die. Socrates also tells us that that conception distinguishes worthy philosophers from less worthy philosophers.

Cebes is familiar with that conception and its implication that philosophers should be willing to die, for he is not at all puzzled by the implication. Rather, Cebes is puzzled how that conception can be consistent with a prohibition against suicide. He says:

How can you say this, Socrates? How can it both be forbidden to do violence to oneself, and be the case that the philosopher would be willing to follow the dying? (61d)

Socrates asks:

Have you and Simmias, who have been with Philolaus, not heard (*akêkoate*) about such things? . . . I myself speak from hearsay [*akoês*] about them. But what I happen to have heard (*tugchanô akêkoôs*), there would be no ill will (*phthonos*) at [my] telling you. (61d6–10)

Because Simmias and Cebes have been studying with the Pythagorean Philolaus, Socrates expects that they are aware of a Pythagorean proscription against suicide. Because Cebes is indeed aware of the proscription (61d8), though unaware of the reasons for it, we may infer that Cebes is not a fully informed Pythagorean.[9] However, Cebes' worry about possible

---

[7] Ebert (2001) argues convincingly that Evenus belonged to a Pythagorean community and that Socrates is relying on a distinctive Pythagorean understanding of what being a philosopher involved, and "is able to develop the connotations of this term" (2001, 434). Ebert puts it that Socrates is "made to assume in this dialogue . . . the role of a Pythagorean *philosophos*." I will argue that Socrates is reminding his interlocutors of what is involved in their aspirations to being philosophers of the Pythagorean sort.

   The fact that Evenus, despite membership in a Pythagorean community, doesn't live as one would expect a Pythagorean to live (as we learn from Cebes' remark that Evenus wouldn't want to die) shows that Evenus isn't a full or consistent Pythagorean.

[8] That Evenus (though inconsistently) considers himself a Pythagorean philosopher seems to me a more likely explanation of Socrates' advice to Evenus than the proposal in Peterson (2003) that Socrates scathingly implies that Evenus would be better off dead because, as a sophist, Evenus was living out fraudulent pretensions. It seems a mistake to think that that sort of bitter remark would fit into the mild tone that Socrates adopts in the *Phaedo* as he attempts to comfort friends that are more distressed at the prospect of Socrates' dying than Socrates is.

[9] Gadamer (1980a, 23–24) concludes from Cebes' ignorance of the prohibition of suicide: "they are no longer interested in the religious content of the Pythagorean teachings and . . . they therefore genuinely represent the modern scientific enlightenment." That is, they belong to the mathematical group among followers of Pythagorean philosophy.

inconsistency is a dead giveaway to his familiarity with the Pythagorean preoccupation with the afterlife.[10] That well-known preoccupation plus the story of Pythagoras' coinage of the word "philosopher" to describe himself – a story that gives Pythagoreans a special claim to the designation "philosopher" – provides an explanation why Socrates expects that Cebes would understand that as a philosopher, i.e., a Pythagorean, Evenus would want to die. To claim to be a Pythagorean philosopher is to imply strong interest in presumed life after death.[11]

Some of Socrates' phrasing indicative of hearing – "have you . . . heard," "from hearsay," and "what I happen to have heard" – is worth comment. "[H]ave you heard" (61d6) would be natural to refer to the relation of the students or hearers, Simmias and Cebes, to their teacher Philolaus. It is suggestive of Pythagorean *akousmata*, the things heard, the pregnant sayings supposedly of the founder Pythagoras preserved through his followers' memorization. Socrates' phrase "from hearsay," on the other hand, may suggest a greater distance from the doctrines he is about to report than having heard lectures from a teacher. And his phrase "what I happen to have heard," which applies to what Socrates will next say, suggests greater distance than an inner circle of hearers. Socrates happens to have heard why certain mystery rituals forbid suicide:

> The reason given in mysteries (*aporrêtois* – "unspeakable matters" or "forbidden matters")[12] on the subject, that we men are in some sort of prison, and that one ought not to release oneself from it, seems to me a big one and not easy to see through. (62b)

That Socrates happens to have heard this, and that there would be no ill will if he mentions it, indicates that what he mentions is not a secret revealed in a ritual available only to an initiate, publication of which the gods might resent. It is rather something that an outsider, such as we readers, might happen to hear.[13]

The mention of mysteries alludes to Orphism. It resembled Pythagoreanism in its obsession with death: Orphic mysteries were rituals that gave

[10] Burkert (1972, 185) comments on the Pythagoreans' preoccupation with death in their *akousmata*: "It is striking how constantly attention is oriented toward the world of the dead."

[11] Nightingale (1995, 14) finds no evidence that Pythagoras introduced "philosopher" as a technical term. To me the *Phaedo* suggests that Pythagoreans use the term in a selective or exclusive way.

[12] Archer-Hind (1883) says that ancient commentators take this to refer to Orphic tradition. Also see Burkert (1985, 296–304) for the association between Orphism and Pythagoreanism.

[13] I disagree with Rowe (1993). He says that "from hearsay" is misleading, and that Socrates is saying new things (probably created by Plato). I think Socrates' phrasing – "no ill will" – is not just a way of saying "I don't mind telling you" (Gallop's translation). I think rather the phrasing defends against violating the mysteries mentioned at 62b.

a glimpse of what happened after death and that gave advice for ensuring safety in the afterlife.[14] The topic of mysteries may seem a new topic, but Socrates' and Plato's contemporaries would have seen a connection with Pythagoreanism, which was early on linked with Orphism.[15] Socrates is suggesting that the Pythagorean prohibition of suicide might rest on the story from the mysteries that in ordinary life we are in a sort of prison: the body is a sort of prison for the soul; escape is not our right.[16]

Though Socrates finds the cultic reason for the prohibition of suicide hard to fathom, he is receptive to a different reason:

but . . . this much seems to me well said: that the ones who take care of us are gods, and we men are one of their belongings. (62b)

Socrates' thought, still not easy to understand, would apparently be that if gods are caring for us, then whatever is happening to us must be nothing to be worried about.

Socrates' thought approaches sufficiently answering Cebes' question why a philosopher might be willing to die, but Cebes worries anew about possible inconsistency (62c–d): if philosophers are the wisest of people (*phronimôtatous*), and if gods care for people, then if philosophers are willing to die, they are willing to leave the best care. Cebes finds that unreasonable (62d). Cebes' phrasing shows that he thinks philosophers exceptionally wise, as does Simmias' reiteration of Cebes' objection:

Why indeed should men so truly wise (*sophoi*) want to escape from masters who are better than themselves, and be separated from them lightly? So I think it's at you that Cebes is aiming his argument, because you take so lightly your leaving both ourselves and the gods, who are good rulers by your own admission. (63a)

Readers might wonder why dying means leaving the care of the gods. Couldn't gods care for us after death also? But Socrates doesn't object to Simmias and Cebes on that point. Instead he diagnoses the intention behind their questions. He thus sets the agenda for the rest of the *Phaedo*.

---

[14] See Plato, *Rep.* 364–365: Adeimantus describes the promise and threat of initiation rituals concerning the afterlife. Burkert (1972, 125): Orphic mysteries vividly depicted punishments awaiting the uninitiated after death.

[15] Burkert (1972, 39): Orphism and Pythagoreanism "were almost inextricably intertwined in the fifth century." See Burkert (1972, 178–179, especially n. 96) on Pythagorean secrecy. See Burkert (1985, 296–301) on Orpheus and Pythagoras.

[16] There is controversy about how the Pythagoreans would have explained a prohibition against suicide. Burnet's note on 62b4 (Burnet 1911) finds the "genuinely Pythagorean origin" of the explanation that the body is a prison. Strachan (1970, 220) concludes differently that Plato is not referring to a Pythagorean explanation of why one should not commit suicide at 62b. Strachan accepts that Socrates, as depicted, tells us that Philolaus forbade suicide, but does not tell us why.

6.3 THE EMPHASIS ON PERSUASION

Several passages show that Socrates intends his speech in the *Phaedo* as a speech in the manner of a law-court speech of persuasion.[17]

(i) First, Socrates responds to Simmias and Cebes:

> I take you to mean that I should defend (*apologêsasthai*) myself against these things [*pros tauta*] as if in a court of law (*hôsper en dikastêriô(i)*) . . . Very well, then . . . let me try to defend myself more persuasively before you than I did before the jury. (63b1–5)

Socrates understands Cebes and Simmias to request from Socrates a law-court-style persuasive defense against the charge of being too tranquil in the face of death.[18] Socrates' saying that he will present a defense as if in a court, and "more persuasively" than he did at his trial, is, I believe, a most important clue about what he says in the rest of the *Phaedo*: it shows that he intends to comply most literally with their request. A conventional speaker in a law-court does not necessarily say what he believes but aims at persuading his audience. So Socrates will speak to persuade Simmias and Cebes whether or not Socrates himself believes his speech. The speech that Socrates gives from here on may thus be unlike the speech of the Socrates of the *Apology*. That speech, though in a law-court, did not aim at persuasion in the conventional way.

Socrates' reference here to an unpersuasive speech he gave to his jurors I take as reference to that very speech we know from Plato's *Apology*. Such reference inclines me to take the Socrates of the *Phaedo* to be the same as the Socrates of the *Apology*. However, in discussing the *Phaedo*, I will not assume that.

(ii) A second passage again comparing Socrates' *Phaedo* talk to a speech in a law-court is this:

> Now with you for my jury I want to give my speech (*ton logon apodounai*) – how it seems to me likely that a man who has really spent his life in philosophy is cheerful when about to die, and is hopeful that when he has died, he will get the greatest goods there. So I'll try, Simmias and Cebes, to tell how this might hold. (63e–64a)

---

[17] Rowe (2007, 99–100) observes with emphasis that the *Phaedo* is a law-court-style defense, but draws a different result from the observation than I do.

[18] In *Phaedrus* 242a–b Socrates says that Simmias has elicited more speeches than anyone else, even than Phaedrus, who is "far ahead of the rest."

It is appropriate for Socrates here to invoke what follows for the "man who has really spent his life in philosophy." He addresses Simmias and Cebes as people especially interested in Pythagoreans. Pythagoreans are distinctively philosophers. Simmias and Cebes aspire to be philosophers, as they understand what philosophers are. (At 101e Socrates says to Cebes, "if you are indeed among philosophers, I think you would do as I say." He suggests that Cebes aspires to be a philosopher. Cebes and Simmias assent in unison.)

(iii) Socrates continues:

> It is likely to have escaped the notice of others that those who rightly engage in philosophy practice (*epitêdeuousin*) nothing other than dying and being dead. Now if this is true, it would be out of place to be eager in one's whole life for nothing else than this, but when this arrived, to be vexed about what they have long been eager for and have practiced. (64a)

"Others" are people other than Simmias and Cebes and other students of Pythagorean ways who are aware of the Pythagorean view Socrates is about to discuss. Others are unaware that philosophy is practicing being dead.[19] Socrates addresses his current defense speech to these particular interlocutors who are inclined toward the Pythagorean views that Socrates will build on, including a certain conception of who counts as a philosopher. Their impression of philosophers comes partly from Pythagorean views, but they think of Socrates as a philosopher. They are receptive to instruction from him on how philosophers should live. (Socrates, however, says he is "mythologizing" (61e; 70b). And he doesn't create his own myths (61b5).)

(iv) Socrates makes a short attempt to persuade Simmias and Cebes that he should not resent death, and concludes by repeating his comparison to a courtroom defense:

> With these things I make my defense (*apologoumai*]) ... To the many it offers no credibility (*apistian parechei* (69e3)).[20] If then I am somewhat more convincing (*pithanôteros*) to you in [my] defense than to the jurors among the Athenians, it would be well. (69d7–e5)

---

[19] This slogan can be spelled out variously, but in connection with Pythagoras as philosopher one thinks of his legendary descent underground (*katabasis*: Burkert (1972, 147–165)): after some years Pythagoras reappeared, much thinner, to tell the story that he had been in Hades. This would be a most straightforward example of the philosopher practicing being dead.

[20] Ast deleted the clause, "to the many it provides no credibility." Burnet (1911) deletes. The new Oxford Classical Text (Duke *et al.* 1995) relegates to the apparatus. Archer-Hind (1883) deletes, finding the clause "utterly pointless." I find, on the contrary, that the words have much point. Rowe (2007) keeps them.

The aside (69e3), "To the many it offers no credibility," again makes clear that Socrates is appealing to these particular interlocutors, who do not consider themselves among "the many," that is, ordinary people. Cebes and Simmias do not consider themselves among "the many" because they think they are or will be part of an exclusive group of philosophers.[21] Socrates' speech relies on premises he attributes to these interlocutors, premises that most people do not accept.

When Socrates says that what will persuade Simmias and Cebes would not be persuasive to "the many," I do not take that either as praise of Simmias and Cebes or as a put-down of them. As Socrates says in the *Crito* and *Gorgias*, majority beliefs have no special status. The same holds for minority beliefs. Socrates is making a straightforward observation. Simmias and Cebes have an uncommon framework of beliefs. Socrates undertakes to produce a speech persuasive to people of Simmias and Cebes' distinctive beliefs.

(v) An especially telling passage that gives ownership of the overall structure of Socrates' speech to Cebes is at 95 b–c, where Socrates states what Cebes requires:

> The bottom line of what you seek is [this]:[22] you require it to be proved that our soul is indestructible and deathless, if a man [who is] a philosopher is going to die while being cheerful, and thinking that as he dies he will do well, differently than if he ended his life in another way of life, and if he isn't being cheerful with a thoughtless and foolish cheer. (95b8–c4)

Cebes requires a made-to-order argument to a conclusion that he assigns to Socrates.

(vi) Again at 95e Socrates attaches the structure of what he is going to say to Cebes:

> It is appropriate for anyone, if he is not thoughtless, to be afraid who does not know nor is capable of giving an argument (*logon* (Gallop (1975): "proof")) that it [the soul] is immortal. Such things as these, Cebes, are what you say, I think. And I take them up again carefully, so that nothing might escape us, and if you wish, you might add or subtract something. (95d6–e3)

Cebes agrees that Socrates' summary is accurate. Cebes already believes that one should not be cheerful about death unless it is

---

[21] See Burkert (1972, 178) on Pythagorean exclusivity.

[22] "Bottom line" translates the Greek *to kephalaion* (95b5–6), literally, "the heading (or top line)." It is a metaphor from addition that relies on the ancient Greek practice of writing the sum at the top of the page instead of at the bottom as we do. See Burnet (1911).

the prospect of another better kind of life. Cebes wants a proof that the soul is immortal. As Socrates creates his persuasive speech, Socrates works with what Cebes requires.

(vii) Of Socrates' several arguments for the immortality of the soul only the final one satisfies Simmias and Cebes (for the time being). At its conclusion Socrates again refers to his arguments' believability to this particular audience:

> Our first assumptions ought to be considered again more clearly even if they are credible (*pistai*) to you. (107b)

(viii) Still later Socrates observes that even the final argument, though it persuaded the interlocutors it addressed, did not persuade Crito, for Crito asks how he should bury Socrates (115c2). Socrates responds:

> I do not persuade Crito . . . but he thinks that I am that dead body which he will see a little later, and he asks how he shall bury me. As for the fact that I have been making a big speech (*logon:* argument) for a long time that when I drink the drug I will no longer remain by you, but will have gone away to some (*tinas:* some unspecified) joys of the blessed, to him I seem to be speaking these things in some other way (*allôs:* Rowe (1993a), Burnet (1911), "in vain"). (115c6 ff.)

The unpersuaded Crito evidently doesn't share all the premises of Socrates' persuaded interlocutors.

These several passages show that the metaphor of persuasion in a court of law, persuasion "more convincing" than Socrates' speech to his jurors at his trial, permeates the *Phaedo*.[23] They show that Socrates intends his speech to convince his particular interlocutors and that Socrates recognizes that his speech would be quite unconvincing to others. His speech is unlike the proof of a geometry theorem, for example, which should carry conviction for anyone who understands it.

Although we have now firmly attached a somewhat Pythagorean conception of philosophy to the Pythagorean hearers and aspiring philosophers, Simmias and Cebes, and have shown that Socrates intends to say what will be persuasive to them though not perhaps to others, we have not yet detached it from the Socrates who articulates it. We have not shown that Socrates is one of the unpersuaded "others" and is not expressing his own

---

[23] More vocabulary of persuasion in the law-court setting is at 63d7, where Simmias says: "Your defense will be made, if you persuade us of what you say" (63d).

   Persuasion appears at 77e. Cebes wants Socrates to assuage their fear of death. He asks Socrates to "reassure" (*anapeithein*) and "win us over" (*metapeithein*), using words related "to persuade" (*peithein*).

beliefs as well when he gives his several arguments. I will now argue that Socrates in fact does not express his own beliefs at the same time as he articulates Simmias' and Cebes'.

6.4 REMARKS ON THE LOGICAL STRUCTURE OF SOCRATES' PERSUASIVE ARGUMENT

I'll first show that the persuasive task Simmias and Cebes assign to Socrates is quite confused. Nevertheless, Socrates carries out very literally exactly what is assigned to him. Its very confusion will be part of my evidence that it does not represent Socrates' convictions.

As background for my discussion I mention some highlights of the *Phaedo*, most of which I will not discuss in detail.

At 63b–c Socrates gives his first very short defense of his willingness to die – that he will be with gods who are good masters. It does not satisfy Simmias. He asks again to be persuaded. Socrates then gives a related somewhat longer argument for the conclusion that it is reasonable for him not to be resentful at dying (63e–69e). At 70b Simmias and Cebes want reassurance that when a man has died, his soul exists and possesses power and wisdom. Socrates asks (70b6) if they want to "thoroughly mythologize" ("to mythologize through and through").[24] Cebes replies somewhat inappropriately, "I would with pleasure hear (*akousaimi*) whatever belief (*doxan*) you have about them," as though he were expecting a doctrinal lecture rather than a story.

At 70–77 Socrates conforms to the expectations of Simmias and Cebes. Socrates uses the language of conclusive demonstration rather than of mythologizing (for example: 76c11: *ara*; 76e5: "the same necessity"). Simmias and Cebes use the language of demonstration (for example: 72a9–10: "from what was agreed on, it holds necessarily thus"; 73a5–7; 77a5: "sufficiently demonstrated"). At 72d Socrates concludes a first argument that the souls of the dead exist. At 76d he concludes a second argument that for those who have knowledge of items such as equality itself their souls must have existed before they were born. At 77d Simmias and Cebes are still afraid of death. At 78b–80b Socrates gives a third argument that concludes,

---

[24] 70b6: *diamuthologômen*. I take the prefix *dia* to be intensifying here. "Through and through" would be a literal way to capture its effect. Since Socrates has previously used *muthologikos* (61b5) clearly to mean "one who makes up stories" (61b4: *poiein muthous all' ou logous*), it seems incomplete just to render *diamuthologein* at 70b6, as some translators (and LSJ) do, as "converse." And since Socrates is going to tell most of the stories, it also doesn't seem right to think of the prefix as adding the sense "across," so that it would be translatable as, "tell stories to each other."

"[the] soul must be completely indissoluble, or something close to it." The three arguments are labeled in the literature "the cyclical argument," "the argument from recollection," and "the affinity argument." At 87c–88b Cebes imagines an objector to the previous arguments: the objector will say they still haven't shown that the soul lasts forever, and even if they had shown it will last forever, they haven't shown it doesn't suffer. Cebes also comments that no one can know about the destruction of the soul since no one perceives it. Cebes imagines that the objector continues:

Well, if that's so, then it is not appropriate for anyone who is cheerful about death not to be cheerful foolishly, who is not able to prove that soul is altogether deathless and indestructible; if not, it is necessary for one who is going to die to be afraid about his own soul lest in the instant of the unyoking from the body it perish altogether. (88b3 ff.)

This statement gives Socrates a structure from which he will give a final argument that the soul is immortal (95b–106e).

So much for background. Socrates' first attempt at persuasion was at 63b, part of which I quoted earlier as item (i) in my list of most important passages. Socrates does not explicitly phrase it as coming from Cebes and Simmias as he does so decidedly in the later passages in my list above. (i) leaves open that Socrates might be stating his own views. He says:

Let me try to defend myself more convincingly before you than I did before the jurors. For, Simmias and Cebes, if I didn't suppose (*mê ô(i)mên*), that first, I shall arrive alongside other gods both wise and good, and then alongside men who have died better than those here, then I should be wrong not to be vexed at death. But now, be assured that I hope (*elpizo*) to arrive among good men – but even this I would not altogether insist on – but indeed that I will arrive among gods who are altogether good masters, be assured that if I would insist on anything else (*ti allo*) of such matters, [I would insist on] this. So because of these things, I'm not so resentful, but I'm hopeful that there is something for those who have died, and as is said of old, much better for the good than for the wicked. (63b4–c7)

Note that the verb "suppose" is quite a tentative one. It does not mean "have a conviction of certainty." Notice also that Socrates here mentions vexation (*aganaktein*: resentment, anger, irritation) as a possible reaction to the prospect of dying. He does not mention fear. Simmias and Cebes bring up fear later.

Socrates' reference to gods in the afterlife responds to Simmias' criticism (63a) that to commit suicide is to leave the gods here that care for us. Though Simmias apparently does not envisage that there might be good gods, or even the same gods, both here and in whatever location one finds oneself after death, Socrates does.

Socrates does not explain what counts as arrival among good men. But on one natural understanding of it, his expectation that he will arrive among good men omits an obvious possibility, that death might be like a dreamless sleep that should be welcomed (as Socrates in the *Apology* speculates). He can omit that possibility when talking to would-be Pythagoreans who expect an afterlife of some sort.

Finally, Socrates' statements in his first attempt to persuade Simmias and Cebes are very mild. He speaks of hope and not of assurance that he will arrive among good men. Then he makes a conditional point: if he would insist on anything *else* about such matters, he would insist that he will arrive alongside gods that are good masters. The word "else" is logically important although some translators omit it. Socrates has not said that he *would* insist on anything else. And he has just told us something he would *not* insist on (that he would arrive among good men). Since we don't know what counts as arrival, the most we can get from this passage is that Socrates would insist (if he would insist on anything else – which we have no evidence he would) that the gods are good masters. That is, they are masters that would care well for him even through death. He offers that thought to explain his hopefulness. His hopefulness explains why he is not angry.

His first attempt at persuasion is then very short, just the few sentences I've quoted. It is a believable explanation of why he faces death so calmly. In brief: he hopes, but is not certain, that he will arrive among good men. If he were to insist on anything else, which he has said he wouldn't do, he would insist that he would arrive among good gods. It fits with his having said earlier that it was "well said" that we are in the care of good gods.[25]

I emphasize that Socrates' conviction here is conditional: he is convinced that the gods (if any) are good and that whatever happens to him in the charge of good gods must be good. That good gods treat him well does not imply immortality or survival after death. If, like Cebes, you count as good only what implies your immortality, then you take Socrates' claim to involve the further point that he will survive death forever.

The rest of the *Phaedo* offers arguments for immortality. It does not mention the gods' goodness nor Socrates' acceptance of whatever they have in store for him.

---

[25] Woolf (2004, 125) sees the rest of the *Phaedo* as arguing for the conviction Socrates states here.

This first attempt at defense, Socrates' own explanation of his calm, decidedly does not satisfy Simmias. Simmias says:

Do you mean to go off keeping this thought for yourself, or would you share it with us too? We have a common claim on this benefit as well, I think; and at the same time your defense will be made if you persuade us of what you say. (63c–d)

Simmias' question reveals that Simmias seems to discount Socrates' *stated* reasons for his own calm. Simmias speaks as though he thought Socrates has unrevealed reasons ("keeping this thought for yourself"). Simmias' question also reveals that Simmias has now turned his attention from Socrates' calm to Simmias' own fear: he wants reasons that pertain to Simmias and Cebes. Socrates now enters conventional persuasive mode; he begins to search out considerations to convince Simmias and Cebes. Such considerations Socrates himself need not believe.

The much later passage, 95b–e3, especially shows Socrates' care to get from Cebes a statement of exactly what Cebes requires. (I've introduced letters into the quotation below to separate distinct points.)

The bottom line of what you seek is [this]: [a] you require it to be proved (*epideichthênai*) that our soul is indestructible and deathless, if a man [who is] a philosopher is going to die while being cheerful, and thinking that as he dies he will do well, differently than if he ended his life in another way of life, and if he isn't being cheerful with a thoughtless and foolish cheer . . .

You say . . . [b] . . . It is appropriate for anyone, if he is not thoughtless, to be afraid who does not know nor is capable of giving an argument (*logon*: Gallop (1975): "proof") that it [the soul] is immortal. Such things as these, Cebes, are what you say, I think. And I take them up again carefully, so that nothing might escape us, and if you wish, you might add or subtract something. (95b8–e3)

There are several contrasts with Cebes' initial request at 63b. First, the demand is now not just that Socrates make a defense of *his own* cheer, but is a general demand for *any* philosopher (as Cebes and Simmias understand what a philosopher is). Second, there is now mention of fear instead of vexation and anger. And third, there is now talk of proof instead of supposition. Cebes thinks that if Socrates does not have proof that the soul is immortal, then he is wrong not to be vexed at his approaching death. Socrates emphasizes to Cebes that he is trying to formulate carefully "what you say."

In the passage quoted above Socrates gives two formulations – [a] and [b] above – of a belief of Cebes:

(1) If one is non foolishly cheerful about approaching death, then one has a proof that the soul is deathless.

(2) If one does not have a proof that the soul is immortal, then one should be afraid of approaching death.

To focus our thought on the form of the argument Cebes wants, as Socrates carefully states it at 95b–e, I'll introduce some letters to represent sentences. Let "P" represent: we have a proof that the soul is immortal. Let "V" represent: one should be vexed or afraid or not cheerful (vexation, fear, and non cheer of course differ, but for our present purposes may be grouped). Cebes wants Socrates to prove that one should not be vexed by the prospect of death. Cebes wants a proof that not-V. The sparest indication of the equivalent formulations that Socrates gives in the passage quoted above are:

(a) If not-V, then P.

(b) If not-P, then V.

By the time Socrates has arrived at these careful formulations of Cebes' demand, Socrates has already made three attempts (the cyclical argument, the argument from recollection, and the argument from affinity) to get the proof that would entitle him to claim that P. These have all failed to satisfy Cebes. Socrates is about to embark on his final argument (from causation/entailment) as he gets his last confirmation of why Cebes wants a proof of immortality. Socrates' final argument (95e–107b) is still under consideration as the prison conversation ends at 115a. Given that the final argument is still standing at the end of the *Phaedo*, let us grant Socrates for Cebes' sake that they at last have a proof. We grant that P. However, that is of no help whatsoever toward getting the conclusion Cebes requested, that one should not be fearful. The argument

If not-P, then V,

P

Therefore, not-V.

is not a valid argument. Not only is it bad, but it is egregiously bad. It shows confusion about "if . . . then," a basic connective. (To see its failure easily, consider the argument of the same form that results if we take "P" to abbreviate "Life is painful" and "V" to abbreviate "Death is vexing.")

The argument Socrates gives has exactly the structure that Cebes so firmly agreed he wanted at 95b, yet it is clear at the simplest level that that argument fails to prove that one should not be vexed. Obviously Socrates is in fact not vexed at the prospect of death. But this structurally confused argument cannot possibly be his reason for his calm.

There is also the further problem that the final argument (95e–107b) we have granted to get the premise P is an unsuccessful proof, though it is quite interesting.[26]

One might think to help Socrates out with the overall structure of his response to Cebes' request by adding a new implicit conditional premise:

If P, then not-V.

But such addition here seems unwarranted, because Socrates was so very careful to confirm at 95b that Cebes does not want to add or subtract anything. (Moreover, such a premise is not so obvious that it can be accepted without support. Even if you last permanently, unless you are doing something you like, your permanence is no comfort – as Cebes fleetingly recognizes at 87c–88b, but apparently forgets by 108.)

So we must conclude that the overall structure of the discussion that generates the final argument for immortality, which precisely meets Cebes' request, is confused at an elementary level. I take its confusion as strong evidence that the overall argument of the *Phaedo* is not one Socrates, as depicted, would endorse. Here I do assume – I think no one will deny me this – that the Socrates of the *Phaedo* has at least in common with the Socrates of other dialogues that he has a grasp of "if . . . then" and "not."

---

[26] For assessment that the arguments fail, see Gallop (1975, 192–222); Bostock (1986, 135–189); and Beck (1999, 132–138). See Yi (2009) on the cyclical argument.

Sedley (1995) thinks that Socrates as depicted (and hence Plato) endorses the final argument. Sedley thinks (1995, 17–20) that the final argument requires understanding of forms, and no one but Socrates has that understanding, since Socrates alone has adequately tested the hypothesis of forms:

I cannot imagine that Plato did not consider the very last argument with which he credited Socrates to be a cogent one, especially as it is the foundation for Socrates' optimistic acceptance of his own death. (1995, 17)

If there remains in the reader any doubt that Socrates fully knows and understands the premises from which he argues for the soul's absolute imperishability, . . . these doubts must be dispelled by the death scene. Such is Socrates' grasp on his conclusion that he can remain totally calm in the face of his own death. (1995, 21)

My imagination goes in the opposite direction from Sedley's. Since the final argument is bad (though interesting), I can well imagine that Plato saw that. I cannot imagine that Socrates, as depicted, didn't see that. Since I believe that Socrates indicates early on (62b–63c) that the foundation for his cheerfulness about death was his belief that he is in the care of good gods, I do not need to explain his calm at his own death by citing a conviction of "the soul's absolute imperishability" – especially since the argument from the claim that P to the claim that not-V is flimsy, and the connection between immortality and unending happiness is not obvious. That explanation ascribes low critical standards to Socrates, and seems to me to trivialize Socrates' calm. The alternate explanation credits Socrates with an interesting attitude toward the world and an entirely appropriate (and consistent) recognition that he is not entitled to instruct others to have that attitude, since it is an attitude, not the conclusion of publicly compelling reasons.

Cebes' request for this kind of proof shows that he isn't thinking clearly. Because Simmias does not comment on the confusion, he is apparently not thinking clearly either. Since except for the impression provided by the *Phaedo* plus the *Phaedrus'* information that Simmias elicits lots of speeches (*Phaedrus* 242a–b) I have no other impression of Simmias and Cebes, I do not necessarily expect them to retain their grip on "if . . . then" and "not" at a time of great distress. Their distress might explain their confusion. And, after all, perhaps Simmias' residual doubt at 107 shows also residual common sense or a recoverable grasp of "if . . . then" and "not," which the two have somehow lost sight of when Cebes asks for a proof that the soul is immortal to further their persuasion.[27]

At 107c–114d Socrates spontaneously relates a myth he has heard about the fate of the soul after death. The myth is not his own invention (107d). It is to illustrate Socrates' statement at 107c that if a soul is immortal, it needs care for the whole of time. For someone with Cebes' concerns the final myth usefully supplements the supposed proof. The myth's account that some souls after death do not suffer but have a pleasant existence answers Cebes' fleeting worry about suffering, as the proof does not. But Cebes is satisfied with his structurally flawed argument well before Socrates relates the myth.

The secondary literature has been rightly severe in objecting to many statements that Simmias and Cebes agree to as Socrates argues for the immortality of the soul. The explanation that Socrates is revealing Simmias and Cebes seems more likely to me than the putative explanation that Socrates as depicted or Plato as author accepts these arguments.

6.5 "TRUE PHILOSOPHERS"

I now return to a central premise of Socrates' persuasive speech to Simmias and Cebes – their view of what philosophy is and what philosophers do. We have reason to think Simmias and Cebes understand the designation "philosopher" to refer especially to Pythagoreans. The first exchange between Cebes and Socrates suggests that philosophers should be willing,

---

[27] Rowe (2001, 40) thinks Plato's return to the theme shows he endorses the soul's immortality. I wouldn't say so. On my hypothesis Socrates returns to it because it is a life-guiding idea of certain interlocutors that needs examination. Plato returns to it (as in *Laws*, without Socrates), because he has arguments (that fit Plato's new characters) that are interesting to look at and might be worthwhile for his readers to ponder. We can give Plato credit for either inventing or transforming to get arguments that, though they are not good, are perhaps as good as they can be, and are nevertheless interesting and engaging.

even eager, to die. Socrates articulates in what way those who are "truly philosophers" (64b9) "are sick with longing for death" or "dying to die" (*thanatôsi*)²⁸ (64b5). 64b is evidence that the conception of philosophers as people making a preparation for death was familiar even to non Pythagoreans. Simmias says that "most people" and "our own countrymen" (his fellow Thebans) would think it very well said that philosophers are dying to die (64b3–5).²⁹ Socrates explains that the sense in which it is true (which not everyone grasps) that philosophers are dying to die is that they want to get separated as much as possible from the distractions of the body even while they are alive. Simmias and Cebes agree.

At 64c2 Socrates, having already brought up that true philosophers are sick with longing for death (64b5), extracts from Cebes an account of death:

Then isn't it nothing else than the separation of the soul from the body? (64c4–5)

This is a controversial view of death, one that Pythagoreans hold. Because he is building his persuasive case on the beliefs of people inclined toward Pythagorean views, Socrates doesn't have to mention the alternative possibility that after death there is simply a dead body but no other trace of the dead person, such as a separate soul.

At 65a Simmias and Cebes agree that the body is a hindrance in the acquisition of wisdom (*phronêsis*), which true philosophers, as the wisest (*phronimôtatoi* (62d4)), wish for. Simmias and Cebes agree that sight and hearing have no truth in them. The poets are always babbling (*thrulousin*) that we neither hear nor see anything accurately. It is odd that at 61b1–4 the poets' babblings are the sole (and self-refuting) support offered here for the extreme view that sight and hearing have no truth in them. The poet babbles: "Nothing you see or hear (such as this poem) has any truth in it." It is a puzzle too how poets who have this view

---

²⁸ *Thanatôsi* is from *thanataô*, which might be a desiderative verb from the related verb "die." Thus some translators render it "want to die." Gallop has "verging on death." Burnet (1911) prefers "are moribund," and doesn't find the desiderative use here, but a form of verb indicating illness. Burnet makes an analogy with *nautiân* – "are sea-sick." We don't have the same devices for creating related verbs in English, but we do have the nice idiom "am dying to" to mean "intensely want to," as in "I am dying to meet your friends," or in the children's punning joke: "Cemeteries are very popular. People are dying to get in." If the verb has a connection with illness, perhaps "are sick to death [of living] would approximate it.

²⁹ Burnet's interesting note on 64b3 says:

[P]robably we have a reflexion of the impression made by the Pythagorean refugees on the *bon vivants* of Thebes . . . It is distinctly implied that the word *philosophos* in its technical sense was well known at Thebes before the end of the fifth century, and this confirms the view that it was originally Pythagorean.

think they can ever detect a meter. We readers may wonder if the circumstance that we get nothing accurately from hearing would have been an especial problem for Pythagoreans relying on *akousmata*. But no one mentions these worries here. That we neither see nor hear anything accurately would, however, explain – no wonder! – why Cebes and Simmias hadn't heard anything clear about the prohibition of violence against oneself from Philolaus.

Socrates gets the agreement of Simmias and Cebes to this:

In reasoning (*logizesthai*), if anywhere, something of what actually is becomes clear to it [the soul] . . . It reasons best, presumably (*de ge pou*), whenever none of these things bothers it, neither hearing nor sight nor pain nor any pleasure either . . . but whenever, disregarding the body, . . . it strives for that which is. (65c)

The soul of the philosopher most of all despises the body and flees from it, and seeks to come to be alone by itself. (65c–d)

Readers again might find it odd that Pythagoreans both despise the body and live in Pythagorean communities: it needs some explanation why fleeing from the body is advanced by getting together with somebody else. Readers who remember that Phaedo has said that for him recalling Socrates is most pleasant of all things (58d) will wonder if the great pleasure of recalling Socrates was a distraction from reasoning. If not, then it is likely that the point that pleasure and pain distract from reasoning is restricted to bodily pleasure and pain.

Socrates says more about what true philosophers think about pleasure:

Lovers of knowledge (*philomatheis*: "lovers of learning") realize that when philosophy takes their soul in hand, it has been literally bound and glued to the body . . . when philosophy takes it in hand . . . and tries to release it by showing that inquiry through the eyes is full of deceit, and deceitful too is inquiry through the ears and other senses and by persuading it to withdraw from these . . . and by urging it to collect and gather itself together and to trust none other but itself whenever alone by itself it thinks of any of the things that are, alone by itself . . . It is, then, just because it believes it should not oppose this release that the soul of the true philosopher abstains from pleasures and desires and pains, so far as it can, reasoning that when one feels intense pleasure . . . one incurs the greatest . . . of evils . . . It's that the soul of every man, when intensely pleased . . . is forced at the same time to suppose that whatever most affects it in this way is most clear and most real, when it is not so. (82d–83e)

The claim that great harm ensues when one is "intensely pleased" because one's soul is "forced . . . to suppose that whatever most affects it in this way is ... most real, when it is not so" is stated generally, but is perhaps restricted again to pleasures of the body. (If not, readers might ask if Phaedo's great pleasure in recalling Socrates was a sign that Socrates was not real.)

Simmias and Cebes agree that real philosophers want nothing to do with the body (65d–67b and 82e–83d) but want to reason about things like justice itself and beauty itself (65d–66a), the being of things, what each thing actually is. They agree when Socrates asks if the person who would come closest to knowledge of what each thing is "most purely" is not the one

who approaches each thing as far as possible with thought itself, and who neither puts any sight into his thinking nor drags in any other sense along with his reasoning, but instead, using pure thought itself by itself, he attempts to hunt down each of the beings that is pure and itself by itself, and when he is freed as far as possible from eyes and ears and practically his whole body because it disturbs the soul and does not allow the soul to attain truth and thoughtfulness whenever it is in communion [with it], isn't this the one, Simmias, if anyone, who will hit upon what is? (65e ff.)

An example of a being itself by itself is the beautiful itself by itself (100b6), as well as simply the beautiful itself, the good itself, the just and the holy, and the equal itself:

everything on which we set this seal "what it is" in the questions we ask and the answers we give. (75c)

Socrates presumably has in mind question-and-answer discussions whose topic is what holy is or what beautiful is, elsewhere in Plato called "forms" (*eidê*) or "aspects." They are what it is for something to be holy or what it is for something to be beautiful. At 76d these are "what we always babble about" (*ha thruloumen aei*). Those beings each of which is "itself by itself" are what Socrates will later call "the buzz-words" ((100b5) *poluthrulêta*: "much babbled about").

Socrates' phrasing suggests that Socrates and his friends often talk about items such as justice itself. There is evidence external to the *Phaedo* that Pythagoreans used the phrase "nature itself."[30] We don't know any details

---

30 (a) Philolaus, the Pythagorean contemporary of Socrates, says: "the being of the objects, being eternal, and nature itself, allow divine and not human knowledge" (DK44B6). The author of *On Ancient Medicine* (420–410 BC) in Schiefsky (2005) has vocabulary appropriate to forms: *eidos*, "itself," and "shares in" (see also Taylor (1911b)). At 15.1 the author writes critically of some who give treatment according to a hypothesis but have not discovered "a certain hot by itself or cold or dry or wet sharing in (*koinôneon*) no other form." (At 1, 1–3 also the author

of what Pythagoreans said about these items, nor if they talked about them coherently. Our interest here, however, is the limited interest of seeing how what Simmias and Cebes assent to about such items fits into Socrates' persuasive speech.

Commentators sometimes speak of this passage and others in the *Phaedo* as a reference to "the theory of forms." The phrase "*the* theory of forms" is somewhat misleading, as Plato scholars widely recognize. The dialogues do not put forward just one collection of statements about forms. To debate here about who first invented a theory of forms would be unfruitful.[31] No matter who first arrived at interesting claims about forms that figured in interesting arguments or explanations, it is clear that phrases including "itself" were associated with certain thinkers and teachers before Plato wrote his dialogues. The phrase "itself by itself" had enough pre-Platonic currency that Aristophanes could use it in *Clouds* in an exchange to the

criticizes those who "hypothesize a hypothesis" on medical matters. In 20 the author objects to some doctors and experts who think it necessary for medicine to know what a man is. He says that to know what a man is is a matter for philosophy (his example: Empedocles). Broackes (2009, 17), perhaps correctly doubts that "itself by itself" in 14 is technical. The accompanying vocabulary of 15 inclines me to think it technical in 15.)

   Burnet (1930/1971, 308) claims too strongly that "the doctrine of 'forms'" began in Pythagorean circles. Burnet is confident that the use of the words *eidê* and *ideai* "to express ultimate realities" was pre-Platonic. Burnet finds it "natural" to suppose the use was originally Pythagorean.

   The character Timaeus in Plato's *Timaeus*, and perhaps the Pythagorean listed by Iamblichus (Nails (2002) s.v. "Timaeus") asks: "Is there some fire itself by itself? And all the other things we always speak of thus, each being themselves by themselves?" (51b8–c1).

   (b) Pythagoreans asked "What is it?" questions. Iamblichus VP (82, DK58C4) lists among Pythagorean maxims several such questions and (quite unsocratic) answers.

[31] I am not asking the question whether there was a Pythagorean influence on Plato or whether Plato believed Pythagorean views. I think those also are not useful questions for organizing thought. Better is the question whether Socrates, as depicted, or Plato, was aware of anything one could at that time be aware of about Pythagorean thought. To that question I think the answer must be yes. Socrates, as depicted, is acutely aware of the influences – the life-guiding strategies – that were available to the young people of his time.

   Kahn (1996, 83) on this point says:

Aristotle's account of Pythagorean influence [on Plato] is . . . incredible as a historical report . . . That Plato's doctrine of participation was borrowed from a Pythagorean theory of imitation is not only implausible on its face; it is contradicted by Aristotle's own statement that the Pythagoreans before Plato made no distinction between sensible things and numbers . . . It is Aristotle who attributes to them a doctrine of resemblance . . . for which there is no independent evidence. And there is nothing in the fragments of Philolaus that could be correctly construed as an anticipation of the theory of forms.

I think to put a question in terms of the theory of forms, as though there were some identifiable group of doctrines, is to make it impossible to answer it clearly.

comic effect that the anus itself by itself of a bent-over student was learning to do astronomy.[32]

For our purposes it is enough to notice simply that Socrates as depicted relies on Simmias' and Cebes' receptivity to some statements about items such as justice itself. Socrates' phrase (100b5), "the buzz-words," suggests that forms were a trendy topic. We do not know if Cebes and Simmias were careful thinkers about forms. The *Phaedo* does not tell us whether or not all three share the same collection of beliefs about items such as justice itself. Since Socrates in the *Phaedo* is engaged in persuasion, we cannot without further clues use what Socrates says in his exchange with Simmias and Cebes as straightforward evidence for Socrates' own convictions. We are only entitled to say that Socrates will use as part of his persuasive project what Simmias and Cebes will assent to.

Socrates gets the agreement of Simmias and Cebes to these claims. First,

> Therefore it's a necessity, ... that from all these [considerations] the genuine philosophers would be won over to some such belief, and so would say some such things to one another: that ... as long as we have the body accompanying the argument in our investigation, and our soul is combined together with a bad thing of this sort, we will not ever sufficiently attain what we desire. And we say that this is the truth. For the body offers countless demands because of its necessary nurture ... so that the proverb is truly [said] that really because of it [i.e. the body] no thinking (*phronêsai*) is possible (*eggignetai*) for us ever about anything. (66b11–66c5)

Second,

> We are compelled to gain wealth because of the body, being slaves to its service. And from this because of all these things we have no leisure for philosophy ... (66c8–d3)

---

[32] Aristophanes (Dover (1968, lines 193–194)). The word translated "anus" is straightforwardly clinical or descriptive, not an obscenity:

> STREPSIADES: Why is [his] anus (*ho prôktos*) looking at the heavens?
> STUDENT: It itself by itself [*autos kath' hauton*] is teaching [itself] to do astronomy.

The original play was performed in 423. The version we have is revised, and circulated unperformed during Aristophanes' lifetime (Dover 1968, xcviii). Aristophanes died about 386 BC.

   The play of course features Socrates who, as depicted by Plato, did use the word "itself." But Aristophanes is not clearly carefully parodying Socratic mannerisms in distinction from those of just any intellectuals he happened to think of. See Dover (1968, xxxix–lvii).

   Broackes (2009) studies the passage in Aristophanes usefully, concluding (2009, 14, 15, 20) that Aristophanes associated the phrase "alone by itself" ("a doctrinal catch-phrase," 2009, 21) with Socrates, well before Plato's writing.

Socrates makes entirely explicit that he is describing what follows from the beliefs of the genuine philosophers (here called "those who are lovers of learning in the right way"):

It really has been shown to us that if we are ever going to know something purely, we must get rid of it [the body], and we must view things themselves with the soul . . . And in [the time in] which we live, thus, as it seems, we will be closest to knowing if as much as possible we not at all consort with the body or commune with it – unless there is a total necessity . . . Such things, Simmias, I think, all those who are lovers of learning in the right way (*tous orthous philomatheis*) will, I think, necessarily say to each other and believe – or doesn't it seem this way to you? (66e–67b)

Simmias strongly assents.

Later Socrates articulates the implication that true philosophers live the way they do in order to become god-like:

It is not permitted to one who has not practiced philosophy and departed utterly pure to arrive into the race of the gods [– not permitted –] except to the lover of learning. It's for these reasons, Simmias and Cebes, that true philosophers abstain from all bodily desires.[33] (82b10–c4)

Pythagoras was considered close to a god. Pythagorean *akousmata* were aimed at "following the divine." This may have meant simply taking directions from god, but may have meant trying to be like god.[34]

---

[33] Gallop (1975) translates as "The company of gods may not rightly be joined," which is of course possible but doesn't convey the strong thought that Socrates is talking about actually becoming a god. But it seems clear that that is the possibility envisaged, because of what has preceded. The discussion has been about people whose souls enter into donkeys, wolves, and ants, for example. That amounts to the person's becoming a donkey, a wolf, or an ant after his death as a person.

[34] Iamblichus *VP* 86 says:

All such injunctions . . . which define what is to be done or what is not to be done, are directed toward the divine, and this is a first principle, and their whole way of life (*ho bios hapas*) is arranged for following the deity (*pros tô(i) akolouthein tô(i) theô(i)*), and this is the rationale of their philosophy. (Translation of Hershbell and Dillon (1991)).

This passage seems to relate more to doing what God wants one to do, but could possibly be the basis for a directive to become like God.

Some Bacchic mystery rituals (Burkert 1985, 293–295) offered the promise of becoming god-like or a god. Comparing Empedocles B146 and B112, Burkert says:

With the promise of *apotheosis* these texts go beyond everything else that is known from Greek mysteries of the Classical Age. (Burkert 1985, 295, n. 25)

Whether or not the mystery ceremonies were a step toward *apotheosis*, the theme of becoming god-like was present in Pythagoreanism at least in the person of Pythagoras, called "the Apollo from the North" (Burkert 1972, 141).

There are recurrent reference to "those who are truly philosophers" and to "genuine philosophers" – 63e9–10: "a man who has truly spent his life in philosophy"; 64a4–5: "those rightly going in for[35] philosophy"; 64b4–5: "those who really philosophize"; 64e2–3: "the one truly a philosopher"; 66b2: "those who are genuinely (*gnêsiôs*) philosophers"; 67b4: (a similar phrase) "those who rightly are lovers of knowledge" (*philomatheis*)[36]; 67d8: "those who philosophize rightly"; 69d1: "those who have philosophized rightly"; 80e6: "rightly philosophizing"; 82c2: "those who truly philosophize"; 83e5: "those who are justly lovers of knowledge." Given this concentration on who counts among "true philosophers" even simple references to philosophers call up the picture of philosophers that Simmias and Cebes bring to the conversation. We should also remember that at 62d4 they identify philosophers with the exceptionally wise (*phronimôtatous*).

These recurrent references to "true philosophers" could seem mocking to an unsympathetic ear. However, I don't think that Socrates is mocking. He is simply carrying out a most literal compliance with Simmias' and Cebes' wish for a defense speech that will be persuasive to them in particular, given the exact conditions they specify and given the inclinations they display.

Here I tally some other items besides the conception of the philosopher that Plato's readers of his era would have recognized as Pythagorean that Socrates invokes to carry out his persuasive project for Simmias and Cebes. There is the immortality of the soul, which the aspiring Pythagoreans are not yet fully convinced of at the beginning of the *Phaedo*.[37] There is the recollection of things seen in a previous lifetime. On that topic the aspiring Pythagoreans show their incomplete grasp of Pythagoreanism.

[35] *haptomenoi*: Burnet (1911) note explains that this means "engage in" or "study."

[36] Burnet (1911) on 67b4 says that *orthôs* refers to the rightness of an appellation. It means those to whom the word applies "in the true sense of the word." Given the story of Pythagoras' invention of the word, Pythagoreans would have some claim on the word, as amounting to "Pythagorean." Some later Pythagoreans denied the label "Pythagorean" to certain groups. This would be to deny them the label "philosopher" also.

[37] Sedley observes (1995, 11) the "paradoxical spectacle" of Socrates persuading Pythagoreans of Pythagorean views. That spectacle testifies to Simmias' and Cebes' incomplete assimilation of Pythagoreanism (Sedley 1995, 11): "the shortcomings of Simmias' and Cebes' Pythagorean training"; (1995, 13): "hopelessly confused"). Sedley says further: "Plato wants us to see how inadequately Pythagoreanism has prepared his speakers for appreciation of the soul's immortality" (1995, 12).

That is possible. (It is also possible that Simmias and Cebes are unconvinced of some corollaries of a confused Pythagoreanism because they retain enough common sense to feel the flimsiness of the so-called arguments.) Sedley goes further, however, and thinks it is a sign that Plato believes he has a better argument. I think not. To reveal that Pythagoreanism does not adequately imply the soul's immortality is consistent with Plato's believing that nothing presently known to him implies it either.

Simmias doesn't know much about recollection, and Cebes associates it with Socrates (*eiôthas*).[38] Other Pythagorean themes are the connection with mysteries, the transmigration of souls (81d5–82b9), becoming god-like (82b10), the tripartite division of the soul (implied at 68c2 and closely related to the Pythagorean doctrine of the three lives, according to Burnet (1911)), talk of items such as justice itself, and the extensive Pythagorean myth at the end of the *Phaedo*.[39] Socrates in fact out-Pythagorizes his young friends. Although they are interested in Pythagoreanism, they are not as clear on what it involves as he is.[40]

I conclude that this whole discussion of what philosophy is and what the true philosopher does, addressed as a persuasive effort to the aspiring Pythagoreans, Simmias and Cebes, represents their beliefs and inclinations particularly.

6.6 SOCRATES IS NOT AMONG THE "TRUE PHILOSOPHERS" HE DESCRIBES

There remains to consider whether Socrates as depicted in the *Phaedo* considers himself one of the "true philosophers," as Simmias and Cebes understand them. In fact the *Phaedo* makes very doubtful that Socrates,

---

[38] Pythagorean recollection was of one's experiences in a previous lifetime. Plato adds in the *Phaedo* that one also recollects truths about justice itself, for example (75c–d). Kahn (2001, 51) thinks that Plato innovatively added recollection of forms to the Pythagorean notion of recollection. Possibly: but I would not agree that Plato added it because he wished to advocate it. Rather, I would think more likely that Plato adds it because it serves Socrates' purposes in this particular dialogue of encouraging his interlocutors to examine their life-guiding beliefs (and, also, it is an interesting idea).

Burnet (1911) on 72e4 thinks that "you are accustomed" and Simmias' unawareness of this are evidence that the doctrine of recollection did not belong to fifth-century Pythagoreanism, though it had Pythagorean origins. He thinks that Socrates made an original application of recollection to scientific and mathematical views. I think the more likely explanation is that Simmias and Cebes don't know as much as they might about the views of the circle they aspire to be part of. Socrates, however, has taken the trouble to become quite familiar with the views of many thinkers with life-guiding pretensions. He naturally leads conversation around to these views to encourage further exploration of them.

[39] Kingsley (1995, 148) after extensive discussion concludes that the myth comes very closely from a composition by Zopyrus of Tarentum, a Pythagorean.

[40] The *Meno* introduces recollection as something that Socrates has heard from "wise men and women." (The mention of women suggests Pythagoreans, since women were accepted into Pythagorean circles.) The appellation "wise," coming from Socrates, is not a compliment or recommendation. I do not take it as an expression of the depicted Socrates' own views. It is better explained as something that appeals to his particular interlocutor, Meno, there. Socrates' appealing to Meno's views is one of the themes of Ebert (2007). Ebert says Socrates makes use of Meno's "reverence for what he knows about Western philosophy" (2007, 197) and is "quoting, as it were, from the Pythagorean tradition of his time" (2007, 198) but not advocating it.

as depicted, satisfies the description of Simmias' and Cebes' "true philosopher" – so doubtful as to imply that Plato intends to convey that Socrates does not satisfy it.

Consider first the description that the true philosopher despises the body and consorts with it only when there is "total necessity" (64e1). Counting everybody (59b–c) visiting prison to see Socrates, we find at least fourteen other bodies present with Socrates throughout the conversation of the final day. Socrates has spent the night with his wife Xanthippe, who has brought along their infant (59e–60a). Even if we imagine that Socrates spent his last night with Xanthippe discussing *post-mortem* household management (which anyway indicates concern for matters of the body), the infant is still evidence of a fairly recent involvement in sex, instead of the true philosopher's "not at all" (64d7). Socrates has got an insight from his body early in the dialogue (60a): the sensation that ensued when he was released from his fetters gave him the idea that pleasure and pain, though opposites, are closely connected. At 74–6 he will use an argument from bodies – sticks and stones – or from what it seems to him (to his sight) about their length – to get a conclusion about the equal itself: the body is not distracting him from thoughts of the equal itself, but rather provoking them. He has been composing poetry, which involves a close attention to sound (60d–61a). He has been spending the last thirty days, not to mention his previous life, as Xanthippe comments (60a), talking with friends. He can't think of anything better to do for his last hours of life (61e) than engage in conversation, which involves hearing and other participants. If he strongly wanted his soul to be alone by itself undistracted by the body the better to think of items like justice itself, this is all odd behavior.

Does he believe the extreme statement – something that true philosophers say to one another (66c4–5) – that because of the body no thinking is possible for us ever about anything? That is unlikely. It does not apply to Socrates. Socrates spends lots of time thinking. Does he believe the extreme claim that "we" (at least the present company, but presumably all those with a body) have no leisure for philosophy? It is the sort of thing that true philosophers say to one another (66d2–3), but it collides with Socrates' previous remark that he has been engaged in philosophy his whole life (61a), together with Xanthippe's remembering his previous conversations with his friends (60a).

True philosophers say to one another that one's body forces one to gain wealth (66c7–d3). Socrates, though he has a body, has taken no interest in wealth. The *Phaedo* reminds us that Crito offered to pay Socrates' fine at his trial (115d); it thus confirms Socrates' lack of wealth. These claims about philosophers that are not true of Socrates are strong clues that Socrates does not consider himself one of Simmias' and Cebes' "true philosophers."[41] From Cebes' and Simmias' agreement, it is clear that the claims correspond to the Pythagorean beliefs they profess or aspire to.

The hypothesis that Socrates is now in persuasive mode, drawing out the implications of the convictions of his Pythagorean friends and saying what appeals to them, would explain Socrates' extreme claims more plausibly than the putative explanation that Socrates now believes his extreme claims about philosophers to which he is an obvious counter-example.[42]

Besides the evident indications from Socrates' self-presentation in the dialogue that Socrates is not the Pythagorean "true philosopher" of his persuasive speech there may of course be other allusions to Socrates' non Pythagoreanism that we can't now well recognize. Some details that may signal Socrates' non-Pythagoreanism are these. Socrates sits on his unmade bed for most of the *Phaedo*: Pythagoreans are supposed to smooth out their bedclothes upon getting up.[43] Socrates takes a bath: there is some – inconveniently inconsistent – evidence of a Pythagorean taboo

[41] Woolf (2004) distinguishes between what he calls "an ascetic reading" and "an evaluative reading" of Socrates' talk of keeping away from one's body. Woolf thinks Plato intended to keep both readings possible. Taken as ascetic, Socrates' recommendations are absurd (2004, 101); they are out of accord with Socrates' own life (2004, 104); and Woolf finds that the ascetic reading "fails to make sense of the idea that the philosopher strives to separate himself from his body" (2004, 106–108). Woolf concludes that the evaluative reading is better for interpreting what Socrates says about a philosophical way of life (2004, 110). However, Woolf finds the ascetic reading better for interpreting what Socrates says about death in connection with the affinity argument (2004, 110–122). The ascetic reading "is needed to secure the appealing vision of immortality on offer [in the affinity argument]" (2004, 123).

[42] For example Bostock (1986, 34–35) says:

The morality which our "true philosopher" lays claim to is thoroughly egocentric ... [T]he philosopher clearly pursues *his own* wisdom. That is the one thing he wants, and the one thing that will get him where he wants to be, off the cycle of reincarnation and ... to bliss everlasting. To this one overriding ambition *everything else* is subordinate, not only the demands of his own body but also all sympathy for others, all concern for justice, and in short practically everything that we consider important to morality.

[43] Burkert (1972, 173) cites Stobaeus 1 49, 59 (from vol. 1 of Wachsmuth and Hense (1958)). The *akousma* from Stobaeus says to roll your bedclothes up every day with the suggestion that that is so you are ready for the journey to the next life. Burkert (1972, n. 55) cites Aristophanes' *Clouds* 975 (as a parallel?). Hewitt (1935, 10–16) discusses Pythagorean and earlier sources for the injunction to straighten up one's bedclothes to remove one's traces.

A later version or perhaps a different *akousma* discussed by Plutarch, *Moralia* ("Table Talk" VIII, 7, 727) summarizes a precept as: "on rising from bed to shake up the bedclothes" (727c). Plutarch's characters (728 B–C) decide that the *akousma* has the commonsense meaning that it is proper to conceal the evidence of bedtime activity with one's wife, or proper to get bedding put away to discourage napping during daytime work hours.

involving baths.[44] Socrates makes a final request for a sacrifice (presumably it is a sacrifice) of a cock: there is evidence (again inconveniently contradicted by other evidence) that Pythagoreans did not approve of animal sacrifice; the white cock was especially sacred to them.[45]

One may still wonder why Socrates as depicted didn't point out the logical flaw in Cebes' request instead of following it out so doggedly and literally. It is a partial answer to remember that Socrates is speaking in order to comfort his friends on an occasion that distresses them deeply (58e–59b; 115d5).

Their questioning him about his calmness in the face of death at the scene of his dying would ordinarily be somewhat callous or insensitive. They worry about that mildly at 84d. But they can see that Socrates is utterly undismayable about his approaching death (58e3: *eudaimôn ephaineto*). So they can see that their questions do not disturb him.

They are not themselves comforted by his simple explanation of his own calm at 63b – his impression that he is in the care of good gods. Socrates sees their distress. Although he does say they are mythologizing through and through, it would perhaps have been insensitive on his part to call their attention to invalid argument. He can leave it for them to discover in a calmer moment. His young friends in the *Phaedo* are seeking instruction about the attitude they should have toward death. They have been with a community intensely preoccupied with what happens after death. It is appropriate and useful for Socrates to spell out in more detail than they have apparently done yet what their inclinations commit them to. It is useful for them to see what life-guiding beliefs persuade them at the moment. It will give them something to examine in the future. Socrates says that their investigation will continue (107b).

---

[44] An *akousma* reported by Iamblichus *VP*, 83 is: "Do not use the public baths." This and a related prohibition that one must not walk on roads traveled by the public are grounded in the explanation that it is unclear if those sharing these things are clean. This reference to a public bath doesn't immediately imply that Pythagoreans shouldn't take a bath in prison. (See Burkert (1972, 172, 186, and also 177, n. 86) for other cults' prohibition of baths.) For one thing, we don't know what the prison bathing facilities were.

In fourth-century comedy, later than Socratic times, "the Pythagorean" was a stock comic figure, and by the time of Aristophanes Pythagoreans were associated with asceticism (Dover (1968, xxxix)).

[45] Iamblichus *VP* 84.

Socrates' interest in his friends' continuing to examine their life-guiding beliefs, his agreement to persuade them, and his careful, repeated, retrieval of what they want to be persuaded of, gives us a sufficient explanation of why Socrates says what he says in the *Phaedo*. It gives us no reason to think that he endorses it all.

And we have reasons for the stronger point that Socrates, as depicted, would in fact reject his apparent recommendations for a way of life in the *Phaedo*. One reason is that the account of philosophy that emerges – that it is something that having a body makes impossible – is incompatible with what Socrates has previously said or shown in the *Phaedo* about how he lives. Another reason is the confusion of the arguments Socrates presents.

I have not used the *Apology* to arrive at my interpretation of the *Phaedo*. I have not considered the much-noticed incompatibility of the *Phaedo*'s conception of philosophy with the *Apology*. The *Phaedo*'s conception involves information about what happens after death, and offers the life-guiding principle of getting out of ordinary living. The *Apology*'s Socrates disclaims any knowledge of what happens after death, and urges focused care for how to live here and now. The *Phaedo* philosopher's asceticism is ludicrously incongruous with the *Apology*'s proposal of free lunch for life in the Prytaneum. To interpret the *Phaedo* I have also not assumed that Plato presents the character Socrates of the *Phaedo* to be dramatically the same character who gave a defense in the *Apology* and talked with Crito in the *Crito*. I observe, however, that Plato gives no hint that the thirty-plus days that separate the *Apology* from the *Phaedo* saw so momentous a change of belief.[46]

But it might now be useful to compare the Socrates of the *Phaedo* with Socrates' self-description in the *Apology*. Given that self-description, we should not be surprised if Socrates devotes a whole conversation to articulate for his friends Pythagorean ideas to which they aspire, even though he does not embrace what he articulates. It is not surprising that he is better acquainted with such ideas than his would-be Pythagorean friends. It is not surprising that Socrates would have thought in some detail and would want to think anew about life-guiding ideas that were in the air around him. If someone asks if it would not have been a better alternative for Socrates to give his friends a straightforward lecture to the effect that we have no reason to believe any claims that supposed authorities such

---

[46] Woolf (2004, 125) concludes that we need see no great change in Socrates' views between *Apology* and *Phaedo*. I agree with his conclusion, but not for his reasons.

as Pythagoras make about what happens after death, we can observe that Socrates as self-described would not have thought that a better alternative. The Socrates of the *Apology* evidently starts from where his interlocutors are, not from where he is. He doesn't supply unexamined premises to arrive at life-guiding results for others.

CHAPTER 7

Others' conceptions of philosophy in the Euthydemus, Lovers,[1] *and* Sophist

7.1 COMPARISON OF SOME ACCOUNTS OF PHILOSOPHY

The dialogues that chapters 2–6 considered present several different conceptions of philosophy. At *Apology* 29d–e Socrates says that his philosophizing involves challenging, examining, and reproaching. The *Apology* also shows awareness, however, that some audience members conceive of philosophizing differently from Socrates. Their different conception counts considering what is in the heavens and under the earth as philosophizing (*Apology* 23d).[2] Socrates denies conversing on those topics.

The *Theaetetus'* Socrates gives Thales as example of a philosophizer (174a–b). Thales' doing astronomy would put him into the group that the

---

[1] For the *Lovers* (also known as *Rival Lovers, Erastai, Anterastai,* and *Amatores*) I use the text of Carlini (1964). The *Lovers'* authorship is disputed. I judge that the reasons so far given against it are insufficient. On the side of authenticity are Grote (1867, vol. I, 452); Crombie (1962, vol. I, 225); Guthrie (1978, vol. v, ch. 6); Davis (1984/1985, 5); Annas (1985, 112); Bruell (1987). See also Sprague (1976, 119–121). Against authenticity are Schleiermacher (1836/1973); Shorey (1928); Souilhé (1930, 107–110); and Centrone (2005).
This is not the place for a full discussion. Here I mention only two of the arguments against authenticity. (a) The thought that various constituents are unworthy of Plato seems to me irrelevant because Socrates is extracting the discussion from a confused and somewhat shallow interlocutor. (b) An unsystematic use of the dual I have heard given as a ground for dismissal. But the dual is optional and the plural is an acceptable alternative (Smyth 1920, §955 and §956). Plato mixes dual and plural in the same passage elsewhere (*Phaedrus* 256c).

[2] *Apology* 23d. Socrates (26d) mentions Anaxagoras as someone who talks about the sun and the moon, but Socrates doesn't use a word related to "philosophy" of him. At *Phaedo* 96b, not using "philosophy," he says that in his youth he was interested in the kind of wisdom they call "inquiry into nature"; 97e gives Anaxagoras as an example.
Phaedo 96b is sometimes considered incompatible with *Apology* (19a–d), which says that no one has ever heard Socrates conversing (*dialegomenou* (19d3)) on these topics. But in fact the passages are compatible. The *Phaedo* does not say Socrates conversed about nature, but that he investigated it. I take it that he observed things heating, chilling, and growing. He observed the stars. Because such investigation was confusing, he turned to studying statements (*logoi*) – their consequences and starting points. To move from objects to statements is presumably to begin *dialegesthai*.

Socrates of the *Apology* says he is not part of. The *Theaetetus* digression describes a philosopher with interests very different from the philosophizing Socrates claims in the *Apology*.

In the *Republic* Socrates says philosophers focus on forms and on being itself. Socrates has to explain for his interlocutors what he means. Adeimantus' preconception that philosophers give inescapable argument to unwelcome conclusions interferes with Adeimantus' keeping Socrates' new explanation in mind.

In the *Phaedo* Socrates describes philosophers who practice dying.[3]

Various details of *Theaetetus*, *Republic*, and *Phaedo* block any immediate inference that Socrates as depicted includes his own practice under the conceptions of philosophy that he articulates in those dialogues. The *Theaetetus'* description of philosophy was best understood to be part of a revealing extraction-by-declaration from the unexaminable Theodorus. Socrates offers the *Republic* and *Phaedo* descriptions as part of a task of persuading his interlocutors of a conclusion they assign to him.

Moreover, unacceptable implications of these three accounts of philosophy that Socrates offers to his interlocutors are reason to think that the Socrates of each of these dialogues, as depicted, would in fact reject them as descriptions of what he, as depicted, does in each dialogue.

These alien accounts of philosophy, however, show that Socrates acknowledges several quite different spheres of application for the "philosophy" word-group. Socrates raises no objections to the ways of applying "philosophy" words that his interlocutors accept from him. His interlocutors, on the other hand, when they accept such phrases as "true philosophers," suggest that conceptions other than theirs are diminished or even fraudulent.

In the *Euthydemus*, *Lovers*, and *Sophist*, differently from the *Theaetetus*, *Republic*, and *Phaedo*, certain conceptions of philosophy are first spoken not by Socrates, but instead by others. We have then even no initial reason to attach those conceptions to Socrates. But we naturally ask how others' accounts of philosophy are related to Socrates' activity in the containing dialogues and also to the philosophizing that he says in the *Apology* is his life's work. We naturally ask also if Socrates recognizes others' accounts of philosophy as unobjectionable applications of the word-group.

---

[3] Ebert (2001, 423) wonders if the philosopher of the *Phaedo* could really enter into the life of the philosopher-king of the *Republic*.

7.2 THE CONCEPTION OF PHILOSOPHY OF AN UNNAMED
OBSERVER IN THE *EUTHYDEMUS*[4]

The *Euthydemus* calls attention to an application of "philosophy" to an activity very different from the practices Socrates describes in the *Theaetetus, Republic*, and *Phaedo*. Crito and an unnamed observer label the trick-argument skills, the eristic craft, of the brothers Euthydemus and Dionysodorus "philosophy" (305b).

Crito uses the word "philosophy" (304e) as he hears the report from an unnamed observer of Socrates' conversation with Euthydemus, Dionysodorus, Cleinias, and Ctesippus. Unable to hear the conversation itself because of the surrounding crowd, Crito got his first report of its content from the observer.[5] The observer first says that Euthydemus and Dionysodorus were conversing (*dialegomenôn* (304e)) and that they are the wisest about "arguments of such a sort" (304e), arguments which the observer finds worthless. Socrates later narrates the conversation to Crito.

In the dialogue Euthydemus and Dionysodorus do not themselves utter the words, "philosopher," "philosophy," or "philosophize." However, after they have made their claim to teach virtue (273d), they assent when Socrates asks if they are the best men of the present time to exhort the young toward "philosophy and care for virtue" (*philosophian kai aretês epimeleian*: 275a1–2). I take Socrates' "and" as appositive or epexegetic, equivalent to "i.e." Socrates indicates some link between philosophy and care for virtue; he repeats the link a few lines later when he asks the brothers to persuade the young Cleinias that "he ought to philosophize and care for virtue" (275a6). Agreeing, the brothers accept a reputation as teachers of philosophy.

Socrates is interested in the brothers' claim to teach virtue because he wants Cleinias to "become as good as possible" (275a) which is, by definition, what virtue will lead its possessor to do. Socrates says that if Euthydemus and Dionysodorus have that knowledge of how to teach

---

[4] I have often consulted Chance (1992). I mostly quote the translation of Sprague (1993).

[5] Wolfsdorf (2008, 255–256) finds the Socrates of the *Euthydemus* a psychologically inconsistent or unrealistic character because in the framing dialogue of the *Euthydemus* Socrates praises the wisdom of Euthydemus and Dionysodorus, yet in their internal conversation that Socrates later narrates, which took place some time before the frame, Socrates learned that these interlocutors were not wise. So in the frame he praises as wise people whom he knows are not wise. My explanation is that in the frame Socrates is speaking as other people, such as Crito, speak when they call Euthydemus and Dionysodorus wise. Crito refers to the brothers' reputation for wisdom in the frame at 272d, although he certainly has some doubts. Speaking to Crito, Socrates continues Crito's way of referring to the brothers.

virtue, Socrates is prepared to address them as gods (273e–274a), that is, as having a divine power.

Although Euthydemus and Dionysodorus, assenting to Socrates' question whether they can exhort someone to philosophy and care for virtue, thereby link philosophy and the care for virtue, and although Socrates and the brothers would agree further that virtue is the disposition for living well, we have no evidence that Socrates and the brothers agree on what counts as the best sort of life. Failure to agree on what the best life is will have the result that their conceptions of philosophy as the care for virtue will not genuinely coincide.

The brothers begin their display of the eristic art by asking Cleinias whether the wise or the ignorant learn. At 275d–276d they employ a series of fallacious arguments that take advantage of incomplete and ambiguous expressions to refute both of Cleinias' attempted answers: the brothers argue that the wise cannot learn because you learn what you do not already know, so a learner must be ignorant; the ignorant cannot learn because someone who is ignorant – presumably to the extent of not understanding what he is being told – cannot learn.

Socrates comments that this must be the "frivolous part" of the brothers' study, a sort of initiation rite. He says: "Even if a man were to learn many or even all such things he would know nothing more with regard to the way things are" (278b5). He would only be able to trip other people up. By "the way things are" Socrates means the weighty matter of how best to live.

Socrates gives a sample of the sort of serious argument he would like to see from the brothers: the gist of a very complex argument that he extracts from Cleinias is that everyone wants to be happy and to have good things; good things are useless unless one has knowledge or wisdom to accompany the good things to enable use of them for good results; therefore to be happy Cleinias ought "to love wisdom" (*philosophein*: to philosophize (282d)). When it is the brothers' turn to take up questioning again, however, they persist in the same sorts of fallacious arguments far from Socrates' example of what he hoped for.

The unnamed observer's brief report of the conversation to Crito is this:

You would have heard men conversing who are the wisest of the present day in such arguments . . . the sort of thing one can hear from such people at any time – chattering and making a worthless fuss about what is worth nothing. (304d–e)

Having heard the unnamed observer's scornful opinion of the conversation, Crito immediately calls it "philosophy":

But surely . . . philosophy is a charming (*charien:* accomplished, tasteful) thing to do at least. (304e)

And the observer answers:

Both the thing itself and the men who engage in it are worthless and ridiculous. (305a)

Crito's comment on this to Socrates is:

To me, Socrates, he did not seem to blame the activity correctly – neither he nor if anyone else blames [it]. But to be willing to converse with such people in the presence of many men seemed to me to be blamed correctly. (305b)

Socrates then asks:

What sort of man was he – the one who came up to you and blamed philosophy? (305b–c)

Here Socrates speaks as the observer spoke, using "philosophy" for what the observer blamed. So Socrates also understands that "philosophy" can apply to the specialized conversational skills the brothers teach.

Though the unnamed observer has contempt for philosophy, under-stood, as he understands it, to be the eristic of the brothers, he nevertheless believes, according to Socrates, that philosophy as he identifies it is a way of gaining prestige that outshines his speech-writing expertise (305d). According-ing to Socrates the unnamed speech-writer plans to learn as much of (what he calls) philosophy as he can in order to be the best in the competition for prestige:

These are the persons, Crito, whom Prodicus describes as the border ground between philosopher and politician, but they think that they are the wisest of men, and that they not only are but also seem to be so in the eyes of a great many, so that no else keeps them from enjoying esteem among everyone than these men occupied with philosophy. (305c)

Socrates explains why the speech-writers lack esteem in some circles:

In private discussions, whenever they are deficient, they are cut down by those around Euthydemus. (305d)

The speech-writers' strategy to establish their superiority is to criticize those like Euthydemus without actually competing with them:

Therefore, they think that if they place these persons in the position of appearing to be worth nothing, then victory in the contest for the reputation of wisdom will be indisputably and immediately theirs and in the eyes of all (305d) ... while outside of risks and conflicts, they reap the fruits of wisdom.[6] (305d–e)

Crito has serious misgivings whether philosophy understood as skill in argument-debates is valuable (307a). He is disinclined to recommend philosophy for his own son:

I am not disposed that I turn the boy toward philosophy. (307a)

Socrates' response bears some reflection. He says:

Let go those who make a profession (*epitêdeuontas*) of philosophy, whether [they are] good or bad, but testing the deed itself (*auto to pragma*) well and finely, if it seems to you to be trivial (*phaulon*), turn every man away from [it], not only your sons; but if it seems such as I think it to be, take courage and pursue it and work at it – and as the saying goes – yourself and your children. (307b)

I would rephrase Socrates' advice thus. (a) Forget those who profess to be doing what they or others call "philosophy." (b) Look at what people do who are doing something they or others call "philosophy." (c) If some activity that someone calls "philosophy" seems a bad thing, avoid it. (d) If some activity that someone calls "philosophy" seems as Socrates thinks, a good thing, then practice it.

Socrates seems in a very deliberate way not to be reforming Crito's or anyone's vocabulary. He recognizes that there are a variety of ways to use the word "philosophy." Socrates' statement contrasts with the attitude of, for example, his younger contemporary, the speech-writer and teacher Isocrates. Isocrates later declares that the word "philosophy" should not be applied to skilled disputers or to astronomers (*Antidosis* 261–266) but rather to the supremely useful teachings of Isocrates.

7.3 THE *LOVERS* AS A COMPENDIUM OF CURRENT CONCEPTIONS OF PHILOSOPHY

Plato's dialogue *Lovers* (or *Erastai*) is his only dialogue whose central question is: "What is philosophy?" Testing various candidates for philosophy, the interlocutors reveal what they are at first inclined to think philosophy is. The conceptions revealed and tested in the dialogue turn out to be unsustainable. No final positive account appears. But we readers learn from the conversation what initially counts as philosophy for some people in the era Plato depicts.

---

[6] Morrison (1958, 209–210) discusses this passage usefully.

At the opening of the dialogue Socrates notices that two youngsters who are the objects of attention of two rival lovers are disputing (*erizonte*) about some astronomical topic. When Socrates asks one of the rival lovers, a wrestler, what the youngsters are so interested in, the wrestler immediately says that they are babbling (*adoleschousi*) and they are driveling on, philosophizing (*phluarousi philosophountes*). So the dialogue's opening gives a trace of philosophy as astronomical thought and as disputation.

Besides the wrestler Socrates has as interlocutor "one who has pretensions to be wiser" (132d). For short, I will refer to him as "the intellectual." The intellectual thinks that philosophy is something fine (133b). The wrestler derides the intellectual (134b) as unslept, unfed, and thin from care or thoughts. Here we perhaps see a trace of the expectation that philosophers are Pythagorean ascetics.

The intellectual offers as his first account that philosophizing is learning as many things as possible in one's life:

What else [would it be] except what [it was] according to Solon; Solon said, "I am growing older while I always am being taught many things," and it seems to me to be fitting for someone going to be philosophizing always to be learning some one thing, whether he is young or old, so that he might learn as much as possible in his life. (133c)

The intellectual perhaps evokes Herodotus' story about the philosophizing of Solon, a story that has one of the earliest occurrences of the word "philosophize."[7] (By 425 BC Herodotus' historical work was familiar enough in Athens that Aristophanes could make a comic allusion to the history in *Acharnians* (lines 523–529).[8] *Laches* 188b also alludes, without mention of philosophy, to Solon's learning many things.) In the story (Herodotus 1, 30) Croesus said to Solon:

You have traveled over much of the earth for the sake of spectating (*theôriês*), because of your philosophizing (*hôs philosopheôn*).[9]

---

[7] An early (controversial) occurrence of "philosopher" in Heraclitus (approximately 540 to 480 BC) connects philosophy with much learning: "Men who are philosophers must be inquirers into many things indeed" (DK22B35).

With two other comments it adds up to a sarcastic dismissal of those he calls philosophers:
(i) Polymathy does not teach insight. Otherwise it would have taught ... Pythagoras. (DK22B40)
(ii) Pythagoras practiced inquiry more than all other men, and making a selection of these writings, constructed his own wisdom, polymathy, evil trickery. (DK22B129)

Heraclitus is saying that philosophers (as Heraclitus conceives of them) – inquire into many things, and learning about many things is a bad thing. These passages also indicate that Heraclitus called Pythagoreans "philosophers."

[8] Forrest (1963, 8).   [9] Hadot (2002, 15) considers this the likely earliest occurrence of *philosophein*.

Croesus expects that as a result of his philosophizing Solon has learned a lot. Croesus then questions Solon as a sage.[10]

When the intellectual's proposal that philosophy is much learning proves unacceptable, he offers that philosophy is learning a moderate amount (134d). The intellectual then professes to be able to support the weaker of two arguments and to win a contest (134d), although he says he won't do that in this conversation. If he considers himself a philosopher, he thinks philosophy involves skill in disputation and in defending implausible theses. Mention of disputation skill evokes the conception of philosophy of the outside observer in the *Euthydemus*. Mention of defending implausible theses suggests the conception of the rhetor Gorgias of Leontini (*c.* 485–380 BC), who refers to "contests of philosophers' speeches" (DK82B11, 13–14) in his speech defending the faithless Helen.

When perplexity about moderate learning ensues because no one can specify whom to consult on which are the appropriately measured studies for the soul (135a), Socrates asks what sorts of things those who philosophize should learn. The intellectual answers that they would be the finest and most fitting kinds of learning that would bring the most reputation (*doxan*) for philosophy (135b) – learning them to such a degree that the philosopher has understanding (135b: *suneseôs*) of these subjects but not to such an extent that he actually produces the product of the study. The philosopher is not like a carpenter who turns out an actual physical product. He is more like an architect who directs others. The architect's greater price apparently indicates his greater prestige (135b–c).

We may compare the intellectual's proposal that philosophy brings prestige to a pronouncement attributed to Gorgias:

Those who do not care for philosophy (*tous philosophias . . . amelountas*) but engage in ordinary (*egkuklia*) studies are like the suitors who, wishing for Penelope, had sex (*emignunto*) with her slave-girls. (DK82B29)[11]

This remark treats philosophy, like marriage to Penelope, as a marker of prestige. The label "philosopher" is then an honorific.

The intellectual next offers that in discussion the philosopher should be able to "contribute an opinion of his own which will make him appear the most elegant (*chariestaton:* most charming, most accomplished) and

---

[10] Plato's *Timaeus* has another use of "philosopher" connected with Solon. The narrator Critias relays his grandfather Critias' account of a narration of Solon's (*Timaeus* 20–21): Solon said he learned in a visit to Egypt some ancient Greek history. According to an Egyptian priest (24c–d) Athena chose for the society she would found a region that would produce men who were most like herself: she was (24d1) a "warlover and a wisdomlover" (*philopolemos te kai philosophos*).

[11] Diels (1882/1960) lists this as of doubtful authenticity.

wisest of whoever is present among those talking or acting concerning the skills" (135d). But in the presence of an expert at any discipline, the philosopher would be useless and hence not good on that topic (137a–b). So this proposal proves unacceptable because the intellectual also believes that philosophers are most useful (136b–c).

The result that philosophers are useless is reminiscent of an implication in another early occurrence of "philosophize" that gives the flavor of the word in the era that Plato depicts in *Lovers*. Thucydides depicts Pericles as saying in 431 BC in praise of Athenians:

We philosophize without weakness (*malakias*). (*History*, 2, 40.1)

That Pericles finds it appropriate to disarm the suggestion that philosophizing involves weakness shows that in his time, as depicted, some people considered philosophers weak – that is to say, presumably, as lacking the vigor for the demands of an active political and military life.[12]

At 137b Socrates comments on the result that philosophers are bad and useless, "It might not be that way, and philosophizing might not be this – being zealous about the arts, conducting one's life minding other people's business (*polupragmonounta*) and poking around and learning many things (*polumathounta*) – but something else." Here he raises a possibility that he will return to at the end of the dialogue.

Socrates then starts another line of discussion about which art makes a creature, whether an animal or a human being, the best (137c ff.). He extracts from the intellectual these admissions. (i) The art that makes some creature the best is the art that knows how to punish rightly, and knows the good and bad, whether one or many (137c) – that is, presumably, whether there is one variety of bad and one of good, or many varieties. (ii) The knowledge that rightly punishes people is the judicial art, the same art that recognizes good and bad people (137d). (iii) If one does not recognize which are good and bad people, one does not know what sort one is oneself (138a). (iv) Knowing oneself is being temperate (138a). (v) Temperance and justice and the judicial art are the same (138b). (vi) This art is the same as the political art (138b), which is the same as the art by which one manages one's household. (vii) It would be shameful if the philosopher spoke or acted in a second-rate way compared to a judge or king or someone else who has the arts just mentioned (138e). (viii) It would be disgraceful if

---

[12] Rusten (1985, 14–19) interprets Pericles' comment not to suggest that all Athenians do philosophy, but that that was one of the things Athenians could take up, as well as their activities as citizens. The date of Thucydides' writing was before 396 BC. The date of Pericles' depicted speech was 431 BC.

the philosopher appeared second best at managing his own household (138e). (ix) It would be disgraceful if the philosopher were second or third best at carrying out some civic assignment. Again the intellectual thinks philosophy brings prestige or highest ranking in an imagined competition.

Socrates in conclusion reports this result from the intellectual's combination of beliefs: "Philosophizing is very far from being much learning (*polumathia*)[13] and busyness (*pragmateia*) about the technical skills (*tas technas*)" (139a).

From the several threads in the *Lovers* there emerges that various conceptions of philosophy are current in Socrates' time, as Plato depicts it. There stands out the (Gorgianic) theme that the philosopher has the most prominent reputation. He shouldn't be in second place in a ranking of pastimes or studies.

Obviously we are given no reason to think that the collection of the intellectual's beliefs that he cannot coherently maintain represents Socrates' conception of philosophy. It is of course possible that some details by themselves might survive further examination.

7.4 THE SETTING OF THE *SOPHIST*

The *Sophist* gives us a Socrates who takes a particular interest in conceptions of philosophy external to him. The main character is an Eleatic visitor or guest never named in the dialogue. It is a small item of similarity with Pythagoras that the participants in the *Sophist* do not speak the name of the visitor.[14]

Socrates asks the visitor, "what the people where he comes from (*ton ekei topon* – 'in the locale there') are accustomed to apply the names ['sophist', 'statesman', and 'philosopher'] to, and what they thought about these things" (216d). The *Sophist* and the *Statesman*, a conversation between the same people on the very next day, together give the impression that there will be another conversation in which the Eleatic visitor holds forth on the topic of the philosopher. But none of Plato's dialogues relates that conversation. However, Socrates' request for the visitor's conception of the philosopher gives us the useful information that Socrates is ready to acknowledge what the visitor will say as a current use of "philosopher" possibly different from the use in Socrates' locale. We have no initial reason to say that Socrates would deem himself a philosopher of the visitor's kind.

---

[13] Manuscript B has *polumathia*. T has *philomathia* instead of *polumatheia* in this sentence, and W has *philomatheia*. (See Souilhé (1930).) The point remains the same on any of the readings.

[14] Translations from the *Sophist* are from Cooper (1997a) with occasional changes.

Theodorus has introduced the Eleatic guest as "very much a philosopher" (216a). Socrates' immediate reaction is to ask if the visitor might be a "god of refutation" (216b). That reaction shows Socrates' awareness of a conception of philosophers as masters of refutation. It also suggests that Socrates might think that Theodorus thinks that is what philosophers are. Theodorus responds that the visitor is no refuter, and is not at all a god (*theos*), but "certainly divine (*theios*: godly), but I call all philosophers that." Theodoros is echoing Socrates' description in the digression of the *Theaetetus* of the god-like philosopher. Theodorus was receptive to that description.

Theodorus' response elicits this reaction from Socrates, who is then silent for most of the rest of the *Sophist*:

And [you do] well, friend. But his kind probably is almost not much easier to distinguish than that of the god. For these men, appearing altogether in all sorts [of ways] through the ignorance of the others haunt our cities – not the fictional (*plastôs*) but the real (*ontôs*) ones, viewing from above the life of those below, and to some they seem to merit honor (*timioi*) for nothing, but to others worthy (*axioi*) of everything. Sometimes they appear as politicians, sometimes as sophists, sometimes they offer the impression of being in every way mad. But certainly I would gladly learn from our visitor – if it's what he would like – what they are used to thinking and what they where he is from are used to naming these . . . sophist, politician, philosopher . . . Did they think that all these are one, or two, or, just like the names, three, and did they by distinguishing three kinds, attach to each a kind corresponding to [the] one name? (216c–217a)[15]

Socrates recognizes several different appearances of what he calls "real" philosophers. I think "real" makes an opposition between "real-life" and "fictional" (*plastôs*), not between real and fake, as some translators have it. Fictional philosophers appear for example in comedy. The translation "fictional" is preferable to "fake" because it would be premature for Socrates to assess some people as fake philosophers. For Socrates has just said that philosophers are almost as difficult to discern as gods are; that puts philosophers at an extreme of difficulty. Having pointed out the difficulty, Socrates then immediately goes on to ask the visitor what he counts as a philosopher. Socrates shows awareness that some people group together sophists and statesmen and philosophers. Socrates does not assume that that grouping can't be correct. He wants to understand what the visitor's people think.

---

[15] There is a textual problem with the last sentence. Schleiermacher (1836/1973) would delete the occurrence of *genos* in a9.

7.5 THE ELEATIC VISITOR'S CONCEPTION OF PHILOSOPHY

Theodorus' introduction and the visitor's evident acceptance of it are strong initial signs that the visitor considers himself a philosopher. If so, what he does in the dialogues in which he appears shows us one conception of what philosophy is. What he does turns out to be, among other things, conceptual analysis, definition by division, and crisp arguments for differences in meaning or differences among kinds.[16] He also makes several explicit statements about philosophy that show what he thinks philosophy is.

First, at 249c–d the Eleatic visitor identifies the philosopher with "the person who values all these – knowledge (*epistêmên*), thoughtfulness (*phronêsin*) and understanding (*nous*) – most." The philosopher therefore, he says, has to refuse to accept the claim that everything is at rest, either from defenders of the one or defenders of forms, and also has to refuse to listen to people who say that that which is changes in every way. He has to say that that which is, everything, is both the unchanging and what changes. The philosopher, as the Eleatic visitor describes him, has a definite position about the constituents of the entire universe. (In that respect the philosopher so described is similar to the natural philosophers like Anaxagoras and Thales.) If the philosopher must have the definite position the visitor states – that being is both the unchanging and what changes, then it would follow according to the visitor that no one among the two groups of theorists of being whose dispute the visitor has described at 246–248 is a philosopher.[17] For one side of the dispute has it that being is the same as body (246b), the other that true being is exclusively "certain thinkables and bodiless forms" (246b).

Second, the visitor asks whether someone who is going to show which kinds blend would not require some knowledge (*epistêmês*). Theaetetus responds: "How does it not require some knowledge – perhaps the greatest (*megistês*)?" The visitor responds:

What shall we call this, Theaetetus? Or by Zeus! Did we fall without noticing upon the knowledge of the free? And is it likely that while seeking the sophist we have first found the philosopher? (253c)

The visitor's response suggests agreement that the knowledge that is a necessary condition of showing which kinds blend with which would be the most important knowledge; he connects having "the greatest" knowledge

---

[16] Ackrill (2001, 96).
[17] It is controversial exactly what position the visitor ascribes to the philosopher. See Politis (2006).

with being free; and he connects having this greatest knowledge and being free with being a philosopher.

The visitor's connection of freedom with philosophy calls to mind and perhaps alludes to the story about Pythagoras related much later by Cicero (*Tusculan Disputations* v, 3, 8)[18] quoted above in chapter 6, section 6.2 (pp. 166–167), and by Diogenes Laertius (*Lives* I, 12; VIII, 8). In Cicero's story the philosopher is the nonslavish, most free one, while the others, the athletes and the merchants, are slaves either to prizes or to profits.[19] According to Cicero's story, men who were most free were interested in being spectators of nature. According to the visitor the knowledge of the free, the greatest knowledge, is a knowledge that would lead to clarity about which kinds blend with which.

Third, the visitor says:

To discriminate by kinds how things can associate and how they can't:... you'll assign this dialectical [skill] only to the one who purely and justly philosophizes... We'll find that the philosopher will always be in a location like this if we look for him. He's hard to see clearly too, but not in the same way as the sophist... The philosopher, always through reasoning staying near the form (*idea*) of being, on account of the brightness of the place, is not at all easy to be seen. (253d–254a)

The visitor adds:

For the eyes of the soul of most people are incapable of bearing up while looking at the divine. (254a–b)

The visitor evidently thinks that philosophers look at the divine, and that most people are not capable of that.

This passage indicates that the visitor's conception of philosophy differs from the conception of the Socrates of the *Apology*, who was clear that he did not have divine knowledge (23a). Socrates' philosophizing, as he understands it at *Apology* 29d–e, involves recognizing that he doesn't know anything important. That would not seem to involve the rare capacity to look at the divine.

Fourth, the visitor says:

It's not harmonious to try to separate everything from everything else. It's the sign of someone completely unmusical (*amousou*) and unphilosophical (*aphilosophou*)... To dissociate everything from everything else is to destroy totally

---

[18] The translation of Cicero by King (1972).

[19] In D.L. *Lives*, VIII, 8 (Hicks, 1925/1991), Pythagoras says more briefly that the best people are spectators while the slavish go after reputation and gain.

everything there is to say. The weaving together of forms with one another is what makes speech possible for us... If we were deprived of that [of speech being among those things that are], the biggest thing is, we'd be deprived of philosophy. (259d–260a)

The visitor's connection of philosophy with harmony makes us think of Pythagoreans. His emphasis that destroying speech would be the end of philosophy is something that the Socrates of *Apology* 29d–e would have to agree with.

In discussing sophists at 230–231, the visitor also reveals how he thinks of philosophy even though he does not use the word "philosophy." The visitor describes thinkers who cleanse souls by refutation. The visitor is in some doubt whether to call them "sophists" (230e–231a) "so we don't pay them [i.e. the refuters] too high an honor."[20] The appellation "sophist" would pay them too high an honor because it seems to connect them with having wisdom (*sophia*), which the refuters deny they have. They claim only to rid people of the false belief that they are wise. The visitor finally settles on calling their activity "noble sophistry": "The refutation of the empty belief in one's own wisdom is nothing other than our noble sophistry" (231b).[21] Perhaps the visitor implies that these cleansing refuters are sophists of a kind or, differently, perhaps he implies that a noble sophist is not a sophist, as an impending disaster is not yet a disaster.

The visitor thinks that the noble sophist is a beneficial educator among a large group of educators most of whom are not beneficial. He says that the noble sophist confers two benefits: he purges others of the false belief that they know something important, and he makes them gentler. (Compare Socrates' assessment of his effect on Theaetetus (*Theaetetus* 210c).) The visitor's account of noble sophistry fits Socrates' practice as the *Apology* describes it.[22] However, the visitor does not mention that. He gives no evidence that he knows what Socrates does. And the visitor does not call these cleansing refuters "philosophers." Rather, he reserves that word for the people he discusses in the four passages that I considered above.

At 232 the visitor summarizes several characterizations of a certain sub-type of sophist – the controversialist: (a) he teaches others to be competent to engage in controversies about the gods; (b) he teaches people to engage

---

[20] It is controversial whether he is concerned that he would pay sophists too high an honor, or pay the refuters too high an honor. Cornford (1957b, 180) opts for the latter, citing Jackson (1885, 175).

[21] He describes Socratic practice under a branch of his account of sophistry as a sophistry *genei gennaia* – perhaps "well-bred breed." To capture the wordplay Brann, Kalkavage, and Salem (1996) have "the bred-to-kind kind."

[22] Trevaskis (1955) argues that the description fits Socrates and not conventional sophists.

in controversies about objects on the earth and in the sky; (c) he teaches people to make general statements in private discussions about being and nonbeing; (d) he teaches people to engage in disputes about laws and political matters; (e) in fact, a controversialist teaches one to engage in disputes with any expert on any subject. The visitor's accounts are reminiscent of the conceptions of philosophy in the *Euthydemus* and the *Lovers*. However, the visitor again does not use the word "philosophy" for the activity of any of these groups. His not using it seems a deliberate avoidance. He has in mind a quite definite conception of what philosophers do, the conception that surfaces in the several passages previously considered from 249–260.

Unlike the Socrates of Plato's dialogues who has described philosophers of several different types the visitor does not seem to acknowledge that there are a number of uses of the word "philosophy." He has, however, seven definitions of the word "sophist" – at (i) 221c–223b; 231d; (ii) 224c1–2; 224d1–2; 231d; (iii) 231d; (iv) 224d; 231d; (v) 225a–226a; 231d–e; (vi) 226a–231b; 231e; and (vii) 232b–236e; 264c–268c.

In his apparently restricted application of "philosopher" the visitor seems much more of a linguistic legislator than Socrates in the *Euthydemus* and *Lovers*. Or perhaps the visitor is just accurately informing us that where *he* comes from, people use "philosophy" as he describes. If the visitor does wish to legislate, he would be similar to Simmias and Cebes in the *Phaedo*, whose interest in Pythagoreanism is connected with their receptivity to talk of "true philosophers."[23]

7.6 WHY DOES THE ELEATIC VISITOR NOT COUNT SOCRATIC CLEANSING REFUTATION AS PHILOSOPHY?

The Eleatic visitor apparently would omit to count people like Socrates as philosophers. Part of the explanation is evidently that the visitor, as depicted, thinks that Socratic practice does not make grand enough claims. Those who refute the vain conceit of wisdom do not call themselves wise. Hence they wouldn't claim the "greatest" knowledge that the visitor claims for philosophers.

Some interpreters think that Plato would say about philosophy what the visitor says and that the omission of Socrates as a philosopher is to be explained by Plato's new view of philosophy. For example, here is one assessment:

---

[23] See chapter 6 (pp. 182–190) and Ebert (2001).

When Theodorus denies Socrates' suggestion that the visitor is either a god or a specialist in elenchus but instead a *philosopher* who, as such, is nonetheless divine, the implication is that one who engages in the elenchus is not yet a fully-fledged philosopher . . . Plato thus signals here the demotion of Socratic elenctic purgation that is soon to follow . . . This, then, explains why immediately following the introduction Socrates is quickly moved offstage and the spotlight shifted to the new model of the Real Philosopher, the Eleatic Stranger.[24]

I'd agree that Theodorus implies that one who specializes in elenchus, as opposed to going beyond it to some grander accomplishment, is not a fully-fledged philosopher. But we do not know that Plato agrees with Theodorus. Our earlier discussion of the *Theaetetus* digression in chapter 3 raised the question whether Theodorus, who is not a self-critical person, is a reliable source of good views. Given Theodorus' failings, we should hesitate before we attribute Theodorus' views to Plato.

Long (1998) identifies Plato's view of philosophy with the Eleatic visitor's practice and account. I divide Long's discussion into two points:

(i) Long finds the secondary role of Socrates in the *Sophist* remarkable, given Socrates' prominence in the *Theaetetus*:

> In the *Theaetetus*, as generally before, Plato draws no distinction between philo-sophical activity and the life and interpersonal discourse of Socrates. That is what makes the dropping of Socrates so remarkable, especially after his appear-ance in the *Theaetetus* as the paradigm philosopher yet again. Up to this point, Plato has forged a virtually continuous link between his method of present-ing the philosopher to the public and his own representations of Socrates. He has repeatedly defined the philosopher, ostensively, via these representations. Yet in the *Sophist* Plato chooses another philosopher, the Eleatic Stranger, to mastermind a conversation which has the object of distinguishing between the sophist, the statesman, and the philosopher. (117)

We may agree with Long that Plato's preferred presentation of the philoso-pher in the majority of dialogues is that presentation of which Socrates serves as an instance. But we must not agree that in the *Sophist* the object of the conversation is to distinguish between sophist, statesman, and philoso-pher. Rather, the stated object of the conversation is to inform Socrates about how people where the visitor comes from distinguish those three types.[25]

---

[24] McPherran (1993, 118).

[25] Cornford (1957b, 168) proposes that *Statesman* 258a suggests that Socrates would question Socrates the younger on the philosopher in another dialogue on the philosopher, to complete the trio of clarifications that Socrates requests at *Sophist* 216. Although Socrates does allude at *Statesman* 258a to talking with Socrates the younger on some future occasion, it seems unlikely that that conversation

(ii) Long (1998, 121) assesses:

> By the time he wrote the *Sophist*, Plato discards Socrates because his own Socratic figure, many-sided though Plato has made him out to be, cannot represent more than a preliminary feature of the philosophical paradigm, as Plato now construes it.

Long says:

> The Eleatic Stranger ... stands for philosophy, but for a philosophy that is formal, mathematical, detached from historical contingency.

> The philosophy that he stands for is Plato's philosophy, or rather, Plato's post-Socratic philosophy ... [26]

> At some point – I identify this with the composition of the *Parmenides* – he [Plato] decides that his own intuitions and philosophical techniques have outstripped anything he could plausibly attribute to his own Socrates. He also recognizes that philosophy, as he now conceives of it, is unambiguously "elitist" as distinct from demotic, academic, and separate from practical life.[27]

> ... [T]he *Sophist* presuppose[s] that philosophers *have the knowledge* that Socrates in the *Theaetetus* so resolutely disclaims.[28]

Indeed the Eleatic visitor of the *Sophist* presupposes that philosophers have knowledge that the Socrates in the *Theaetetus* disclaims (210c). The Eleatic visitor of the *Sophist* thinks philosophy has much to do with collection and division, and it involves knowledge of kinds and a glimpse of divine things. The engaging issues that the visitor takes on are not central to the conception of philosophy of the Socrates depicted at *Apology* (29d), for example; they are central to someone else's ("in that place there").

We may not, however, immediately infer from Plato's depiction that Plato now thought that Socrates' conception was inferior to the visitor's. I would say, contrary to Long, that we have so far no reason to say that for Plato Socrates now no longer counts as an up-to-date philosopher. We have no more reason to say that Plato thought that the role of the visitor

---

would coincide with the projected conversation about which people *where the visitor comes from* ("in that place there") count as philosophers. Socrates wants to be informed by the visitor. Theaetetus answers the Eleatic visitor's guiding questions in the *Sophist*. Guided by the visitor, with whom he has often talked before (*Sophist* 218a), he can inform his audience about what people, where the visitor comes from, say about sophists. But it is not obvious how Socrates the younger, an Athenian, could, by answering Socrates' questions, show the conception of philosophers where the visitor comes from. See also Notomi (1999, 24).

[26] Long (1998, 131). Long finds useful precedent in Stenzel (1940), who says (1940, 76): "Plato's philosophical interest has entirely changed its direction."

[27] Long (1998, 132).   [28] Long (1998, 133).

as main speaker in the *Sophist* was too advanced to give to Socrates than we have to say that Plato thought that the role simply was not relevant – or even, that it was not good enough. We need further reason if we are going to say that the conception of philosophy-as-important-knowledge is Plato's preferred one. If we propose that (a) the Eleatic visitor's conception is better and that (b) Plato is likely to have the better conception, we need fresh argument for (a).

There is in fact some relation between Socratic practice and what the Eleatic visitor does. Socrates as depicted in other dialogues was perfectly capable of any of the visitor's logical maneuvers. The visitor's method of division is at bottom the multi-step distinction of kinds within larger kinds. Socrates does division on a small scale – usually one-step – in *Euthyphro*: the holy is one part of what is just; number is distinguished into scalene and isosceles; one part of justice has to do with ministering to gods, another with ministering to humans (12d); there are different kinds of ministering (13a). Socrates does division in the *Gorgias*: oratory and pastry-baking and cosmetics and sophistry are part of the practice of flattery (462–463). Socrates distinguishes kinds of fitness – of body and of soul; Socrates distinguishes sorts of apparent fitness – of body and of soul.[29] In the *Protagoras* Socrates elicits arguments to identify, that is, to blend in one way, kinds: cowardice is ignorance of what is and is not to be feared; courage is wisdom about what is and is not to be feared (360c). *Republic* 454a mentions dividing by kinds. In the *Meno* (72–76) Socrates, though not using the vocabulary of blending, shows how certain kinds blend. So the visitor's capacities do not outreach those of Socrates in other dialogues.

Rather, the visitor's important difference from the Socrates of the *Apology* is that when the visitor takes as central the "greatest" knowledge at 253c, he takes as central some techniques that Socrates took as subsidiary to his main project of reflecting self-critically on how to live. The visitor differs in another way from Socrates in that the visitor accepts near-divine status for philosophers.

So we have no more reason to say that Socrates' role in the *Sophist* is a demotion than we have to say that it is an entirely neutrally presented fact, or even a tribute. We have no more evidence that the Socrates of other dialogues now did not measure up to Plato's new standard for philosophers than we have evidence that Plato deemed an alien but rather interesting

---

[29] Allen (1984, 197) observes that *Gorgias* 465 uses the method of division and *Euthyphro* 11e–12e in effect distinguishes species and genus.

conception of philosophy not quite worthy of the Socrates of the *Apology*.

The brute fact is that Plato's Socrates in the *Sophist* and elsewhere reasonably acknowledges several different ongoing conceptions of philosophy in his ambience. He recognizes that "philosophy" is used for more than the activities that the Socrates of *Apology* 29d–e said his philosophizing comprised. Since the acknowledgment is reasonable, it seems likely that Plato also acknowledged the point. Similarly, Socrates' initiating question to the visitor shows that Socrates recognized that the word "sophist" might be used differently elsewhere. As the visitor explains the word "sophist," it can apply to Socrates. And where the visitor comes from ("that place there") the word "philosopher" apparently does not apply to Socrates as he characterized his life in the *Apology*. We readers can conclude that Socrates would not have been the visitor's kind of philosopher, just as the visitor is not quite Socrates' kind. We do not have sufficient reason to say that Plato is using the Eleatic visitor of the *Sophist* to promote Plato's own favorite conception of philosophy. Plato has left it up to us to decide where to apply the word "philosopher."

In summary: Socrates in these dialogues recognizes many uses of "philosophy" as current. And in these dialogues he shows that he can speak as those who primarily have those uses speak. He can include all these things that others consider philosophy as philosophy of a sort:

- (i) skill at eristic disputation (in *Apology* –"making the worse argument the stronger"; in *Euthydemus*; allusion in *Lovers*)
- (ii) speculation about nature, such as the heavens (in *Apology, Theaetetus, Lovers*)
- (iii) prestigious general informedness (*Lovers*)
- (iv) "practice of dying" (*Phaedo*)
- (v) consideration of elevated topics, especially what divine beings would be interested in (*Theaetetus, Republic, Sophist*)
- (vi) collection, division (*Sophist*)
- (vii) arguments concerning the blending of kinds (*Sophist*)
- (viii) claims about the totality of being (*Sophist*).

A conception of philosophy that I have not yet considered –

- (ix) making laconic pronouncements (*Protagoras* (342a–343c)) –

will come up in chapter 9 (pp. 240–241).

These conceptions of philosophy do not at all fit the way Socrates comports himself in the dialogues that contain them. And they certainly do not fit the way the Socrates of the *Apology* (29d–e) describes his philosophizing. (However, the *Sophist*'s activities of collection and division and analysis of meaning are something that the Socrates of some dialogues uses on a small scale as a part of an examination.)

We may conclude from this look at others' conceptions of philosophy that they provide so far no evidence that the Socrates of Plato's dialogues ever moves from the philosophizing as examining that he claims for himself in the *Apology*.

CHAPTER 8

Socrates and Plato in Plato's dialogues

8.1 SOCRATES IN PLATO'S DIALOGUES

Consideration of Socrates' behavior in putatively doctrinal dialogues confirms so far my hypothesis that within the dialogues of Plato Socrates stays the same examining figure of the *Apology*. I do not say that my hypothesis is conclusively established. I think it at least as likely as the alternative hypothesis that Socrates speaks doctrine of a developing Plato.

The hypothesis that the Socrates of Plato's dialogues is deeply the same explains, for the dialogues I have considered, what Socrates is doing – he is engaging in the activity in which, as he says in the *Apology*, he spent his life. In the *Apology* he calls it his philosophizing; he says it comprises asking whether people care for the condition of their souls, and examining or testing them to find out if they do if they say that they do. He discerns their care or lack of it by observing their reaction to being shown not to know what they think they know. He reproaches if they seem untroubled. And all of that, he says, is persuading people to care about the way they live.

In the *Theaetetus* digression, the *Republic*, and the *Phaedo* we saw only a certain stage of the process of examination – the stage of the interlocutor's revealing himself by his reaction to Socrates' apparent teaching. Disclosing to his interlocutors what they are inclined to believe is the first step of the process of examination that he is always encouraging. As it happens, in other dialogues we do not often see direct challenge, the earliest stage that Socrates mentions in the *Apology*. Nor do we often see the later stage of reproach.[1] What we always see is the early necessary stage of the interlocutor's revealing himself. What we sometimes see, as in the elenctic dialogues, is the next stage of exploring the consequences of what is revealed.

---

[1] Cleitophon gives the stage of challenge and the stage of reproach prominence at *Cleitophon* 407b. On *Cleitophon*, see Slings (1999), Bailly (2003), and Bowe (2007). We see praise at *Theaetetus* 210c for Theaetetus' unpretentiousness.

216

On the hypothesis of Vlastos, Socrates' conversations are Plato-centric: Socrates voices Plato's convictions. On my hypothesis, Socrates' conversations center around the interlocutor. If an interlocutor is unwilling to speak out his convictions, Socrates finds them by stating trial positions for the interlocutor to react to.

My interlocutor-centered hypothesis has the advantage of accounting for some details that Vlastos' Plato-centered hypothesis neglects. Mine accounts for Plato's care to identify the Socrates of the *Theaetetus* digression with the Socrates of the *Euthyphro* and hence with the Socrates of the *Apology*. My hypothesis explains Socrates' saying in the *Theaetetus* that *not one* of his arguments comes from him but *always* from the wise person he is currently speaking with (161a7 ff.). It explains that no one, as Theodorus says (169b), can talk to Socrates without getting stripped. My hypothesis accounts for the detail that Socrates calls the conversation of *Republic* book 1 an agreement-based question-and-answer conversation, while he understands the conversation starting in book 2 to be a speech against-speech competition in which the entrants are like litigants in a court. My hypothesis accounts for the detail that Socrates is careful to attach the logical pattern of his *Phaedo* argument to his interlocutors, Cebes and Simmias, for whom he consents to give a defense that is "more convincing" (*Phaedo* 63b4) than his defense in the *Apology*. Notoriously what a litigant says to convince hearers in court is no reasonable guide to the litigant's convictions. Socrates' very literal compliance with his interlocutors' request for persuasion reminds one of the saying, "Be careful what you pray for: you might get it."

My hypothesis had the outcome that for certain views commonly taken to be doctrines of Plato's we have only reason to believe that they attach to Socrates' interlocutors. We do not have reason to attach the views to Socrates. For example there now attaches to Socrates' interlocutors a "grandiose metaphysical theory"[2] of transcendent Platonic forms – items such as Beauty itself and Justice itself – that are the sole objects of knowledge and that are accessible only to a specially educated few. Similarly an "elitist" political program[3] with an account of philosophers as otherworldly sorts

---

[2] Vlastos (1991a, 48): "grandiose metaphysical theory of 'separately existing' Forms"; (1991a, 53): "boldly speculative metaphysical system . . . the transcendent Forms."

[3] For example, Nussbaum (1997, 25–26):

Plato . . . was certainly an elitist about reason, and openly hostile to democracy . . . Plato argues for the restriction of Socratic questioning to a small, elite group of citizens, who will eventually gain access to timeless metaphysical sources of knowledge; these few should rule over the many.

who have a vision of the forms[4] that entitles them to control the lives of nonphilosophers attaches to the interlocutors that occasion it. Similarly for the arguments for the immortality of the soul in the *Phaedo*. I have argued that the grandiose, elitist, and visionary proposals, and the arguments for the immortality of the soul, are various reflections of Socrates' various interlocutors, revealed as he examines them.

Though I confirmed only for selected dialogues my hypothesis that the apparently doctrinal Socrates is still the examining Socrates, I think the reader can easily extend it to dialogues I did not consider, for example, to the *Phaedrus* and *Symposium*. The reader can straightforwardly extend my treatment to points on which the depicted Socrates might seem to differ from dialogue to dialogue.[5] I believe the reader will find confirmation that in all the dialogues of Plato in which Socrates appears he is the same examining Socrates with his conviction of his and our profound human ignorance. He is never a newly confident Socrates teaching novel and elaborate doctrines. He is the Socrates to whom belongs the life of constant examining that he reviews in the *Apology*.

8.2 WHAT DOES SOCRATES BELIEVE?

A central part of Socrates' examining and philosophizing life, as he describes it in the *Apology*, is his profession of ignorance about the greatest thing. The Socrates of all the dialogues does not have knowledge of that greatest thing, how one should live one's life. His considered conviction that he knows nothing important, nothing that would put him in a position to teach others or to advise others how best to live their lives – and neither does anyone else – has been well tested. The insight that neither he nor anyone else has knowledge about the greatest thing turned out to be one part of

---

[4] Vlastos (1991a, 54): "this strange visionary doctrine that the soul has had many births and many deaths, and . . . its epistemological pendant, that *all* knowledge is innate, all learning in our present life being but the recovery of what our soul carries along from its primordial past."

Kahn (1996, 66) attributes to Plato "the frame of mind of a metaphysical visionary" and says:

Such a person is convinced that the unseen, intangible world, accessible only to rational thought and intellectual understanding, is vastly more meaningful, more precious, and more real than anything we can encourage in the realm of ordinary experience . . . Philosophy is essentially the practice of spiritual liberation by which the rational psyche prepares itself for a successful voyage back to its transcendental homeland.

[5] For example, consider Vlastos' list of differences between the Socrates of the early dialogues and the Socrates of the middle dialogues in Vlastos (1991a, 48–49). His ten Theses notice several dimensions of difference between the Socrates in some dialogues and the Socrates in others. Vlastos' summary of the differences in Socrates' conception of philosophy in different dialogues is in his Theses IIA–IIB, VIA–VIB, and XA–XB. My hypothesis would account well for these differences.

the content of the Delphic oracle's answer, "No," to the question whether anyone was wiser than Socrates. The message was about everyone equally, not just about Socrates. Given his experience of examining, he apparently expects the message to withstand further testing by others as well as it has withstood his own testing. Socrates of course cannot elevate his expectation into a teaching – something he knows. He cannot coherently say: "Here are some directions for how to live: neither take nor give directions for how to live."[6] He does, however, always invite his interlocutors to join him in the life of examination. The proposition that no human being has that greatest knowledge that would qualify him to issue directives for how to live has so far survived examination. It implies that no human being should accept such direction from another.

8.3 SOCRATES AND PLATO ACCORDING TO KAHN

Different from my hypothesis that the Socrates of all the dialogues is the examining Socrates of the *Apology* and in opposition to Vlastos' view that the depicted Socrates is of two – or more – minds because Plato uses Socrates to present Plato's developing views there is the view of Charles Kahn[7] that Plato uses even the Socrates of the aporetic dialogues to build toward or to unfold gradually a grand vision of Plato's that will appear

---

[6] Beversluis (2006, 110, n. 34), commenting on Vlastos, thinks there is a serious objection to the thought that Socrates cannot just state moral knowledge:

This thesis [that Socrates wants each of us to find out moral truth for ourselves] in addition to being textually unsubstantiated, . . . has two unfortunate consequences. First, it makes the incommunicable thesis textually unfalsifiable. Second, it frustrates Socrates' alleged wish . . . [*T*]*elling us* that . . . each of us must find out moral truth for ourselves . . . makes it impossible for us to find it out for ourselves.

Beversluis also comments:

What [Socrates] *does* say is that *he* cannot impart moral knowledge because he has none. And neither, he suspects, does anybody else. However, if they did, he would certainly want them to impart it . . . The early dialogues abound with that request . . .

[In] the *Crito* . . . Socrates exhorts Crito to attend to the views of the moral expert – the person who "understands justice and injustice and who represents truth itself" . . . – if such a person exists – and "who should be respected and feared above all others" (*Crito* 48a5–10). The fact that, in all likelihood, such a person does not exist does not alter the fact that he would be the person to consult if he did. There is not the slightest hint in this passage that moral knowledge is incommunicable and that everybody must "find it for themselves." (2000, 109–110)

(a) In this connection we should also keep in mind the (almost) assertion from the *Apology* that the unexamined life is not worth living for a human being. That is some textual evidence. (b) Communicating the content of a claim is different from imparting knowledge of the claim. (c) If consultation with an expert were available, the person who consulted the expert would apparently not be living a human life.

[7] Kahn (1996).

fully in the middle dialogues, particularly the *Republic*. For Kahn Socrates
in Plato's dialogues – with the sole exception of the *Apology*, to which
Kahn accords some likelihood of representing the historical Socrates – is a
constant character speaking Plato's novel vision.[8] I will not here give Kahn's
view the detailed consideration it merits, but will only indicate that I have
thought about it.

Kahn separates the *Apology* even from what most interpreters think to
be quite kindred dialogues such as the *Euthyphro*. One of his reasons is
especially interesting: the *Apology* makes no mention of the "What is it?"
question that is prominent in other dialogues. Kahn observes:

> There is no trace [of definition] in either the *Apology* or the *Crito*, nor in the other
> two short dialogues that may reasonably be regarded as among Plato's earliest
> writings: the *Ion* and *Hippias Minor*. In the absence of appropriate documentation,
> do we have any reason to follow Aristotle in ascribing the practice to Socrates? Or
> should we regard the *What-is-X?* question of the *Laches, Euthyphro*, and *Meno* as
> a Platonic innovation? I believe that the answer to this second question must be
> "Yes."[9]

Kahn's observation about the absence of the "What-is-X?" question is
accurate, acute, and thought-provoking. And it calls for some explanation.
But we need not explain it via the proposal that Plato invented the "What is
it?" question as a step in the direction of "essential definition."[10] We might
also draw from the *Apology*'s silence about the "What is it?" question the
likely conclusion that the Socrates of the *Apology* is not treating the "What is
it?" question as his sole or even central prompt for an examination. Rather,
he leaves open that he had other ways of initiating examinations: he had
other opening questions, and he had the useful modes of extraction by
declaration and of acquiescing to an interlocutor's request to be persuaded,
as in a law-court, of an assigned conclusion.

8.4 THE DELPHIC ORACLE AND A PROBLEM FOR TWO VIEWS ABOUT PLATO'S DEVELOPMENT

Anyone who believes, as do Kahn and Vlastos, that Plato developed, either
early or somewhat later, beyond the views of the Socrates of the *Apology*,

---

[8] See Kahn (1996, 88–93) on the *Apology*. Kahn thinks the *Crito* less likely to reflect the historical
Socrates, but at least more likely than any of Plato's other writings except the *Apology*. Even the
dialogues that Kahn counts earliest after the *Apology*, the *Ion* and *Hippias Minor*, Kahn takes to begin
the unfolding of Plato's own project: "with the *Ion* and *Hippias Minor* we encounter something new"
(1996, 101).

[9] Kahn (1996, 93).   [10] Kahn (1996, 94–95).

has some questions to answer. Should we believe that Plato, as he wrote the *Apology*, was at that time convinced by Socrates' stance of the importance of acknowledging one's own ignorance? That is, should we believe that Plato accepted Socrates' considered interpretation of the message of the Delphic oracle that no human being was wiser than Socrates? Or should we believe, despite Plato's powerful portrayal, that the Socrates of the *Apology* and his interpretation of the Delphic oracle did not convince Plato as he wrote of it? No matter how we answer these questions, if we accept Vlastos' or Kahn's interpretation, we think that Plato came to reject the interpretation of the message of the Delphic oracle that Socrates arrived at after much testing.

Then we have the question: why did Plato do that? Plato depicts Socrates as taking the message of the Delphic oracle very seriously, starting at some point in Socrates' mid-life and up to the important occasion of the defense speech in which he explains his life. People who interpret Plato as at any time offering his own elitist doctrine understand Plato to have rejected entirely the message of the Delphic oracle. Yet the message was about Plato – as well as about you and me – as much as it was about Socrates. If Plato developed to present the positive and extraordinary doctrines with which interpreters commonly credit him, Plato came to believe that the Delphic oracle's message was wrong. He came to believe that there was or could be someone wiser than Socrates, someone much wiser, and about the greatest things. Plato then believed that there could be or were people so wise that they could direct others and thus approach the divine wisdom that Socrates disclaimed. Did Plato believe that this wiser person was himself? Did he have some new basis for that belief? Had he personally survived Socratic examinations? Or did he merely believe or hope that there was likely to be some other wiser person? And did he have some basis for that belief or hope? Had he observed anyone who could survive a Socratic examination and who could thus establish a capacity to instruct others on how to live their lives? I think the answer to all these questions is likely to be, "No." So I find it to be very unlikely that Plato ever rejected Socrates' interpretation of the message of the oracle as Plato depicts it.

8.5 DEVELOPMENT AND PLATO'S CREATIVITY

As part of his overall interpretation of the author Plato, Kahn makes another thought-provoking observation. He says, as one of his principal objections to the idea that even the group of so called "Socratic" or "early" dialogues of Plato's can be taken as reliable testimony to the philosophy of the historical Socrates:

[I]t is highly implausible to assume that a philosopher as creative as Plato should remain fixed in the position of his master for a dozen years or more after Socrates' death.[11]

In connection with the observation of Plato's creativity Kahn asks an arresting question:

If the argument of the previous section is correct, any historical account of Socrates' philosophy (as distinct from his personal actions, appearance, and character) must be drawn from the writings of Plato alone. But Plato is one of the most original thinkers of all time, as well as a great creative artist. How can we distinguish the history from the art? How can we tell where Plato's memory of his master's teaching ends, and his own development and transformation of this teaching begins?[12]

Kahn's question seems to assume that if we admit Plato's creativity, we must therefore look for some point at which Plato strikes out on his own into something new – to develop and transform Socrates' ideas. According to Kahn Plato arrives at the novel viewpoint that "the unseen, intangible world, accessible only to rational thought and intellectual understanding" is "more precious and more real" than "anything we can encounter in . . . ordinary experience."[13] In Kahn's view the creative Plato has a vision of an unseen world that is "the place of origin from which the human spirit or the rational psyche has come, and to which it may under favorable circumstances return."[14] This creative Plato also thinks philosophy is the preparation for a journey to a "transcendental homeland."[15]

Kahn's creative Plato then contrasts fully with the Socrates of the *Apology* who doesn't know sufficiently to teach about the things in the place of the

---

[11] Kahn (1996, 74).   [12] Kahn (1996, 88).   [13] Kahn (1996, 66).

[14] Kahn (1996, 384–385) further summarizes Plato's distinctive views:

From early on Plato's conception of philosophy is guided by a strong metaphysical vision. The objects of knowledge in a strong sense are not the objects of ordinary experience. Plato never gave up the otherworldly vision of reality that he presented in the *Symposium* as the teaching of Diotima, developed in the *Phaedo* in Socrates' characterization of philosophy as a preparation for death, and confirmed in the *Republic* by the allegory of the Cave, where ordinary experience is represented by the prisoners who sit in darkness. Whatever developments and revisions may appear in later dialogues, the basic scheme of metaphysical and epistemic dualism is everywhere presupposed . . . I mean the radical distinction between Being and Becoming, between eternal verities that remain unchanged and variable appearances that come and go. The former are accessible to knowledge and rational understanding . . . And although the metaphysics of invariant Being is scrupulously excluded from the *Theaetetus*, Plato's otherworldly vision is nowhere more strikingly expressed than in Socrates' outburst in that dialogue about escaping from the evils of this mortal life by "assimilation to the divine."

I conclude that Plato never wavers in his metaphysical vision. The reality which is the object of the philosopher's quest is always located in the unseen world of eternal, invariant Being, to be grasped only by rational discussion and intellectual understanding.

[15] Kahn (1996, 66).

unseen, and counts himself fortunate that he doesn't think he knows about them (29a–b).[16] And this creative Plato with his vision of prospective existence in an otherworldly realm contrasts fully with the Socrates whose only concern was that he practice nothing unjust or impious (32d) while leaving aside any thought of death (28d). That Socrates was concerned exclusively with the here and now. Plato's creativity, as Kahn sees it, has led him to place himself as the polar opposite of Socrates.

But Plato might show his creativity in ways other than the way Kahn proposes. For example, it would also be an exercise of creativity if, as I think, Plato started from not fully thought-out ideas in the air in his time or in Socrates' time and then developed them – sometimes by drawing out unforeseen consequences but sometimes by supplementing them in wildly original ways. Plato's attaching these ideas to especially receptive interlocutors to reveal dramatically the characters of those interlocutors would be a creative achievement. These available ideas that Plato creatively extended might be not only ill-thought-out or half-baked, but even far-fetched, cock-eyed, lame-brained, and self-serving. And Plato might even have invented some entirely on his own for his revelatory purposes if he didn't find them ready to hand.

In contrast to Kahn I believe it is most likely that Plato exercised his creativity writing what would appeal to the depicted interlocutors of Socrates. So Plato created the city in the *Republic*, and so he portrayed the arguments of the *Phaedo*. Plato very creatively displays a *modus operandi* of his character Socrates perhaps in the spirit of the conversations he had heard from the historical Socrates.

I would resist Kahn's phrasing of "master" and "teachings," in favor of "much-admired friend" and "convictions." And in contrast to Kahn I would not assume that Plato's memory of his friend's convictions ended. If these convictions stood up to examination, there would be no need to transform or develop them to the extent of espousing their negation. It would be worthy of Plato's creativity for him to spend his writing

---

[16] To fear death, men, is nothing other than to seem to be wise, while not being so. For it is to seem to know what one does not know. No one knows if death is, as it happens, the greatest of all goods for a human being; but people fear it as though they knew well that it is the greatest of evils. And how is this not reproachable ignorance – thinking that one knows what one does not know? But in this, men, I perhaps differ from the many human beings also here and if I were to say that I am wiser than someone in something, [it would be] in this: that since I do not know enough about the things in [the domain] of Hades, thus I also think that I do not know. (29a5–b6).

Because "Hades" is close to the word for "unseen" and because "know" translates a perfect of "see," the whole creates a mild joke; not having seen enough about things in the domain of the unseen, thus I also think that I have not seen.

career depicting discussions of widely different kinds with widely various kinds of people to further subject to examination Socrates' minimal but central conviction of the *Apology* that he failed to know the greatest things.

8.6 THE TESTIMONY OF ARISTOTLE ABOUT DOCTRINES OF PLATO

It may be objected that to suggest that Plato's dialogues do not recommend the famous putative doctrines Socrates articulates is to discount the testimony of Aristotle. Aristotle writes as though he had the impression that Plato was recommending as doctrine some definite ambitious views that go far beyond the Socratic profession of ignorance about the greatest things. If Aristotle were doing that, that would be relevant evidence for how to understand Plato. Or, more exactly, it would be relevant evidence if Aristotle had more information about Plato's convictions than a reader of the dialogues can get from the dialogues. Perhaps Aristotle got information during his time as a student in Plato's Academy from his personal acquaintance with Plato. This is not the place for a full treatment of the bearing of the Aristotelian testimony, but I will make some observations.[17]

First, as Cherniss reminds us, "the external evidence for the nature of the Academy in Plato's time is extremely slight."[18] One of Cherniss' reasons for thinking that Aristotle had no special information about what Plato thought about forms I mention because it is interesting, though I cannot use it myself. Cherniss says that if one takes the educational program of the *Republic* as a genuine recommendation (as I do not) and thinks that the Academy was modeled upon it, then since Aristotle was only thirty-seven years old when Plato died, Aristotle would not have been learning about the theory of ideas:[19]

If this section of the *Republic* is in any way applicable to Plato's own activity in the Academy, it certainly forbids us to suppose that he there came before pupils under thirty years of age, who did not have and could not get the training which he believed to be a necessary preliminary even for the carefully selected students of his ideal state, and glibly lectured to them on the doctrine of ideas; in fact, it

---

[17] See the balanced treatment of Aristotle's testimony in Irwin (2008, especially 77–78). He decides, as I do not, that Aristotle's distinction of Plato's views from the views of the historical Socrates is a convincing basis for the distinction. Although I fully accept Irwin's view of the likely compositional order of the dialogues, I do not follow him in taking compositional order as a clue for separating the historical Socrates and Plato.

[18] Cherniss (1962, 62).

[19] In the *Republic* it is only mature people who are at least fifty years old who are "allowed to devote themselves to the highest philosophy" (Cherniss 1962, 69).

makes it seem highly improbable that he lectured on the doctrine or tried to *teach* it formally at all.[20]

A second reason of Cherniss' to think that Aristotle had no information about what Plato believed that was not derived from the dialogues seems more weighty to me. Cherniss thinks that Aristotle's admitted lack of information about some points of interpretation of the *Timaeus* shows that Aristotle did not get from Plato a definitive interpretation of that dialogue. Cherniss generalizes to make a point about all the dialogues:

Plato did not expound any physics or natural philosophy beyond that which he wrote in the *Timaeus*, and he did not give his students or associates any further exegesis of the doctrines which he set down in his dialogues.

This is not only the necessary inference from Aristotle's confession of uncertainty concerning the intention of the *Timaeus*: it is also implied by the fact that Plato's associates could and did disagree in their interpretations of many of his doctrines. Some of these debates can be reconstructed; for others the evidence remaining is too slight to show more than that they did take place; but those which have left distinguishable traces make it highly probable that there were many more, no sign of which remains.[21]

Another instance of Aristotle's uncertainty about a point in a dialogue that is evidence that Aristotle did not get special clarification from Plato is Aristotle's statement about the *Republic*:

But indeed, what will be the mode of the whole state for those who take part in it, Socrates has not said, nor is it easy to say. For pretty much the majority of the state arises from the citizens other [than the guardians], about whom nothing has been determined. (Aristotle, *Politics* (1264a 11–14))

Aristotle goes on to give quite a list of points left undetermined.

I agree, then, with this particular conclusion of Cherniss': that Aristotle does not have any more information about what Plato believed than is given in the dialogues. (On other matters I have a number of strong disagreements with Cherniss about interpretation of Plato and Aristotle.)

---

[20] Cherniss (1962, 69–70).
[21] Cherniss (1962, 72).The quoted material follows this:

> Aristotle . . . says that he cannot decide precisely what was intended because the *Timaeus* does not clearly state whether the receptacle is separate from the elements or not. It seems not to have struck anyone as strange that Aristotle could make such a statement, although he had been a member of the Academy continuously from the time the *Timaeus* was written until Plato's death. Yet, if he was uncertain about Plato's meaning, did it never occur to him to ask the master for an explanation? Or did he ask and receive no answer? And if so, why did Plato keep silent when he must have known that he was thus inviting misrepresentation of his opinions and misinterpretation of his theories? Whatever the reason may have been, however, the fact itself is certain, and its significance for the so-called "school" is momentous.

For reasons somewhat different from Cherniss' Kahn infers that Aristotle's account of the difference between the historical Socrates and Plato is not reliable. Part of Kahn's evidence is a passage in Aristotle's *Metaphysics*, one of the few in which Aristotle states a difference between Socrates and Plato. Aristotle says (Kahn's translation with one change):

Plato afterwards took Socrates as his teacher, who was concerned with moral philosophy and not with the study of nature; but in these matters Socrates sought for the [said] of a whole [group] (*to katholou*) and was the first to focus attention on definitions. Plato therefore came to the conclusion that this [what is said of a whole group] referred to something else and not to sensible things. For it was impossible that the general definition should be of the sensible things, since these were always changing.

Plato, accordingly, called such entities Forms (*ideai*) and held that sensible things were distinct from these and named by reference to them. For things are named after Forms (*eidê*) on the basis of participation [in the corresponding Forms]. But he only changed the name "participation" (*methexis*). The Pythagoreans say that things exist by imitation (*mimêsis*) of numbers; Plato changed the name to participation. (A6, 987a32–b12)[22]

Kahn finds here no evidence that Aristotle had special information about Plato's early intellectual development. Kahn thinks Aristotle's source for Plato's views was mainly the dialogues plus perhaps information from Xenophon.[23]

From Cherniss and Kahn I take two points about Aristotle's testimony:
(1) Despite proximity to Plato, Aristotle probably did not learn from him personally what Plato's convictions on various philosophical points were.

---

[22] Kahn (1996, 81).
[23] Kahn (1996, 81–82):

There is no reason to suppose that Aristotle had any good evidence for the early development of Plato's thought. When he arrived in Athens as a youth of seventeen, Plato was sixty years old . . . Aristotle had in front of him, as given, all the early and middle dialogues. (Of the dialogues in which Socrates is the chief speaker, only the *Philebus* was composed after Aristotle's arrival in Athens.) . . . [T]he exaggerated estimate of Pythagorean influence certainly corresponds to the intellectual atmosphere of the Academy in Plato's later years.

It is sometimes supposed that Aristotle is relying here on an oral tradition in the Academy, or even that he had discussed these matters with Plato himself. Such an assumption seems entirely gratuitous. We know nothing of the personal relations between Plato and Aristotle . . . And what we do know of Plato as a writer does not suggest any readiness to speak openly about his intellectual development. The only solid piece of historical information here is that the theory of Forms belongs to Plato, not to Socrates . . . The rest of Aristotle's report is more likely to represent his own speculation, based upon his reading of the dialogues and supplemented in some cases by information from Xenophon.

(2) Aristotle probably got his views about what Plato thought from the dialogues, just as we do.[24] If so, then if he reports that Plato thought such and such, his evidence is that such and such a character in a dialogue said it. Where Aristotle reports (in the few passages where he does actually mention Plato by name) that Plato held a certain view, it would be best to take Aristotle as entitled to say that *in some dialogue or other such and such a view is put forward by the main character of that dialogue for discussion.*[25]

If so, then until we take account of what Plato is doing with his dialogues, it is not appropriate to use Aristotle's few reports as reports of Plato's convictions.

To these two points I add a further point that I draw from Stephen Halliwell's study of a passage in Aristotle:[26]

(3) Aristotle himself is aware that what the main character of a dialogue says might not be what Plato believes. Aristotle does in fact sometimes maintain a rather careful distinction between what Socrates says in a dialogue and what Plato might believe.

Halliwell closely studies this striking passage:

Now all the Socratic dialogues display extraordinary flair (*to peritton*), sophisticated stylishness (*to kompson*), ground-breaking radicalness (*to kainotomon*), and indefatigability in tracking philosophical problems (*to zêtêtikon*); but [to do] everything well is perhaps (*isôs*) difficult. (*Politics* 1265a 10–13)[27]

Halliwell comments:

[T]aken both individually and as a group these terms imply very little at the level of philosophical *doctrine*, and much more at that of philosophical ethos, mentality, and in the broadest sense, style . . . The sentence . . . says nothing about specific ideas, positions, or doctrines. (2006, 199–200)

Halliwell also notes passages[28] in which Aristotle's phrasing is a constant reminder that the character Socrates is putting forward certain views. The phrasing is entirely neutral about whether Aristotle attributes the views to Plato. Halliwell then concludes after his consideration of the statement in the *Politics*:

---

[24] On this point but with special reference to the so-called "unwritten" doctrines, see Allen (1984, 20–25).

[25] Irwin (1995, 5–6) lists Aristotle's references to Plato's views. See also Ross (1924/1958, xxxiii–lxxi).

[26] Halliwell (2006).

[27] The translation I gather from Halliwell's summing up (2006, 200). Since *isôs* also means "equally," another translation of the last clause might be: "But to do everything equally well is difficult."

[28] Halliwell (2006, 200–210).

I conclude... that at this (early?) stage of his career Aristotle had a strong sense of, and some considerable respect for, the dialogic finesse and dramatic form of Plato's writings – so much so that he went out of his way to discuss the *Republic* in a fashion which avoids equation of its ideas with the author's personal beliefs, while following a similar though slightly less sustained hermeneutic method in the case of the *Laws* as well. All this is in keeping with the conception of Socratic dialogues attested at *Poetics* 1 1447b11 and *On Poets* fr. 15 (Gigon) as a mimetic genre of writing and therefore, by Aristotelian criteria, a medium for something other than first-person authorial statement. *Politics* 2, in other words, manifests a marked inclination to argue dialectically with Plato's texts, treating their contents as material for serious philosophical debate, but not primarily or predominantly as the expression of authorial tenets.[29]

Halliwell shows that Aristotle can exercise care in treating Plato's writings. Given Aristotle's subtlety in his treatment of the *Republic*, I would say that Aristotle acknowledges that the dialogue form distances Plato from what his characters say.

Aristotle does not, however, always display the subtlety of his understanding. Halliwell's study also calls our attention to the fact that in his treatment of the *Republic* Aristotle seems focused on how certain ideas bear up under scrutiny and how they fit with thoughts that he is working out, and shows no interest in assigning credit or discredit for the ideas he discusses. He is sometimes not careful about ascribing speeches to their correct presenters in the dialogues. For example, he seems to include the *Laws* among "Socratic" discourses even at *Politics* 1265a10–11, since he has just been talking about the *Laws*. And when in the same context he reports some of the content of the *Laws*, his "he says" (1265a5; 1265a29; 1265b19) does not have a named subject.[30]

Continuing with the objection that Aristotle's testimony about Plato has a special importance and should indeed be used as a clue to Plato's thought, one may say that Aristotle himself definitely recommended *his* doctrines. If Socrates' nondoctrinal stance so impressed Plato that Plato was deliberately nondoctrinal, why didn't Socrates similarly impress Aristotle, through Plato's writings, so that Aristotle wrote nondoctrinally? To this there are two responses, the second of which will carry more force.

The first is that there is plenty of puzzlement and tentativeness in Aristotle.[31] He retained the Platonic and Socratic belief in the usefulness of being puzzled, and in stirring puzzlement in students. I say this is

---

[29] Halliwell, (2006, 202–203).

[30] I note that Halliwell (2006) is more inclined than I am toward other explanations of the Aristotelian testimony that separates Plato from Socrates, see Halliwell (2006, 208, n. 48; 209, n. 55).

[31] Aristotle, *Metaphysics* book III, ch. 1; *Nicomachean Ethics* book VII, ch. 1; book IX.

the less convincing response because one can get from Aristotle a strong impression of positive doctrine being enunciated without an invitation to question it – to the extent that one of my students once, to my surprise and disappointment, reacted, "What I can't *stand* about Aristotle is that he thinks he *knows everything!*"

The second response is that Aristotle does not seem as sensitive as Plato seems to the danger of any influence – such as indoctrination – in a direction away from the direction of being self-critical. Socrates as depicted by Plato was acutely sensitive to the capacity for being misled on the part of youngsters who were receptive to – sometimes overeager for – guidance by those they took to be wise authorities. Plato's care to record Socrates' perception of danger is of course evidence for Plato's own sensitivity to it. (See *Republic* 491d–493c. Further evidence for Plato's sensitivity is, as I understand it, the poignancy of the *Theaetetus*.) We do not have to suppose that Plato was sensitive because he had at some point been indoctrinated, and had got over it. We may leave that as a possibility, but we may also entertain as a possibility that Plato had seen the effects of indoctrination on others. We may also entertain as a possibility that Plato was convinced by the argument we discerned in the *Apology*: that those reputed to be wise about the greatest things who were thus perceived as life-guiding authorities were in a position to do the worst harm to others.

A part of this second response is that Aristotle may have been less sensitive to the dangers of indoctrination because he himself was temperamentally not susceptible to it. He was not the sort of person to submit with docility to the guidance of a perceived authority. He was more likely to take any idea presenting itself as authoritative wisdom and to give it a good drubbing. Aristotle's relative insensitivity to the influence of reputed authorities may help to explain why he didn't follow Plato's pattern of deliberately avoiding in his own writings the stance of an authority.

8.7 MORE ABOUT PLATO

We have seen that Socrates as depicted in the *Apology* was horrified by the appellation "wise" that some people gave him (chapter 2, pp. 33–36). He thought it was shameful to seek for reputation and honor more than to care for one's way of life (*Apology* 29d): he was indifferent to and even resistant to honors and reputation.[32] Thus he did not seek out the reputation

---

[32] He projects in a way we can take seriously his lack of interest in victory and his willingness to be refuted and defeated in argument if he is improved by that (*Gorg.* 457e–458b).

and honor that some people presumed the label "wise" indicated. Plato's recurrent depiction indicates the importance Plato attached to the character Socrates' shrinking from conventional honor.

If Plato attached such importance to Socrates' horror of reputation, we have a possible explanation of something else about Plato: Plato's nearly total absence from his dialogues. He is of course absent from the dialogues of Socrates set in Plato's childhood, but we still have the question why he is absent from the dialogues set late in Socrates' life. We still have the question why Plato didn't write dialogues in which he himself took part. At least one contemporary, Xenophon, did show himself in conversation with Socrates. So Plato's keeping himself out of the dialogues so deliberately calls for explanation.

It is only a partial explanation of Plato's absence to say that Plato didn't want to appear to be an authoritative teacher and instead wanted the reader to think about the issues for himself, not simply to accept without examining it what Plato recommended.[33] That would not be a full explanation because to avoid the reader's submission to Plato's authority Plato could have written himself into his dialogues as a character who always said, like Socrates, that he didn't know anything important. There would have been room for one other self-critical person in the dialogues. Yet Plato absented himself. A fuller explanation for his care to be absent would be that Plato was trying to avoid self-promotion, honor, and reputation as much as did the Socrates Plato depicts.[34] And no wonder, if reputation decreases the likelihood that you will be thoughtful about your life.

As it happens, Plato's stratagem of avoiding notice and reputation did not succeed, at least not in the most obvious way or in the long run, any better than Socrates' stratagem did.[35] But – as Aristotle says – it is difficult to do *everything* well.

8.8 SOMETHING ELSE TO EXPLAIN AND A PURE SPECULATION

We may also use Plato's admiration for and imitation of Socrates' distaste for honor and reputation, Socrates' opting out of the competitive

---

[33] Frede (1992, especially 214–219).   [34] Contrast Michelini (2003b, 59) on Plato.

[35] *Apology* 23a: "Each time the people who are present think that I myself am wise about the things on which I refute another person."

Possibly Plato's stratagem worked in the short term. Kahn (1996, 4) says:

In the fifteen years after Socrates' death, Antisthenes was probably regarded as the most important follower of Socrates. The dominant position of Plato, both as author and as leader of a school, was only established later, probably after 385 BC.

glory-seeking way of life of his contemporaries, to explain a possible fact about Plato. As reported by some sources, though the report is controversial, Plato changed his name. We are now in a position to explain this putative fact. His original name, according to D.L. (*Lives*, III, 4) was "Aristocles."[36] Its etymology gives it the meaning "best fame" or "best reputation." If Plato was as horrified by reputation as the Socrates he depicts, Plato would have found that name entirely inappropriate to Plato's aspirations.[37] The name by which we know him, "Plato," which was a common Greek name, has its own interesting etymology. Among the meanings of the source *platus* is "flat." What is flat does not stand out. It is not outstandingly noticeable. "Plato" would thus be a subtle opposite of "best fame." It would be a most appropriate name for someone to choose who wanted to avoid notice and reputation, or for an author who wanted to disappear from his writings.

8.9 A POSSIBLE OBJECTION: THE TRADITIONAL INTERPRETATION OF PLATO

My overall interpretation may seem to have the result that the many generations of previous interpreters of Plato are mistaken. Those who have taken the very famous views that Socrates articulates in the *Theaetetus* digression, the *Republic*, and *Phaedo* as doctrine of the depicted Socrates and hence doctrine of Plato have misunderstood both the fictive Socrates and Plato. Julia Annas raises the objection forcefully against interpreters who say that Plato does not embrace the picture of the philosopher in the *Theaetetus* digression. She says:[38]

Many readers have been tempted to share the alleged view of the philosopher's fellow citizens, who consider him arrogant in his self-sufficiency.

So unattractive is this as an ideal of the philosophical life that there has been...attempt to deny that Plato is recommending it...Apart from other

---

[36] See Riginos (1976). Nails (2002), in her "Plato" entry, doubts that "Aristocles" rather than "Plato" was the given name. Part of her reason is Notopoulos' (1939) demonstration that the name "Plato" was not uncommon, and that etymologies were widely used in apocryphal anecdotes. Notopoulos goes beyond those demonstrated facts to argue that the story of the name change was a fiction. Sedley (1998, 145) deems the story more likely than not. Notopoulos reminds us usefully that Socrates names Plato thus at Socrates' trial.

[37] Sedley (1998, 145–146) "finds irresistible the conjecture that the name change is to be linked to Plato's early association with Cratylus." Sedley thinks that Plato took seriously the topic of etymology and correctness of names. Adding to Sedley's conjecture, I conjecture that partial inspiration for the name change was what Plato learned from Socrates.

[38] Annas (1999, 55–56).

objections, if this were right then ancient Platonists would have grievously mis-understood Plato's intentions here.[39]

I do respectfully disagree with those ancient Platonists who took Plato to be endorsing the declarations of the digression because they took the depicted Socrates to be endorsing them. And though they perhaps misunderstood Plato's intentions, they were nevertheless affected in one of the ways that Plato intended. Plato intended to depict a Socrates capable of appearing to his interlocutors to be an edifying lecturer or sage who could therefore bring about an extraction or revelation by declaration or by a persuasive speech. The ancient Platonists were taken in by the Socrates Plato depicts, just as Theodorus was, and just as some of us may for years have been taken in.[40]

Though I speak of being taken in, I decidedly do not say that Socrates misled the interlocutors I have discussed. In the *Republic* he takes them at their word and gives them exactly, literally, what they ask for: a legalistic counter-speech under conditions they impose. In the *Phaedo* again he takes his interlocutors exactly at their word and gives them what they ask for: an argument to persuade them that has exactly the dubious form that they request. In the *Theaetetus* digression he fulfils Theodorus' prediction that no one in talking to Socrates can avoid being stripped bare. If the interlocutors misunderstood Socrates, it is because they did not listen carefully to themselves or to Socrates.

Annas points out that there was a very large tradition of taking Plato as not advocating anything in the way of doctrine, and in fact as a skeptic.[41]

---

[39] The ancient Platonists that Annas mentions as taking Plato to endorse the advice to imitate god (2002, 52–53) are the first–second-century AD Alcinous and the first-century BC Arius Didymus.
    Compare Beversluis (2006). Beversluis takes as stimulus for his arguments in support of the view that "the Platonic dialogues contain Plato's philosophical views" (2006, 85) that there is a "venerable interpretative tradition" (2006, 91: he lists twenty-nine of the "biggest names in the history of Anglo-American classical scholarship") that would need to be tackled.

[40] However, despite having a disagreement with the ancient Platonists, I can at least agree whole-heartedly with the insight of Annas (2006, Introduction and c. 1). She observes that the ancient Platonists had no need to think of Socrates' different manners in different dialogues as evidence of the development of Plato's doctrines.

[41] See, for example, Annas (1992, 60, n. 28):

> [S]cholars...are often implicitly accepting something like Arcesilaus' view, particularly if they stress the characters of Socrates' interlocutors and Socrates' occasionally dubious-seeming ways of arguing. If an argument is *ad hominem* then fully to understand it we must know about what the interlocutor thinks, and focus on the actual moves and why they are made, rather than seeing the argument as part of a built up "Socratic ethics." Much recent focus on "the dialogue form" and treatment of Socratic arguments piecemeal with stress on the particular context implicitly revives Arcesilaus' Socrates...[A]n interest in oratory developed in the Academy, and Socratic arguments provide much material for studying how to (and how not to) convince various types of people.

Although she finds the skeptical interpretation of Plato overall unconvincing, she recognizes that it has reasonable sources and can be a useful corrective to some excesses of doctrinal interpretations. The tradition of skeptical interpretation is congenial to my own project at least in that it does not take some famous allegedly Platonic doctrines to be actual Platonic doctrines.[42]

8.10 PLATO'S DOCTRINES

I have argued that Socrates, as depicted, was not advancing the famous doctrines of the political arrangements of the *Republic*, the "baroque monstrosity"[43] version of a theory of forms, the arguments for the immortality of the soul, and the conception of the philosopher in the *Theaetetus* digression, the *Republic*, or in the *Phaedo*. If I am right, we do not have sufficient reason to think that Plato was advancing those famous doctrines through his character Socrates.

I do believe, however, that Plato had philosophical views. What I cannot believe, given his reasoning skills, is that he ever had views that are indefensible and that collapse under commonsense examination.

Moreover, as I have said, I assume along with others that the character Socrates does indeed convey convictions of Plato's. My discussion in fact strongly suggests that the author Plato was himself convinced throughout his writing career of the convictions he gives to the Socrates he depicts in the *Apology*, and as my argument has it, to the Socrates depicted throughout the dialogues. The *Apology's* compelling portrait together with the totality of the dialogues is for me forceful indication of some strong convictions of Plato's. They are strong convictions that we may attribute to the Socrates of all the dialogues: for example, that it is important to acknowledge that one does not have knowledge of the greatest matters; that the greatest harm one can do to someone else is to offer as knowledge teachings about how to live that are less than genuine knowledge; and that continually subjecting oneself to examination – possibly by examining others – is a requirement of a thoughtful life. Those connected points are convictions of Socrates, as depicted, and of Plato.

---

[42] It is a relief to find that my interpretation falls into a tradition. Harold Cherniss liked to say (for example, Cherniss (1957, 225)), "There is little or nothing under the sun that is entirely new in Plato scholarship." If so, then something that appears new would be alarmingly suspect. So I am glad to fit into the tradition of the skeptical interpretation of Plato. I am grateful to Elizabeth Belfiore for suggesting that I consider my relation to this tradition.

[43] Meinwald (2008). See chapter 1, n. 16, p. 6.

If my interpretation is correct, many interpreters have misunderstood Plato's writing in two respects: they misunderstand the depicted Socrates sometimes as doctrinal, when he isn't; they misunderstand the author Plato as having doctrines that Plato most likely did not have. The question naturally arises: would Plato have cared that Socrates as depicted and Plato were thus misunderstood? I think in the light of the preceding section the answer to the question about Plato would certainly be, "No, not at all." Plato was apparently not writing to give readers a glimpse of himself. He might even have been pleased to see how well he had disappeared into the text. Surely he would have been pleased to see how well the text provokes revealing reactions from its readers. The answer to the question about Socrates in the dialogues is more complicated. In giving Socrates the appearance of a doctrinaire lecturer, Plato creates an appearance that the character gives himself. So when readers accept that appearance also, to the extent that readers accept it, Plato realizes perfectly his own intention to depict Socrates as he seems to his interlocutors. Readers misunderstand Plato's Socrates exactly as Socrates' interlocutors, for their potential benefit, do.

8.11 THE ARGUMENT OF LOVE; PLATO AND THE HISTORICAL SOCRATES

According to my chapters 3–6 Plato's character Socrates disappears into his conversations with his interlocutors. That is to say, the topic of Socrates' conversations is never primarily Socrates himself. It is always the soul of his interlocutors.[44] We might well ask: why would he spend his life by disappearing in that peculiar way? One form of the question, and one answer, is this:

Why didn't he lead a more ordinary life or a moderately pleasurable one? The answer can be, finally, that he could not help living as he did. I mean that he was driven irresistibly . . . Driven by what? By the one positivity that perhaps can be attributed to him: that he was driven by affection and compassion for others.

---

[44] So, as I understand him, argues Sharp (2006). Particularly interesting is Sharp's discussion in his ch. 4 of three revealing comments about Socrates in the dialogues: Nicias in the *Laches*, Terpsion in the *Theaetetus*, and Alcibiades in the *Symposium*. Sharp says of Alcibiades' declaration in the *Symposium* that nobody is like Socrates:

It may well be that what is unprecedented about Socratic dialogism as Alcibiades knows it and cares about it is Alcibiades himself. He has never felt about or judged the *logoi* of another man as he does Socratic discourse, because no other's discourse contains as much of Alcibiades himself and his own discourse. (2006, 168, ch. 4)

Indeed, all Socrates' negativity stems from that one positivity and is dictated by it. It is his energy, his eros. He is more than just the friend of the Athenian jurors that he says he is . . . He cared for them more than he cared for himself.[45]

Socrates' life of self-submerging conversation shows the love that he claims for his interlocutors (*Apology* 29d1–2: *humas . . . philô*). He cares for them by turning the conversation toward them.

As Socrates disappears into his conversations with his interlocutors Plato disappears into his writing. As the topic of Socrates' conversations is the interlocutor's soul, the topic of Plato's dialogues is the soul of the reader. Plato bares the soul of the reader who responds when Socrates bares the soul of his interlocutor.

We might now ask further about the author Plato a question similar to our question about the character Socrates: why would anyone spend his life – or in Plato's case, his writing career – by disappearing in this peculiar way? The answer I would suggest is the same as our answer for Socrates: a compelling love, and perhaps only that, would explain it. However, since Plato would not ever know most of his readers, we cannot suppose that Plato's disappearance shows his love for the reader as Socrates' disappearance shows his love for the interlocutor. More probably we readers are accidental beneficiaries as Plato uses his dialogues to memorialize Socrates, to continue the Socratic practice of examination, and so to show his love for Socrates. The reader may decide whether so compelling an impulse was likely to be occasioned by the actual historical Socrates or rather by a phantom of Plato's creation only lightly connected to the historical figure.[46]

---

[45] Kateb (2006, 242).

In contrast, Beversluis (2000, 37) says:

> Socrates' frequent use of faulty arguments and unscrupulous dialectical tactics calls into question his announced seriousness and concern for the souls of his fellows.

I would disagree. Of course a full treatment of this point would require discussion of each exchange that Beversluis considers in detail. My impression is that Socrates usually uses a valid pattern – unless, as in *Phaedo*, his interlocutors request an invalid one. When Socrates extracts dubious premises from his interlocutors, he does them the valuable service of showing them the sorts of thing to which they are inclined to assent, revealing them to themselves.

[46] See Segvic (2009, 184) on the historical Socrates.

CHAPTER 9

Socrates and philosophy

9.1 WHICH OF PLATO'S DIALOGUES CALL SOCRATES A PHILOSOPHER?

Socrates, defending himself when on trial for his life, imagines his accusers saying:

"Socrates, for now we will let you go on this [condition]: that you no longer spend your time in this investigation in which [you have been spending your time] and do not philosophize... and if you should be caught doing this, you will die." (*Apology* 29c–d)

Socrates rejects the imagined offer:

I would say to you . . . as long as I breathe and am able to, I will certainly not stop philosophizing, and urging you, and making an exhibit of myself to whoever of you I happen on, saying what I usually [say]: "Best of men, who are an Athenian, from the city greatest and most reputed for wisdom and strength, aren't you ashamed for caring about money – how you will have as much as possible – and reputation and honor, while you don't think of or care for thoughtfulness and truth and your soul – how it will be the best possible." (29d–e)

Using the word "philosophizing" for the activity in which he spent his life, he says that his philosophizing was urging his fellows to care for how they might best live.

To further understand that passage, I'll look at other passages in which Plato uses "philosophy" words. I seek evidence that Plato is, or is not, depicting Socrates as a philosopher. This project will not seem odd if we recall our evidence so far that the Socrates of various dialogues is aware of several distinct conceptions of philosophy and several different activities someone calls "philosophizing." For each such conception there is the question: is Socrates a philosopher under that conception?

236

I group selected passages as types of evidence that Socrates is depicted as a philosopher according to the conception of philosophy salient in each passage.

Most interesting are passages of clear self-description in which Socrates says outright that he philosophizes or is a philosopher.

Also of interest are passages in which Socrates articulates an account of philosophers. We can then consider if the containing dialogue depicts him as such a philosopher.

Also passages in which an observer, other than Socrates, says or strongly implies that Socrates is or is not a philosopher according to the observer's conception of philosophy are of interest.

9.2 CLASSIFICATION OF PREVIOUSLY CONSIDERED PASSAGES

We have already noticed passages in the *Theaetetus*, *Republic*, and *Phaedo* in which Socrates articulates a conception of philosophers.

Given Socrates' professions in the *Theaetetus* that he always gets what he says from the wise person he is talking to (161a–b), and given Theodorus' information that everyone who comes near Socrates gets stripped (169b), the best explanation of Socrates' account of the philosopher in the digression was that it was Theodorus' conception. The failings of the philosopher described in the digression made it likely that Socrates was not that sort.

In the *Republic* Socrates articulates a conception of the philosopher to which Glaucon assents in books 2 and 5. Socrates says more about the philosopher to Adeimantus in book 6. The structure of books 2–10 as a contest of persuasive litigant-speeches gave grounds to say that what Socrates says about philosophers belongs to the eager listeners. It is no grounds to say that Socrates would aspire to it as self-description. Moreover, the inconsistency of the account Glaucon accepts and the confusion of the account Adeimantus accepts give us reason to doubt that the highly self-critical Socrates could be endorsing them.

The *Phaedo*'s Socrates again gives an assigned persuasive speech containing an account of philosophy. Because it is a constituent of an assigned persuasive speech, we cannot straightforwardly take Socrates' account of the "true philosophers" that Simmias and Cebes aspire to be as a self-description of Socrates. The account's failure to survive scrutiny gave us positive reason to think that it did not represent the convictions of the *Phaedo*'s Socrates about himself.

We considered from the *Euthydemus* an observer's conception of philosophy. What the unnamed observer deemed philosophy and thought Socrates

practiced was pernicious and clearly not the practice of the *Euthydemus*'
Socrates.

The *Apology* passage in which Socrates reports that his accusers think
he does philosophizing (23d) of the sort that includes teaching about the
heavens and teaching bad arguments gives another observer's conception
of philosophy.

When the Eleatic visitor of the *Sophist* omits the Socratic practice of
cleansing examination from philosophy as the Eleatic visitor understands
it, we see the visitor's conception of philosophy, according to which the
philosopher has the greatest knowledge, the knowledge of which kinds
blend with which (253c).

Also to be counted as observers' and alien conceptions of philosophy
are the several impressions of philosophy that the young intellectual interlocutor of the *Lovers* explored: for him, philosophy involved wide-ranging
but less than expert knowledge that confers much prestige. The wrestling
interlocutor, in contrast, thinks that philosophy is useless prating and babbling (132b) that wears you thin from anxious thoughts (134b) and is not
an accomplishment (132d).

9.3 SOME MORE STATEMENTS FROM OBSERVERS

Parmenides in the *Parmenides* speaks of Socrates and philosophy in
Socrates' youth. After Socrates displays inability to talk coherently about
forms such as largeness itself and likeness itself, Parmenides says that if
someone won't allow that there are forms of beings and won't mark off a
form for each, he will destroy the possibility of conversation (*dialegesthai*)
(135b–c). Parmenides then asks Socrates, "What then will you do about philosophy?" (135c): Parmenides implies that Socrates as an adolescent has been
doing philosophy.[1] We do not know precisely what Parmenides, as depicted,
thought philosophy was. However, his question suggests either that Parmenides thinks Socrates has been philosophizing, or that Parmenides thinks
Socrates thinks Socrates has been philosophizing. If some of Parmenides'
evidence is what he saw Socrates do when he first addressed Zeno and Parmenides, then Parmenides at least allows philosophy to involve deducing
contradictory claims from an interlocutor – though in an effective way, not

---

[1] Mansfeld (1990, 64–68) decides that the *Parmenides*' chronological indications have only "pseudo-
precision" for Plato's own purposes and we are somewhat free to assume a date. The *Parmenides*
depicts Parmenides at the Great Panathenaea, which occurred at four-year intervals. We then know
four possible dates of the *Parmenides*. The earliest was 462/461 BC, when Socrates would have been
seven or eight. I opt for the festival at which Socrates would have been fifteen or sixteen.

deviously.[2] When Parmenides comments that he noticed when listening to a previous conversation of Socrates that Socrates has been trying to mark off or define (*horizesthai*) forms too soon before being properly exercised (135c), Parmenides gives evidence that he allows definitional – "What is it?" – questions that he has heard Socrates asking to be part of philosophy. Parmenides' asking what Socrates will do about philosophy if there are no forms and hence no conversation suggests that Parmenides thinks (or thinks that Socrates thinks) that to do philosophy implies that conversation (*dialegesthai*) is possible (135c).[3] The sort of philosophy that Parmenides associates with the adolescent Socrates, then, involves conversing, asking "What is it?" questions, and deducing contradictions from the responses of an interlocutor. Such philosophizing is compatible with the philosophizing that the elderly Socrates attributes to himself in the *Apology* (29d).[4] For one thing, it does not suggest that Socrates knows the answers to any of the questions he asks: it permits the *Apology*'s profession of ignorance about the greatest things. The *Parmenides*, however, gives no evidence that the adolescent Socrates would make that profession.

A passage from the *Gorgias* gives an observer's conception. At *Gorgias* 484d–485e Callicles advises Socrates to leave philosophy because it is only appropriate for a certain time of life, and it leaves one "never uttering anything, free, great, or competent" (485e). His advice "stop refuting" at 486c and his scorn for "those who refute these minutiae" suggest that he thinks of philosophy as question-and-answer refutation, perhaps only with the goal of winning a contest. Callicles thinks philosophy is appropriate for youngsters: it shows they are liberal, not slavish, and that they will be later interested in prestige. He says:

---

[2] For (a) discussion of the content of Socrates' conversation with Parmenides – what Parmenides sees as philosophy – and for (b) the assessment that Socrates' arguments against Zeno are excellent ones, see Peterson (2008).

[3] Some interpreters think that Socrates as a youth in the *Parmenides* thinks he knows a fully-fledged theory of forms. Against that Peterson (2008, especially 383–388 and 406–409) argues that to 129b1 Socrates merely deduces problems from Parmenides' and Zeno's professions and does not employ a technical theory of forms. Later Parmenides' questions introduce proposals about forms that Socrates, as part of the question-and-answer convention, is constrained to answer quickly. These go far beyond his simple but effective statements up to 129b1. But Socrates' readiness in answering Parmenides' questions – Socrates' momentary commitments – is not the same as an expression of confidence in convictions that he holds deeply.

[4] Kahn (1996, 93–95) observes that the *Apology* does not mention that Socrates asked "What is it?" about key notions in his interlocutors' claims to expertise. Although other early Socratic dialogues of Plato's show Socrates putting penetrating, as opposed to merely clarificatory, "What is it?" questions as part of the testing of professed experts, Kahn does not allow himself this other evidence. He thinks the *Apology* uniquely reveals Socrates the historical figure. In Plato's other dialogues Socrates serves Plato's own purpose of progressively unfolding his own philosophy.

When I see philosophy in a young boy, I approve of it; I think it's appropriate, and consider this man a liberal one, whereas I consider one who doesn't engage in philosophy illiberal, one who'll never esteem himself worthy of any fine or well-bred deed. (485c)

Callicles might be suggesting that the young who take an interest in minor verbal competitions show an inclination for the greater competitive activities of politics.[5]

Hippias Minor 363a gives an observer's conception. Eudicus asks why Socrates doesn't either praise or refute the speech Hippias has just given because "we [Socrates and Eudicus] . . . most claim to have a share in philosophy." Eudicus thinks Socrates, as a philosopher, critiques speeches and refutes them.

9.4 MORE PASSAGES IN WHICH SOCRATES SUGGESTS A CONCEPTION OF THE PHILOSOPHER

At *Protagoras* 342–343 Socrates sketches a conception of philosophy under which he clearly does not fit. Socrates has entered into a little contest with Protagoras to explicate a poem of Simonides. Socrates says:

Philosophy is most ancient and most prevalent among the Greeks in Crete and Sparta, and the most sophists (*sophistai*) on earth are there. But the natives . . . pretend to be unlearned in order not to reveal that in wisdom (*sophia(i)*) they stand out among the Greeks . . . like the sophists whom Protagoras was speaking of [at 316d–317a] . . . (342a2–b5)

You would know that I say these things as the truth and that the Spartans are the best educated with respect to philosophy (*pros philosophian*) and speeches in this way: if someone would meet with the most ordinary one of the Spartans, in discussions he will find him in most ways an evidently ordinary [person], and then, whatever happens [to be the topic] of what is being said, he throws in a saying worthy of remark – short and compressed, like a skilful javelin-thrower, so that the one he is talking with appears no better than a child. Now there are those – both among people of the present and of the past who have realized this very thing: that spartanizing [laconizing] is much more philosophizing (*philosophein*: loving wisdom) than [it

---

[5] Dodds (1959, 14) says:

One is tempted to believe that Callicles stands for something which Plato had it in him to become (and would perhaps have become, but for Socrates) . . .

The similarity of the name "Callicles" (literally "fine fame") to Plato's putative given name "Aristocles" (literally "best fame") would fit with Dodds' speculation about why Plato had Callicles (real or imagined – Dodds thinks real) as a character.

is](342d4–e4) loving exercise (*philogumnastein*), knowing that being able to utter such sayings belongs to a completely educated person. Among these was Thales of Miletus, Pittacus of Mytilene, and Bias of Priene, and our Solon, Cleobulus of Lindus, Myson of Chen, and seventh is mentioned among these the Spartan Chilon. All these were zealots for, lovers of, and learners of Spartan education, and anyone might see that their wisdom is such – short sayings, worthy of remembering, having been attributed to each one. (342d4–343a8)

Why am I saying these things? Because this was the manner of the philosophy (*tês philosophias*) of the ancients – a certain Spartan brevity. (343b3–4)

It is unlikely that the *Protagoras'* Socrates thinks this account of the awkward-in-dialectic but apothegmatic philosopher applies to himself or that his interlocutors think it applies to Socrates. In the first place, at 336b–c Alcibiades says he would be surprised if Socrates "gives way to anyone among human beings in . . . conversation (*dialegesthai*)." And in the second place, Socrates is not associated with memorable one-liners. In this he contrasts with most of the figures he mentions for their laconic brevity. Their much later biographies in Diogenes Laertius, which at least somewhat represent the lore about them in Socrates' time, often include for each a little collection of pregnant short sayings. Socrates' biography does not. Although there are a number of anecdotes in which Socrates makes witty rejoinders, Diogenes Laertius lists no apothegms for him.[6]

In a qualified way we may say that Socrates' description of philosophy at *Euthydemus* 275a gives a conception of philosophy not applicable to Socrates. Socrates is addressing Euthydemus and Dionysodorus: he gets their assent when he asks if they are best able to exhort a man to "philosophy and the care for virtue." The remark apparently identifies philosophy and the care for virtue. The necessary qualification is that since Socrates is aware that the brothers think of virtue as success and honor in public life, he is aware that the philosophy that interests them is different from what interests him. He is speaking as he thinks they would speak.

In the *Theaetetus* Socrates makes a short allusion to philosophy as crucially involving wonder or puzzlement. Theaetetus says (155d) he feels wonder and gets dizzy when considering how something can be such and

---

[6] Xenophon (*On Hunting* 13.4) links philosophy and apothegms by saying that certain people are not philosophers on the ground (among several) that they don't have any gnomic sayings (*gnômai*). *Contra* Goldman (2009) I would not say that Plato attempts to put Socrates in the tradition of the sages with gnomic sayings.

such at one time and at a later time be the opposite of such and such without having ever *come-to-be* the opposite, i.e. without having undergone a process of change. Socrates says:

> That experience, that feeling of wonder, is very characteristic of a philosopher: philosophy has no other starting point. (155a)

Socrates does not explicitly say here, "I am a philosopher of this sort." He does not elsewhere in the *Theaetetus* say he is dizzied, or equivalently, that he is at an impasse. But he does say that the experience of people who keep company with him is that they are full of puzzlement (*aporias*: 151a). Theaetetus acknowledges impassible points at 158c3 (*aporon*) and 196c9. Other dialogues in which Socrates says he is at an impasse (*aporia*) present Socrates as puzzled (*Meno* 80c–d; *Hippias Major* 286c–d; 304c). In *Protagoras* (61d) and *Hippias Minor* (376c) Socrates is torn between two positions but doesn't use the phrasing "I am in *aporia*" for his state. It seems reasonable to supply it, however.

At *Lysis* 213d Socrates is pleased, watching Lysis, by "his philosophy." Lysis has just involuntarily exclaimed that he thinks there was something wrong with the way they have been doing their inquiry.

In sum, Socrates sometimes connects philosophy with the recognition of a problem. It seems likely that Socrates would include his own practice under that kind of philosophy.

9.5 PASSAGES OF SOCRATES' SELF-DESCRIPTION

Of the four occurrences of "philosophy" words in the *Apology*, two are reported from Socrates' accusers, who do not understand what his philosophizing is. They do not echo him when they say he philosophizes. Rather, he echoes them when he takes up at 29d their imagined condition at 29c: "no longer to philosophize." When he replies that he won't stop philosophizing, he might have said, "I won't stop doing what you just called 'philosophizing' – although you don't understand what I actually do." Nevertheless, I think we can take it that Socrates claims philosophizing for himself at 29d. Indeed, that seems to me the most important passage of Socrates' self-description as a philosopher in Plato's dialogues.

Although *Apology* 28e, in which Socrates says that the god ordered that he "ought to live philosophizing," is the first point in the *Apology* at which Socrates takes on a "philosophy" word for himself, it is somewhat doubtful as a full self-ascription. It comes as a surprise, since previously in the

Apology we have only heard about those whose philosophizing is nothing like what Socrates does. He uses the word "philosophizing" to indicate the false charge against him (23d): his detractors say of him what is handy to say "against all who philosophize" – that he teaches about what is in the heavens and under the earth and not believing in gods and making the weaker speech the stronger. But he has said at 18b–c and 19a–e that he does none of those things. That is to say, he does not philosophize in the way in which his detractors understand what philosophizing is. He does not say that his detractors use "philosophize" incorrectly.

It seems most reasonable to understand 28e to say that the god ordered him to live "as you would say, 'philosophizing'."

Socrates' account of his philosophizing at *Apology* 29d–e is particularly revealing of himself. He is not examining and revealing an interlocutor. Although he is giving a law-court speech, it is because he is in a law-court, not because interlocutors have asked him to speak in law-court persuasive style. And he says that he will speak the truth (17b). The *Apology* speech is different from his speeches in such dialogues as the *Republic* and *Phaedo*, which are intended to reveal his audience more than to reveal Socrates. In contrast, in the *Apology* he wants to explain himself. It is also relevant that at *Phaedo* 62b Socrates suggests that his defense speech in court was less than persuasive. I understand him to mean that the speech did not appeal to the predilections of his audience of Athenian jurors.[7] Naturally, their reaction to his speech reveals the audience somewhat, but his *Apology* speech does not aim primarily at effecting such revelation. He is fulfilling a solemn obligation to explain himself in court (17b–c; 18a; 18e; 19a).

Another passage in which Socrates suggests that he describes himself as a philosopher is *Gorgias* 481–482. Speaking to Callicles, Socrates says that philosophy is one of his beloveds:

Each of us is the lover of two objects, I of Alcibiades, Cleinias' son, and of philosophy, and you of the *dêmos* of Athens and the Demos who's the son of Pyrilampes . . . [M]y beloved, philosophy, . . . always says what you now hear me say, my dear friend, and she's by far less fickle than my other beloved. As for that son of Cleinias, what he says differs from one time to the next, but what philosophy says always stays the same . . . So either refute her . . . or else if you leave this unrefuted, then . . . Callicles will not agree with you, Callicles, but will

---

[7] I agree with Kahn (1996), ch. 3 that the *Apology* is in some ways different from the other dialogues of Plato: it tells us about Socrates in a unique way, and not much about his audience. I agree with much of Kahn's sketch of the "minimal" picture of Socrates that the *Apology* gives us (except for 1996, 89 on Socrates' search for wisdom, which I would put differently).

244 Socrates and Philosophy in the Dialogues of Plato

be dissonant with you all your life long. And yet for my part . . . I think it's better to have my lyre or a chorus that I might lead out of tune and dissonant, and have the vast majority of men disagree with me . . . than . . . to contradict myself, though I'm only one person. (481d2–482c2. Translation of Zeyl (1987))

His statement occurs after conversation with Polus and before he tests Callicles. This is the first mention of philosophy in the dialogue. Up to that point Socrates has several times shown his eagerness for question-and-answer conversation, *dialegesthai* (447c; 448d–e; 449b; 453b; 454c; 457c–458b; 462a) and for testing or refutation (471e–472d; 475e). So here his audience would understand that his "philosophy" is question-and-answer conversation.

We learn later (487d) that Socrates has previously overheard Callicles saying that one shouldn't go into philosophy too far. Callicles shows what he understands philosophy to be at 484d–485e. And he thinks Socrates philosophizes (484c; 486a). Though Socrates says his philosophizing aims at consistency by means of testing, and Callicles shows he understands that as he criticizes Socrates at 485c, Callicles nevertheless thinks that Socrates' questioning is on trivial points (497b–c).

So *Gorgias* 481 seems a somewhat diminished self-ascription. What Callicles calls the "philosophy" of Socrates – which Callicles sees only superficially – is a commitment to consistency.

At *Phaedo* 60e–61a Socrates says he at first understood a recurrent dream that told him to practice music to mean that he should go on as usual, since philosophy is the highest music. Speaking to his Pythagorean friends, he includes his habitual activity as what he and they would call philosophy.

9.6 WHY DID SOCRATES, AS DEPICTED, CALL HIS ACTIVITY "PHILOSOPHIZING"?

On the basis of our spare evidence we may say that in Plato's dialogues Socrates sometimes presents himself as – calls himself – a philosopher. It is of interest that the evidence is spare. Neither Socrates nor anyone else mentions philosophy in for example, *Euthyphro, Crito, Ion, Cleitophon, Alcibiades Major, Hippias Major, Meno,* or *Laches.*

More precisely speaking, we may say that when Socrates does call himself a philosopher, he calls himself a philosopher of exactly one particular kind of many kinds called "philosophers." He is one who tests and examines by questioning and who when appropriate reproaches those examined on the matter of life-conduct.

On the other hand, in the *Apology* Socrates specifically denies that he does one kind of philosophizing, the kind that involves thinking about things above and below the earth. This is the kind of philosophizing that certain detractors attribute to him.[8] Moreover, not only that kind of philosophizing, but several of the other activities that fall under someone's conception of philosophy clearly are not what Socrates was engaged in. For example, Callicles is not accurate when (484c–486d) he describes Socrates' philosophizing as refutation about "minutiae." Nor is the external observer of the *Euthydemus*.

Socrates does not legislate that others incorrectly use the word "philosophers." Yet given these several uses of "philosophy" words for activities that do not at all fit Socrates as he describes his life in the *Apology*, the question naturally, even urgently, arises: why does not Socrates, as depicted in the *Apology*, do for "philosopher" what he does for "wise man"? In the *Apology* he firmly denies that he is a wise man (e.g. 38c). He takes the unqualified term "wise" as a term of terrible slander. (See chapter 2, pp. 33–36.) He allows himself only human wisdom. Why does he not also do the same for "philosopher" and accept the term only in some very qualified way?

If we take the Socrates of Plato's *Apology* to be an accurate rendition of the historical Socrates, there is also a parallel question about the historical Socrates: why, if there were these various competing conceptions of philosophy in current circulation, would he accept the word "philosophize" for his activity, especially when his old detractors' use of it fueled the formal charge against him (*Apology* 23d)? If we do not take the Socrates of the *Apology* to be an accurate rendering of the historical Socrates, we would be free to speculate that Plato invented the fiction that Socrates called himself a philosopher.[9] Yet we still have the question why the depicted Socrates did so.

That, rather than the historical question, is what I am first asking here. I am asking a question about Plato's authorial choices and what explanation for them we can find within the dialogues. That is, I am asking if we can tell from the dialogues why Socrates, as depicted, sometimes calls himself a philosopher. That question is challenging enough.

---

[8] At 23d Socrates implies that three things – speaking of things aloft and under the earth, not believing in gods, and making the weaker speech the stronger – were part of someone's conception of philosophy.

[9] Xenophon's writings generally do not particularly attach the label "philosopher" to Socrates, although "philosophy" words (rather rarely) occur in Xenophon's writings. Nightingale (1995, 17) reports that Xenophon never singles out Socrates as properly called a "philosopher."

9.7 ONE POSSIBLE REASON WHY SOCRATES CALLS HIS OWN ACTIVITIES "PHILOSOPHIZING"

When we dwell on the fact that the Socrates of the *Apology* so emphatically distinguishes himself from the wise man, the *sophos*, and on the fact that to be called "wise" horrifies him, we can see that the word "philosopher" has two features that make it useful for Socrates. First, there is the story of its invention by Pythagoras. The story may or may not be accurate, but it was presumably known in Plato's and Socrates' time.[10] On one interpretation of that story the inventor of the word meant it to indicate that he had no art, no special teachable knowledge. Second, there is the etymology of the word – "lover of wisdom" or "amateur wise man" (the latter phrase from a student's essay). Its etymology lends itself to a somewhat appealing argument that philosophers are not wise, an argument Plato's dialogues record three times.

For example Socrates in the *Symposium* relates that Diotima contrasts the philosopher with the wise (*sophos*) person by calling attention to etymology. Socrates' story of Diotima follows an earlier exchange between Socrates and Agathon. Both are part of Socrates' contest-speech entry into the after-dinner entertainment of competing encomia to *Erôs*. Socrates extracts from Agathon the statement (200a) that whatever desires (*epithumei*) and loves (*era(i)*) something lacks what it desires. Socrates says (200b1), "To me this looks amazingly necessary." Questioning Agathon, Socrates mostly uses the verb *epithumein*, a strong word for wanting or desiring or yearning. Socrates closely connects it with *eran*, a strong word for "love," centrally for erotic love. However, Socrates twice uses "wish" (*bouloito* (200b4, b9)). Socrates and Agathon reach agreement on this important point:

> What one does not have, what one is not, and what one lacks, these are what desire (*epithumia*) and love (*erôs*) are of. (200e)

Having extracted this agreement from Agathon, Socrates then relates what Diotima ("wise in these things and much else" (201d1–2)) said to him when she tested Socrates (*êlegche* (201e5)) in just the way that Socrates examined Agathon. As Socrates tells it, Diotima got him to agree on these points:

  (i) Correct belief is something between wisdom and ignorance.
  (ii) *Erôs* lacks good and beautiful things and thus desires (*epithumei* (202d2)) what he lacks.

---

[10] Our report descends from Heraclides of Pontus, an associate of Plato's. Chapter 6, section 6.2 (p. 167) discusses the source.

(iii) *Erôs* is a great spirit (*daimôn*), neither god nor mortal, but in between (202d).
(iv) Its power (*dunamin* (202e2) is to carry things between men and gods.
 (v) A god does not mix with men (203a).
(vi) The person who is wise about such things (perhaps divine things; perhaps communicating with the divine) is a spirit-like or semi-divine (*daimonios*) man (203a).
(vii) The person who is wise about anything else is an ordinary smith (*banausos*: 203a).

Diotima then describes *Erôs*. He is (203d) a "schemer after the beautiful and good," "a clever hunter," "always weaving some devices," "desirous (*epithumêtês*) of thoughtfulness (*phronêseôs*), philosophizing through all his life, a clever magician, sorcerer and sophist, who 'dies and comes to life again,' and who is 'in the middle between wisdom and ignorance'." After these pronouncements, Diotima says:

This is the way it is: none of the gods philosophizes (*philosophei*) nor desires (*epithumei*) to become wise, for he already is – nor if anyone else is wise [does he philosophize]. Nor again do those who lack learning philosophize or desire to become wise. For lack of learning is this difficult thing: the seeming to oneself, while one is not fine or good or thoughtful (*phronimon*), to be sufficiently [so]. The person then who does not think that he is in need would not desire what he does not think he is in need of. (203e–204a)

To Socrates' question who does philosophize, if it isn't those who are wise nor those who lack learning, Diotima answers:

This is already clear even to a child: those [who are] between both of these. (204b)

Diotima relies on the etymology of "philosophize." It is as though she argues that one who philosophizes, or loves wisdom or *sophia*, cannot actually have wisdom because to love it is to acknowledge that you lack it.[11]

---

[11] In the *Lysis* Socrates apparently infers that those who do philosophy cannot be wise from Lysis' previously granting Socrates at 217e–218a that what is neither good nor bad but has the bad present with it desires the good. The passage apparently equates *philia* – friendship – with *epithumia* – yearning.
 In the *Phaedrus* Socrates again comments that only gods are wise, but people can be philosophers. (And being wise is something better than being a philosopher.) There's no explicit statement that gods cannot be philosophers. At 278a Socrates is discussing a certain sort of person who takes seriously for understanding and learning only "what is truly written in the soul," and who thinks other writing is of little worth. Phaedrus asks what name should be given to such a man, Socrates answers: "To call him wise, Phaedrus, seems to me too much, and proper only for a god. To call him wisdom's lover – a philosopher – or something similar would fit him better and be more seemly" (278d).

Diotima's putative argument would actually be unconvincing. The verb *philein* that is a constituent of *philosophein* is not necessarily a strong verb for yearning or erotic desire in the way that *epithumein* and *eran*, which first appear in Diotima's discussion, are. It is somewhat plausible to say that if one has erotic longing or yearning for something, an intense want, *erôs*, then one must lack it at the moment. Such a strong claim about *philia* is not plausible. To have *philia* – a friendly love – for something does not imply that one lacks it. Indeed, one definitely must have – in an appropriate sense of "have" – some of those for whom one has *philia* – friends, children, or family members. So when Diotima says that one who philosophizes recognizes a lack, she does not successfully argue from the etymology of the word "philosophizes." Someone sensitive to etymology would have to allow that someone friendly to wisdom might actually have it in some sense of "have." It is only someone with a needy craving or yearning for wisdom who necessarily lacks it. To argue successfully from etymology, Diotima should start from such words as *erôsophos* or *sopherastês* – unfortunately both nonexistent.

So the word "philosophize" is merely suggestive of and not on etymological grounds conclusively implicative of "not wise." Yet, in that it is suggestive, Diotima's thought could be part of the explanation of why the word might appeal to Socrates, as depicted. It almost fits with Socrates' claimed eroticism. *His* love of wisdom is a response to a want, a felt lack, something brought on, no doubt, by his constant *aporia*. He has an *erôs* – something different from many varieties of *philia* – that would imply that he lacks wisdom.

9.8 ANOTHER POSSIBLE REASON WHY SOCRATES CALLS HIS ACTIVITIES "PHILOSOPHIZING"

In several of Plato's dialogues some young people around Socrates were very interested in philosophy – whatever they thought it was. For some of the young people Plato depicts it has the approximate sense of "intellectualizing."[12] They are aware that others might call it "idle intellectualizing."

For example, the young intellectual of the *Lovers*, who answers with much love of honor (133a), treats his intellectualizing, which his wrestler

---

In the *Phaedrus* he treats the word "philosopher" as appropriate for a person he prays to be like – so he treats being a philosopher in the sense in which he understands it when speaking with Phaedrus as valuable.

[12] See Nightingale (1995, 14–15).

acquaintance thinks useless, as setting him apart from others. The intellectual is proud of it even if he can't explain exactly what it is: he can offer only that it would give one the "most reputation for philosophy" (135b) and make him "seem the most accomplished and wisest" in a conversation (135d) and that it implies thinking about the "finest" things (135b). He perhaps thinks that it sets him apart because some of the specialized activities termed "philosophizing" lend themselves to contest and competitive display. Not everyone can arrive at novel cosmological speculations, or understand the arcane ones. Not everyone – even someone who can operate in the ordinary business of life quite competently with logical apparatus such as "if," "then," and "not" – can invent arguments quickly in debate. Not everyone can think easily about geometry.

There may of course have been youngsters, different from the intellectual, who engaged in argumentative disputation or astronomy-talk or whatever simply for the sheer joy of it and not as an opportunity to sneer at others. The *Parmenides* shows a young Socrates eager for challenge in disputation. Perhaps as a youth he also had an interest in thinking about the finest things – in having the most important knowledge – without having understood quite what that would be.

Philosophy also interests the young interlocutors of the *Phaedo*. They admire "true philosophers," perhaps because they admire Pythagoreans who claim that denomination. The young people of the *Charmides* also take interest in philosophy, as Socrates signals when upon his return to Athens after an extended absence he inquires (153d) about the state of philosophy and then immediately about the young people.

That the young people in Socrates' setting are interested in philosophy as they conceive of it gives us another possible reason why Socrates as depicted accepts "philosophize" as a description of his own activities. Socrates as depicted engages with what interests the young people he wants to encourage to examine their lives. If they are interested in philosophy and if they think he is a philosopher and of use to them for developing their philosophical skills, they will be interested in talking to him.

We should not think of Socrates' associating himself with philosophy in this sometimes indeterminate way as a marketing ploy. Socrates has nothing to market. Nor is he interested in surrounding himself with young admirers. He is interested in improving the young people he knows. He goes around "always doing the thing that belongs to you . . . as a father or older brother persuading [you] to care about virtue" (31b3–5).[13] Their interest

---

[13] Christopher Moore called my attention to this phrasing.

in thinking about the most important things – though their conception of that is quite different from Socrates'– is Socrates' starting point. In *Alcibiades* I, Socrates can tell that Alcibiades is interested in having the most honor and power (105b, 105e). Socrates does not mention philosophy. He intrigues Alcibiades by saying that no one but Socrates is capable of giving Alcibiades the power he wants (105e). Socrates then proceeds to question Alcibiades about relevant knowledge. (The older Alcibiades of the *Symposium* (218a), saying that he has been bitten by discussions (*logôn*) in philosophy, which "take hold more fiercely than a snake," thinks of Socrates' practice as philosophy of a kind that makes him pained and ashamed (215e–216a).)

For Socrates in the *Apology* and, I have argued, for the constant Socrates everywhere else, the most important matter for people to think about is how to conduct their own lives most thoughtfully. It is to examine how to live. Young interlocutors like the intellectual in the *Lovers* do not have such examination in mind as the greatest or most important thing. They just want to be doing something important. Socrates can take advantage of some vagueness to present himself not inaccurately to such interlocutors as one who will philosophize with them.

9.9 PLATO AND PHILOSOPHY: ONE VIEW

My understanding of Socrates' conception of his own practice as depicted throughout the dialogues – which he is willing to call his "philosophizing" – has consequences for my understanding of the author Plato, who presents for us the multiple conceptions, some overlapping and some irreconcilable.

One consequence is that unlike many interpreters I do not consider the conception of the philosopher that Socrates articulates in the central books of the *Republic* to represent what Plato aspired to. Yet we can discern Plato's favored conception of philosophy in the dialogues. The totality of the dialogues featuring Socrates show that Plato thought that philosophizing as Socrates claims it in the *Apology* was the best practice in which to spend one's life. That then was Plato's favored conception of philosophy.[14]

I will discuss two interpreters, representative of many, to make more vivid by contrast my picture of Plato's understanding of philosophy. The particular authors merit discussion in some detail. But my project in this

---

[14] In the Seventh Letter, if it is by Plato, I don't find anything to disconfirm my view about Plato's favored conception of philosophy. But that is of course a different topic.

book is not to respond directly to them, but only to present an alternative worth considering.

For example, Alexander Nehamas says in a thought-provoking study:

[D]ifferent authors seem to have fought with one another for the purpose of appropriating the term "philosophy," each for his own practice and educational scheme. In the long run, of course, Plato ... emerged victorious. He thereby established what philosophy is by contrasting it not only with sophistry but also with rhetoric, poetry, traditional religion, and the specialized sciences. This was a grandiose project.[15]

Nehamas takes Plato – of course via the Socrates Plato depicts – to give his own practice the distinctive label "philosophy" in the course of differentiating himself from various other types of educators.

Nehamas poses a problem for any attempt to distinguish the elenchus-wielding Socrates from sophists:

If ... the test of truth in the elenchus is essentially dialectical, then the truth can be established only to the extent that you continue to win the argument ... Both Socrates and his opponents, therefore, necessarily aimed at victory. In this respect at least, Socrates cannot have differed in method from those sophists who practiced the method of question-and-answer and who did not intentionally use fallacious reasoning.[16]

Nehamas solves this problem of how to distinguish Socrates, who aimed at victory in argument, from the sophists, who also aimed at victory in argument, by saying that what set Socrates apart was that Socrates refused to present himself as a teacher of virtue.[17] But Plato could not distinguish himself from the sophists in that way because Plato according to Nehamas came to think of philosophy as the teaching of the true art of virtue. Plato,

---

[15] Nehamas (1990, 5).
[16] Nehamas (1990, 10). Nehamas (1990, 8) thinks it impossible to talk about fallacious reasoning without a theory of fallacious reasoning, which Plato lacked. I would say that we do not need anything large enough to be called a theory to identify an invalid argument pattern. We only need one counter-example to a pattern. In general, I believe, Socrates does not extract invalid inferences from his interlocutors. The operative form of his arguments is *modus ponens*. He often extracts likely false (and sometimes large and implicit) conditional premises. But that is the interlocutor's problem, not his. And no one expects any theory to enable us to distinguish true from false premises on a fully general scale.
[17] Nehamas (1990, 11):

From our point of view ... we can distinguish between Socrates and the sophists by means of his refusal to present himself as a teacher of others ... The difference between Socrates and the people with whom he was often and not so unreasonably confused is ultimately a difference in purpose, in the sort of life he chose to follow.

being like the sophists in both arguing and in teaching, would have been indistinguishable from them.[18]

According to Nehamas, Plato solves the problem thus:

Plato's magnificent solution to this problem [is that] . . . [h]e defines dialectic as a method of argument which aims at the discovery of the real nature of things and is not guided by the merely verbal distinctions which at best indicate how the world appears to us. (*Rep.* 454a–c; *Tht.* 164c–d) . . . [H]e insists that the real nature of things is constituted by the Forms in which these things participate. The dialectician studies the Forms and therefore the theory of Forms, which Plato introduces in his middle works and which constitutes a deeply controversial metaphysical theory, also functions to under-write the nature and practice of dialectic: the dialectician and the sophist now do something fundamentally different and in different ways; their methods are no longer the same, even though they may appear identical.[19]

Plato of course does not use the word "metaphysical," but I take it that Nehamas means by "metaphysical" approximately "what has to do with the account of reality" or "what really is as distinct from how it might seem to us."[20]

Nehamas describes Plato's new understanding of philosophy and its claims:

Sophistic influence can be securely avoided, Plato argues in the *Phaedo*, the *Republic*, and the *Sophist*, only by supplementing the elenchus with the study of the unchanging nature of the world, which demonstrates both how argument should ideally proceed and how life should properly be lived. But distinguishing philosophy from sophistry in this manner is no longer neutral. It presupposes accepting a specific and deeply controversial philosophical theory . . .

But to agree too quickly with Plato on this issue may commit us to a restrictive and perhaps problematic conception of philosophy – at least insofar as Platonism is a view of limited appeal.[21]

To summarize: Nehamas holds that in certain dialogues Plato recommends a conception of philosophy (though "grandiose," "restricted,"

---

[18] Nehamas (1990, 12):

> For Plato became convinced that, in contrast to Socrates, he *did* know what virtue is and undertook to teach it to others: he came to the conclusion that virtue and happiness consist in the life of philosophy itself. But Plato's ambitious and controversial conception of the nature, function, and value of philosophy, articulated in detail in the *Republic*, creates a new problem for him. If philosophers aim to teach the true art of virtue (that is, philosophy itself) then their purpose appears to be at least superficially identical with the purpose of many of the sophists.

[19] Nehamas (1990, 12).
[20] Dancy (1991, xii): "[A] metaphysical theory called 'the Theory of Forms ' . . . located the foundation of reality in abstract entities."
[21] Nehamas (1990, 13–14).

"problematic," and "of limited appeal") that can account for Plato's new confidence that philosophers can "teach the true art of virtue (that is, philosophy itself)."[22]

My very brief comments on this are these.

Against the view that Plato thought that accepting the Theory of Forms – as standardly understood as a "deeply controversial metaphysical theory" – "demonstrates . . . how argument should ideally proceed" is, I believe, the example of the Socrates of the short aporetic dialogues. He manages many inferential transitions quite adequately. He pretty much shows us how argument should very respectably or even ideally proceed without accepting (as Nehamas agrees he does not in those dialogues) the fully-fledged metaphysical theory of Forms. Nehamas would say that that Socrates never makes progress or gets important results. I disagree.

Against the view that Plato thought it important to accept the standardly understood Theory of Forms to see "how life should properly be lived" is, I believe, again the Socrates of the early dialogues. Devoid of the Theory of Forms sketched in the *Republic* for Glaucon and Adeimantus, that Socrates seems to me a strong and never retracted example of how life should properly – that is, decently and justly – be lived.

Also against the view that Plato thought that accepting a "deeply controversial metaphysical theory" helps us live properly is the fact that Plato does not give an actual example (nor does anyone else) of a person who has lived a more just life because of believing the "baroque monstrosity" Theory of Forms of the scholarly literature.[23] The *Republic* implicitly claims a better life for its philosopher-kings, but it does not seriously examine how contemplating forms leads philosophers to live more decently. Though book 9 argues – dubiously and for the benefit of his interlocutors – that philosophers have many times more pleasure, Socrates as depicted gives no sign he takes pleasure as a goal. (The Socrates of the *Apology* would not object to bliss (41a–c) provided it could be achieved without injustice (32d).) Nehamas' saying that Platonism – that is, presumably, the monstrous Theory of Forms – is "of limited appeal" perhaps signals that he knows of no convincing examples of lives lived more justly via the *Republic*'s metaphysical theory.

According to my argument of chapters 3–6 there is an explanation of accounts of philosophy in the *Republic* and in other dialogues more effective than the proposal that Plato is newly confident that he can teach the art of virtue. The *Republic*, for example, instead shows that Socrates'

---

[22] The last-quoted phrase is from Nehamas (1990, 12).
[23] Meinwald (2008). See chapter 1, n. 16 (p. 6).

rather confused interlocutors were willing to accept the apparently confident account of philosophy within a speech that they had requested from Socrates to persuade them.

Thus I think it unlikely that Plato thought that believing the grandiose Theory of Forms was important either for argument or for life.

9.10 PLATO AND PHILOSOPHY: A SECOND VIEW

In a careful study of Plato's use of several genres of writing in his dialogues, Andrea Nightingale[24] examines some early occurrences of words from the "philosophy" word-group and draws a conclusion. She employs the word "metaphysical" – again, not Plato's – to indicate talk about Forms:

Plato was born into a culture which had no distinct concept of "philosophy," in spite of the fact that various kinds of abstract and analytic thinking had been and were being developed by the Presocratics, the mathematicians, different kinds of scientist, and the sophists. Previous to Plato, these intellectuals, together with poets, lawgivers, and other men of skill or wisdom, were grouped together under the heading of "*sophoi*" and "*sophistai*" ... As a careful analysis of the terminology will attest, ... [*philosophein*] does not take on a specialized and technical meaning until Plato appropriates the term for his own enterprise. When Plato set forth a specific and quite narrow definition of the term, I will suggest, he created a new and specialized discipline. In fact, "philosophy" as Plato conceived it comprised not just an analytic inquiry into certain types of subjects, but a unique set of ethical and metaphysical commitments that demanded a whole new way of living.[25]

Nightingale finds Plato's account of philosophy in the *Republic*:

[T]he *Republic* ... contains the most explicit and detailed definition of "philosophy" in the Platonic corpus. Indeed it is not until the middle dialogues that we find any attempt to appropriate or to define the term "philosophy."[26]

There was, however, a rather specific – and apparently new – content given to the word "philosophizing" at *Apology* 29d.

---

[24] Nightingale (1995).   [25] Nightingale (1995, 10).
[26] Nightingale (1995, 17). Also relevant is this from 17–19:

> The "definition" of philosophy found in the *Republic* does not ... offer a "simple" identification of the philosopher. To be sure, Socrates has a good deal to say about the epistemic aspects of philosophy. In particular, he indicates, the true philosopher will develop the rational part of his soul in order to make the journey from appearance to reality, from opinion to knowledge, from the physical world of particulars to the immaterial realm of the Forms. But ... the "definition" articulated in books 5–7 ... ranges far beyond the intellectual activities that characterize philosophy ... [W]hile the *Republic* offers the most detailed definition of the "true" philosopher, one should not forget that the nature of philosophy and the philosopher is addressed ... in the great majority of the middle and late dialogues.

Nightingale assumes that when Socrates speaks in the *Republic* he voices for Plato beliefs that Socrates, as depicted, has accepted and is recommending to his interlocutor. She says:

Plato makes no mention of philosophic predecessors in the *Republic*. His definition is exclusive, not inclusive ... [I]n spite of his deep engagement with the ideas of many of these [Presocratic] thinkers, Plato did not consider them to be "philosophers" in his sense of the term.[27]

As Nightingale says, the conception of philosopher articulated in the *Republic* excludes the Presocratics. Indeed, it excludes the Socrates of the *Apology*.

I have argued that we do not have sufficient reason to say that the exclusivity was Plato's recommendation. The most we are entitled to say without further argument is that the exclusivity is what appealed to his interlocutors. It is an outcome of my previous argument that the phrase "[Plato's] sense of the term" is less accurate for the account of the philosopher in the *Republic* than the phrase "the sense that Socrates gives to the word 'philosopher' as he creates a persuasive speech that will appeal to Glaucon and Adeimantus."

Nightingale comments on her procedure:

[M]y investigation deals with what *Plato says about what he is doing* – with his explicit and deliberate attempts to define and defend his own peculiar way of thinking and living in the context of a culture which had no distinct concept of "philosophy."[28]

Most strictly speaking the phrase "what Plato says about what he is doing" must amount to "what Socrates or others say about philosophy in Plato's dialogues."

Nightingale implies that Plato thought of the philosopher as a new kind of sage[29] and philosophy as a special kind of wisdom that he had:

---

[27] Nightingale (1995, 18 with n. 14).   [28] Nightingale (1995, 10, n. 31).

[29] Nightingale (1995, 92):

It is, finally, to define and dramatize ... this new kind of sage called the "philosopher" ... that Plato clashes with his tragic predecessors. Socrates, the *Gorgias* urges, is heroic but not tragic.

As I have contended, the creation of "philosophy" was not simply a matter of giving a name to a new method of inquiry and argumentation. Rather, philosophy had to make a case for itself as a discipline that offered a unique kind of wisdom which rivaled the other brands on offer. This was by no means a simple enterprise, as Plato's frequent attempts to define and legitimize philosophy clearly attest ... Plato introduces "philosophy" not just as an intellectual activity but as a new kind of social practice. For philosophy as Plato conceived it was not simply a distinct mode of inquiry and argument, but rather a unique way of living based on specific ethical and political commitments. (193–194)

In order to create the specialized discipline of philosophy, Plato had to distinguish what he was doing from all other discursive practices that laid claim to wisdom.[30]

According to my hypothesis, in contrast, we should take most seriously the point that Plato depicts Socrates near the end of his life in the *Apology* as having been consistently horrified by the label, "sage" or "wise man."[31] Plato's depiction of Socrates' horror there represents Plato's equal horror.

Nightingale thinks that Plato's work gave the discipline of philosophy a high status:

[B]ecause history has conferred upon the discipline of philosophy the legitimacy and the high status that Plato claimed for it, we moderns tend to overlook the effort it took to bring this about.[32]

She says:

Although this study deals with the original construction of the discipline of philosophy in the West, it addresses many of the same issues that are being discussed in contemporary dialogues about the present state of philosophy. What constitutes "true" philosophy in the 1990s? What is at stake when professional philosophers insist (in good Platonic fashion) that certain thinkers are not philosophers?[33]

I would say, rather, that it is not good Platonic fashion to insist that certain thinkers are not philosophers. Plato does not make that sort of linguistic decree. Rather, we find Plato depicting a considerable variety of uses for the word "philosopher." Plato – or his Socrates – was not trying to do linguistic legislation. Plato was depicting Socrates as observing or proposing conceptions of philosophy – some of them exclusive – that were operative or appealing in Socrates' time. I have argued that, for example, the phrase "true philosophers" belongs to Socrates' interlocutors, probably relying on a Pythagorean distinction, and not to Socrates as depicted. I have argued that Plato shows Socrates developing – in the *Republic* perhaps rather wildly – his interlocutors' conceptions of philosophy in ways that appeal to them.

These are some brief comments on Nightingale's proposals.

---

[30] Nightingale (1995, 10–11).
[31] See also on the seriousness of Socrates' denial of wisdom Cooper (2007, 31–40).
[32] Nightingale (1995, 11). Nightingale also says (1995, 61): "In Plato's day ... philosophy reached a relatively tiny group of literate elites."
  Her phrasing suggests that it is already settled what philosophy is. One might more accurately say: in Plato's day a number of rather different activities – geometry, astronomy (both observation and speculation), verbal disputation, and rhetorical studies, for example – were typically called "philosophy." Only a small group of literate and privileged people had the time to practice these.
[33] Nightingale (1995, 195).

"The discipline of philosophy," the activity of the "professional philoso-phers" that she refers to, is presumably the activity practiced in academic settings, in institutions, in philosophy departments. I would assume that Nightingale allows there to be a fairly wide range of practices included in this discipline that she says has a high status.

We can ourselves distinguish the discipline of philosophy, so understood, from the totality of many activities, some not professional, currently and widely called "philosophy." In our time this totality has an ambiguous status somewhat similar to the ambiguous status of the totality of activities called "philosophy" that Plato informs us of in his dialogues. In our time one usage of "philosophy," a usage that might be called "popular" or "ordinary," but which is not to be entirely discounted in favor of academic usage, has it that anyone who has an attitude toward life has a philosophy or counts in that respect as a philosopher.[34] In our time there are on the one hand people who think that most of what is called "philosophy," not excluding academic philosophy, is, to varying degrees, useless verbosity and speculation. Others like Nightingale consider it a specialized discipline of high status.

It does not seem to me that we have sufficient evidence that Plato claimed a high status for philosophy or made an effort to bring that about, although even today some people may invoke him to defend a high status for philosophy conceived in one way. Rather, Plato portrays that a high status (at least in some circles, and for some conceptions of philosophy) was already there in Socrates' time. Some people where the Eleatic visitor came from thought that what philosophers knew was the "greatest" kind of knowledge. The intellectual youth of the *Lovers* thought that philosophy was a fine thing and that anyone who scorned philosophy shouldn't be counted as a human being (*Lovers* 133a). Outside Plato's dialogues some people (perhaps Gorgias of Leontini previous to Plato) considered philosophy a study in comparison with which others paled.[35] Isocrates in Plato's era wanted the label "philosophy" exclusively for his study of useful thought about how best to act and speak (*Antidosis* 270–271). In the earlier era Plato depicts in his dialogues philosophy had a high status for some and a low status for others. Plato does not seem to me to be attempting to change that.

Indeed for most people envisaged in Plato's dialogues what is called "philosophy" does not have a high status. If we count up the people

---

[34] Popper (1986, 211): "All men are philosophers, because in one way or other all take up an attitude towards life and death."

[35] DK82B29, quoted in chapter 7 section 7.3 (p. 203).

present or alluded to in Plato's dialogues who disapprove of what they call "philosophy" (think of the majority in the *Republic*), there are more people who think it useless or pernicious than who think it valuable.[36] Socrates fully recognizes the various forces of the word "philosophy," and in speaking to his interlocutors Socrates can use "philosophy" to mean "what you call 'philosophy'" without committing himself to any high evaluation of it. An example of his use of "philosophy" in widest application is his saying to Callias in the *Protagoras*:

I am always astonished (*agamai*) at your philosophy (*sou tên philosophian*). (335d)

Callias' claim to what some people would call "philosophy" is that he has hired prominent sophists as his teachers.[37] Translators perhaps unwilling to connect Callias with philosophy render *philosophian* here as "love of wisdom" or "love of learning." That translation of course is also correct. But I think it important to see that Socrates can apply the word "philosophy" as casually and widely as anyone else.

In summary, many, not just one, of the conceptions of philosophy from Plato's dialogues survive today. Their accompanying diverse statuses that Plato portrays in his dialogues also survive. Among the survivors, but not a unique survivor, is the conception that Plato sketched in the *Republic* of philosophy as the study of things very much beyond the ordinary (such as the Platonism that Nehamas says is "of limited appeal"). Adeimantus' idea that philosophy has something to do with arguments has survived.[38] The

---

[36] Compare Xenophon, *Memorabilia* I, 2, 31. Xenophon relates that Critias made a law not to teach "the art of arguments." Xenophon says that Critias was attributing to Socrates what was commonly held against philosophers, and "[thus] slandering him in the eyes of the many": that is, Critias made use of majority ill-will against philosophers.

[37] On Callias, see Nails (2002) *s.v.*

[38] Maintaining an early connection of philosophy with argument Cooper (2007, 23–24, n. 4) says:

Thus, already, before any effect that Plato's writings might have had, there was in play a well-developed notion of a "philosopher" as someone engaged in logical argument and trusting to reason in pursuit of the truth about how things actually are, while, if that pursuit of the truth requires it, disregarding experience and convention. Thus Plato drew upon a preexisting tendency to use the term specifically for those devoted to logical argumentation and prepared to follow reason, in pursuit of the truth, wherever it led, even if it conflicted with custom and experience. He was able to establish that usage.

"Tendency" seems to me less accurate than would be "possibility."

An anecdote of Xenophon's connects philosophy with argument. Xenophon relates his response to the Persian envoy Phalinus, who happened to be a Greek. Phalinus has asked the Greek mercenaries in service to Cyrus to surrender their weapons now that Cyrus is killed. Xenophon says to Phalinus:

Phalinus, at this moment, as you see for yourself, we have no other possession [literally: no other good] if not arms and virtue. Now if we have our arms, we think to make use of our virtue also, but if we give them up, that we shall likewise be deprived of our lives [literally: our bodies]. Don't think,

Eleatic visitor's conception that philosophy centrally involves argument about meaning and conceptual mappings has survived. The conception of the *Phaedo* that philosophers are ascetic wise men has survived in some circles. But also the compelling conception of the *Apology* that philosophy is serious reflection on how to live – available to and crucial for any human being – survives today. It is practically the opposite of the *Republic*'s conception of something out of reach except to an elite few.

9.11 SOCRATES, PHILOSOPHY, AND PLATO

I return to my question why Socrates accepts the word "philosophizing" at *Apology* 29d for his own activities as he looks back over his entire life, the very life, I have argued, that Plato depicts in the other dialogues in which Socrates appears.

It should be clear that it makes no difference to my argument in which order Plato composed his dialogues, so I deliberately omit discussion of that.

So far I have suggested two possible reasons for Socrates' rather puzzling acceptance of a label that in its previous occurrences in the *Apology* – as in many occurrences in the other dialogues – was derogatory or trivializing and not deferential. In its mildest use it had the approximate sense of our "intellectualizing."

The first reason I suggested was the etymology of the word which, if Diotima's argument intrigues you, can almost imply lack of wisdom. It then has a wry appropriateness for the Socrates who, consistently throughout the dialogues, as my hypothesis claims, acknowledges his ignorance about the most important things, to know which would be wisdom. Given also the storied explanation that Pythagoras gave to the word "philosopher" when he putatively invented it, the word indicates someone with no teachable art. It is again fitting for Socrates.

The second reason I suggested was that Socrates sees that his young friends are interested in philosophy, which they think is the study of the

then, that we shall give up to you our only possessions. But with these and for your possessions we will fight.

Phalinus replies, "You seem like a philosopher, young man, and what you say is not inelegant" (*Anabasis* II, I 12–13).

What seems philosophical about Xenophon to Phalinus (one Greek to another) is evidently that Xenophon is arguing, using several "if . . . then" claims that are implicit in the Greek's participial constructions: if we don't have our arms and our virtue, then we don't have anything; if we have our arms, then we can make use of our virtue; if we give up our arms, then (we can't make use of our virtue, and) we lose our lives; so we won't give up our arms.

most important things. In that case Socrates is not averse to mentioning philosophy or being called a philosopher as a device to effect their conversing about what he thinks the most urgent topic – how to conduct your life. Even if what Socrates thinks the most important thing is not necessarily what his younger interlocutors of the moment think most important, Socrates can still allow that "philosophizing" applies to his activity as an inviting self-description. To allow the label for that tactical reason would have been, though not inaccurate, somewhat sly. It would not have been to claim the word as an honorific.

I'll suggest now a third possible source of Socrates' accepting the accusatory label "philosophize" at his trial. At 29d when he says he philosophizes, he is responding to his accusers, whom he has just imagined (29c) offering the condition – "not to philosophize"– under which they will release him. So when he responds to them he is speaking as they speak, but accepting their derogatory word. I suggest that he now fully accepts the label out of defiance or stubbornness. It is as though he says to his detractors: "You don't understand what I am doing – which you call 'philosophizing', meaning to derogate it as pernicious intellectualizing. Fine. I'll call what I am doing (which actually happens to be examining and reproaching if necessary) 'philosophizing' too: and it is *that* that I won't stop doing." That acceptance of the description "philosophizing" might be comparable to acceptance in our era of the label "queer," which started as a term of derogation, but which was claimed and made their own as a self-classifying term by those whom it originally derogated.

If the Socrates of *Apology* 29d now out of defiance fully makes his own this quite ordinarily derogatory or trivializing description, "he philosophizes," then Plato's depiction in the *Apology* is of a surprising, even shocking, event.

My hypothesis of chapters 3–6 has been that the dialogues of Plato's in which Socrates appears bear out the description that the Socrates of the *Apology* gives as he summarizes his life near its end. All of Plato's dialogues depict that same Socrates who accounts for himself in the *Apology*. My hypothesis has now been reasonably enough – of course not decisively – confirmed for me to use it to explore a consequence.

In depicting Socrates saying in the *Apology* that he "philosophizes," Plato has Socrates making a gesture that at once acknowledges its striking apparent etymology and storied origins, imitates the vocabulary of the young people he hoped to attract to a life of examining, and throws back at his accusers their accusation. From Plato's depiction of this gesture at once wry, concessive, and defiant, I would now draw a conclusion about Plato: Plato's dialogues also do not show us Plato appropriating "philosophy" as an honor-conferring title for his own work, a title that applies only to a few select people. By depicting Socrates' final acceptance of the dubious term "philosophizing" for his practice, Plato himself accepts the hitherto sometimes severely derogatory and sometimes merely trivializing or deflating term for his own practice, which imitates Socrates'. Socrates' conversations give interlocutors the opportunity to see themselves: interlocutors take at least the first step of a self-examination as they react to Socrates' provoking and revealing words. Socrates thus invites them into what he takes to be the most serious business of life. Plato's dialogues invite the reader to philosophize in that way.

Bibliography

Abel-Rappe, Sara and Kamtekar, Rachana (eds.), 2006. *Blackwell Companion to Socrates*. Oxford

Ackrill, J.L., 2001. *Essays on Plato and Aristotle*, 2nd edn. Oxford

Adam, Adela Marion, 1918. "Socrates, quantum mutatus ab illo," *Classical Quarterly* 12: 121–139

Adam, James, 1963. *The Republic of Plato*, 2 vols., 2nd edn. Cambridge

Allen, R.E., 1971. "Plato's Earlier Theory of Forms," in Vlastos (ed.), 1971: 319–334
    1984. *Plato: Euthyphro, Apology, Crito, Meno, Gorgias, Menexenus*. New Haven
    2006. *Plato: The Republic*. New Haven

Annas, Julia, 1981. *An Introduction to Plato's "Republic."* Oxford
    1985. "Self-Knowledge in Early Plato," in O'Meara (ed.), 1985: 111–138
    1992. "Plato the Sceptic," *Oxford Studies in Ancient Philosophy*, Supplementary vol. 9: 43–72
    1999. *Platonic Ethics, Old and New*. Ithaca
    2002. "What are Plato's Middle Dialogues in the Middle of?," in Annas and Rowe (eds.), 2002: 1–23
    2006. "Ethics and Argument in Plato's Socrates," in Reis (ed.), 2006: 32–46

Annas, Julia and Rowe, Christopher (eds.), 2002. *New Perspectives on Plato, Modern and Ancient*. Washington, DC

Archer-Hind, R.D., 1883. *The "Phaedo" of Plato*. London

Armstrong, A.H., 1966. *Plotinus, Ennead I*. Cambridge

Aune, Bruce, 1997. "The Unity of Plato's Republic," *Ancient Philosophy* 17: 291–308

Ausland, Hayden, 2000. "Who Speaks for Whom in *Timaeus/Critias?*," in Press (ed.), 2000: 183–198

Babbitt, Frank Cole (trans.), 2000 [reprint of 1928]. *Plutarch's Moralia with an English Translation*, vols. I and II. London

Bailly, Jacques, 2003. *Plato's "Euthyphro" and "Cleitophon."* Newburyport

Bambrough, Renford (ed.), 1965. *New Essays on Plato and Aristotle*. New York

Barnes, Jonathan, 1995. *The Cambridge Companion to Aristotle*. Cambridge
    (ed.), 1984. *The Complete Works of Aristotle: The Revised Oxford Translation*. Princeton

Basore, J.W., 1985. *Seneca: Moral Essays*, vol. I. Cambridge

Beck, Martha, 1999. *Plato's Self-Corrective Development of the Concepts of Soul, Forms, and Immortality in Three Arguments of the "Phaedo."* Lewiston

Benardete, Seth, 1984. *The Being of the Beautiful.* Chicago

    1997. "Plato's Theaetetus: On the Way of the Logos," *Review of Metaphysics* 51: 25–53

Benson, Hugh, 2000. *Socratic Wisdom: The Model of Knowledge in Plato's Early Dialogues.* Oxford

Beversluis, John, 2000. *Cross-Examining Socrates: A Defense of the Interlocutors in Plato's Early Dialogues.* Cambridge

    2006. "A Defense of Dogmatism in the Interpretation of Plato," *Oxford Studies in Ancient Philosophy* 31: 85–110

Blondell, Ruby, 1998. "Reproducing Socrates: Dramatic Form and Pedagogy in the Theaetetus," in Cleary and Gurtler (eds.), 1998: 213–238

    2000. "Letting Plato Speak for Himself: Character and Method," in Press (ed.), 2000: 127–146

    2002. *The Play of Character in Plato's' Dialogues.* Cambridge

Bloom, Allan, 1968. *The "Republic" of Plato.* New York

Boardman, John, Griffith, Jasper, and Murray, Oswyn (eds.), 1988. *The Oxford Illustrated History of Greece and the Hellenistic World.* Oxford

Bostock, David, 1986. *Plato's "Phaedo."* Oxford

Bowe, G.S., 2007. "In Defense of Cleitophon," *Classical Philology* 102: 245–264

Bradshaw, David, 1998. "The Argument of the Digression in the Theaetetus," *Ancient Philosophy* 18: 61–68

Brann, Eva, Kalkavage, Peter, and Salem, Eric (trans.), 1996. *Plato's Sophist: The Professor of Wisdom.* Newburyport

Brickhouse, Thomas C. and Smith, Nicholas, 1989. *Socrates on Trial.* Princeton

    1994. *Plato's Socrates.* Oxford

    2000. *The Philosophy of Socrates.* Boulder

Brisson, Luc, 2001. "Vers un dialogue apaisé: Les transformations affectant la pratique du dialogue dans le corpus platonicien," in Cossutta and Narcy (eds.), 2001: 209–226

Broackes, Justin, 2009. "*autos kath' hauton* in the *Clouds*: Was Socrates Himself a Defender of Separate Soul and Separate Forms?," *Classical Quarterly* 59: 1–21

Brown, Eric, 2000. "Justice and Compulsion for Plato's Philosopher-Rulers," *Ancient Philosophy* 20: 1–18

    2003. "Plato: Ethics and Politics in the Republic," *Stanford Encyclopedia of Philosophy*, http://plato.stanford.edu/entries/plato-ethics-politics/

    2004. "Minding the Gap in Plato's Republic," *Philosophical Studies* 117: 275–332

Brown, Lesley, 1998. "How Totalitarian is Plato's *Republic*?," in Ostenfeld (ed.), 1998: 13–27

Brownson, Carleton, 1922. *Xenophon: Anabasis*, rev. John Dillery, 1998. Cambridge, MA

Bruell, Christopher, 1987. "On the Original Meaning of Political Philosophy: An Interpretation of Plato's Lovers," in Pangle (ed.), 1987: 91–110

Brunschwig, Jacques, 1986. "Aristotle on Arguments without Winners or Losers," *Wissenschaften Jahrbuch* 1984/85: 31–40

Brunschwig, Jacques and Lloyd, Geoffrey E.R. (eds.), 2000. *Greek Thought: A Guide to Classical Knowledge.* Cambridge

Burkert, Walter, 1960. "Platon oder Pythagoras? Zum Ursprung des Wortes 'Philosophie'," *Hermes* 88: 159–177

  1972. *Lore and Science in Ancient Pythagoreanism.* Cambridge

  1985. *Ancient Religion.* Cambridge

Burnet, John, 1901–1907. *Platonis Opera*, vols. 1–5. Oxford

  1911. *Plato's "Phaedo,"* Oxford

  1924. *Plato's "Euthyphro," "Apology of Socrates," and "Crito."* Oxford

  1930/1971. *Early Greek Philosophy*, London

Burnyeat, M.F., 1990. *The Theaetetus of Plato with a translation of Plato's "Theaetetus" by M. J. Levett revised by Miles Burnyeat.* Indianapolis

  1992. "Utopia and Fantasy: The Practicability of Plato's Ideal City," in Hopkins and Savile (eds.), 1992: 175–185

  2003. "By the Dog," *London Review of Books* August 7: 23–24

  2004. "Fathers and Sons in Plato's Republic and Philebus," *Classical Quarterly* 54: 80–87

Bury, R.G., 1966. *Plato with an English Translation: Timaeus, Critias, Cleitophon, Menexenus, Epistles.* Cambridge

Byrd, Miriam, 2007. "The Summoner Approach: A New Method of Plato Interpretation," *Journal of the History of Philosophy* 45: 365–438

Carlini, Antonio, 1964. *Alcibiade, Alcibiade Secondo, Ipparco, Rivali: Testo Critico e traduzione.* Turin

Centrone, Bruno, 2005. "Die Anterastai und Platons Erotische Dialoge," in Döring, Erler, and Shern (eds.), 2005: 37–49

Chance, Thomas, 1992. *Plato's "Euthydemus": Analysis of What Is and Is Not Philosophy.* Berkeley

Chappell, Timothy, n.d. Archelogos Commentary, http://archelogos.com/xml/toc/toc-theae.htm

Cherniss, Harold, 1957. "The Relation of the Timaeus to Plato's Later Dialogues," *American Journal of Philology* 78: 225–266

  1962. *The Riddle of the Early Academy.* New York

Cicero, see King (trans.), 1927

Clark, P.M., 1955. "The Great *Alcibiades*," *Classical Quarterly* 5: 231–240

Clay, Diskin, 2002. "Reading the Republic," in Griswold (ed.), 2002: 19–33

  2007. "Plato Philomythos," in Woodard (ed.), 2007: 210–236

Cleary, John J. and Gurtler, Gary, S.J. (eds.), 1998. *Proceedings of the Boston Area Colloquium in Ancient Philosophy* 14. Leiden

  2000. *Proceedings of the Boston Area Colloquium in Ancient Philosophy* 16. Leiden

  2003. *Proceedings of the Boston Area Colloquium in Ancient Philosophy* 18. Leiden

  2008. *Proceedings of the Boston Area Colloquium in Ancient Philosophy* 23. Leiden

Cleary John J. and Wians, W. (eds.), 1993. *Proceedings of the Boston Area Colloquium in Philosophy* 7. Lanham

1995. *Proceedings of the Boston Area Colloquium in Ancient Philosophy* 9. Lanham

Cohen, S. Marc, 1971. "Socrates on the Definition of Piety: Euthyphro 10A–11B," in Vlastos (ed.), 1971: 158–176

Cooper, John (ed.), 1997a. *Plato: Complete Works*. Indianapolis

1997b. "The Psychology of Justice in Plato," in Kraut (ed.), 1997: 17–30

2004a. "Method and Science in On Ancient Medicine," in Cooper, 2004b: 3–42

2004b. *Knowledge, Nature, and the Good*. Princeton

2007. "Socrates and Philosophy as a Way of Life," in Scott (ed.), 2007: 20–43

Corlett, J. Angelo, 2005. *Interpreting Plato's Dialogues*. Las Vegas

Cornford, Francis M., 1957a. *Plato's Cosmology: The "Timaeus" of Plato Translated with a Running Commentary*. New York

1957b. *Plato's Theory of Knowledge*. New York

1965. *Principium Sapientiae*. New York

Cossutta, Frédéric and Narcy, Michel (eds.), 2001. *La forme dialogue chez Platon: Évolution et réceptions*. Grenoble

Crombie, I.M., 1962. *An Examination of Plato's Doctrines*, 2 vols. London

Dancy, R. M., 2004. *Plato's Introduction of Forms*. Cambridge

Davidson, Donald, 2005a. "Plato's Philosopher," in Davidson, 2005b: 223–240

2005b. *Truth, Language and History*. Oxford

Davidson, James, 1997. *Courtesans and Fishcakes: The Consuming Passions of Classical Athens*. New York

Davis, Michael, 1984/1985. "Philosophy and the Perfect Tense: On the Beginning of Plato's Lovers," *Graduate Faculty Philosophy Journal* 10: 75–97

de Boo, Edward, 2001. "*ho theos plattôn*": Puns on Plato's Name in the "*Republic*," PhD dissertation, Department of Classics, Brown University. Providence

De Lacy, Phillip, 1976. "The Concept of Function in *Republic* I," *Paideia* (Special Plato Issue)

De Lacy, Phillip and Einarson, Benedict (trans.), 1959. *Plutarch. Moralia*, vol. VII. Cambridge, MA

De Vogel, C.J., 1955. "The Present State of the Socratic Problem," *Phronesis* 1: 26–35

Denniston, J.D., 1996. *The Greek Particles*. Cambridge, MA

Denyer, Nicholas (ed.), 2001. *Plato: "Alcibiades."* Cambridge

Destreé, Pierre and Smith, Nicholas (eds.), 2005. *Socrates' Divine Sign: Religion, Practice, and Value in Socratic Philosophy*. APEIRON 38. Kelowna

Diels, Hermann, 1882/1960. *Die Fragmente der Vorsokratiker*, 3 vols., 9th edn., ed. Walther Kranz. Berlin

Dillon, John, 1993. *Alcinous: Handbook of Platonism Translated with an Introduction and Commentary*. Oxford

Dodds, E.R., 1959. *Plato: "Gorgias": A Revised Text with Introduction and Commentary*. Oxford

Dollard, John, 1939. "The Dozens: Dialectic of Insult," *American Imago* 1: 3–25

Döring, Klaus, Erler, Michael, and Shern, Stefan (eds.), 2005. *Pseudoplatonica.* Stuttgart

Dorion, Louis-André, 2005. "The Daimonion and the Megalêgoria of Socrates in Xenophon's 'Apology'," in Destreé and Smith (eds.), 2005: 127–142

Dougherty, Carol and Kurke, Leslie (eds.), 1993. *Cultural Poetics in Ancient Greece.* Cambridge

Dover, K.J. (ed. and trans.), 1968. *Aristophanes. "Clouds."* Oxford

    1994. *Greek Popular Morality in the Time of Plato and Aristotle.* Indianapolis

Doyle, James, 2004. "Socrates and the Oracle," *Ancient Philosophy* 24: 19–35

Duke, E.A. *et al.* (eds.), 1995. *Platonis Opera,* vol. 1. Oxford

Ebert, Theodor, 1973. "Plato's Theory of Recollection Reconsidered: An Interpretation of Meno 80a-86c," *Man and World* 6: 163–181

    2001. "Why Is Evenus Called a Philosopher at *Phaedo* 61c?," *Classical Quarterly* 51: 423–434

    2007. "'The Theory of Recollection in Plato's Meno': Against a Myth of Platonic Scholarship," in Erler and Brisson (eds.), 2007: 184–198

Edmunds, Lowell, 2004. "The Practical Irony of the Historical Socrates," *Phoenix* 58: 193–207

    2006. "What Was Socrates Called?," *Classical Quarterly* 56: 414–425

Emlyn-Jones, Chris (trans. and comm.), 2007. *Plato: Republic 1–2. 368c4.* Oxford

Erler, Michael and Brisson, Luc (eds.), 2007. *Gorgias-Menon: Selected Papers from the Seventh Symposium Platonicum.* Sankt Augustin

Ferrari, G.R.F. (ed.), 2007. *The Cambridge Companion to Plato's "Republic."* Cambridge

Festugière, A.J., 1970. *Proclus: Commentaire sur la République. Traduction et notes,* vol. 1. Paris

Fine, Gail, 1979a. "False Belief in the Theaetetus," *Phronesis* 24: 70–80

    1979b. "Knowledge and Logos in the Theaetetus," *Philosophical Review* 88: 366–397, repr. in Fine, 2003

    1993. *On Ideas: Aristotle's Criticism of Plato's Theory of Forms.* Oxford

    1994. "Protagorean Relativisms," in *Boston Area Colloquium in Ancient Philosophy* 10: 211–43, repr. in Fine, 2003

    1996. "Conflicting Appearances: Theaetetus 153d–154b," in Gill and McCabe (eds.), 1996: 105–33, repr. in Fine, 2003

    1998. "Plato's Refutation of Protagoras in the Theaetetus," *APEIRON* 32: 201–234, repr. in Fine, 2003

    (ed.), 1999. *Plato 2: Ethics, Politics, Religion, and the Soul.* Oxford

    2003. *Plato on Knowledge and Forms: Selected Essays.* Oxford

    (ed.), 2008a. *The Oxford Handbook of Plato.* Oxford

    2008b. "Does Socrates Claim to Know that he Knows Nothing?," *Oxford Studies in Ancient Philosophy* 35: 49–88

Forrest, W.G., 1963. "Aristophanes' 'Acharnians'," *Phoenix* 17: 1–12

Forster, Michael, 2006a. "Socrates' Demand for Definitions," *Oxford Studies in Ancient Philosophy* 31: 1–47

    2006b. "Socratic Refutation," *Rhizai* 3: 7–57

2007. "Socrates' Profession of Ignorance," *Oxford Studies in Ancient Philosophy* 32: 1–35

Fowler, H.N. (trans.), 1914. *Plato's "Euthyphro," "Apology," "Crito," "Phaedo," and "Phaedrus."* Cambridge

Frank, Jill, 2007. "Wages of War: On Judgment in Plato's *Republic,*" *Political Theory* 35: 443–467

Frank, J., Minkowski, H., and Sternglass, E. (eds.), 1963. *Horizons of a Philosopher: Essays in Honor of David Baumgardt.* Leiden

Frede, Michael, 1992. "Plato's Arguments and the Dialogue Form," *Oxford Studies in Ancient Philosophy,* supplementary vol. 9: 201–219

1996. "The Literary Form of the *Sophist,*" in Gill and McCabe (eds.), 1996: 135–151

2000. "The Philosopher," in Brunschwig and Lloyd (eds.), 2000: 1–19

2004. "Aristotle's Account of the Origins of Philosophy," *Rhizai* 1: 9–44

Gadamer, Hans-Georg, 1980a. "The Proof of Immortality in Plato's *Phaedo,*" in Gadamer, 1980b: 21–38

1980b. *Dialogue and Dialectic: Eight Hermeneutical Studies on Plato. Translated and with an Introduction by P. Christopher Smith.* New Haven

Gallie, W.D., 1964a. *Philosophy and the Historical Understanding.* New York

1964b. "Essentially Contested Concepts," in Gallie, 1964a: 157–191

Gallop, David, 1975. *Plato: "Phaedo" Translated with Notes.* Oxford

Gentzler, Jyl (ed.), 1998. *Method in Ancient Philosophy.* Oxford

Giannantoni, Gabriele (ed.), 1990. *Socratis et Socraticorum Reliquiae.* Naples

Gifford, Mark, 2002. "Dramatic Dialectic in Republic Bk 1," *Oxford Studies in Ancient Philosophy* 20: 35–106

Gill, Christopher, 2002. "Critical Response to the Hermeneutic Approach from an Analytic Perspective," in Reale and Scolnicov (eds.), 2002: 211–222

Gill, Christopher and McCabe, Mary Margaret (eds.), 1996: *Form and Argument in Late Plato.* Oxford

Gillespie, C.M., 1912. "The Use of eidos and idea in Hippocrates," *Classical Quarterly* 6: 179–203

Goldman, Harvey, 2004. "Re-examining the 'Examined Life' in Plato's Apology of Socrates," *Philosophical Forum* 35: 1–33

2009. "Traditional Forms of Wisdom and Politics in Plato's *Apology,*" *Classical Quarterly* 59: 444–467

Gomez-Lobo, A., 1994. *The Foundations of Socratic Ethics.* Indianapolis

Gordon, Jill, 2003. "Eros and Philosophical Seduction in *Alcibiades 1,*" *Ancient Philosophy* 23: 11–30

Griffith, Mark, 1990. "Contest and Contradiction," in Griffith and Mastronarde (eds.), 1990: 185–206

Griffith, Mark and Mastronarde, Donald J. (eds.), 1990. *Cabinet of the Muses.* Atlanta

Griffith, Tom (trans.), 2000. *Plato, "The Republic."* Cambridge

Griswold, Charles (ed.), 2002. *Platonic Writings, Platonic Readings.* University Park

Grote, George, 1867. *Plato and the Other Companions of Sokrates*, vol. 3. London

Grube, G.M.A., 1935/1964. *Plato's Thought*. Boston

Gulick, Charles Burton, 1928/1982. *Athenaeus: The Deipnosophists with an English Translation*, 7 vols. Cambridge, MA, repr. 1987

Guthrie, W.K.C., 1962. *A History of Greek Philosophy*, vol. I: *The Earlier Presocratics and the Pythagoreans*. Cambridge

    1975. *A History of Greek Philosophy*, vol. IV: *Plato: The man and his Dialogues, Earlier Period*. Cambridge

    1978. *A History of Greek Philosophy*, vol. V: *The Later Plato and the Academy*. Cambridge

Hadot, Pierre, 1995. *Qu'est-ce que la philosophie antique?* Paris

    2002. *What is Ancient Philosophy?* English trans. by Michael Chase of Hadot, 1995. Cambridge

Halliwell, Stephen, 1995. "Forms of Address: Socratic Vocatives in Plato," in de Martino and Sommerstein (eds.), 1995: 87–121

    2006. "An Aristotelian Perspective on Plato's Dialogues," in Herrmann (ed.), 2006: 189–211

Harte, Verity, 1999. "Conflicting Values in Plato's *Crito,*" *Archiv für Geschichte der Philosophie* 81: 117–147

Havlicek, Ales and Karfik, Filip (eds.), 2001. *Plato's "Phaedo": Proceedings of the Second Symposium Pragense*. Prague

Heinaman, R., 2004. "Why Justice Does Not Pay in Plato's Republic," *Classical Quarterly* 54: 379–393

Helm, James J. (ed.), 1981. *Plato: Apology. Text and Grammatical Commentary*. Wauconda

Helmbold, William, 1939. *Plutarch's Moralia with an English Translation*, vol VI. London

Herrmann, Fritz-Gregor (ed.), 2006. *New Essays on Plato: Language and Thought in Fourth-Century Greek Philosophy*. Swansea

Hershbell, Jackson and Dillon, John (eds. and trans.), 1991. *Iamblichus: On the Pythagorean Way of Life. Text, Translation and Notes*. Atlanta

Hesk, Jon, 2007. "Combative Capping in Aristophanic Comedy," *Cambridge Classical Journal* 53: 124–160

Hewitt, William, 1935. "The Image in the Sand," *Classical Philology* 30: 10–22

Hicks, R.D., 1925/1991. *Diogenes Laertius: Lives of Eminent Philosophers with an English Translation*, 2 vols. Cambridge, MA, repr. 1991

Hitchcock, David, 2000. "The Origin of Professional Eristic," in Robinson and Brisson (eds.), 2000: 59–67

Hobbs, Angela, 2007. "Plato on War," in Scott (ed.), 2007: 176–194

Hopkins, Jim and Savile, Anthony (eds.), 1992. *Psychoanalysis, Mind, and Art*. Oxford

Irwin, Terence, 1977. *Plato's Moral Theory*. Oxford

    1995. *Plato's Ethics*. Oxford

    1998. "Common Sense and Socratic Method," in Genzler (ed.) (1998): 28–66

2008. "The Platonic Corpus," in Fine (ed.), 2008a: 63–87

Isnardi, Margherita, 1954. "Note al dialogo pseudoplatonico antereastai," *La parola del Passato* 9: 137–143

Isocrates, see Norlin (trans.), 1929

Jackson, Henry, 1885. "Plato's Later Theory of Ideas, v: The *Sophist*," *Journal of Philology* 28: 173–230

Jäkel, Siegred, and Timonen, Asko (eds.), 1994. *Laughter Down the Centuries*, vol. 1. Turku

Joly, Robert, 1970. "Platon ou Pythagore? Héraclide Pontique, fr. 87–88," in Joly, 1994: 15–31

1994. *Glane de philosophie antique*. Brussels

Jouanna, J., 1990. *Hippocrate II, 1 (De l'Ancienne Médecine)*. Paris

Jowett, B. and Campbell, Lewis, 1894. *Plato's "Republic": The Greek Text*, vol. 3. Oxford

Judson, Lindsay and Karasmanis, Vassilis, 2006. *Remembering Socrates: Philosophical Essays*. Oxford

Kahn, Charles, 1996. *Plato and the Socratic Dialogues: The Philosophical Use of a Literary Form*. Cambridge

2001. *Pythagoras and the Pythagoreans: A Brief History*. Indianapolis

Kamtekar, Rachana, 2001. "Social Justice and Happiness in the Republic: Plato's Two Principles," *History of Political Thought* 22: 189–220

2005. "The Friendship of Politics: Callicles, Democratic Politics, and Rhetorical Education in Plato's *Gorgias*," *Ancient Philosophy* 25: 319–339

Kateb, George, 2006. *Patriotism and Other Mistakes*. New Haven

Kenny, Anthony, 2004. *Ancient Philosophy*. Oxford

King, J.E. (trans.), 1927. *Cicero in Twenty-Eight Volumes: XVIII. Tusculan Disputations*. Cambridge, MA

Kingsley, Peter, 1995. *Ancient Philosophy, Mystery, and Magic*. Oxford

Klosko, G., 1983. "Criteria of Fallacy and Sophistry for Use in the Analysis of Platonic Dialogues," *Classical Quarterly* 33: 363–374

Kraut, Richard (ed.), 1992. *Cambridge Companion to Plato*. Cambridge

(ed.), 1997. *Plato's "Republic": Critical Essays*. Lanham

Lamb, W.R.M. (trans.), 1927/1986. *Plato in Twelve Volumes: XII Charmides, Alcibiades I and II, Hipparchus, The Lovers, Theages, Minos, Epinomis*. Cambridge, MA

Lee, Desmond, 1977. *Plato: "Timaeus" and "Critias."* London

Leroux, Georges (trans. and comm.), 2002. *Platon: La République*. Paris

Levett, M.J., see Burnyeat, 1990

Liddell, H.G., Scott, R., and Jones, H.S. (eds.), 1843/1961. *A Greek–English Lexicon*. Oxford

Lloyd, G.E.R., 1979. *Magic, Reason, and Experience: Studies in the Origin and Development of Greek Science*. Cambridge

1989. *Revolutions of Wisdom: Studies in the Claims and Practice of Ancient Greek Science*. Berkeley

Lloyd-Jones, Hugh, 1983. *The Justice of Zeus*. Berkeley

Long, A.A., 1998. "Plato's Apologies and Socrates in the Theaetetus," in Gentzler (ed.), 1998: 113–136

Long, Alex, 2007. "The Form of Plato's *Republic*," in Osborne (ed.), 2007: 224–241

Majors, Richard and Billson, Janet Mancini, 1992. *Cool Pose: The Dilemmas of Black Manhood in America.* New York

Mansfeld, Jaap, 1990. *Studies in the Historiography of Greek Philosophy.* Assen

Marchant, E.C. and Todd, O.J. (trans.), 1923/1979. *Xenophon in Seven Volumes: IV. Memorabilia and Oeconomicus. Symposium and Apology.* Cambridge, MA

Martin, Richard, 1993. "The Seven Sages as Performers of Wisdom," in Dougherty and Kurke (eds.), 1993: 108–128

de Martino, Francesco and Sommerstein, Alan (eds.), 1995. *Lo Spettacolo delle Voci.* Bari

Matthews, Gareth, 1997. "Perplexity in Plato, Aristotle, and Tarski," *Philosophical Studies* 85: 213–228

McCabe. M.M., 2006. "Is Dialectic as Dialectic Does?," in Reis (ed.), 2006: 70–98

McDowell, John (trans. and comm.), 1973. *Plato: "Theaetetus,"* Oxford

McKirahan, Richard, 1994. *Philosophy before Socrates: An Introduction with Texts and Commentary.* Indianapolis

McPherran, Mark, 1993. "Commentary on Morgan," in Cleary and Wians (eds.), 1993: 112–129

  1996. *The Religion of Socrates.* University Park

Meinwald, Constance, 1992. "Good-Bye to the Third Man," in Kraut (ed.), 1992: 365–396

  2008. "The Metaphysics of the Republic," Arizona Colloquium in Ancient Philosophy at the University of Arizona, Tucson, unpublished

Menn, Stephen, 1992. "Aristotle and Plato on God as Nous and as the Good," *Review of Metaphysics* 45: 543–573

  1995. *Plato on God as Nous.* Carbondale

Merlan, Philip, 1963. "Das Problem der Erasten," in Frank, Minkowski, and Sternglass (eds.), 1963: 297–313

Michelini, Ann (ed.), 2003a. *Plato as Author: The Rhetoric of Philosophy.* Leiden

  2003b. "Plato's Socratic Mask," in Michelini (ed.), 2003a: 45–65

Minar, Edwin L., Jr., Sandbach, F.H., and Helmbold, W.C.(trans.), 1961. *Plutarch: Moralia With an English Translation*, vol. 9. Cambridge, MA

Montuori, Mario, 1981. *Socrates: Physiology of a Myth.* Amsterdam

Morgan, Michael, 1992. "Plato and Greek Religion," in Kraut (ed.), 1992: 227–247

  1995. "Philosophy in Plato's *Sophist*," in Cleary and Wians (eds.), 1993: 83–106

Morrison, Donald, 2000. "On the Alleged Historical Reliability of Plato's Apology," *Archiv für Geschichte der Philosophie* 82: 225–265

Morrison, J.S., 1958. "The Origins of Plato's Philosopher-Statesman," *Classical Quarterly* 8: 198–218

Nails, Debra, 1995. *Agora, Academy, and the Conduct of Philosophy.* Dordrecht

  2002. *The People of Plato.* Indianapolis

Nehamas, Alexander, 1990. "Eristic, Antilogic, Sophistic, Dialectic: Plato's Demar-
cation of Philosophy from Sophistry," *History of Philosophy Quarterly* 7: 3–16
1998. *The Art of Living: Socratic Reflections from Plato to Foucault.* Berkeley
1999a. *Virtues of Authenticity.* Princeton
1999b "Socratic Intellectualism," in Nehamas, 1999a: 27–58
Nietzsche, Friedrich, 2006. *Thus Spoke Zarathustra*, ed. Robert Pippin trans.
Adrian de Caro. Cambridge
Nightingale, Andrea, 1995. *Genres in Dialogue: Plato and the Construct of Philosophy.*
Cambridge
Norlin, George (trans.), 1929. *Isocrates*, vol. II. Cambridge, MA
Notomi, Noburu, 1999. *The Unity of Plato's Sophist.* Cambridge
Notopoulos, J., 1939. "The Name of Plato," *Classical Philology* 34: 135–145
Nussbaum, Martha, 1997. *Cultivating Humanity.* Cambridge, MA
O'Connor, David K., 2007. "Rewriting the Poets in Plato's Characters," in Ferrari
(ed.), 2007: 55–89
O'Meara, Dominic (ed.), 1985. *Platonic Investigations.* Washington, DC
Olson, Halsten, 2000. "Socrates Talks to Himself in Plato's *Hippias Major*," *Ancient
Philosophy* 20: 265–287
Osborne, Robin (ed.), 2007. *Debating the Athenian Cultural Revolution.*
Cambridge
Ostenfeld, Erik Nis (ed.), 1998. *Essays on Plato's Republic.* Aarhus
Owen, G.E.L., 1986a. *Logic, Science, and Dialectic: Collected Papers in Greek Phi-
losophy*, ed. Martha Nussbaum. London
1986b. "The Platonism of Aristotle," in Owen, 1986a: 200–220
Pangle, Thomas (ed.), 1987. *The Roots of Political Philosophy.* Ithaca
Parke, H. W. and Wormell, D.E.W., 1956. *The Delphic Oracle.* Oxford
Parker, Robert, 1988. "Greek Religion," in Boardman, Griffith, and Murray (eds.),
1988: 248–268
Penner, Terry, 1992. "Socrates and the Early Dialogues," in Kraut (ed.), 1992:
121–169
2005. "Platonic Justice and What We Mean by Justice," internet *Journal of
the International Plato Society* 5, http://gramata.univ-paris1.fr/Plato/article
60.html
Penner, Terry and Rowe, Christopher, 2005. *Plato's "Lysis."* Cambridge
Peterson, Sandra, 2003. "An Authentically Socratic Conclusion in Plato's *Phaedo*:
Socrates' Debt to Asclepius," in Reshotko (ed.), 2003: 33–52
2008. "The *Parmenides*," in Fine (ed.), 2008a: 383–410
Philip, James A., 1966. "Platonic Diairesis," *Transactions and Proceedings of the
American Philological Association* 97: 335–358
Phillips, A.A. and Willcock, M.M. (eds. and trans.), 1999. *Xenophon and Arrian:
On Hunting.* Warminster
Plotinus, see Armstrong, 1966
Polansky, Ronald, 1992. *Philosophy and Knowledge: A Commentary on Plato's
"Theaetetus."* Cranbury

Politis, Vasilis, 2006. "The Argument for the Reality of Change and Changelessness in Plato's *Sophist* (248e7–249d5)," in Herrmann (ed.), 2006: 149–175

Popper, K., 1986. "How I See Philosophy," in Shanker (ed.), 1986: 198–212

Press, Gerald (ed.), 2000. *Who Speaks for Plato?* Lanham

Prior, William (ed.), 1996. *Socrates: Critical Assessments*, vol. II. New York
  2001. "The Historicity of Plato's Apology," *Polis* 18: 41–57

Reale, Giovanni and Scolnicov, Samuel (eds.), 2002. *New Images of Plato: Dialogues on the Idea of the Good.* Sankt Augustin

Reeve, C.D.C., 1988. *Philosopher Kings: The Argument of Plato's "Republic."* Princeton
  1989. *Socrates in the "Apology": An Essay on Plato's "Apology of Socrates."* Indianapolis
  (trans.), 1998. *Plato: "Cratylus."* Indianapolis
  2000. "The Role of TEXNH in Plato's Conception of Philosophy," in Cleary and Gurtler (eds.), 2000: 207–222
  (trans.), 2004. *Plato: "Republic." Translated from the New Standard Greek Text with Introduction.* Indianapolis

Reis, Burkhard (ed.), 2006. *The Virtuous Life in Greek Ethics.* Cambridge

Reshotko, Naomi (ed.), 2003. *Desire, Identity, and Existence: Essays in Honor of T.M. Penner.* Kelowna

Riddell, James, 1877/1973. *The Apology of Plato with a Revised Text and English Notes and a Digest of Platonic Idioms.* New York

Riginos, Alice, 1976. *The Anecdotes Concerning the Life and Writings of Plato.* Leiden

Robinson, Richard, 1953. *Plato's Earlier Dialectic.* Oxford
  1969a. *Essays in Greek Philosophy.* Oxford
  1969b. "Dr. Popper's Defense of Democracy," in Robinson 1969a: 74–99

Robinson, Thomas M. and Brisson, Luc (eds.), 2000. *Plato: "Euthydemus," "Lysis," "Charmides."* Sankt Augustin

Roochnik, David, 2003. *Beautiful City.* Ithaca

Ross, David, 1924/1958. *Aristotle's Metaphysics: A Revised Text with Introduction and Commentary.* Oxford
  (trans.) 1958/1980. *Aristotle: Nicomachean Ethics* (trans. rev. J.L. Ackrill and J.O. Urmson). Oxford

Rowe, C.J., 1983. "Plato on the Sophists as Teachers of Virtue," *History of Political Thought* 4: 409–427
  1993a. *Plato: "Phaedo."* Cambridge
  1993b. *Plato: "Symposium."* Warminster
  2001. "The Concept of Philosophy (Philosophia) in Plato's Phaedo," in Havlicek and Karfik (eds.), 2001: 34–47
  2006. "The Literary and Philosophical Style of the Republic," in Santas (ed.), 2006: 7–24
  2007. *Plato and the Art of Philosophical Writing.* Cambridge

Rue, Rachel, 1993. "The Philosopher in Flight: The Digression (172c–177c) in Plato's 'Theaetetus'," *Oxford Studies in Ancient Philosophy* 11: 71–100

Rusten, J., 1985. "Two Lives or Three? Pericles on the Athenian Character (Thucydides 2.40. 1–2)," *Classical Quarterly* 35: 14–19

Rutenber, Culbert Gerow, 1946. *The Doctrine of the Imitation of God in Plato*. New York

Ryle, Gilbert, 1965. "Dialectic in the Academy," in Bambrough (ed.), 1965: 39–68

1966. *Plato's Progress*. Cambridge

Santas, Gerasimas (ed.), 1979. *Socrates: Philosophy in Plato's Early Dialogues*. London

(ed.), 2006. *The Blackwell Guide to Plato's "Republic."* Oxford

Schiefsky, Mark, 2005. *Hippocrates on Ancient Medicine*. Leiden

Schleiermacher, F., 1836/1973. *Introductions to the Dialogues of Plato Translated from the German by William Dobson*. New York

Schofield, Malcolm, 1999a. *Saving the City: Philosopher-Kings and other Classical Paradigms*. New York

1999b. "Plato on the Economy," in Schofield, 1999a: 69–81

2006. *Plato: Political Philosophy*. Oxford

Scott, Dominic (ed.), 2007. *Maieusis: Essays on Ancient Philosophy in Honour of Myles Burnyeat*. Oxford

2008. "The *Republic*," in Fine (ed.), 2008a: 360–382

Sedley, David, 1995. "The Dramatis Personae of Plato's *Phaedo*," *Proceedings of the British Academy* 85: 3–26

1998. "The Etymologies in Plato's Cratylus," *Journal of Hellenic Studies* 118: 140–154

1999. "The Ideal of Godlikeness," in Fine, (ed.), 1999: 309–328

2002. "Socratic Irony in the Platonist Commentators," in Annas and Rowe (eds.), 2002: 37–57

2003. "A Socratic Interpretation of Plato's *Theaetetus*," in Cleary and Gurtler (eds.), 2003: 277–313

2004. *The Midwife of Platonism: Text and Subtext in Plato's "Theaetetus."* Oxford

2007. "Philosophy, the Forms, and the Art of Ruling," in Ferrari (ed.), 2007: 165–2001

Segvic, Heda, 2009. *From Protagoras to Aristotle*, ed. Myles Burnyeat. Princeton

Shanker, S.G. (ed.), 1986. *Philosophy in Britain Today*. Albany

Sharp, Kendall, 2006. *Socrates and the Second Person: The Craft of Platonic Dialogue*, PhD dissertation, University of Chicago. Chicago

Shields, Christopher, 2003. *Classical Philosophy: A Contemporary Introduction*. London

Shorey, Paul, 1917. "Note on Republic 368a," *Classical Philology* 12: 436

1928. "Review of Lamb 1986/27," *Classical Philology* 23: 303–305

(trans.), 1963. *Plato, The Republic*. Cambridge, MA

Slings, S.R. (ed. and comm.), 1999. *Plato: Clitophon*. Cambridge

2003. *Platonis Rempublicam recognovit, etc. S.R. Slings*. Oxford

Smith, Nicholas (ed.), 1998. *Plato: Critical Assessments*, vol. III. London

Smith, Nicholas, and Woodruff, Paul (eds.), 2000. *Reason and Religion in Socratic Philosophy*. Oxford

Smith, P. Ch., 2000. "Not Doctrine but Placing in Question," in Press (ed.), 2000: 34–125

Smith, Robin, 1997. *Aristotle: Topics Bks I and VIII Translated with a Commentary.* Oxford

Smyth, Herbert Weir, 1920. *Greek Grammar.* Cambridge, MA, rev. Gordon M. Messing, 1956, repr. 1974

Souilhé, Joseph, 1930. *Platon: Oeuvres complétes, tome XIII–2e partie.* Paris

Sprague, Rosamond Kent, 1962. *Plato's Use of Fallacy: A Study of the "Euthydemus" and Some Other Dialogues.* New York

 1976. *Plato's Philosopher-King.* Columbia

 1993. *Plato: Euthydemus.* Indianapolis

 1994. "Platonic Jokes with Philosophical Points," in Jäkel and Timonen (eds.), 1994: 53–58

Stenzel, J., 1940. *Plato's Method of Dialectic,* D.J. Allan, trans. and ed. Oxford

Stokes, Michael, 1986. *Plato's Socratic Conversations.* Baltimore

 1998. "Plato and the Sightlovers of the *Republic,*" in Smith (ed.), 1998: 266–291

 2005. *Dialectic in Action: An Examination of Plato's Crito.* Swansea

Strachan, C.G., 1970. "Who Did Forbid Suicide at *Phaedo* 62b?," *Classical Quarterly* 20: 216–220

Strauss, Leo, 1978a. *The City and Man.* Chicago

 1978b. "On Plato's Republic," in Strauss, 1978a: 50–138

de Stryker, E. and Slings, S.R., 1994. *Plato's Apology of Socrates.* Leiden

Tarrant, Dorothy, 1946. "Colloquialisms, Semi-Proverbs, and Word Play in Plato," *Classical Quarterly* 40: 109–117

 1958. "More Colloquialisms, Semi-Proverbs, and Word-Play in Plato," *Classical Quarterly* NS 8: 158–160

Taylor, A.E., 1911a. *Varia Socratica.* Oxford

 1911b. "The Words, *eidos, idea,* in Pre-Platonic Literature," in Taylor 1911a: 178–267

Taylor, C.C.W., 2008. "Socrates the Sophist," in Judson and Karasmanis (eds.), 2006: 157–168

Thesleff, Holger, 1990. "Theaitetos and Theodorus," *Arctos* 24: 147–159

Tomin, Julius, 2001. "Socrates in the *Phaedo,*" in Havlicek and Karfik (eds.), 2001

Trevaskis, J.R., 1955. "The Sophistry of Noble Lineage (*Sophist* 230a5–232b9)," *Phronesis* 1: 36–49

Tuplin, Christopher (ed.), 2006. *Xenophon and His World.* Stuttgart

Vanderwaerdt, P.A. (ed.), 1994. *The Socratic Movement.* Ithaca

Vasiliou, Iakovos, 2008. *Aiming at Virtue in Plato.* Cambridge

Vegetti, Mario (ed. and comm.), 1998–2007. *Platone: La Repubblica,* 7 vols. Naples

Vlastos, Gregory (ed.), 1971. *The Philosophy of Socrates.* Garden City

 1991a. *Socrates: Ironist and Moral Philosopher.* Ithaca

 1991b. "Socratic Piety," in Vlastos, 1991a: 157–178

1994a. *Socratic Studies*. Cambridge

1994b. "Socrates' Disavowal of Knowledge," in Vlastos, 1994a: 39–67

1995a. *Studies in Greek Philosophy, vol. II: Socrates, Plato, and Their Tradition*, ed. Daniel Graham. Princeton

1995b. "The Theory of Justice in the Polis in Plato's Republic," in Vlastos, 1995a: 69–103

Wachsmuth, Curt and Hense, Otto (eds.), 1958. *Stobaeus (Joannis Stobaei)*. Berlin

Waterfield, Robin, 1987. Plato: "Theaetetus." London

1993. *Plato: "Republic."* Oxford

2006. "Xenophon and Socrates," in Tuplin (ed.), 2006: 79–113

Waymack, Mark, 1985. "The *Theaetetus* 172c–177c: A Reading of the Philosopher in Court," *Southern Journal of Philosophy* 23: 481–489

Wehrli, Fritz (ed.), 1945. *Die Schule des Aristoteles: II. Aristoxenos*. Basel

Weiss, Roslyn, 1996. "Virtue without Knowledge: Socrates' Conception of Holiness in Plato's *Euthyphro*," in Prior (ed.), 1996: 195–216

2001. *Virtue in the Cave*. Oxford

2006. "Socrates, Seeker or Preacher?," in Abel-Rappe and Kamtekar (eds.), 2006: 243–253

2007. "Wise Guys and Smart Alecks in *Republic* 1 and 2," in Ferrari (ed.), 2007: 90–115

West, Thomas G., 1979. *Plato's "Apology" of Socrates*. Ithaca

2004. "Leo Strauss and American Foreign Policy," *Claremont Review of Books*, Summer, www.claremont.org/writings/crb/summer2004/west.html

West, Thomas G. and West, Grace Starry, 1998. *Four Texts on Socrates: Plato's "Euthyphro," "Apology," and "Crito," and Aristophanes' "Clouds."* Ithaca

White, Nicholas, 1979. *A Companion to Plato's Republic*. Indianapolis

Whitman, Walt, 1993. *Leaves of Grass*. New York

Wildberg, Christian, 2003. "The Rise and Fall of the Socratic Notion of Piety," in Cleary and Gurtler (eds.), 2003: 1–28

Williams, Bernard, 1981. *Moral Luck: Philosophical Papers 1973–1980*. Cambridge

Wolfsdorf, David, 2004. "Socrates' Avowals of Knowledge," *Phronesis* 49: 75–142

2008. *Trials of Reason: Plato and the Crafting of Philosophy*. Oxford

Woodard, Roger (ed.), 2007. *The Cambridge Companion to Greek Mythology*. Cambridge

Woodruff, Paul, 1982. *Plato: "Hippias Major" Translated with Commentary and Essay*. Oxford

1983. *Plato: Two Comic Dialogues, "Ion" and "Hippias Major."* Indianapolis

1986. "The Skeptical Side of Plato's Method," *Revue Internationale de Philosophie* 40: 22–37

Woolf, Rafael, 2003. "Commentary on Sedley," in Cleary and Gurtler (eds.), 2003: 314–323

2004. "The Practice of a Philosopher," *Oxford Studies in Ancient Philosophy* 26: 97–129

2008. "Misology and Truth," in Cleary and Gurtler (eds.), 2008: 1–16

Xenophon: for *Anabasis*, see Brownson, 1922; for *Memorabilia*, see Marchant and Todd (trans.), 1923/1979; for *On Hunting*, see Phillips and Willcock (eds. and trans.), 1999

Yi, Byeong-Uk, 2009. "The Cyclical Argument and Principles of Change in Plato's Phaedo," *Logical Analysis and History of Philosophy* 12: 85–102

Yonezawa, Shigeru, 1995. "Socratic Knowledge and Socratic Virtue," *Ancient Philosophy* 15: 349–358

2004. "Socrates' Conception of Philosophy," *British Journal for the History of Philosophy* 12: 1–23

Yunis, Harvey, 2007. "The Protreptic Rhetoric of the Republic," in Ferrari (ed.), 2007: 1–26

Zeyl, Donald, 1987. *Plato: "Gorgias."* Indianapolis

2000. *Plato: "Timaeus."* Indianapolis

Index of passages cited

ARISTOPHANES
Acharnians
  523–529 202
Clouds
  193–194 187

ARISTOTLE
Magna Moralia
  1182a 158
Metaphysics
  985b27 158
  987a32–b12 226
  1092b10 ff. 166
Nicomachean Ethics VI
  ch. 5 77
Nicomachean Ethics X
  1178b8–12 78
  1178b15–18 80
On Poets
  fr. 15 228
Poetics I
  1447b11 228
Politics
  1264a11–14 225
  1265a5 228
  1265a10–13 227, 228
  1265a29 228
  1265b19 228

CICERO
Tusculan Disputations V
  3, 8 167, 207–208

DIOGENES LAERTIUS
Lives of Eminent Philosophers
  I, 12 167
  I, 27–33 28–29
  I, 28–29 29
  I, 108 28
  III, 4 231
  VIII, 8 167, 208

EURIPIDES
Iphigenia in Tauris
  1247ff. 29

HERACLITUS
  DK22B35 202
  DK22B40 202
  DK22B129 202

HERODOTUS
Histories
  I.30 202–203

IAMBLICHUS
De Vita Pythagorica
  58–59 167
  82 156, 186
  83 193
  86 188

ISOCRATES
Antidosis
  261–266 201
  270 201
  270–271 257

PHILOLAUS
  DK44B6 185

PLATO
Alcibiades Major
  105b 250
  105e 250
  112d–113c 69, 94–95
  113a–b 8
  114d 99–100
Apology
  17a 37
  17b 243
  17b–c 243
  17c 62

PLATO *Apology* (cont.)

18a 38, 243
18b 19, 22, 35
18b–c 243
18c 19, 22–23, 24
18e 19, 22, 35, 243
19a 23, 243
19a–e 243
19a8–b2 23
19b–c 24
19b–d 62
19b5 23
19c 25, 62
19c4–5 42
19c7 25
19d 26, 38, 196
20b–c 26
20b4 18
20b5 18
20c1–e3 34
20d 19, 36, 43
20d–e 26
21a 48
21b 19–20, 42
21b5–6 50
21b8–c2 20
21c3–d7 20–21
21c6–7 21
21d 36, 42, 62
21e 48
21e3–22a8 21
22a 35, 53
22a3–6 52
22a5 21
22a8–c 22
22c9–d1 42
22d 22, 43
22d–e 53
22d7 32
22e 22, 53
22e–23b 36
22e6–23a3 23
23a 208, 230
23a5–6 36
23a6–b4 51
23b 22, 32
23b3–4 42
23c4 49
23d 38, 39–40, 196, 238, 243, 245
24a6 43
24b 19, 23, 40, 73
24c 32, 65
24c6 32
24d 32

24d4 40
24d7–9 18
25b 65
25c 18, 31
25d 32
26b 65
26b1–2 18
26c7 37
26d 38, 196
26d–27 32
27a 64
27b 64
28a 43
28b 33
28d 223
28e 2, 39, 242–243
29a 166
29a–b 223
29a5–b6 223
29a6–b1 42
29b 18, 43, 45, 46, 89
29b5 42
29b6–7 43, 45
29c 242, 260
29c–d 236
29d 1, 34, 39, 229, 235, 239, 242, 254, 259, 260
29d–e 31, 65, 166, 196, 208, 209, 214, 236, 243
29d–30a 52
29d–30b 30, 62
29d2–30b2 34
29d8 46
29e 1, 62
29e–30a 1, 39
30a 47
30a1–2 32
30b3–4 33
30c 46
30d 89
31a 46
31a2 54
31a6–7 53
31b3–5 249
32b 62
32d 1, 30, 62, 223, 253
33b9–c4 49
34a 151
35d 37, 55
37b6–7 42
38a 2
38c 245
39c 64
40a2–3 38
40c 37

41a–c 253
41b 64
41c 53
41d 64
41e 2
42a 42, 166
Charmides
31b3–5 249
153d 249
154d 64
Cratylus
400d 81
Crito
44d 35
46b6 84
46c1 84
46d6 84
48b3 84
48c–d 81
48c1 84
48d3 84
50a 162
Euthydemus
272c 142
272d 198
273d 198
273e–274a 199
275a 198, 241
275d–276d 199
278b5 199
278e 44
279a 44
282d 199
293e 44
295b 70
304d–e 199–200
304e 198
305a 200
305b 198, 200
305c 200
305d 200–201
307a 201
307b 201
Euthyphro
2b 78, 79, 80
4b7–c3 78
4e–5a 81
5d8–6a5 78
6a 78
6a–b 81
7b7–9 78
9e 74, 84
11c5 69
11d 68
11e–12e 213

12d 213
12e 76, 77
12e–15a 77
13a 213
15e 81
Gorgias
447c 244
448d–e 244
449a 26
449b 244
453b 244
454c 244
457c–458b 244
457e–458b 229
459d–460a 26
462–463 213
462a 244
463a 18
465 213
465d–466a 162
467d6–e1 8
471e–472d 244
475e 244
481–482 243–244
484c 244
484c–486d 245
484d–485e 239–240, 244
486a 244
486c 239
487d 244
497b–c 244
506c 57
508e–509a 45
509 56
513b–c 118
515c–d 31
516b 31
519d–e 162
522c1–2 38
Hippias Major
286c–d 242
286d–e 95
287a 95
304b–c 26, 40
304c 242
364b 105
Hippias Minor
363a 240
369c6 97
376c 242
Laches
186c4 25–26
187e 64
188b 202
190b–c 97

PLATO *Laches (cont.)*
  Laws
    886d 24
    889a–d 24
  Lovers
    132b 238
    132d 202, 238
    133a 248, 257
    133b 202
    133c 202
    134b 202, 238
    134d 203
    135a 203
    135b 203, 249
    135d 203–204, 249
    136b–c 204
    137a–b 204
    137b 204
    137c 204
    137d 204
    138a 204
    138b 204
    138e 204
    139a 205
  Lysis
    210e 34
    213d 242
    217e–218a 247
    218 123
  Meno
    72–76 213
    80c–d 242
    91a–b 31
    91b–c 27
    92e–94c 31
    99e–100a 31
  Parmenides
    129b1 239
    130b 48
    135b–c 238–239
    135d 48
  Phaedo
    58d 184
    58e–59b 193
    58e3 193
    59a 167
    59b–c 191
    59e–60a 191
    60a 191
    60d–61a 191
    60e–61b 168, 244
    61a 168, 191
    61b1–4 183
    61b4 176

61b5 168, 173, 176
61b6 168
61c 168
61d 169
61d6 170
61e 168, 173, 191
62b 170, 171, 243
62b–63c 181
62c–d 171
62d4 183
63b 172, 193
63b–c 176, 177
63b4 217
63c–d 179
63d 175
63e–64a 172
63e–69e 176
63e9–10 189
64a 166, 173
64a4–5 189
64b 183
64b4–5 189
64c 183
64d7 191
64e1 191
64e2–3 189
65a 183
65c–d 184
65d–67b 185
66b2 189
66b11–c5 187
66c4–5 191
66c8–d3 187, 191
66d2–3 191
66e–67b 188
67b4 183, 189
67d8 189
68c2 190
69d1 189
69d7–e5 173
70b 168, 173, 176
70c 139
72a9–10 176
72d 176
72e4 190
73a5–7 176
74–76 191
75c 185
75c–d 190
76c11 176
76d 176, 185
76e5 176
77a5 176
77d 176

77e 175
78b–80b 176–177
80e6 189
81d5–82b9 190
82b10 190
82b10–c4 188
82c2 189
82d–83e 184–185
83e5 189
84d 193
87c–88b 177–179, 181
95b 174, 181
95b–c 174
95b–e3 179
95b–106e 177
95d–e 174
96b 196
97e 196
100b5 185, 187
100b6 185
101e 173
107b 175, 193
107c–114d 182
108 181
115c 175
115d 191, 193

Phaedrus
229–230 39
242a–b 172, 182
269e 139
278a 247

Protagoras
61d 242
335d 258
336b 18
336b–c 241
338d–e 94
342a–343c 214, 240–241
343 214, 241
343a4 29
343b6–7 20
348a 94
352a 64
360c 213
362a 18

Republic
328b 101
328d 101
331a 126
336c 93, 162
336e 163
337b–c 93
337c 136
337c–e 93

337c–339b 160
338c 136
344e 163
348 96, 98
348b 94, 98
354a 126
357a 99, 100
357a–d 158
358b 147
358c 102
358c–d 98
358d 106
358e 98
359b 103
359c 103
360b 78
360d 103
361b 99
361d 103, 105
365d 99
365e–366a 99
366 156
366a 106
366b–d 103
367b 147
367e 106
368a 150, 155
368b 162
368b–c 100, 161
368c 99, 100, 102, 162
369b 159
372 151
372b 109
372c 108, 110
372c–d 125
372d 108
372e 113
372e–373 108–109
373c 110
374c4–e1 111
374e1 121
375a 121
375a2 121
375b4 121
375c 122
375d–e 122
375d1 121
375e1 121
375e6 121
375e8 121
376 151
376a–c 122
378b 111
383c 155

PLATO *Republic (cont.)*

386a 111
386c 111
387 159
387b 111
387d 111
388a 111
388e 163
395c–d 111
398c 112–113
398d 153
398e 110
399a 110, 111
399c 110
399d 110
399e 109, 110
400a 151
401b 110
402b9–c 138–139
403b 107, 110
404a 111
404b 111
404c 110
404d 110
407d 110
409c 107
410a 113
412c 111
414–415 135
414b–415d 111
414c 161
415b 111
415d 111
416a–c 111
416b–c 161
416d 111
421a–b 107
423 113
424b 156
427e 102–103, 113
429a 161
430e 161
432c 161
432e 104
433a 161
434c 163
434e 113
435c–d 161
437d–e 126–127
438a–c 127
439 113
439–441 158
439a–b 127
441d–e 107
443b 107

449–450a 113
450b 104
450c–d 161
450d 149, 152
450d–e 104
450e–451b 149
451–453 111
452a–453b 161
454a 213
454d–e 113
456a 111
457b–c 161
458b 111
458c6 147
459a 122, 151
459d–e 111
463e 107
464a 111
466e–467c 111
468b 150
469a 155
470e6 147
472 114
472a 161
472e 113
473b 147
473c–e 124
473d5–6 152
473e 161
474 147
474a 113, 124
474b 161
474b–c 124
475d 151
475e 135
475e–476a 133
475e–476d 152
476a 125, 127, 128
476a–b 125
476b 125
476c 125, 129
476d 125, 128
476d4 130–131
477a2–3 144
478a–b 125
478a11–13 144
479 130
479–480 137
479a 131
479a–b 133–134
479d–e 125–126
479e–480a 131
479e6 137
480a 132
480e 130

484a 134–135
484b 131–132
485a–b 132–133
485b–487a 141
485c3–4 135
485d–e 125
486e1–487a8 136
487c4–e 136
487d 140
487e–488a 138
487e7–488a1 147
488–489 146
488a–489c 138
489d–e 140
489e 104
490d 140
491a–492a 141
491b 146
491d–493c 229
492 142
492a 141
493d–494a 140
493e–494a 146
494b 140, 141,
  142
494b–495a 140–141
494d5–9 141, 147
494e–495a 142
495b 141
495c–d 142
495d–e 146
496a 143
496a11–12 144
496b 137
496c 143
497b 155
497b–c 145, 146
497d–e 161
498d 164
499a–b 161
499c–d 139
499e–500a 145
500b 146
500c–d 146, 155–156
500d 145
503c–d 112
506c–507a 161
509b 160
509c 107, 160
509d–511e 158
510c–e 152
517a8 152
517b5–6 147
521d 112
522e 112, 153

525b 112, 153
525c 112
525d 152
526a 152
526d 114, 153
527c 112, 114, 153
528d 151
530b 149
530d8 152, 158
531d–534a 135
532d 164
532e–533a 152
536e 104
537a 111
537c 112
537d–e 137
539c 137
539d–e 112
541 112
541a–b 112
543a 114
543c7–544a1 113
544 113
546a–d 153
548d–e 151
580b 158
583b 104–105, 154
587b–588a 153
588e 158
590 120
592b 114
595–596 101
595c 104, 161
596a 104, 149
596a–597 133
596b 128
597b–c 158
597c3 126
597c9 126
600b 156, 158
602c 158
603a1 96
608b 104, 152
608d 149, 156
610a–b 164
611 156
612c–d 107
614b 149
618a–620d 154
618b 152
Sophist
216a 206
216b 206
216c–217a 206
216d 205

PLATO (*cont.*)
  221c–223b 210
  224c1–2 210
  224d 210
  224d1–2 210
  225 139
  225a–226a 210
  226a–231b 210
  230–231 209
  231d 210
  231d–e 210
  231e 210
  232 209–210
  232b–236e 210
  246b 207
  249c–d 207
  253c 207, 213, 238
  253d–254a 208
  254a–b 208
  259d–260a 208–209
  264c–268c 210
Statesman
  258a 211–212
Symposium
  172e–173a 159
  173a 151
  177c 67
  185 18
  198c 18
  200a 246
  200b 246
  200e 246
  201d1–2 246
  201e5 246
  202d 246–247
  202e2 247
  203a 247
  203d 247
  203e 247
  204 123
  204b 247
  215e–216a 250
  218a 250
Theaetetus
  142a–b 88
  143d 66
  143d–144c 62
  144a–b 66
  145a6 66
  145d4 88
  146b 73
  146c 66
  148b3 88
  149b 88
  150c4–7 69

151a 242
151d 53
151e4 88
152 60
155 65
155a 242
155d 70, 241–242
156a2 88
157c–d 68
158a5 88
158c3 242
161a 86
161a7 68, 217
162b 73
162d3 88
165b 66, 73
167c4–6 60
168a 66
169b 64, 67, 73,
  217
169c–183a 67
169c6–7 73
171d 60
171d3–5 84
172a 60
172b–177c 13, 85
172c 61
172c3 67
173b 66, 72
173c 72, 73
173d 61
173e–174a 61
174a–b 196
174b 61
175b–c 62
175c 81
175c1 66
175d 62
175e 72
176a–b 76
176a2–4 72, 73
176b–c 76, 77
176c 81
176d–e 82
176e–177a 82–83
177b 86–87
177b8 59
177c2–4 73
183–184 67
184d1 88
184e 70
190b 68
195d 139
196c9 242
200c7 88

210 65, 70
210b 65
210b–c 68
210c 89, 209, 212
210c5–6 74
210d 62
216a ff. 67
Theages
126–127 33–38
126a 82
Timaeus
17b 115–116
17c 115–116
17d 116
17e 116
18a 116
18b 116
18c 116
18c–d 116
18d–e 116
19a 116
19b 116, 117
19c 117
19d 117
19e 117
20–21 203
20b 117
24c–d 203

29d–e 79, 80
51b8–c1 186

PLOTINUS
Ennead I
2 77, 79

PLUTARCH
Moralia
"Advice About Keeping Well" 129d 16
"How to Profit from One's Enemies" 88e
    16
"On Listening to Lectures" 40c–d 16
"On the Control of Anger" 463e 16
"Table Talk" 727–728 192
"The Divine Vengeance" 550a 78

THUCYDIDES
History
2, 40.1 204

XENOPHON
Apology
3 18
Memorabilia
I.2.31 258
I.2.46 48
III.vi 151

General index

Ackrill, J.L. 6, 115
Adam, James 113, 126–127, 135, 155, 164
Adeimantus (interlocutor) 13, 53, 103, 105–107,
    117, 120, 136–147, 154–157, 237
  biographical background 150, 151
  confusion/error 138, 140, 146–147, 159
  presentation of character 149–150,
    159–160
  revelation through Socrates' speech 107–109,
    118–119, 147–148, 163, 165
  suitability for philosophy 141–142, 144,
    146–147
Aeschinus Socraticus 27
afterlife
  benefits of 177–178
  debates on 33, 83
  initiation rituals 171
  see also immortality of the soul
Agathon (interlocutor) 246
Alcibiades 6, 234, 241, 250
Alcibiades Major 94–95, 99–100, 250
  authorship 94
Alcinous 75, 79, 109
Allen, R.E. 142
Anacharsis 28, 48, 49
Anaxagoras 25, 196–202, 207
Annas, Julia 80, 112–113, 231–232, 233
Antisthenes 230
Anytus (interlocutor) 31
Apology 7–8, 17–58, 220, 239
  compared with Phaedo 166, 172, 194–195,
    196
  compared with Theaetetus 59, 62–66, 68,
    71–72, 74, 84
  composition 18
  conflicts with "grand hypothesis" 220–221
  as exceptional case 220–221, 243
  factual accuracy 17–18, 19
  treatment of life/philosophy 1–2, 12–13, 14,
    196, 208–209, 214, 216–218, 222–223,

229–230, 233, 238, 242–243, 245–246, 250,
    259
  wordplay 17–18
Ariston (father of Plato) 155
Aristophanes 193
  Acharnians 202
  Clouds 42, 62, 186–187, 192
Aristotle 77, 78, 80, 186
  commentary on Plato 224, 225, 226, 229;
    sources 224–227
  doctrinaire approach 228–229
  scholastic flaws 228
  Topics 94
Aristoxenus 166
Arius Didymus 75
Athenaeus 18
Athens/Athenians
  civic characteristics 31, 54, 236
  harm resulting to from Socrates' demise/exile
    53

Barnes, Jonathan 6
bathing, advice against 193
beauty, nature/discussion of 125–126, 127–136,
    185
  dichotomy with ugliness 128, 130, 133–135
  distinguished from beautiful things 125,
    128–130, 133–135, 140, 185
Belfiore, Elizabeth 110, 233
Benardete, Seth 69, 85
Benson, Hugh 27, 34, 55–57
"betters," guidance by 43–45, 46
Beversluis, John 10–11, 219, 232, 235
Bias of Priene 241
"biggest things" 22–24, 30–33
  inappropriate claims to knowledge of 33–36,
    46–47
  Socrates' claims to ignorance of 43–46, 54–55,
    56, 57, 218–219; (apparent) contradiction
    47, 52–53

Blondell, Ruby 69, 85, 110–111, 149, 161–162
Bloom, Allan 122, 142
body, as obstacle to philosophy 185, 187–188, 192, 194
    contradicted by Socrates' behavior 191–192
Bostock, David 192
Bradshaw, David 85
Brickhouse, Thomas C. 5, 43, 45, 46, 50
Brunschwig, Jacques 94
Burkert, Walter 157
Burnet, John 19, 20, 25, 37, 186, 189, 190
Burnyeat, Miles 59, 87, 155

Callias (interlocutor) 258
Callicles (interlocutor) 31, 57, 239–240, 243–244
caring, failure of 39, 64–65
Cebes (interlocutor) 166–167, 168–194
    lack of clarity of thought 182
    "ownership" of Socrates' speech 174–175
    Socrates' ascertainment of requirements 179–182
Cephalus (interlocutor) 88, 101
Chaerephon 19, 29, 48, 49, 50, 51
Charmides 249
Cherniss, Harold 224–225, 233
children, role in "ideal" city 111, 116
Chilon of Sparta 241
Cicero, M. Tullius 167, 207–208
city, "just," depiction of 108–115
    "purging" 109–110
    Socrates' first choice 108, 109, 113
    in *Timaeus* 115–118
Cleinias (interlocutor) 198–199
Cleobulus of Lindus 241
conclusion, preassigned, reasoning towards 13–14
conditional reasoning 9
    in *Republic* 110–111, 112–115, 118–119
controversial ideas (in *Republic*) 2–3, 5–6, 90–91, 233
    commentators' distaste for 90, 91, 120, 148, 164–165
    failure to stand up to examination 121, 148, 160–161
    as "ironic" 92, 162
    pious purpose 163–165
    as "reduction to absurdity" 92, 120–121, 162
    revelatory purpose 163, 165
    Socrates' distancing from 118–119, 120, 147–148, 161–162, 164–165
    (supposed) backtracking 92, 162
controversialists 209–210
"conversion," absence of 7–8
Cooper, John 6, 258

Corinth, battle of (391 BC) 88
Cornford, Francis M. 211–212
courage, definitions of 56
courtroom style (of speechmaking) 98–99, 172–174, 175
craftsmen, claims to wisdom 22, 35
Cratylus 18
Critias 258
Crito 194
    compared with *Theaetetus* 62–63, 74, 84
Crito (interlocutor) 35, 175, 191, 198, 199–201
Croesus 202–203
Cyrus the Great of Persia 258–259

Dancy, R.M. 5
de Lacy, Phillip 121
de Stryker, E. 18, 34, 37, 40, 49, 51
death
    as dreamless sleep 178, 183
    fear of 177, 179–180
    readiness to face 166, 168–171, 173–174, 176–183, 193–194
    Socrates' ignorance about 7–8, 33
    vocabulary of 183
    see also afterlife; soul, immortality of
definition, questions of 220, 226
    see also division
Delphic oracle 19–20, 22, 28–29, 36, 48–51, 218–219, 221
    as basis/impetus for Socrates' mission 51, 53, 54
    impact of pronouncement on Socrates 48–49
    inscriptions at site 50
    lack of positive significance 49–51
    negative interpretation 50–51
    Socrates' interpretation 51
Demodocus 33–34
"digression" (*Theaetetus*) 13, 59–89, 211, 216–217, 232
    (apparent) inconsistency with other dialogues 59, 62–66, 85–89
    commentaries 85–87
    criticized for philosophical shortcomings 59
    failure of claims to stand up to examination 74–82, 86
    internal inconsistency 81
    "likeness to God" passage 75–82
    nonexamination of controversial claims 74, 84
    nonorigination of statements with Socrates 69
    as rhetoric 87
    setting 60–61
    structure 61

Dillon, John 79
Diogenes Laertius 18, 28–29, 35, 208, 241
Dionysodorus 48, 198–199
Diotima (interlocutor) 246–248
divine mission, philosophic
    examination/instruction as 47–56, 144
  grounds for belief in 47, 51–54
  mandatory nature 54
  specific application to Socrates 53–54
division, definition by 207, 213
doctrinal approach 2–3, 6–7, 231–234
  anti-doctrinal interpretation 11–12
Dodds, E.R. 240
dogs, philosophers compared with 121–123,
  151
dreams/dreaming
  as anti-philosophical activity 125, 130
  messages conveyed by 168

Ebert, Theodor 169
Echecrates (interlocutor) 166, 168
Eleatic Visitor (character in *Sophist*) 205–214,
  238, 257, 258–259
  divergences from Socratic practice 213
  links with Socratic practice 213
  as model of Platonic philosophy 210–213
  as philosopher 207–210
eristic approach 199
erotic interests 67, 150–151, 191
Euripides, *Iphigenia in Tauris* 29
Eurytus 166
Euthydemus 14, 70, 197–198, 201, 203, 210, 214,
  237–238, 241
Euthydemus (character) 48, 198
Euthyphro 8, 76–77
  compared with *Theaetetus* 62–63, 68, 71, 73,
  74, 78, 81, 84
  temporal link with *Theaetetus* 63
Evenus of Paros 26–46, 168–169
examination 1–2, 4–5, 8–13, 31–32, 34–35, 64–65
  by declaration 69–70, 74, 85–86
  partial 73–74, 86, 216
  as Socrates' life-work 39, 47–56, 67–71, 216,
  219

fallacious reasoning, theory of 251
familiar things, attachment to 122–123, 124
flawed arguments, nature of 9
forms, theory of 5–6, 126, 127–128, 135–136, 152,
  181, 185–186, 187, 226, 252–254
  lack of practical application 253
  overstatement of importance in Plato's
  thought 253–254
  see also ideas, theory of
Forster, Michael 43

Frede, Michael 8, 11
freedom, links with philosophy 207–208

Gifford, Mark 88
Glaucon (interlocutor) 13, 103, 106–108, 117,
  120, 125–136, 137, 161, 164, 237
  biographical background 122, 150–151
  choice of modes of argument 96, 97–99
  confusion/inconsistency 122–123, 124–125,
  127, 131, 132, 133, 135–136, 147
  mathematical interests 151–152, 153–154,
  158–159
  overreceptivity 149
  presentation of character 149–160
  reasons for change of choice 101
  relationship with Socrates 159
  responses to Socrates' prompts 151–152
  revelation through Socrates' speech 107–109,
  118–119, 122–125, 147–148, 160, 163, 165
  suitability for philosophy 141–142, 144
  use of vocative towards 152–153
god(s)
  in the afterlife 176, 177–178
  benign attitude 52–53, 55, 76
  contemplation/aspiration to resemble 75–82,
  144–145, 154–156, 188, 208
  debate on existence of 39–40, 47, 52–53,
  54–55
  naming 81
  nonbelief in, accusations of 23, 24, 37
  ordering of human behavior 47–56
Goldman, Harvey 36
Gomez-Lobo, A. 24
good men, (anticipated) encounters in the
  afterlife 178
goodness
  of character/life *see* virtue
  creation of, as god-like attribute/human
  aspiration 80
  need for badness as counterpoint 75–76
Gorgias 79, 118, 160, 239–240, 243–244
Gorgias of Leontini 26, 27, 38, 203, 257
"grand hypothesis" 3, 4, 5–7, 14–15, 217
  criticisms 4–5, 217, 219–220
Griffith, Mark 25
Grote, George 103
Guthrie, W.K.C. 3, 85

Halliwell, Stephen 7, 88, 152–153, 227–228
happiness, nature of 83
harm, role in definition of right/wrong 46–47
harmony, links with philosophy 208–209
Heraclitus 202
Herodotus 202–203
Hicks, R.D. 18

Hippias 26
Hippias Major 8, 95
Hippias Minor 97, 240
Hippias of Elis 26–27
Hitchcock, David 48

Iamblichus 154, 155, 156, 186, 188, 193
ideas, theory of 126
ignorance, acknowledgment of 35, 42–43,
    161–162
injustice
    penalties of 82–83, 86–87
    preferability to justice 96 *see also*
    unscrupulous person
innovation, avoidance of 156
"intellectualizing" 248–249
interlocutors
    drawing out, as constant feature of Socratic
    method 68–71, 72, 234–235
    resistance/challenges from 70
    revelation 7, 12, 71–74, 159–160, 216–218, 256
    (*see also* Adeimantus; Glaucon; Theodorus)
    tailoring of Socratic style to 4–5, 7, 13–14, 31,
    110–111, 232
irony
    ascribed to Plato/Socrates 10–11 *see also*
    controversial ideas
    Socrates' use at trial 40–41
Irwin, Terence 15, 224
Isocrates 201, 257
"itself," as philosophical term 126–127, 129,
    130–135, 156–157, 185–186, 187
    as constant 132
    satirized 187

"judges," in Socratic terminology 37–38
jury, role in speech-against-speech arguments
    98–99
justice 60–61, 149, 185
    divine 76, 77–78, 81
    as expedient 99–100
    internal querying as to 62
    planned defence (in *Republic*) 98, 106–107
    preferability to injustice, quantified
    153–154
    slandering of 102–103
    see also injustice

Kahn, Charles 4, 33, 56, 63, 186, 190, 218,
    219–220, 221–222, 224, 226, 239, 243
Kallipolis 114–115, 162
Kenny, Anthony 2
Kingsley, Peter 154
Klosko, G. 9
"knock knock" jokes 96

knowledge
    different senses of 42–43, 55–56
    distinguished from belief 125–126
    nature of 42–56, 59
    role in philosophical make-up 130–132
    seeking of 56–57
    Socrates' (limited) claims to 55–56, 58, 62
Kraut, Richard 4

Laches 97
Laws 15
learning
    false conundrum of "impossibility" 199
    love of, as characteristic of philosopher
    122–125, 132–133, 184–185
Liddell, Henry, and Scott, Robert, *Greek Lexicon*
    77
Lloyd, G.E.R. 20, 25
Long, Alex 106
Long, Anthony A. 63, 211–212
Lovers 14, 197, 201–205, 210, 214, 238, 248–249,
    257
    authorship 196
luxury, as component of ideal city 108–109,
    110–111, 118–119
Lysis 242, 247

majority, judgmental capacities 143, 145
    see also philosophers, popular opinion of
Martin, Richard 28
mathematics *see* Glaucon; Pythagorean theory
McKirahan, Richard 155–156
McPherran, Mark 24
Meinwald, Constance 6
Meletus (prosecutor) 31–32, 38, 40–41, 65
Meno 94, 190
metaphysics 252–254
midwifery, analogy with 68
militarism
    role in "ideal" city 108–109, 110–112, 114,
    117–118, 150
    role in Pythagorean theory 154
Miller, Mitchell 81
"misplaced charity," accusations of 10–11
Montuori, Mario 49, 50–51
Morgan, Michael 4
Morrison, Donald 18
mud 132
Myson of Chen 28–29, 30, 50, 241
"mythologizing," Socrates' use of term 168,
    176

Nails, Debra 88, 151, 231
nature theorists 24, 25, 39–40, 196, 207
    conflation of Socrates with 24

Nehamas, Alexander 45, 251–252, 254, 258
  criticisms of theory 253–254
Nietzsche, Friedrich, *Also sprach Zarathustra* 82
Nightingale, Andrea 254–256, 257
Notopoulos, J. 231
numerology 153–154, 158–159
Nussbaum, Martha 217

O'Keefe, Tim 74
opsa 108
"ordinary people," contrasted with "wise" 21–22
Orphic traditions 170–171

Parmenides 8, 132, 151, 238–239, 249
Parmenides (personage) 48
Pericles 31, 48, 204
persuasion
  constraints on 105–107
  dependence on persuadee 99–100, 107–109
  as function of speech in *Republic* 99, 100,
    102, 160
  as Socrates' purpose in *Phaedo* 172–175, 176,
    178
Phaedo 5, 7–8, 13–14, 166–195, 196, 197, 210,
    216–217, 223, 243, 244, 249, 259
  confused nature of argument 176, 180–182,
    193–194, 195
  doctrinal content 2–6
  logical structure of argument 176–182
  precise fulfillment of assignment 176, 189,
    232
  setting/participants 166–171
  tailoring of speech to audience 172, 173–174,
    175, 190, 193–194, 217
Phaedo (character) 166–168, 184
Phaedrus 5, 218, 247–248
Phalinus (envoy) 258–259
Philolaus 166, 167, 169–170, 184
philosopher(s)
  appropriate environment 144–145
  coinage/early use of term 167, 170, 182–183,
    189, 190, 202, 246, 259
  exclusions from definition 209–210
  extent of knowledge 125–136
  extraction of description from interlocutors
    71–74
  leadership of imagined city 92, 112–113, 117,
    121–122, 124–125, 135, 138–146; objections
    136–137, 145
  means of avoiding corruption 144
  personality suitable for 135, 141–142, 146–147,
    154, 207
  popular opinion of 138–140, 142–143, 145–146
  prestige 138–139, 142–143, 200–201, 257–258

pronouncements on nature of 5–6, 237–242;
    in *Phaedo* 237; in *Republic* 121–147, 237; in
    Theaetetus 61, 72, 237
  "real" 173–174, 206, 256; recurrent references
    (in *Phaedo*) 189
  (supposed) otherworldliness 61–62, 139–140
"philosophizing," Socratic use of term 38, 41, 58,
    63–65, 202–203, 214, 216, 242–243
  defined in relation to other kinds of activity
    245–250
  etymology 247–248, 259
  as life's work 38–40, 236
  reasons for choice of 246–250, 259–261
philosophy
  academic status 256–258
  death as gateway to 166, 168–171, 173–174,
    182–183
  debate as to nature of (in *Lovers*) 201–205
  low place in public opinion 199–200, 257
  modern uses of term 256–257
  nonSocratic conceptions 14, 197–203, 215
  Phaedo's account of 167–171, 182–190
  Platonic redefinition 254, 255, 256
  problem-solving element 242
  (range of) Socratic/Platonic conceptions
    14–15, 196–197, 201, 214–215, 236, 256
  Socrates' failure to define precisely 245
  (supposed) change in Plato's view of 210–213
piety
  (im)possibility in gods 76–77
  of Socrates' purpose 163–165
pilot, (flawed) analogy with philosopher 138
Pittacus of Mytilene 241
Plato
  absence from dialogues 230, 235
  (alleged) change of approach/personality 3–4,
    10, 65–66, 92, 210–213, 217–218, 220–221,
    222–224
  anti-doctrinaire stance 229; misunderstood
    231–233
  authorial stance 14–15
  avoidance of self-promotion 230
  creativity 221–224
  criticisms 6–7, 9
  distancing from views expressed 227–228,
    250
  influence in modern world 258–259
  logical acumen 8–9, 10–11, 233
  motives/message in dialogues 220–235
  name: change of 230–231; wordplay on
    17–18
  philosophical views 222, 233–234, 250–259
  (possible) Pythagorean influences 186
  posthumous reputation 230

priorities 5
relationship with readers 15–16
reluctance to pronounce authoritatively 11
pleasure, philosophical view of 184–185
Plotinus 79
Plutarch 16, 78, 192
poets 183–184
claims to wisdom 22, 35
Polansky, Ronald 85
Polemarchus (interlocutor) 101
politicians
claims to wisdom 20–22, 31, 35
Socrates' attempts to educate 21–22
Popper, Karl 257
preliminary studies, need for 139
"Prettycity" *see Kallipolis*
Prodicus of Ceos 26, 27
Protagoras 240–241, 258
Protagoras of Abdera 60
interrogation by surrogate (in *Theaetetus*) 60, 67, 73
Socrates' rejection of thesis 82–85
Pythagoras 188, 207–208, 246
supposed visit to Hades 173
Pythagorean ideas/communities 154–157, 166–190, 202, 205, 209
Glaucon's/Adeimantus' attachment to 152, 153–159, 164
(implied) criticisms 189
Plato's belief/unbelief in 186
popularity at time of writing 157
role in *Phaedo* 167, 168, 169–171, 173, 175–176, 182–184, 185–186, 189–190, 192, 194–195
Socrates' differences with 192–193

"queer," compared to "philosophizing" 260
question-and-answer method 8, 48, 137, 251
contrasted with speech-against-speech mode 96–97
as founded in agreement 97
overlap with speech method (in *Republic*) 103, 104–105, 109
stylized mode 70, 94, 96, 141

recollection, Pythagorean theory of 190
Reeve, C.D.C. 33, 40, 113, 142
refutation, as business of philosopher 206, 209, 239–240
Republic 5–6, 13, 53, 88, 90–119, 120–165, 171, 197, 216–217, 223, 225
account of philosophy 253–254, 255
(apparent) internal inconsistency 91–93, 160
Book 1 93–97
compared with *Timaeus* 115, 118

educational program 224–225
plans to continue discussion 163–164
see also Adeimantus; city; controversial ideas; Glaucon; speech; war
right/wrong, (problems of) definition 46
Robinson, Richard 3
Roochnik, David 92
Rowe, Christopher 6, 12, 115, 182
Rue, Rachel 76, 77–78
Ryle, Gilbert 10–11, 59

sages 27–29, 30
Sedley, David 2, 6, 45, 60, 72, 77, 181, 189, 231
seeming, links/differences with being 60–61, 84–85
Sharp, Kendall 89, 234
Shields, Christopher 2
Simmias (interlocutor) 166–167, 168, 169–172, 179, 182–194
challenges to arguments 179
lack of clarity of thought 182
Slings, S.R. 18, 34, 37, 40, 49
Smith, Nicholas 5, 43, 45, 46, 50, 51
Socrates
agnosticism 53
as answerer 95
anti-doctrinaire stance 229
anti-Pythagorean practices 192–193
(apparent) duality of approach 2–8, 91–93
beliefs 218–219
consistency across dialogues 58, 71, 90, 91, 216–218, 260–261
historical figure, relationship with Plato's presentation 221–222, 245
idiosyncratic use of (accusers') vocabulary 36–37, 38, 42, 57–58, 260
last day 166, 168–195
oratorical abilities 37
presentation of character 5, 14–15
presentation of controversial views 90–91 *see also* doctrinal approach; *Republic*
self-effacement 234–235
trial: accusers 242; defense speech 1, 17–58, 172, 236; persons attending 151, 159
youth 238–239, 249
Socrates, as philosopher 236–261
described as 137, 237, 238–240
divergence from descriptions 62–66, 123–124, 137, 190–193, 197, 210–215, 237, 240–242
educative role 249, 259–260
self-description as 242–244
specific application of term 244–250
suitability for role 142

Solon 28–29, 30, 49, 50, 202–203, 241
Sophist 8, 14, 67, 197, 205–215, 238
sophists 24, 25–26, 27, 87, 143–144, 240
    description in *Sophist* 209, 210
    distrust of 27
    Plato/Socrates distinguished from 251–253
sophos/sophia see wisdom
soul(s)
    arguments for justice focused on 107,
        116–117
    care of, centrality to worldly existence 1–2,
        30–33
    immortality of 5–6, 7–8, 156, 164, 166,
        174–175, 176–177, 181–182, 183, 189–190;
        arguments for 178–182; myths of 182
    transmigration, theory of 154, 164, 188, 218 *see
        also* recollection
Sparta 240–241
speech (in *Republic*) 103
    choice of method 98–99
    construction to order 105–107, 232
    conventions of 105, 160
    rejection in favour of question and answer
        96
    Socrates' preparedness to engage in 101–103
    Socrates' reluctance to engage in 104,
        149
    as technical exercise 102
    unconventional elements 103
    see also controversial ideas
speeches, writers of 200–201
Sprague, Rosamond Kent 9
Statesman 205, 211–212
Stobaeus 192
Strauss, Leo 92
suicide, prohibition/objections 168–169,
        170–171, 177–178, 184
Symposium 5, 218, 234, 246–248, 250

teachers, Socratic examinations 73–74, 87–89,
        198–199, 209
Thales of Miletus 28–29, 49, 196–197, 207,
        241
Theaetetus 8, 196–197, 241–242
    date of composition 65–66
    see also "digression"
Theaetetus (young interlocutor) 61, 65, 73–74,
        86, 88–89, 207, 209, 241–242
    biographical background 88, 89
    praised by other speakers 66, 70, 71
Theages 33–34, 144
Theodorus of Cyrene (atheist) 66
Theodorus of Cyrene (teacher/interlocutor) 13,
        61, 62, 64, 66–67, 83, 85–89, 206, 211, 217,
        232

comparison with Socrates 67–71
    presentation of character 66–67, 87–89
    revelation 71–74
thoughtfulness
    distinguished from "wisdom" 31, 34, 35, 36,
        53
    as feature of Socrates' life 18
    (im)possibilty as divine attribute 77
Thrasymachus (interlocutor) 93–94, 95, 96, 101,
        104, 155
Thucydides 204
Timaeus 79–80, 186, 203
    Aristotelian interpretation 225
    depiction of city, compared with *Republic* 115,
        118
Timon (parodist) 18
Twain, Mark, *The Adventures of Huckleberry
        Finn* 123

unscrupulous person
    outcome of examination 86–87
    philosophical arguments unlikely to impress
        83
unworthy practitioners, practice of philosophy
        by 142, 143–144

Vegetti, Mario 156
virtue
    aspiration to, as basis of good life 30–33,
        56
    care for, identified with philosophy 241
    expert knowledge of 33
    false claims of 39
    training of others in 46, 198–199, 251–253
Vlastos, Gregory 3, 4, 5, 14–15, 42, 52–55, 91, 92,
        109, 217, 218, 220–221

Wagner, Ellen 149
war *see* militarism
Weiss, Roslyn 39, 46, 65, 77
West, Thomas G./Grace Starry 40, 110, 111
Whitman, Walt 82
Williams, Bernard 80
wisdom 19–58
    imputation of, as "slander" 19, 22–23, 24,
        33–36, 57, 71, 229–230, 256
    range of meanings 19–20, 23, 27–28
    rooted in proper conduct of life 30–31
    Socrates' claim to 22, 36–37, 42–43, 57
    as superhuman 27, 34, 56–57
    see also thoughtfulness
Wolfsdorf, David 5, 91, 198
women, in Pythagorean theory/*Republic* 156
wonder, role in philosophy 241–242
Woodruff, Paul 81

Woolf, Rafael 192
wordplay, Plato's use of 17–18
  see also Apology
wrestling, metaphor of 64, 73

Xanthippe 191
Xenophon 18, 151, 226, 230, 241, 245,
  258–259

"Yo' Mama" game 96
Yonezawa, Shigeru 35
young people
  in dialogues 248–250, 259–260 *see also* names
    of specific interlocutors
  pitfalls awaiting 140–142

Zopyrus of Tarentum 190